More praise for *Power Conc*

"Power Concedes Nothing is full of valuable and honest insights from writers who led some of the most important work that contributed to our victories in the 2020 elections. This book is essential reading for all progressive organizers and strategists who are interested in both winning elections and building power for the long term."
– Maria Peralta, National Political Director, SEIU; Co-Founder, Win Justice

"An effective electoral strategy and practice—one that is carried out at scale and makes our base communities stronger and more connected—is absolutely essential for building a powerful US left. By providing a detailed recounting and in-depth analysis of progressive electoral engagement in 2020, *Power Concedes Nothing* makes a huge contribution to getting us there."
– Bill Fletcher, Jr., long-time trade unionist, writer, and a past president of TransAfrica Forum

Power Concedes Nothing documents and reflects on the kind of organizing it will take to build a majoritarian coalition capable of defeating the right. It contains important lessons for everyone who is concerned about accomplishing that vital task.
– Michael Podhorzer, Senior Advisor to the President, AFL-CIO

"Grassroots organizers throughout the country, especially in communities of color, helped us to avert disaster in the 2020 election. Thanks to the contributors and editors of this immensely valuable collection, the lessons gleaned from an array of successful organizing strategies will not be lost to the historical amnesia that often claims such local but transformative work."
– Angela Y. Davis, Distinguished Professor Emerita, University of California, Santa Cruz

"This is the untold story of how people powered grassroots movements in multiple states transformed the political landscape in the 2020 elections and wrote a blueprint for a multiracial democracy in America going forward."
– José La Luz, labor strategist and member of DSA's National Political Committee

"A must-read for those concerned with racial justice and the future of our democracy!"
- Steve Phillips, Author, *Brown Is the New White,* and founder, Democracy in Color

Organizers know best what works and doesn't work to build the sustained grassroots power needed to win elections, state by state. *Power Concedes Nothing* captures the frontline expertise that effective progressive political strategy depends on.
– Anthony Thigpenn, Founder and President, California Calls

"Before 2020, no presidential candidate ever got anything close to the 81 million votes that powered Joe Biden to the White House. A great deal of credit belongs to the wide array of social and economic justice organizations that hadn't always plunged into the difficult task of identifying and mobilizing sometime voters—disproportionately low-income and minority group members—but in 2020, did just that. How they did that and what they learned in the process is the subject of the trenchant reports in this volume by a wide range of savvy organizers. It's required reading for anyone who understands that democracy itself is on the ballot in 2022 and 2024—and who wants to see it preserved and expanded."
– Harold Meyerson, Editor at Large, *The American Prospect*

"*Power Concedes Nothing* is essential reading for anyone seeking to block the forces of patriarchal white nationalism and build a democratic society worthy of our sacrifice and allegiance. The electoral defeat of the Trump regime, achieved in no small measure by people and movements found in these pages, demonstrates that organizations rooted in justice struggles can—and must—build a political coalition ultimately capable of governing the transition to a just, multiracial, and feminist democracy."
– Tarso Luís Ramos, Executive Director, Political Research Associates

"Defeating a patriarchal, white supremacist authoritarian was our task in 2020, crucial for our communities and for people across the globe. We needed a long view, a comprehensive and nuanced power-building strategy. That meant not abandoning the electoral arena to the extreme right and the neoliberals. We needed united fronts and masses in motion. This book tells the behind-the-scenes stories of the planning and on-the-ground work that led to victory. They provide crucial lessons about the transformative, visionary, strategic, and creative civic engagement needed for our long haul road to liberation."
– Cindy Wiesner, Executive Director, Grassroots Global Justice Action Fund

"We need to study, re-study, and then study again the lessons from the Georgia elections in 2018–2021. *Power Concedes Nothing* is a good place to start."
– LaTosha Brown, Co-founder, Black Voters Matter Fund

Power Concedes Nothing

Power Concedes Nothing

How Grassroots Organizing Wins Elections

Edited by
**Linda Burnham, Max Elbaum,
and María Poblet**

OR Books
New York • London

Published by OR Books, New York and London
Visit our website at www.orbooks.com

All rights information: rights@orbooks.com

First printing 2022

Cataloging-in-Publication Data:
A catalog record for this book is available from the Library of Congress.
A catalogue record for this book is available from the British Library.

ISBN: 978-1-68219-330-3 (paperback)
ISBN: 978-1-68219-329-7 (e-book)

Designed and typeset by Hiatt & Dragon, San Francisco, Calif.
Cover design: Guillermo Prado, *8 point 2 design*.
Cover photo courtesy UNITE HERE.

Contents

Part 2: Communities of Color Drive the Win

Part 3: Workers on the Doors

Part 4: Bernie, Democratic Socialism, and the Primary Battles

Part 5: Mobilizing Voters Across the Country

Introduction:
2020 Was an Extraordinary Year

Linda Burnham, Max Elbaum, and María Poblet

The nation had endured four years of a presidential administration led by a white supremacist, anti-immigrant, self-dealing demagogue whose disdain for the institutions and procedures of democratic governance became ever more entrenched as his presidency unfolded. Trump deliberately attacked democratic norms and unleashed a suite of far-right actors prepared to use Congress, the federal bureaucracy, the courts, the Republican Party, state legislatures, right-wing media, and armed militias in their bid for authoritarian rule. Of course Trump's particular brand of toxicity seeped into well-tilled soil. Forty years of Republican anti-tax, anti-regulatory, anti-government ideology and governance; backlash against the election of the nation's first Black president; fear of demographic change; the growth of a far-right, all-encompassing media environment; and long-standing, deeply rooted patterns of white and Christian supremacy set the stage for his election. It took most of us far too long to fully comprehend that Trump's presidency represented a qualitative increase in the determination and capacity of the right to impose minority rule.

And then, in early 2020, the emergent COVID-19 pandemic layered a public health crisis on top of a crisis of democracy. The pandemic exposed, once again, profound inequalities related to class, race, gender, and immigration status. Debates over the public health measures required to halt the pandemic fed on and exacerbated political volatility. The pandemic also underscored Trump's unique blend of incompetence, disinterest in actually governing, and profound indifference to human suffering—character traits ultimately responsible for hundreds of thousands of unnecessary deaths, and which likely contributed to defeat in his bid for re-election.

As if the public health and democracy challenges were not enough, the millions of acres burned in 2020 wildfires, unprecedented flooding and other extreme weather events, deepened awareness of the urgency of climate crisis and the scale of interventions needed to mitigate it. The reckless denialism of the Republican Party is evidence of their willingness to put the lives of current and future generations at mortal risk in exchange for the support of the fossil fuel industry. The election season was haunted by the prospect of environmental collapse.

Left and center against the right

The 2020 elections served as a temperature check on where the country stood after four years of the most intense political polarization since the Civil War. The elections also served as a reading on the relative strength of various political blocs, that is, the capacity of left, right, and center to shape the political terrain. Conservatives, having subordinated themselves to the far right, consolidated the Republican Party around the MAGA agenda of racial and imperial revenge, with Trump as Maximum Leader. White supremacist militias and Q-anon conspiracy theorists were welcomed into the fold. This newly dominant bloc looked eagerly toward another four-year term as an opportunity to double down on white minority, patriarchal rule. Despite a few notable defections from his camp and from the Republican Party, Trump went into the election with the advantages of his incumbency, the dated Electoral College system that confers advantages on white and rural voters, and a roused, highly motivated right-wing base.

Of course, the main question to be settled by the election was whether a broad enough coalition could be forged to rebound from Hillary Clinton's disastrous 2016 loss and toss Trump out of the White House. Mainstream Democrats had to at least nod to the left. Bernie Sanders' 2016 campaign had demonstrated that a substantial swath of the electorate is open to a left-of-center political agenda. The campaigns of both Bernie Sanders and Elizabeth Warren in 2020 generated levels of excitement and support that confirmed the existence of a large constituency in favor of governance and policies well to the left of the Democratic Party mainstream. Their platforms, including a Green New Deal, Medicare for All, the cancellation of student loan and medical debt, a humane immigration policy, and higher taxation rates on corporations and the ultra-wealthy made it clear that neoliberal austerity for the poor and precarious was not the only thing on offer. There *is* an alternative. Though their primary bids failed, their candidacies opened up new realms of possibility and sparked left imagination.

The US left has been neither united nor strategic in its electoral interventions for many, many decades. Since Jesse Jackson's campaigns for the presidency in 1984 and 1988, and the subsequent collapse of the Rainbow Coalition, some sectors of the left have rejected engagement with the two-party system. Instead, they have adopted an abstentionist stance or launched largely symbolic third-party efforts. More pragmatic sectors of the left tended to vote for Democrats based on a harm reduction framework, while putting little energy into electoral politics. Overextended (and underfunded) on community-based or issue-based organizing projects, and often lacking the skill sets and the organizational vehicles to intervene effectively in the electoral realm, they prioritized other battlefronts.

But beginning about 10 to 15 years ago, these dynamics began to change as local and state-based groups—many of them represented in these pages—started to grapple directly with one of the central ways in which US political power is accumulated and wielded. An important set of organizations emerged that combine social justice values with electoral organizing, and that are determined to build political power independent of the Democratic Party. The 2016 election underscored the importance of these initiatives and brought other left forces in from the abstentionist sidelines. The degree of traction achieved by Bernie Sanders' campaign together with Trump's surprise triumph brought home to nearly everyone the unacceptable cost of abstentionism. The 2020 election saw a maturation of the trend toward left electoral engagement in the context of a truly critical contest. The stakes were so self-evidently high that progressive and left organizations of nearly every stripe wrestled with how best to mobilize their constituencies against Trump and in defense of democracy. Though the social justice left has come to the arena relatively late, it is already a key player. With any luck, we are in the early stages of an era in which the left strengthens its capacity for effective intervention from one election to the next, shifting the political alignment in a more progressive direction.

On May 25, 2020, in the midst of presidential primary season, a murderous policeman pressed George Floyd's last breath out of his body. Demonstrations against police violence and the summary execution of Black people spread throughout the country, led and energized by furious young Black protestors. Tens of millions of people took to the streets in the spring and summer of 2020, in demonstrations that were more numerous and located in more cities and towns than at any other point in US history. The protests changed the racial climate. Black Lives Matter signs sprouted in shop windows and on lawns across the country. Corporations and institutions of every kind scrambled to respond to the "racial reckoning." For many, a light bulb had finally been turned on. Others wondered why such belated enlightenment always seems to require the sacrifice of Black lives.

In any case, the ruthless suffocation of George Floyd impacted the presidential contest and set off social and political currents that continue to shape today's national dialogue. Debates over racist policing and incarceration and intractable, racialized economic inequities inevitably filtered into the campaigns. And the right-wing distortion industrial complex mangled anti-racist demands in ways that were guaranteed to energize their base. This continues today, with the Republican base mobilized to discredit any attempt to teach the history of US racism, under the banner of opposition to critical race theory.

In this book

Voters turned out in record numbers in 2020. The 2020 electorate, as compared to 2016, showed the largest increase on record between two presidential elections. Turnout rates increased in every state, in every racial and ethnic group, across gender, and in every age cohort.[1]

The record turnout was driven, at least in part, by the grassroots activists and leaders who tell their stories in this book. This volume of essays provides a close-in vantage point on how many of the organizations that anchor social justice organizing in the US met the challenge of an electoral campaign. The organizations and networks represented here led an array of initiatives across the country. Their work on the ground contributed substantially to the margins needed to defeat Trump.

It is our hope that this volume enables the left to share experiences and insights across organizations, constituencies, issues, and geographies. And that it serves to strengthen the left's orientation to, and practice in, this arena. Each of its chapters sheds light on a distinct set of organizing challenges, protagonists, and approaches to electoral work. Yet a few themes surfaced again and again.

Most of the organizations represented here focused on some combination of registering and motivating new voters and targeting outreach to "low-propensity voters." Communities with high concentrations of low-propensity voters—including communities of color—often reflect the results of entrenched patterns of political investment. A party committed to turning out suburban soccer moms is unlikely to prioritize the kind of work it takes to transform a low-propensity voter into a high-potential voter. The strategies implemented by the organizations in this book were based on the conviction that sufficient investment of time and resources—together with culturally savvy messaging—could tap into the potential of low-propensity voters to determine election outcomes.

While COVID-19 forced organizers to innovate on contacting and mobilizing voters at a distance, there is no substitute for the work on the doors. Engaging prospective voters in conversation, listening hard to their concerns, answering basic questions as to how, where, and when to vote—all this is better served by face-to-face conversations than by phone or text—or, at an even further remove, ads. Every mode of voter communication was needed for the scale of outreach 2020 demanded, and the contributions of the tens of thousands of people who phoned and texted were absolutely indispensable. But high-quality work on the doors, in union halls, places of worship, schools, and community centers—unmediated human connection—brings out leadership qualities in canvassers and volunteers, identifies potential activists and allies, and produces experiences that can be mined for lessons that shape future work in ways that other forms of outreach cannot.

Investment in high-cost, fly-in/fly-out consultants and pollsters is often misplaced spending. Donors need to think long and hard about investing in the local organizations and leaders that are committed to staying in place for the long haul—well beyond this electoral cycle or the next.

There are challenges related to aligning work on electoral campaigns with the robust, ongoing relationship-building, grassroots campaigning, and organization-building required to win progressive change. Those challenges can be anticipated and worked with in productive ways. And the relationships and skills acquired in these distinct forms of work can be mutually reinforcing.

The contributors to this book are busy with the work of creating a more just society. The pressure of that work, especially in these turbulent times, leaves little room for reflection and summation. The next battle looms. We are grateful that our contributors found the space to bring us stories of what they did, and why and how they did it.

Some chapters in *Power Concedes Nothing* focus on electoral organizing in states that were key to the presidential contest. Others reflect on the efforts of progressive networks and alliances engaged in multi-state organizing. The critical role of organized labor in getting out the vote is the subject of several articles. Organizers in communities of color bring attention to the role of Black, Indigenous, Latinx, and Asian American voters in 2020.

No single volume on grassroots electoral organizing could hope to be comprehensive. We have not covered every sector of the social justice movement. Nor have we been able to include the work of many indispensable organizations and networks. We hope that the process of summarizing experiences and sharing lessons will continue in many other forms.

2022 and 2024

While the country took a small step back from a precipice on November 3, 2020, there was barely a pause before Trump loyalists rallied to a new cause—the alleged "steal" of the election. The violent, failed insurrection on January 6 drove home the level of commitment of Trump and his party to remaining in power by any and all means.

The lie that Trump won, and that a Democrat is illegitimately sitting in the White House, serves at least two purposes. The base, feeding on a constant stream of new false narratives, has been provided with a cause, which keeps it inflamed and stokes polarization. And Republican political operatives, in state houses and on election boards across the country have an excuse to introduce laws and procedures intended to constrain democracy and suppress the votes of the constituencies Democrats depend upon.

So here we are in 2022 and the right-wing authoritarians who lost in 2020 are still challenging the results of that election. Each day they demonstrate their dedication to white minority, patriarchal rule. Each day they make clear that they are glad to resort to extra-legal—or even violent—measures, if staying within the bounds of the law serves as a check on their power. As one of our contributors succinctly put it, they are playing for keeps.

The midterm elections of 2022 and the presidential election of 2024 are shaping up to be pitched battles. Trump enablers, acolytes, wannabes, and bankrollers are doing everything in their power to gain ground in 2022 and restore Trump in 2024. A Trump restoration would be far worse than his election in 2016. He has shown all of us who he is and what he stands for. And if health or criminal prosecution takes him out of the running, other would-be strongmen are lining up to take his place. A GOP victory, whether by quasi-legitimate means or by what amounts to a coup, would signal a truly profound degeneration of the political space. As many have noted, right-wing resurgence and the figure of an authoritarian strongman with fascistic leanings are phenomena not limited to the United States. But, given the place and power of the US in global politics, the further shredding of democratic norms and institutions and/or a Trump restoration would likely incur disastrous consequences, both nationally and globally. Said another way, the stakes in 2022 and 2024 remain extraordinarily high.

We may be sure that the social justice organizations that share their experiences in this book are fully alert to what hangs in the balance for the constituencies and issues they represent. Whether the rich lessons of 2020 are absorbed and put to use by an expanded and more united progressive current in US politics will, in no small measure, shape the future of democracy.

Our title

We take our title from a speech given in 1857 by the brilliant abolitionist Frederick Douglass. Here is the paragraph in which the phrase appears:

> This struggle may be a moral one, or it may be a physical one, and it may be both moral and physical, but it must be a struggle. Power concedes nothing without a demand. It never did and it never will. Find out just what any people will quietly submit to and you have found out the exact measure of injustice and wrong which will be imposed

upon them, and these will continue till they are resisted with either words or blows, or with both. The limits of tyrants are prescribed by the endurance of those whom they oppress. In the light of these ideas, Negroes will be hunted at the North and held and flogged at the South so long as they submit to those devilish outrages and make no resistance, either moral or physical. Men may not get all they pay for in this world, but they must certainly pay for all they get. If we ever get free from the oppressions and wrongs heaped upon us, we must pay for their removal. We must do this by labor, by suffering, by sacrifice, and if needs be, by our lives and the lives of others.

We encourage you to read the whole speech.

Notes

1. Jacob Fabina, "Despite Pandemic Challenges, 2020 Election Had Largest Increase in Voting Between Presidential Elections on Record," United States Census Bureau, April 29, 2021, www.census.gov.

Part 1

Building Progressive Power in the States

1

Change a State and Shock a Nation: Georgia in the 2020 Elections

Linda Burnham interviews Cliff Albright, Beth Howard, Adelina Nicholls, and Nsé Ufot

The intensity of contention for political power in Georgia from 2018 through early 2021 was unmatched anywhere else in the country. Stacey Abrams ran a highly competitive campaign for governor in 2018 and came within a hair's breadth of winning what many contend was a stolen election. President Biden won the 2020 presidential campaign by fewer than 12,000 votes, the narrowest margin in the state's history. On January 20, 2021, after a fierce runoff election, Georgia sent two Democratic senators, Raphael Warnock and Jon Ossoff, to Washington. They are the first African American and first Jewish senators to represent Georgia in the state's history. None of this happened by accident. The following interviews recount what it took to "change a state and shock a nation." Cliff Albright of Black Voters Matter, Adelina Nicholls of the Georgia Latino Alliance for Human Rights, Beth Howard of Showing Up for Racial Justice, and Nsé Ufot of the New Georgia Project talk about the deep work their organizations did in 2020.

LB: What is your organization's mission? What is it designed to do?

CA: We have two affiliated organizations. One is our 501(c)(3), the Black Voters Matter Capacity-Building Institute, and the first of our organizations that we started in 2016, the Black Voters Matter Fund, which is our 501(c)(4) organization. Our mission is to build power in Black communities, and we believe that elections and voting is one way of building power, although by no means the only way. We believe that an important part of *how* we build power in our communities is by supporting the incredible collection of grassroots organizations that do this work on a daily basis. We operate in 11 core states. Those are places where we have at least one staff member. There are four other states where we don't have staff, but we do have an anchor partner organization that we provide some level of support to throughout the year.

AN: My organization is Georgia Latino Alliance for Human Rights (GLAHR). We created this organization to advocate and organize Latinos and immigrants in the state of Georgia on issues of civil and human rights. We've been working since 1999, under our first name Coordinadora de Líderes Comunitarios (Coordinator of Community Leaders), and in 2007 we became GLAHR.

BH: Showing Up for Racial Justice (SURJ) is really working to build a political home for people like my family. I grew up on a very small family tobacco farm in rural eastern Kentucky. It was an overwhelmingly majority white community and a very poor and working-class community. My mother worked as a grocery store clerk for decades and my father worked often as a strip miner in coal mining. We all worked on the farm in tobacco. We had a lot of joyful times and a lot of love. And also we experienced a lot of the impact of living in systems where a few people have all the wealth and the rest of us really suffer under capitalism.

All that to say, right now SURJ is focusing on creating an organizing space where working-class poor folks in majority white, rural, small town, Southern and Appalachian communities can start to meet other people who share their class. We know that poor white people are suffering and that the right has doubled down on a strategy to maintain white support so that they can continue to attack our democracy. We have base-building projects in communities like mine across the South that we're layering with electoral work through SURJ Action. And we also have a national network of thousands of members across the US who work on abolition and economic justice campaigns in their states and communities. In all our work with white people of all classes and backgrounds, what we really try to do is organize around mutual interests, talking to our folks about what white people stand to gain from breaking with white solidarity and joining a multiracial movement.

NU: We are actually a constellation of organizations. New Georgia Project, is a 501(c)(3). New Georgia Project Action Fund is our 501(c)(4) and advocacy arm. New South Super PAC works in the 600-plus counties that make up America's Black Belt from East Texas all the way to DC. There are tons of counties across that swath that are majority Black and have never had a Black elected official, never had a Black mayor, never had a Black or Latino person serve on a school board or city council. The way that we change America is by changing the South and supporting elected officials who come from the communities that we care about.

But people probably know us best for registering nearly 600,000 Black and Brown folks to vote in all 159 of Georgia's counties. So there isn't a place in Georgia where the New Georgia Project hasn't organized and where we haven't registered people to vote, even in the parts of the state that people call Deliverance Country. Our goal is to build the Georgia and build the country that our families deserve.

Georgia is changing really rapidly. Black and Brown people are going to make up the majority of Georgians and there's this racial voter registration gap. There are 1.2 million African Americans, Latinos, Asian Americans, and unmarried white women in the state who are eligible to vote, but they're completely unregistered. Stacey Abrams hired me as the first executive director of the organization.

LB: What did your organization set out to do in Georgia in the 2020 elections?

CA: In 2020 we were really just trying to expand and go deeper on the work we'd been doing in Georgia for the past three years. We started in one county in Georgia in 2016. Our first county was Sumter County. There was one legislative seat that we were trying to impact. The first $1,000 we raised went into doing some GOTV on election day. Lo and behold, that seat flipped. It was a Republican-controlled seat in a county that is largely Black. Since then, we've been expanding county by county, mainly in rural areas, connecting with organizations in places no one could find on the Georgia map.

By the time we got to 2020, we were probably in 50 counties across Georgia, most of those rural counties and places like Columbus, Savannah, and Augusta, which also don't get much attention compared to metro Atlanta. So, what we were trying to achieve was to get people to believe that we had the power to do something that had not been done in decades in terms of the presidential election. And to do something, in terms of the Senate races, that had never been done. Not just winning both seats, but the first Black senator and then the first Jewish senator to come from the state.

Remember, after the 2018 gubernatorial election, which literally saw the governor's seat stolen from Stacey Abrams, a lot of people across the country wondered how would Black voters rebound. Overcoming that, to get people to go deeper than we had in 2018, that was the first task. At the end of the day, we weren't just organizing around the presidential election, but around a bunch of local elections taking place across the state, including a DA race centered in Brunswick, Glynn County, Georgia, which is where Ahmaud Arbery was murdered. That race was just as important to us as the Senate and presidential races were.

That's what we were trying to do, get folks to turn out in spite of all the voter suppression efforts, to increase our participation and make our voices be heard.

LB: I really want to get some of the texture of the work. What does the work look like?

CA: The starting point is we connect with folks who are already there, already doing the work. That might be a church group, it might be an

NAACP chapter, it might be a youth arts and culture organization. It might be a group that's not even a formal group, that's not incorporated. The group of mamas on the corner who, when they need to round up the community, they get it done. Then sometimes people reach out to us. Either way, it's about that connection with local groups, the existing infrastructure, and then seeing what we can do together. Are there resources we can get you? Do you need some help with outreach, because we might be able to help you do a texting campaign?

Sometimes we have access to other statewide partners and we can bring them resources from our incredible civic engagement table. Sometimes it's information, sometimes it's technology, sometimes it's media connections. Sometimes we help them get resources for canvassers to go door to door in their community. A lot of people who care about their community would love to go door to door, but the economic reality is, they can't afford to. But if we're able to give a stipend, then these groups can kill two birds with one stone: get good info out to their community and also get some income to folks that probably have been doing a lot of stuff for free. And then sometimes it's strategy, being willing to get on a Zoom with folks to scheme and dream with them, and let them know the ideas they have aren't crazy.

LB: Ade, what did your organization do in the 2020 elections?

AN: If you allow me to go to 2018, that was our first intervention into electoral politics. At that time we were supporting progressive candidates that could move the demands of Latinx and immigrant communities. We also were canvassing and trying to motivate and explain to Latinos statewide their rights, and also that they need to get out to vote.

In 2020, we began again, in another capacity. For the first time we got a 501(c)(4) called GLAHR Action Network. We started first with civic engagement, get-out-the-vote work, informing about the election dates and candidates. We organized, in collaboration with SONG and Mijente, community forums and candidate forums. Our initial approach was to target two counties: Cobb and Gwinnett Counties. Both counties had 287(g) programs with devastating consequences in the Latino or undocumented community.[1] We canvassed around 140,000 doors in both counties reaching Latinx and other communities of color, explaining what 287(g) was, and that we need the support to kick out those sheriffs.

At the end of the day, in both counties we were able to kick out both sheriffs, putting in place for the first time in the history of those counties, two Black sheriffs. Of course, one of the things they did was deliver the end of 287(g), which was the bigger demand. For more than 20 years we have built this network called *comites populares* (people's committees) around the state—a network where more than 19 groups in the state of Georgia have helped us to mobilize, getting out the Latinx vote, in particular in rural communities that nobody cared about. Something has happened in Georgia with the demographics of the Latinx community. We started to have these young voters—18, 19, 20, 25—who, for the first time, wanted to be involved. With the general elections we canvassed more than 330,000 doors statewide, reaching every single Latinx door in the state, mobilizing more young voters through our *comites populares,* and using this capacity that has been built for 20 years at the grassroots level.

We wanted to do something a little different from traditional electoral politics, which tells us we only need to reach those who are able to vote. We thought "No way!" Many in our community do not vote. So we continued trying to motivate and create this movement among the Latino community. We now have the results, but none of this could have been done without the grassroots community organizing of communities of color.

LB: Your organization has been working at the grassroots level for many years. What drew you into the electoral arena?

AN: For us, electoral politics is another strategy to use. For many years, we have been using diverse strategies to push back local law enforcement as well as ICE and DHS; pushing back all these policies that affect many undocumented communities through the 287(g) program. But at the beginning, when we started to work on grassroots community organizing, it was because there were many issues happening around the state, in particular in rural areas, where no one cares. We have witnessed many violations of civil rights, human rights, consumer rights, labor rights, in rural Georgia. We paid attention initially to rural Georgia because we know that here in the Atlanta area there is a lot of information, a lot of resources. But communities in rural Georgia, in particular Latinx communities, are disenfranchised. They don't have access to many informational resources.

One of the main activities in 2000, we decided to organize the collection of signatures to request driver's licenses for undocumented immigrants from then Governor Roy Barnes. I began to visit communities that opened the door for us—Albany, Moultrie, Tifton, Cordele, Glennville, Savannah. We collected more than 40,000 signatures that were delivered to the governor. Of course, we didn't get the driver's licenses, but we were able to identify natural leadership from across the state. They are the ones still pushing all the campaigns from the ground up. But it wasn't until 2018, with Trump in power, that all the little tricks to move around in other administrations were closed. At the same time, the demographics changed, so that gave us the opportunity to be a part of the work in the state in electoral politics.

LB: What was your organization trying to do in Georgia in 2020?

BH: We are really trying to build large-scale base-building work centered in grassroots organizing. We're layering base-building with electoral work through SURJ Action.[2] As white antiracist folks, being in these communities that we've often overlooked, we have really seen the vacuum that's left. The right has invested so much money in making sure that poor and working-class white people will choose the side of the oppressor. And so we're trying to build this base. We do that by creating the kind of welcoming space that is centered in working-class community. We were welcomed into the Black-led electoral table in Georgia to

do our part in this very important election year, to organize white people. We really wanted and needed poor and working-class white people
to turn out and vote against Donald Trump and vote for multiracial solidarity.

For the runoff election, I was with part of our field team in rural
north Georgia. There's really no progressive infrastructure there, or if
there is, it's pretty small. We had a really robust phone-banking program
in the general election that we continued into the runoffs. Thousands of
SURJ leaders made millions of calls. Between the general and the runoff,
we made 1.8 million calls into Georgia to do persuasion, turnout, and
deep listening.

Thank goodness we defeated Donald Trump! And then, for the runoff election we scrambled and rolled out a field and phones program. The
phones were focused mainly on turnout with urban and suburban folks.
For our field door knocking, we had turfs in suburban and urban places
where there were also low-propensity voters plus rural north Georgia
and the rural and semi-rural places around Athens. I was in and around
Canton, in north Georgia.

A lot of what I helped strategize around was our rural canvassing.
We were knocking on doors that are largely ignored by the Democrats.
The only other door-knockers I would see were from the right and from
the Republican Party, and they hit every single door. We did see results
that we're really proud of, and that we've learned a lot from.

NU: We knew that our asterisk governor was going to be a part of a
scheme to suppress as many votes as possible. They were going to try to
make it as difficult as possible for people of color to vote and for those
votes to be counted. And we knew that there was not enough time to
change the composition of the legislature so that we could change the
laws. And so our only tactic in that moment was to overwhelm the system, to have so many Black folks voting and so many young people voting that it would be almost impossible for them to steal the election. Let
me be clear, it did not stop them from trying. Remember the January
2nd phone call between the former president of the United States and

the secretary of state of Georgia. "Please, baby, baby. Please tell me you can find 12,000 votes in the couch cushion somewhere." With 7 million Georgians voting as a high watermark for us in our elections, the win margin between [Trump and] Biden/Harris was 11,000 votes. And so our strategic decisions made on the front end bore fruit.

There was a plan for Metro Atlanta, there was a plan for the rural Black Belt—about 23 counties that are majority Black and mostly rural. I would argue that those are the battleground counties in our new battleground state. And then the straight-up-and-down red counties, Trump country, where we were going in with surgical precision looking for white progressives and people of color and young people, and making what was historically a 70/30 Republican/Democratic district to get it to 60/40, and make ourselves competitive statewide. We are constantly thinking about mobilization. How do we flex our power? How do we test our power and what do we direct our power towards?

My favorite part of the work that we do is art and culture. We want to change the culture of voting. So when we're doing our voter protection and election protection work and we find out that folks have been waiting in line for 2, 3, 5, 10, 12 hours to vote in Georgia, we deploy food trucks, hire mariachi bands, second line bands, stilt walkers, tumbling troops. We are on our seventh or eighth election cycle now where we hire live performers to keep people encouraged while they're in line.

LB: What were the main challenges in the work? What difficulties did you have to overcome?

CA: That period covers COVID. It covers the summer of protests and police violence, which hit us not just in terms of the national stories around George Floyd, but we were dealing with Ahmaud Arbery and incidents that took place even before 2020. So that was a hot issue for folks all throughout Georgia. Then you had the regular challenges of organizing in Georgia: voter suppression, the voter purges. There's the everyday challenge of organizing in primarily rural communities, which mean challenges of resource availability, transportation, wifi access.

COVID threw us for a big loop. We stopped doing door-to-door canvassing. One of the main strategies we wound up using was our caravans, getting not just our big bus, but what we call our "baby busses," the 15-passenger vans, leading caravans throughout communities. They give out information, make noise and raise awareness without going to the doors. Next to the voter suppression itself, COVID was the biggest challenge we had to navigate.

AN: Moving into the runoff was new work for us. The administration of that 501(c)(3), 501(c)(4), and PAC, that was a challenge by itself. And we had these "visitors" from Florida who showed up to the office. They told us, "You can let us know information on where we can put our addresses and register to be able to vote for Ossoff or for Warnock." They came with suitcases in two big vans, they came inside to the office, and they asked tricky questions. It was very challenging for us. They said they wanted to go see Ossoff, and asked where could they go to register.

"Isn't that what the Democrats want? For people to come from outside of Georgia to register?"

We were lucky, but from there, we tried to put more safeguards in place, not only at the office, but also for our canvassers. It also helped a lot the amount of resources that came onboard for the runoff campaign. Without that, I don't think we could have mobilized as well. We had hundreds of volunteers and canvassers working 60 hours a week in the last two weeks without taking days off. It was really challenging in terms of the logistics. It was challenging, but we decided to do what we know how to do, and that is to work with the grassroots, to mobilize community, to have these conversations with Latinos. During the runoff, we canvassed doors of Republicans and Democrats—*all* Latinx communities in the state. Many kicked us out, many things happened! But dealing with COVID, we didn't stop. We provided all the PPE equipment, we started doing the canvassing, and we didn't stop until January 5th. That was, I believe, when we got the results.

We are learning in the process. There are many things we need to move. I hope at the first opportunity, we can change the State Assembly. We need to pass different laws, we need to introduce a different approach, and also push for those politicians that are willing to commit to this progressive agenda that could benefit all of us.

BH: We were the only ones there from the progressive side, and the Republicans were hitting every door. There wasn't a lot of infrastructure we could plug into. We were really in rural turf, so it's going to take twice as long to hit as many doors as you can in an urban or suburban place. It's really tough turf geographically. You're driving from door to door. You can't just park somewhere and then walk city blocks and hit a lot of doors.

We use VAN, the Voter Activation Network, and use a map or an app on our phones to track our turf. And you will hit places where you have no cell service and you can't find that address.

We had volunteers come in to work on phones and on doors in the runoff from across the country. We did a lot of training online for people so that they could be ready when they got there. One of the trainings we did, for example, was a "Welcome to the South" video where we talked about Southern culture and we talked about class, really trying to uproot a lot of the classism that takes hold. It's within all of us.

We really wanted to educate our canvassers and our members, preparing us to go out and be in our culture, love on people, see them in their dignity and embrace the culture as opposed to it being something that is wrong or something we need to change. That's a challenge, and it's so rewarding. Time after time we would hear people say, "I cannot believe you came out here! No one comes out here to talk." Another challenge that we're really struggling with is there's just not a deep bench of white folks who are anti-racist, who have this blend of analysis about class and race combined with really nuts-and-bolts organizing skills who are also from poor and working-class Southern communities and Appalachian communities. We just have to have that if we're going to be at scale.

NU: Our most sophisticated, most effective tactic is high-quality face-to-face conversations. We go door to door, we have in-person meetings in church basements and in housing projects and college campuses all over the state of Georgia. And quarantine didn't allow us to do that. And so we had to get creative. How do we recreate those high-quality conversations in a technologically mediated environment? A huge challenge, and I don't think that we've figured it out yet.

One of the things that we were really proud of is that all of our meetings always had food, always had music, always had childcare. We couldn't meet in person, but we would send people Uber Eats and DoorDash if we needed people to meet with us virtually. Fifteen minutes before we began, we'd make sure that there was food delivery at your house to try to re-create the experience we had if people were coming to meet us at the office. We kept our phonebanks and textbanks alive. But instead of texting people and asking if they registered to vote or reminding them about the upcoming election, we would ask them how they were doing and if they knew where to go to get help, if they needed it. So we were keeping our list warm, but we led with our humanity.

LB: What were your organization's main accomplishments? What did you do well?

CA: Just staying together as an organization is a big accomplishment in and of itself! Like a lot of organizations in the racial justice space, we were able to receive a good amount of financial resources because there were a lot of donations taking place during the summer of protest. There were a lot of companies that were trying to donate their guilt or complicity away. We were able to expand our fundraising efforts and that let us do some of the more creative forms of outreach. We were able to dramatically increase our digital outreach.

Early on in the pandemic, the big thing was educating people around social distancing and using hand sanitizer, and making sure people were safe and fed. When we were doing our phone calls and text banking, we wouldn't just jump into "Hey, are you registered? Hey, are you voting?" It was, "Hey, how are you doing? Are you aware of COVID?" We didn't want to act like we weren't in the middle of a pandemic. That was the first thing to do, welfare checks on people before getting into the logistics of GOTV and voter outreach.

All of that laid the groundwork for the high levels of turnout we saw during the general election, the historic levels of turnout we saw during the runoff election, the levels of turnout we saw of younger voters, the higher level of turnout of voters who had not voted in 2016, but voted in 2020. When we say that voters we contacted had a 64% turnout rate, we weren't just reaching out to folks who were going to come out and vote anyway. We were reaching out to folks who had not previously come out, had not voted in the last presidential election, who were not likely to come out. So when we say that 64% of the folks we reached turned out, that's saying something!

BH: The electoral work we were doing is very different from the Democratic Party approach. We have really embraced bold, progressive reforms and candidates, including candidates of color, because we really believe that poor and working-class white people will turn out and vote for candidates who are bringing meaningful, progressive change. We embrace talking explicitly about race because we lose when the right talks about race and we don't. And they talk about race all the time. What we see in Georgia is a lot of these electoral races aren't won because there's overwhelmingly working-class white people voting for Trump, but more so the races are decided by nonvoters who aren't showing up.

We had long conversations with people about the issues that impacted their lives, talking to them about their day-to-day lives and what's on their minds. COVID would come up, healthcare, just trying to make ends meet, housing, disability, all of those things. This was a year of racial justice uprisings. We had a white supremacist president, so they would bring up race. We got to have conversations about Black Lives Matter, about the removal of Confederate statues. We didn't try to convince them that Democrats were going to save us, or that electoral work or elections are going to save us. We always listen to people's rightful anger, anger about politicians, electoral politics, partisan party politics.

I got to tell them, "Yes, I'm disappointed in the Democratic Party, too. They have let me down, too. And here's why I'm doing this work in this moment." We were able to have those kinds of conversations with people who really welcomed us. I do want to say, people slammed the door in our face, people said hateful things. I've been called every name that you can imagine, but that's the same as any other electoral work I've ever done.

We helped the coalition win twice. We made 1.8 million calls to white voters who we knew were suffering under this administration and who were infrequent voters. Some 3,800 SURJ members had 36,000 conversations with voters and secured 21,200 commitments to vote. We hosted phone banks that had over 500 people on them. We saw shifts in poor and working-class white communities—what they classify as non-college-educated. Biden made major gains in majority white counties among white people who didn't attend college.

And those are the people we called. We know we didn't do that all on our own, but we did do our part, and we consider that a victory. For the runoff, we made 675,000 phone calls. We had 9,576 commitments to vote on the phones. We knocked 28,000 doors and had 7,000 conversations with voters on the doors.

NU: We moved nearly a million young people and people of color to vote, not only in the November 2020 general, but in the January 5 runoff. There was so much hand-wringing, "There's no way that you'll be able to replicate that performance in the runoffs. Everybody knows that the people who show up in runoffs and in primaries are overwhelmingly white and overwhelmingly senior citizens. Young people of color are unreliable. They don't vote. They're definitely not showing back up to vote in January." And we proved them wrong. I'm very proud that 85, almost 90% of the people who showed up to vote in November came back to vote in January. We were able to sustain that level of turnout because people knew and understood the assignment. They say in our community, "You stay ready, you don't have to get ready." Right? In the 72 hours after Georgia was called for President Biden and Vice President Harris we received over 10,000 requests to volunteer, and because of infrastructure that we have in place, we were able to say "yes" and place every single one of those requests. Every single one. Now people flake. Yes, because humans, right? But we were able to place, within 72 hours, every single one of them. So I'm proud that we built the infrastructure that was designed to meet that moment.

LB: What are the main lessons from your work in Georgia? What relevance does the Georgia work have for the nation as a whole?

AN: For many years, in particular with us here in the Latino community, the Southeast of the United States has not been funded; organizations like ours that didn't have participation in electoral politics. We saw the attention going just to the electoral part, diminishing the importance of the role of grassroots organizing. It wasn't until the demographic change that we saw the need to intervene in the electoral world. We already had walked long years in communities and we had their trust. The main lesson for us is to learn, to learn from the Black community that is leading this, and at the same time, educating our community that needs to participate.

I did hear many years ago that the coalition between Black and Brown was "Mission Impossible." I don't think so. I think the new generations of Latinos, but also the Black communities, have opened up. I do believe we have shown, in terms of last year, that this is possible. Communities of color made the impossible possible.

For many years, I was asking for support from other groups regarding immigration reform, or to stop deportations. And someone raised his hand and told me, "But what are you giving us in return?" At that time, I didn't know what to say. We didn't have anything; we didn't even vote. I arrived in 1996 and the mid-1990s is when the big boom of Latinos and immigrants arrived in Georgia because of construction of the Olympic stadium in 1996. I think civic engagement has allowed us to do this intersection, joining the demands of Black and Brown communities. I think civic engagement in 2020 gave us that strength and that solidarity among groups. And also the recognition. The Black community is embracing Latinos with papers or without papers. The homework for us is to continue teaching, educating, forming this political consciousness in our community here in the state of Georgia. It's part of learning that lesson with those who are here, stirring the pot. Letting them know we also have spoons, and we are also able to stir the pot.

CA: Those of us who do this work know demographics is not destiny. It takes work to make those demographics actually show up as electoral power; it takes organizing. So I think Georgia has a lesson to teach a lot of states around Black and Brown unity. We don't always talk to the same communities, right? We have our niches, but when we need to work together, when we need to share information, share contacts or strategies, and sometimes even resources, I think these groups in Georgia demonstrate how doing that well can change a state and shock a nation.

We had some lessons that were really affirmations. The power of culture in our work is something we knew was important prior to 2020. In 2020, it went to a whole different level. We were able to use music and culture and faith and food, and traditions. One of the most powerful activities that we did was, we were giving out food boxes during the holiday season, which included fresh produce, fresh vegetables grown largely by Black farmers in the area. December 31 was the last day of early voting. Well, what are people thinking about on New Year's Eve? They're thinking about New Year's Day, which in our community is a tradition around cooking collard greens and black-eyed peas. Folks are getting ready for New Year's Day. Why don't we help them by giving out fresh collards and black-eyed peas and why not throw in a few boxes of cornbread. But we're going to do it at locations that are across the street from the early vote polling place. As people are going through getting their box of goodies for their New Year's meal, we're like, "Hey, by the way, today's the last day of early voting. How about you go across the street and go vote."

And we did this in 30 counties simultaneously in one day. We believe this is part of the reason the Georgia legislature made sure to forbid giving out food and water to people as they were waiting in line. That didn't just come out of no place.

Another lesson, there was a lot of attention being paid to Georgia, and a lot of our groups got more money than we get in a typical election year. Money is not the end all and be all. But for our groups, having some extra cash matters! That combination of having the resources, combined with some really, really good strategies, credible messengers, culturally based strategies, language-relevant strategies—when those things can meet, that's where the magic happens, and that's what happened in Georgia.

So part of the lesson for the rest of the country is, FUND THESE GROUPS. FUND THESE STATES that are often neglected and ignored and have literally been written off for decades as just conservative bastions that are gonna be red no matter what. Invest in these states, invest in these groups, and some incredible things can happen. That's the lesson, not so much for us—we all knew this—but that's the lesson that the rest of the country needs to take away. Because there are groups in Texas that need funding and if you're really talking about changing Texas from the abomination it is now, you have to invest in groups the same way groups in Georgia were invested in.

All of that—the importance of investment, the importance of unity, the importance of using culture to turn out voters, and the importance of focusing on the issues, not on personalities—all of that is part of the secret sauce.

BH: Some of the main lessons that I continue to sit with go back to, "Who are Trump voters? What is Trump country?" The first stereotype that comes to mind is a poor white person from the South or Appalachia, right? The most angry, volatile Trump-supporting people I talked to were white people with money, mostly white men with money. And so I really want us to think about who keeps Trump in power and who his base really is. I think we need to not continue to scapegoat poor white people and count them out. They are bearing the brunt of these harmful policies and we are taking that fury and that righteous anger and directing it where it belongs, not at other poor and working-class people, Black and Brown people, Indigenous people, people of color.

Back to the question of where we are investing, the question of, "Well, let's put more money into urban and suburban turfs because you're going to hit more doors in the least amount of time," I would also say one-on-one conversations is where it's at. A lot of campaigns depend on lit drops or narrative work or online social media campaigns. I think we can never replace one-on-one conversations.

I would say another thing is investing in leadership. We need such a strong, deep bench of poor and working-class anti-racist white organizers. We just have to have more. And so we just have to continue investing in leaders from these areas, the long-haul investment beyond a single election. That's really what we centered our strategy around, talking to people, knocking doors, doing that deep organizing. We are going to have to do deeper work in more conservative parts of our states. And that's what it's going to take.

NU: That conservative Republicans are playing for keeps. They are not playing any games with us at all. Mitch McConnell did not stutter when he said that he's going to do everything he can to stop the Biden agenda. I think that the violence that we are seeing in this moment by white bad actors is being underreported. I'm really proud of all that we have been able to accomplish. People don't recognize how remarkable it is because they don't appreciate the violence that we are routinely subject to in trying to do this work. And I'm talking about state violence that includes press conferences where they put my photo up and call me a criminal and accuse us of participating in voter registration fraud. Georgia's anti-voting bill created five new voting crimes, and two of them are felonies.

What I need people to know is that what we are building is super-innovative. It's designed to meet the threat of the moment. The level of sophistication of these white supremacists and their campaigns has increased. The response from movement and social justice organizations has to meet that sophistication with their own sophistication. That's why we build video games. That's why we focus on misinformation and disinformation and how it's poisoning the information wells and social media. These Cold War tactics have destabilized entire governments without any loss of blood. It's not just foreign bad actors that are using these tactics. It's domestic ones as well, and they're using them against movement organizations and using them to suppress votes. The world needs to know. You see us protesting and you think that that's it. We are fighting on multiple fronts because we're being attacked on multiple fronts.

When we all watched the governor's race be stolen because the dude that was responsible for counting the votes was the dude that was also running, it could have been a moment where people withdrew and were like, "I told you this politics voting shit doesn't work." But they doubled down and they were pissed and they were angry. We created a container for that anger and used it to propel further civic engagement work. Thinking about our anger and our disappointment as a fuel, as a power source.

And then also centering joy and culture. In 2020, we gave away 50 pairs of Jordans. They were literally the hottest pair of sneakers. We gave them away on National Voter Registration Day, and it helped us register 8,000 young people. We love ourselves, we love our families, we love our communities. That's a renewable resource and that's what we use to power our campaigns. As awful as things are, as angry as we get, as hypocritical as our government is, the thing that keeps us going back to work is that we do this work in community. You've seen people go to the ends of the earth for their loved ones. And that is what we're willing to do for Black families in Georgia.

This article is based on a joint interview with Cliff Albright and Adelina Nicholls and two separate interviews with Beth Howard and Nsé Ufot.

Notes

1. Section 287(g) is the section of the Immigration and Nationality Act that allows formal agreements between the Department of Homeland Security and local and state law enforcement agencies. Under these agreements, local and state law enforcement officers are deputized to perform some of the functions of immigration agents. Section 287(g) has led to increased levels of surveillance, detention, interrogation, and deportation procedures in Latinx and other immigrant communities.

2. A 501(c)(4) organization.

2

The Battle for Democracy in Michigan

How Years of Relationship Building and Months of Scenario Planning Defeated Racist Attacks on Democracy in Michigan

Art Reyes III and Eli Day of We the People Michigan

Most Americans don't know much about the Electoral College vote that follows November's popular vote during presidential election years, and for good reason. The exercise is largely ceremonial, with each state's electors casting votes that reflect the popular will of their state's voters. 2020 was different. We endured a dizzying onslaught of possible nightmare political scenarios, with plot lines that—under different circumstances—might have been fun to watch on the big screen, but were a real hellscape to live through. In Michigan, the electors met alone in the State Capitol, under credible threats of violence, with Republican attorneys and grievance peddlers attempting to lawyer their way into the Capitol and seat a completely different set of electors in order to overthrow the popular will of Michigan voters. In the end, however, Michigan's 16 electors safely cast their votes for Joe Biden on December 14, 2020, closing a volatile post-election period rife with attempts to overturn legitimate election results using disinformation, baseless lawsuits, and damaging political theater at the local, state, and federal levels.

The story of how and why our fragile system was pulled back from the edge in Michigan is a story of independently organized public pressure. Along with several others, We the People Michigan led a multiracial grassroots effort that not only anticipated Trump's desperate strategy months before, but out-organized and outmaneuvered the far right. We learned that state power infrastructure matters in the fight to reshape our country. We also learned that multiracial organizing against authoritarian forces is possible even in one of the most segregated states—but only if we are intentional about campaign structure, deliberate about state strategy, explicit about race, diligent in preparing more than the right, and clear that we must build trust early before the stakes are high. These and other lessons from our effort will be important for anyone looking to stave off future attacks on our fragile democracy, and those building movements to expand and deepen it.

Building the United Front

Imagine a split screen dated April 30, 2020. On one side, we had violent foreshadowing in the form of a few dozen armed white nationalists storming our State Capitol, occupying the gallery with long rifles, and attempting to force their way into the chambers where our elected officials met.

On the other side, a different and virtual gathering was happening. Black, white, Brown, Native, and recently immigrated Michiganders from every corner of the state held an eight-hour-long People's Telethon. This effort was organized by a massive coalition called MI Covid Community that was formed in response to the emergent pandemic. Black and Brown folks in Detroit shared poetry and mourned loved ones they had lost that month to the COVID-19 crisis. White and Native people in rural communities and undocumented people throughout Michigan talked about the mutual aid efforts happening, where our people were taking care of their neighbors and communities. Some 21,000 people tuned in online as we called our elected representatives—the same ones who sat in the State Capitol under siege—and demanded an end to water shutoffs, an end to evictions, and the release of incarcerated loved ones at risk of getting COVID-19 in our county jails and state prisons.

On one side, there was violent and racist backlash. On the other, there was the future: working-class people fighting for their communities and for each other. These opposing themes would continue to play out throughout the year. After the murder of George Floyd in May 2020, people across the state poured into the streets demanding justice for state violence perpetrated against Black folks. Massive waves of street demonstrations took place in cities like Detroit, Kalamazoo, Flint, Lansing, and Grand Rapids, but also in rural places like Traverse City, Cadillac, Cheboygan, and Houghton. Demonstrators marched despite the presence of armed white nationalists committed to intimidation and periodic police violence.

Ironically, the physical isolation of the pandemic opened digital portals to constantly meet with grassroots leaders hundreds of miles away on a more regular basis. It became normal to strategize with people from Detroit, Benton Harbor, Northern Michigan, and the Upper Peninsula all at once. We shared resources, we prepared for actions, we commiserated over COVID-19 struggles and fears, and we mobilized our communities for the 2020 election.

There was a palpable sense of solidarity growing around our movement ecosystem in the face of 2020's monumental challenges, and our organization, We the People Michigan, was a key part of that. After launching in 2017, we spent the next three years building relationships, training organizers and grassroots leaders, and asking the question: Is it possible to build a multiracial, working-class movement in Michigan that can create aspirational vision together, acknowledge our linked fate, and take seriously the work of building governing power? We knew that would require us to build a strong and durable people's organization, but also tend to the ecosystem of other movement organizations across the state. For all its trials and tribulations, 2020 in many ways felt like a harvest year. The relationships, trust, leadership, and capacity that we had worked hard to build were being called into action.

But throughout 2020, we also watched as the right grew increasingly extreme in their white nationalist and violent rhetoric. Armed counter protesters threatened demonstrators, elected officials cozied up to white militia leaders, and a plot to kidnap and execute the governor—that would eventually be thwarted—was being formed by leaders of far-right groups.

So when Angela Peoples—a leader from the nascent national formation called the Democracy Defense Coalition—called in early August 2020 with clarity and urgency in her voice that many were growing increasingly worried about an authoritarian play come November, we were aligned. A set of key states were beginning to build plans for worst-case scenarios, and she asked if We the People Michigan would lead where we were.

We held two weeks of meetings with our team, knowing that wading into this would be time-intensive and dangerous. What other urgent work would we need to set aside? What campaigns would stop in order to start this? How would we keep each other safe in the worst-case scenarios? We are a state-level power organization that is not affiliated with any national organizations or networks for a reason. We believe that state power is necessary in order to transform our society, and too often national progressive organizations see state-based organizations solely as a way to execute the plans and metrics that they've raised money for.

This felt different—existential in many ways—so after hours of discussion and planning internally, we committed to leading the work. We moved swiftly with our close partner Detroit Action to build the initial core team and began building out the structure before Labor Day arrived.

The initial core team formed in late August 2020 and consisted of five people: Art Reyes III of We the People MI, Branden Snyder of Detroit Action, Stephanie Arellano of the Services Employees International Union (SEIU), Jamila Martin of Movement Voter Project, and Joon Kang, a labor organizer formerly with SEIU who joined to support this effort full-time outside of organizational affiliation. We articulated our shared purpose in explicit terms, set agreements for how we would work together and make decisions, got clear on our individual capacity, time, and strengths, and decided on roles. We had simple but clear agreements: we would approach the work with joy; we would treat core team meetings as sacred; we would have agendas for every meeting; we would engage, challenge, and push each other with respect and love; we would assume best intentions but acknowledge the impact of our action; we wouldn't let things fester; we would hold ourselves accountable to maintaining anti-racist values; we would be transparent with each other and we would trust the group. Art would coordinate the core team and overall effort. Branden would function as our political director, organizing elected officials, key validators, and partners. Jamila would assemble the constituencies committee and begin pulling a diverse set of constituencies into the effort, leading regular briefings. Joon would begin assembling geographic-based action councils and prepare a foundation for mobilization. Stephanie would steward mobilization strategy and action planning. We did this before we built robust strategy and plans, so we were committed to how we would work together on this monumental project before the work got too deep.

As the core team grew, we onboarded people to how we operated and how we made decisions. We also named explicit roles that we needed others to take on, adding communications, research, mobilization, and geographic action council capacities to the core team. Over time, the team grew to include leaders from We the People Michigan, Detroit Action, SEIU, Michigan Liberation, 482Forward, Michigan United, and Progress Michigan.

We decided to fly under the banner of We Make Michigan, an existing group of grassroots and labor organizations focused on delivering a clear, consistent, and compelling narrative about what working-class people can accomplish together in order to win long-term progressive power in the state. It also gave us a catchy and memorable banner to rally under when the post-election environment predictably devolved into the dangerous circus that it did.

We built action councils that were the rooted engines for the work in communities. These were distributed leadership teams of local leaders in communities across the state that were committed to organizing their communities around anti-democratic threats. We knew we had to build a popular front. In Detroit, leaders who had led demonstrations demanding an end to state violence against Black people stepped in to help lead the action council with local organizing groups. In Washtenaw County, a broad coalition of leftists-to-centrists formed a council, and in Benton Harbor, a core of Black leaders and activists formed another one. In rural Northern Michigan, community members, activists, Native leaders, and people who had never organized direct actions built nine rural action councils across the region.

Hundreds of leaders had explicit roles as we built a structure firmly on a foundation of relationships across community, across race, and across urban and rural regions in Michigan. We strategized regularly with leaders in other states through the national Democracy Defense Coalition, who provided thoughtful resources. We partnered with some national organizations that sought to support the work, most notably Kairos, who demonstrated humble support and honest value adds. More often than not we had to check anxious, white-led national organizations attempting to swoop in, so they wouldn't mess up our tight strategy and intentional structure. The strategy required relationships, knowledge of local context and culture, specific knowledge of state institutions, regulations and political actors, and a commitment to building long-term infrastructure. We fought off Beltway political operatives, consultants, and organizations that had none of those things, with a clear message often delivered directly on national conference calls—follow state leadership or stay out of our way.

We Make Michigan wanted to be ready for the growing swarm of scenarios that might play out when Election Day rolled around on November 3, 2020. We recognized early that we needed to build a tight web of linked progressive forces across the state in order to match the inevitable conservative backlash. In addition to setting up action councils in every corner of the state, we had teams building communications plans, mobilization plans, safety plans, digital organizing plans, and conducting opposition research. Most importantly, we had a core team of rooted organizers and leaders from grassroots and labor groups that had been meeting at 8 a.m. every single day for months in order to prevent a democratic disaster.

This was built quickly in the grand scheme of things, but was only possible because of a disciplined and committed core team, a strong web of alliances across the state with robust leadership rooted in communities, a foundation of relationships and trust that was built well before this moment, and a series of months in 2020 that forced the movement ecosystem in Michigan to scrap plans and silos and work together like our futures depended on it.

Structure made collective strategy easier, and when the crisis happened, we were able to act nimbly and with clarity. This also meant we had to be explicit about race from the start. Months before the election, we constantly highlighted that if the far right tried to steal this election, they would do it with viciously racist attacks on Detroit in an attempt to disenfranchise Black voters and other voters of color. As early as June, right-wing groups began recruiting conservative activists to "guard the vote" at the TCF Center,[1] the convention center where Detroit's absentee ballots would be counted. We predicted that Trump and his allies would wage divide-and-conquer attacks, tacitly endorse white nationalist threats, and stoke racist fears with law and order rhetoric.

The attack

He didn't disappoint. As Detroiters voted in record numbers on November 3, 2020, a powerful few hatched plans to use lazy and well-worn dog whistles about the nation's blackest city to divide us by race and by place. Instead of accepting the unambiguous will of Michigan voters, Trump and his small band of goons tried to bully and cheat their way through an election where the results were clear. It quickly became evident that the power of everyday people to shape our democracy shook them to the core. In his desperation, Trump pulled out a classic conservative play: stoking fear in order to divide and distract us not only from his failures, but Michigan voters' rebuke of him and his brand of supercharged white nationalism. He encouraged and empowered vigilante violence, while blaming Black people, local elected leaders, and anyone who opposed his agenda.

Trump's Michigan strategy was simple: sow distrust in the election by claiming voter fraud in the Motor City in an effort to disenfranchise Black voters and embolden the GOP-controlled state legislature to do his bidding. While voter suppression and divide-and-conquer politics are not new, this supercharged version of it—where baseless, screeching cries of fraud are made to suppress and wipe out the power of voters of color—will likely become a key weapon in Republican's national strategy. It's important to be careful here. The Republican Party, and conservative forces more broadly, have always fought to block anyone they don't like from participating in political life. The founders of the United States were notoriously anti-democratic zealots who, despite some of their rhetoric, trembled at the thought of "the minority of the opulent" being overpowered by "the majority."[2] They established this country based on the idea that the wealth of the first must be protected from the egalitarian impulses of the second. The South was a one-party authoritarian ethnostate for centuries that required a bloody Civil War and a massive Civil Rights Movement to even begin rectifying. The United States, put simply, only became a semi-credible democracy in 1964.

In the decades since, conservatives based their electoral strategy on the three-legged stool of free-market worship, military supremacy, and white cultural anxiety. But as polling shows, the public is increasingly repulsed by the conservative agenda. As that distaste grows, each leg of the stool is kicked out from under them, leaving today's Republican Party with no choice but to make the destruction of what little democracy we have the centerpiece of their electoral strategy. Along with stoking the embers of white resentment, it is all that remains for them. It should come as no surprise then that the scale and pace of the attack on voting rights is reaching absurd heights. At last count, the Brennan Center for Justice documented that "lawmakers have introduced at least 389 restrictive bills in 48 states in the 2021 legislative sessions."[3] Beyond voting itself, Republican leaders are placing enormous amounts of energy and resources towards strengthening their grip on anti-democratic institutions like the federal courts, the Supreme Court, and the United States Senate.

In Michigan, that playbook was put to ferocious use in 2020. Here, the strategy was a work of highly scripted political theater, in which dog-whistle racism against majority Black cities like Detroit took center stage. Michigan's population is roughly 75% white, while Detroit, Michigan's largest city, is nearly 80% Black.[4]

It wasn't only progressives who saw this for the obvious and cynical stagecraft that it was. In an article published by the *Guardian*, reporters obtained a leaked audio recording of Stuart Foster, a Republican operative who trained ballot challengers prior to the election. In it, Foster told a group of ballot challengers on the eve of the election that he was "confident with our election system … I'll get myself into trouble here … if fraud was so prevalent, then did the Democrats forget to do it in 2016? They just forgot to do it? … I mean, Trump … barely won. And it's not because he didn't win. [Democrats] just didn't show up. Did they just forget? Fraud was so prevalent, but they just forgot to do it?"[5]

In one breath, Foster was basically admitting that accusations of rampant fraud are not serious allegations, but flat out nonsense cooked up as a pretext to fan confusion. He is also fully aware that his acknowledgements of the Republicans' cowardly voter intimidation tactics would not be well received by the party leaders who devised them. With the true nature of their hypocrisy revealed, Foster still encouraged the challengers to focus their energy on "these more defensive precincts, these more Democratic precincts," playing into hideous stereotypes of largely Black cities like Detroit being unable to govern their affairs responsibly.

Following their marching orders on election night, challengers descended on Detroit's TCF Center on November 3, 2020. As dozens of us who were there can confirm, these challengers were allowed to observe the count, and were only addressed when they lurked over the bodies of counters and barked out orders at them in violation of the rules. In a ballroom full of working-class Black and Brown Detroiters, working tirelessly through the night at a difficult and thankless job that underpins our democracy, Foster's strategy led to a grotesque display of racist theater. While a routine count was underway indoors, a small but shrieking mob of white Michiganders from far-flung corners of the state was chanting "Stop the count!" at overwhelmingly Black election officials. You didn't have to look hard to catch the horrific parallel to the countless episodes in American history of fierce white backlash to Black democratic participation.

Thankfully, Detroiters and others who love and stand with this city came out in forceful numbers to defend democracy and ensure that every vote was counted. We know that in recent memory, communities across Michigan—especially Black and Brown ones—have had their voices taken from them. It was just in 2012 that voters defeated the state's dictatorial emergency manager law only to see Republican Governor Rick Snyder ram it back through the legislature.[6] The move gave him the power to install emergency managers that superseded mayors and city councils and had unilateral control over school boards and city finances, under the guise of helping municipalities and school districts that were financially struggling. It crushed local democracy and imposed fiscal tyranny in majority Black cities like Detroit, Flint, and Benton Harbor.

The consequences have literally been poisonous for working-class people in the case of Flint.[7] Many of the organizers and everyday people who recently rose in defense of Detroit's election process were also active on the frontlines of those earlier fights against state-imposed despotism, making them clear-eyed, fierce, and battle-tested defenders of democracy.

So when Republican state legislators subpoenaed the Board of Elections for voting records after the election, based on what even the conservative *Detroit News* calls "unsubstantiated claims"[8] of voter fraud, we were all on high alert to ensure that our voices weren't pushed aside again. And we won.

When Trump began attacking Detroit as one of "the most corrupt political places anywhere in our country," we kicked our statewide organizing machine into gear. The action councils we built positioned us to respond across rural and urban communities and across race immediately, telling a powerful story about the solidarity found in Michigan's diverse communities. Those communities issued a thundering response to Trump. Thousands of people mobilized in events held in communities from Detroit to Hancock, Grand Rapids to Marquette, Ann Arbor to Traverse City, and many places in between. People sang and danced in the streets and joyously celebrated—not in the name of any politician, but in the name of our communities and our ability to stand up for each other.

At every turn, Trump and his Republican allies would seek to drive yet another divide-and-conquer tactic to pit communities against one another, but we were ready for them. When the Wayne County Board of Canvassers met over Zoom on November 17, 2020, initially voting 2–2 to halt certification and stop counting votes prematurely, over 300 people stayed on the conference call for nearly six hours to give testimony expressing their outrage at the clear attempt to disenfranchise Black voters in Detroit. The board's move was deeply bizarre given its narrow purpose and the complete lack of evidence that any election irregularities had occurred. The board, after all, is composed of four governor-appointed members whose main job is to certify election results. After significant public pressure, the board later reversed its vote, certifying the Wayne County results.

On November 20, Trump summoned Republican state legislative leaders to Washington, DC, on the eve of the Michigan State Board of Canvassers meeting to pressure them into doing his bidding. We were able to shed public light on their trip and confronted Republican State Senator Mike Shirkey at the airport as he left Detroit, landed in DC, and returned.

On November 23, a mile-long car caravan rolled through Lansing with slogans like "Certify the Vote" and "The People Have Spoken," while a livestream digital event was taking place with dispatches from across Michigan communities. Hundreds of Michigan residents gave hours of testimony, even after the board voted to certify. Black, white, Brown, Indigenous, Yooper (residents of Michigan's Upper Peninsula), Detroiter, suburbanite, all testified with clarity that the people had spoken, and attempts to halt certification were rooted in racist and unfounded attacks on Detroit. We were able to respond robustly because of months of organizing and scenario planning built upon years of intentional multiracial organizing and relationship building. It is how a mass of multiracial Michiganders stood together and resoundingly rejected attempt after attempt to undermine our democracy by denigrating Detroit voters.

Conclusion

In the end, what stopped the charge of aspiring authoritarians was the same as it has always been and will be in the future: the fierce power of everyday people united behind the vision of a better world. When we build real and lasting solidarity, and fearlessly confront the powerful few who shamelessly stoke fear of poor people, people of color, and immigrants to distract from their own horrific failures, we can outpunch them, and build a world where everyone not only lives with dignity, but flourishes to their full potential. And we will.

The reason we fought so fiercely and with such single-minded dedication was not for any party or politician. We believe that the hope for a better world lies with sources of independently organized working-class power that recognize the importance of having an adversarial relationship to the country's ruling class. We also know that we have to be nimble in our strategy and do what it takes to create the most favorable terrain possible for our movement's long-term success. That will always include defending the few pathways working people currently have to participate in shaping the country's future.

Put simply, we are fighting for breathing room and a better chance to build the future we want. In order to get there, we know that we cannot rely on a political party or politician to deliver the future we deserve or to determine the course of our shared future. We must rely on each other. In Michigan, the voters decided that Black Lives Matter, that we need healthcare for all, that water is life and not a commodity, that our planet must be a place that can sustain life for generations to come, and that we won't allow our planet to be sacrificed for corporate profit. The voters decided that every one of us, no matter where we were born or what documents we have, deserves to live with dignity.

We came together to vote in record numbers, and by doing so, sent a message about the kind of world we want—one where everyone not only lives with dignity, but flourishes. When the will of the people was threatened by scared and desperate demagogues, we worked together to demand that every vote be counted, the voice of the people be respected, and we stood side by side to protect each other, our families, and our communities.

We are at a historical moment in this country, preceded by centuries of people-led movements for things like abolition, and women's, labor, and civil rights. Progress was made in those early battles because people stuck together and protected one another.

2020 showed in a palpable way that we can build the multiracial working-class movements we need to win. It required discipline, and intentional structure with clear roles, agreements, and decision making. It required a thoughtful strategy that could anticipate the moves of the opposition and understand where levers of decision-making power existed. It also required clarity that race and class are central to this fight and that we must work to be explicit about their divide-and-conquer strategies while building multiracial movements. We had to love and trust each other enough to step into uncertainty, knowing that we would have each other's back. If we heed these lessons, we can not only defend our communities and each other, but we can win the world we deserve.

Notes

1. See, for example, the video *Operation Guard the Vote*, Michigan Conservative Coalition, 2020, www.michiganconservativecoalition.com.

2. Max Farrand, ed., *The Records of the Federal Convention of 1787*, 4 vols. (New Haven, CT: Yale University Press, 1911–37).

3. Patrick Berry et al., *Voting Laws Roundup: May 2021*, Brennan Center for Justice, May 28, 2021, www.brennancenter.org/.

4. US Census Bureau (2019), "QuickFacts: Detroit City, Michigan," www.census.gov/quickfacts.

5. Tom Perkins and Peter Beaumont, "Donald Trump's Baseless Vote Fraud Claim Opens Cracks in Republican Ranks," *Guardian*, November 7, 2020.

6. Michigan voters voted to repeal Public Act 4, the state's emergency management law, in 2012. Two months later, Republican Governor Rick Snyder signed a new emergency management law into effect, claiming that this version "heard, recognized and respected the will of the voters."

7. In 2011, Governor Rick Snyder appointed Michael Brown as emergency manager in Flint, Michigan. Brown oversaw the switching of Flint's water supply from treated water from the Detroit Water and Sewerage Department to water from the Flint River. This decision is credited as the cause of the city's water crisis, in which residents of Flint were exposed to lead poisoning and a host of other health tragedies.

8. Craig Mauger, "Michigan Senate Finds No Voter Fraud, but Here's What It Did Find," *Detroit News*, June 24, 2021.

3

LUCHA's 10-Year Road Map to Victory

César Fierros Mendoza of Living United for Change in Arizona (LUCHA)

The headline on Election Day 2020 was that Arizona was too close to call. Not mentioned, however, was the work done by thousands of organizers, canvassers, volunteers, and their families up until the cut-off time to vote. They courageously knocked on doors, blanketed entire neighborhoods with get-out-the-vote flyers, and made endless phone calls to last minute voters. Furthermore, they chased down vote-by-mail ballots, ushered people to the polls, drove folks without transportation to voting centers, and handed out water and snacks to voters waiting in long lines. Despite the pandemic and the threat of violence, our community came together and left no stone unturned in this pivotal election. Arizona took several weeks to certify a razor-thin victory for President Joe Biden. This was a historic electoral victory, and would not have been possible without the unwavering perseverance of our LUCHA (Living United for Change in Arizona) organizers and other grassroots organizations across the state.

The last time Arizona actually went blue was in 1996 for President Bill Clinton, who earned only 46% of the vote. Since then, pundits and Democratic Party officials have repeatedly claimed that Arizona was up for grabs. They called it a purple state, or a swing state, and political operators from both parties claimed that the changing demographics alone in Arizona would inevitably flip the state blue. To no one's surprise but theirs, this "sit back" approach did not work, and even as our state changed, the dramatic shift in politics that was predicted never happened. After 1996, Democrats struggled up and down the ballot in Arizona as the state legislature and the governor's seat remained bright red for years. When our community leaders would urge the Democratic Party to invest in our communities, they ignored us. Instead of organizing the Latinx communities that were central to any path to victory for Democrats, they talked a lot and came around once every four years asking for our votes.

We knew that changing demographics alone weren't enough to shake Arizona's political landscape to its core and build a more equitable government, so we got to work ourselves. If we wanted to mobilize people to elect good leaders and hold them accountable once in office, we needed a massive long-term investment of resources, and a sustained effort that involved registering people to vote, conducting voter education, hosting listening sessions, and developing new leaders that came from our communities. From the fight against SB 1070 in 2010 to the defeat of Donald Trump in 2020, building power has been more than a decade in the making for LUCHA, and the historic victories that occurred in November of 2020 would not have been possible without the organizing and lessons learned over that ten-year span.

The birth of LUCHA

Arizona has been a hotbed for right-wing politics, white supremacists, and Nazi sympathizers for generations. Our state has given birth to politicians who erected Confederate statues, Republican officials who mandated segregation, and legislators who banned Mexican American studies. Barry Goldwater was a national GOP star and one of the central figures in the 20th-century conservative movement who got his start in Arizona trying to preserve voting barriers against Brown voters, saying he was against allowing anyone who doesn't understand English from casting a vote.[1] In the 21st century, Arizona has continued to be rife with

Trump-style politicians who grin at the opportunity to persecute Black, Brown, and indigenous communities. These politicians—like State Senate Majority Leader Russell Pearce, Arizona's notorious anti-immigrant Governor Jan Brewer, and America's most deplorable Sheriff Joe Arpaio—made thriving political careers out of weaponizing their elected seats to pass, sign, and enforce legislation like SB 1070,[2] a law used to tear Brown immigrant families apart.

Despite this relentless barrage of right-wing repression, our state has also birthed champions of civil rights and justice. These champions have fought ferociously to dismantle the status quo, put an end to persecution, and uplift their communities. Fed-up communities of color have also built many organizations that continue to fight against racism and inequality, and for justice and liberation. LUCHA is one such organization, founded in 2010 during the aftermath of an onslaught of attacks from a racist state legislature and governor.

For numerous election cycles leading up to 2010, Democrats had dismissed Arizonans of color as "low-propensity" or "infrequent" voters, and so the state Democratic Party failed to invest heavily in door-knocking programs in Latinx, immigrant, Indigenous, and other communities of color. Even mailers about candidates and reminders to vote were often not sent to these key constituencies. That lack of engagement from the Democrats created a dangerous void that Republicans easily exploited in 2010. While Democrats treated us as outsiders unworthy of the same level of focus and support given to white voters, it became easier for Republicans to foment and exploit racist and anti-immigrant sentiment. This opened up an avenue for racist politicians to ultimately pass SB 1070, the most restrictive anti-immigrant law in the country at the time, which later became known as one of the world's harshest anti-immigration policies.[3] This "show me your papers" law was passed by a Republican majority in the state legislature and signed by Republican Governor Jan Brewer. It required local law enforcement officers to inquire about an individual's immigration status during routine traffic stops if the person stopped was deemed "suspicious" of being undocumented.

SB 1070 was an experiment that allowed the conservative right to consolidate power and fan xenophobia through white supremacist tactics such as depicting immigrants as rapists, criminals, and drug dealers. This led to open displays of white supremacist domination and violence through police raids in homes and at *tiangis* (swap meets),[4] as government officials permitted the active racial profiling of anyone that looked Latinx. This became a nightmare for our community. Places like El Gran Mercado in Phoenix—a massive marketplace where Mexican culture, food, and music thrived for 21 years—became ghost towns overnight. SB1070 instilled fear in our community, and many believed that cultural hubs would attract Arpaio raids. This led to the decline not only of places like El Gran Mercado, but of the overall immigrant population in Arizona as around 100,000 Latinx people fled from Arizona to states with "friendlier immigration laws."[5]

When it became clear that Democrats were not listening or standing with us to defend our communities, we came together and started looking out for each other. LUCHA—founded just the previous year—quickly built the organizing infrastructure and political apparatus that the Arizona Democratic Party had neglected to build with us for so many years. Persecuted communities dealing with the racial profiling and raids ultimately rose up and fought back. Instead of bemoaning our plight, we turned pain into action and scars into change, and began what would become over a decade of organizing and building power in our community

Many members of our community had a choice in 2010: flee the state or stay and fight. Some left in the months after SB 1070 passed in April, but many more stayed and joined the movement to stand up to hate and racism. We began dismantling the GOP's grip on power in Arizona brick by brick. We fought back to not only strip power away from those who wished to do us harm, but to also gain power across the state to defend and lift up our communities. Many who were new to politics and organizing became volunteers and organizers overnight. We worked around the clock, equipped with clipboards and voter registration forms, to talk

to people in our communities and build the trust needed to mobilize
people into action across the state. During the summer of 2010, we began
every day with a 4 a.m. vigil at the State Capitol, followed by all-day voter
registration canvassing at grocery stores, churches, laundromats, and gas
stations. When election day rolled around in November 2010, our over
200 volunteers had knocked on over 50,000 doors and registered 13,000
new voters, many of whom were of Latinx descent. Unfortunately, it was
not enough to create immediate electoral change. After the 2010 elections, Arizona still had a racist governor in Jan Brewer, State Senator
Russell Pearce (the main architect of SB 1070) was still in office, and
Republicans still controlled the State Legislature. This gave now State
Senate President Russell Pearce the absolute power to pass whatever dis-
criminatory legislation the GOP wanted, and that's exactly what they
did. However, with a legitimate organizing apparatus, our community
had the tools and capacity to come together, continue to fight back, and
strip power away from hateful politicians.

After the election, we continued fighting against SB 1070, and the
racist law was eventually stripped down piece by piece through federal
courts and the Supreme Court. In 2011, our coalition of Latinx leaders
began engaging directly with state legislators, flooding the House and
Senate chambers and committee rooms with endless testimony and
protest. After the passage of SB 1070, we defeated many other omnibus
bills that attempted to ban undocumented families from being able to
keep a roof over their heads or having access to basic necessities like
running water.

The momentum we gained from the victories in 2010 and 2011 then
catapulted us into a massive campaign that gathered over 18,000 signatures in support of a recall election against State Senate President Russell
Pearce. The election led to his eventual defeat—the first time in Arizona's
political history that a lawmaker was successfully recalled. At the core
of this victory was relational organizing,[6] which is an organizing model
that is in direct contrast to the Democrats' practice of sending strang-
ers into our communities every four years asking for a vote. Relational

organizing is about utilizing the existing relationships we have with family, friends, and neighbors to help turnout voters. Instead of hiring an organizer from the East Coast and bringing them to the West Valley in Phoenix to talk to community members, we recruit from within the communities we're working in, building a lasting network of organizers and volunteers to mobilize their loved ones to protests, the ballot box, and everything in between.

These early experiences built LUCHA into what we would eventually become. Today, we are an organization led by changemakers fighting for social, racial, and economic transformation. We organize low- and moderate income and minority families to take action on the issues that are most important to them and advance the cause of social and economic justice for all. We use leadership development, grassroots issue-based campaigns, advocacy, and civic engagement to create an Arizona in which every resident has an equitable voice in determining the policies and shaping the decision-making bodies that will govern our lives.

At the center of our organization is our membership. Our members are a part of all the decisions the organization makes, from endorsing candidates to advancing policy or planning actions. We host annual events that bring our members together for our Congreso (People's Congress) and our Asamblea, where we vote on our policy platform, aptly named our People First Economy. These are spaces where LUCHA members can decide for themselves how they want to co-govern, and with whom. It is for that reason LUCHA has a special place in the community, and these values and principles were forged in our early days in 2010 and 2011. Through the fight against SB 1070 and the recall campaign, we learned that organizing can be tedious, but it is fruitful. It requires one door knock at a time, one conversation at a time, and one registered voter at a time. There are no secret weapons or tricks. It takes hard work and grit to make progress, and this type of organizing is what propelled us into the next phase of our work.

Growing the fight

In 2015, LUCHA led the YES for Phoenix budget override efforts that brought $21 million to the Phoenix Union High School District, directly increasing student resources and salaries for district support staff.[7] That same year, LUCHA pioneered the Fight for $15/ LUCHA por $15 campaign in Arizona,[8] leading to historic strikes, sit-ins, and marches in Arizona advocating for a living wage. In 2016, LUCHA led the fight for Proposition 206, also known as the Minimum Wage and Paid Time Off initiative.[9] Despite hand-wringing from both sides of the aisle, it passed with the approval of 58% of Arizona voters and incrementally raised the minimum wage for nearly a million Arizonans from around $7 per hour to $12 per hour. This landmark proposition also currently provides up to five days of paid sick time for all workers. Contrary to opponents' fear mongering, economic forecasters found that Arizona's wage increase benefited the state's economy by lifting many Arizonans out of poverty, creating jobs, increasing people's purchasing power, and raising wages for food service employees.

In 2016, LUCHA also co-founded the BAZTA Arpaio campaign along with two partner organizations, Puente and Poder.[10] The BAZTA campaign was led by a multiracial and multigenerational coalition with one goal in mind: the ousting of Sheriff Joe Arpaio. Arpaio was the menace of Maricopa County, whose divisive and racist ideology terrorized Black and Brown communities for 24 years and led to the deportation and criminalization of thousands of Arizonans during his tenure. We successfully defeated him, and although Donald Trump was victorious in defeating Hillary Clinton in 2016, the passage of Proposition 206, the defeat of Arpaio, and our massive successes in increasing voter registration numbers among the Latinx community set the stage for LUCHA to lead the fight in Arizona in 2018 and 2020.

In 2018, local organizations came together to launch the MiAZ campaign, led by a coalition of six organizations: LUCHA, Mi Familia Vota, Our Voice Our Vote, CASE Action, Chispa AZ, and Progress Arizona. The campaign's goal was to push Arizona over the political and electoral tipping point, by harnessing the grassroots power of our respective organizations and communities to flip Arizona blue. MiAZ launched a massive field program that knocked on 1 million doors across Arizona. In addition to the field efforts, we also launched a massive digital and communications campaign to blanket television and radio with ads in both English and Spanish. These investments in our community exploded turnout in the November midterms, and led to major victories, including the election of our very own *luchadora* (member of LUCHA), board member, and longtime community organizer Raquel Teran to the Arizona House of Representatives in Legislative District 30. Our efforts also further narrowed the Republican majority in the Arizona state legislature, elected Democrats to several statewide offices, contributed to Democrats taking back the United States House of Representatives, and secured the election of Kyrsten Sinema to the United States Senate.

The movement we helped build endured beyond just one election cycle, and increased turnout among Latinos in Arizona from 32% in 2014[11] to a whopping 49% in 2018.[12] Meanwhile, voter registration among Latinx voters has continued to increase since 2014, up to nearly 800,000 by the end of 2018. With only 63% of eligible Latinx voters registered compared to 74% of non-Latinx whites, there is still a lot of room for improvement. Regardless, what LUCHA and the MiAZ Coalition were able to accomplish in 2018 was nothing short of incredible, and it gave us momentum to elect Regina Romero—Tucson's first Latina mayor—in 2019.

Without the progress made between 2010 and 2019, we would not have been prepared to deal with an election year that was as far from typical as we could have imagined, and the events that transpired during the 2020 presidential election would not have been possible.

2020: A critical juncture

As LUCHA was approaching our 10-year anniversary, Trump's first term as president was also coming to an end. After almost four years of a calamitous presidency, we began a heated presidential election cycle that would decide the trajectory of our country for generations to come. At the same time, a deadly pandemic was sweeping the country and destroying lives by the tens of thousands every day, and months of nationwide protests had spilled out over the cruel and unjust murder of George Floyd at the hands of law enforcement in Minnesota. The stakes could not be greater, and we knew Trump would stop at nothing to retain power—even if it meant denying the existence of a pandemic and contesting the results of the election if he lost.

Trump's campaign was completely invested in white supremacy. The same divisive tactics deployed in his 2016 victory were amplified tenfold in 2020. He was now backed by a massive traditional and online media machine spewing hate and disinformation, and blanketing social media 24/7. On top of all that, no incumbent president had lost reelection since 1992, when Clinton unseated Bush. To say the cards were stacked against us would be an understatement. Luckily, LUCHA had almost a decade of experience and lessons fighting white supremacists to build on heading into 2020.

The number of registered Democratic voters in Arizona has trailed behind registered Republicans for well over a decade. Despite the warnings from the Latinx community to Democratic Party leadership over the course of several election cycles, there remained no outreach strategy to the Latinx community in order to close that gap going into 2020. This gap has doomed efforts to flip key seats from red to blue in past elections, but the Democrats seemed doomed to repeat their mistakes. In 2016, Hillary Clinton's campaign in Arizona struggled tremendously to connect with Latinx voters. They brought white organizers from outside of Arizona into our communities just a few months before Election Day. As a result of their lackluster efforts, 31% of Latinx voters in that election cast a ballot for Trump, while 61% voted for Clinton. This was in stark contrast to 2012, when the Obama campaign invested seriously in connecting with Latinx voters and won 74% of their vote, while only 26% of them voted for Romney. We know that in 2016, Trump was so successful nationally in part because he was able to steal away enough votes from key racial minority groups that usually vote Democratic—specifically Latinx voters—to narrow Hillary Clinton's path to victory. If Trump was able to siphon off enough Latino voters again in 2020, we knew that Arizona would not turn blue and Trump would be likely to win a second term.

Regardless of these challenges, we persisted, because at LUCHA we considered the reelection of Donald Trump and his lackeys to be an existential threat to the survival of this country and our people. Trump winning would not only validate his xenephobic and fascist agenda, but we knew it would also result in more violence and death in Black, Brown, and indigenous communities. For over four years, we had a sitting US president who openly persecuted our communities and pulled any political string necessary to score points with his base of majority white male voters. Many of their actions were in response to fears that their political power was fading away due to an increasingly progressive and diverse electorate, a phenomenon which was being driven in part by people who looked like LUCHA members. We knew that for us especially, sitting on the sidelines was out of the question. What would be required of us at LUCHA and other organizations was an unprecedented shift in strategy and effort.

The COVID-19 pandemic forced us to recalibrate our entire 2020 operation in order to defeat President Donald Trump and replace GOP Arizona Senator Martha McSally with Democrat Mark Kelly in the United States Senate. Our MiAZ coalition, which we started in 2018, had an especially strong presence in Arizona's five major counties (Pima, Maricopa, Coconino, Pinal, and Yuma) and was also active across the rest of the state. Not only was this the largest progressive effort in Arizona, it was the only serious field campaign in Arizona with this much capacity.

The Arizona Democratic Party and a lot of other organizations decided to restrict their contact with Arizona voters to just phone calls and text messages. We knew that these methods alone would be insufficient in a presidential election, so we knocked on over 1 million doors from July 2020 all the way through election day on November 3, 2020. We also sent over 130,000 text messages, made over 3 million phone calls, registered over half a million new voters, and hosted over a dozen Facebook live events that provided voter education and fact-checking during the debates. We also trained tribal organizers on how to hold voter registration drives in their communities, and sent them to organize in Arizona's various indigenous communities.

While our staff worked mostly from home, in-person voter registration and outreach was done with strict COVID-19 health protocols in place to keep our organizers, canvassers, and voters safe. This included socially distanced drive-through voter registration events, car rallies, socially distanced outdoor mobilization events, and a lot of investment in personal protective equipment (PPE) for our canvassers. When we started in 2010, our teams of canvassers knocked on doors with clipboards and paper lists. This time around, we knocked on doors with face shields, face masks, iPads, iPhones, and copious amounts of hand sanitizer.

Beyond the numbers and strategy, though, what made the biggest impact was the people who threw down with us. When Asusena—one of our canvassers—knocked on the door of a new mother holding a baby in her arms, she shared with Asusena that she might not be able to vote in this election because the pandemic and financial turmoil impacted her severely, and that her mother had just been detained and deported. Instead of counting her out and walking away, Asusena stayed and listened, then responded with, "That's exactly why you vote, so you can be your mother's voice" in this election. Another talented organizer, Alexis, led a team of volunteers to contact tens of thousands of voters via a relational organizing platform, Outvote. Blanca, another amazing organizer, and her team of 200 volunteers made nearly 3 million phone calls to mainly first-time voters. Our communications and digital team used online and traditional media platforms to earn over 100 million impressions through running ads on social media, streaming platforms, running ads on TV and radio, and even billboards across the state. Coupled with on-the-ground organizing, this helped inform Arizona voters on the stakes of this election, and helped combat disinformation campaigns launched by Trump and his allies.

LUCHA and the MiAZ Coalition left no stone unturned in 2020. Our investments in our field, digital, and communications programs are what pushed Arizona over the top. It is what led 70% of Latinx voters to turn out for Joe Biden over Trump and it's what led Latino majority precincts to increase their participation by 20% between 2016 and 2020. LUCHA and allied organizations were able to accomplish something that was completely unprecedented: flipping two state legislative districts and electing LUCHA-endorsed candidates to the Pima County Recorder and Corporation Commission. In addition, we helped give Democrats a national majority in Congress by electing a Democrat to the United States Senate, defeated Donald Trump, and elected Joe Biden. These historic victories could not have been possible without the heroic work done by regular people in our communities who wanted to make a difference.

Our campaign director, Stephanie Maldonado, was one of many who led the efforts to defeat Donald Trump. After more than a decade of organizing, we were able to overcome immeasurable odds because, as she said, "The work for Arizona that has been done over the last 10 years is what truly got us to this moment. We have a new generation of Latinx voters no longer looking towards political parties for support, but instead building their own power and uplifting their communities." The tipping point, she said, were the relentless racist attacks and immigration raids that tore families apart. Enough was enough. "People came together, and made the decision to fight."

One out of every four voters in Arizona make up the largest nonwhite voting block in the country. The Latinx community wielded enormous political influence in this election, and that influence will only continue to grow. Despite the victories we won in 2020, there is a lot of work to be done to continue enfranchising Black, Brown, and Indigenous communities into the political process and winning liberation, equity, and justice for all. Electorally, the Democratic Party lost seats in the US House of Representatives, and the Arizona state legislature did not flip blue as predicted. That is why we will continue to make the types of investments in electoral organizing that LUCHA and other allies were able to make in 2020.

In the past 10 years, "We never gave up hope," Maldonando said. "We saw losses, but we knew that empowering our community, registering our people to vote, sharing our stories, connecting them to their power, walking them through that process, that's what got us here." It's clear that when you invest time and resources in our community, build relationships, and earn our trust, our people show up.

Conclusion

Getting Arizona to the point in history where we have witnessed a multiracial electorate defeated Arpaio, passed a minimum wage initiative, elected the first Latina mayor of Tucson, elected two Democratic senators, defeated Donald Trump, and flipped the state blue for President Biden would not have been possible without a decade plus of organizing and pushing the needle by organizers and activists.

Over the past decade, we have learned many lessons at LUCHA. One of them is that whether you are fighting for immigrant rights, fighting to defend voting rights, fighting to pay people a liveable wage, or fighting some other fight, the same people and the same systems are standing in the way of progress. We have a common enemy that thrives off our division, because when we are not united they win. Building coalitions and partnerships multiplies our efforts tenfold, and in states like Arizona where Republicans hold many of the levers to power, coalitions are absolutely necessary to stopping conservative movements and right-wing legislators. Zooming out nationally, we believe that intentional coalitions and increasing coordination of the left is vital if we are to repel and ultimately defeat the growing far-right movement in this country.

Another lesson is that elections are an essential site of battle that we cannot afford to sit out. When we don't have a seat at the table—either in the form of our own people getting elected or some sort of account-ability over those who are elected—we are on the menu. It is incumbent that we engage in the electoral process to oust politicians who stand against us and elect those who stand with us, but elections cannot be the only tactic that we engage in. Often, our people are disheartened by what feels like wasted energy spent on elections for politicians who will ultimately betray us, but that is only because we usually fail to make explicit the larger strategy that elections are a small part of. At the end of the day, we're trying to build political power to reshape our commu-nities into places where we can thrive, and electoral power is essential to that project.

Our work at LUCHA has led to transformational changes in our state. While we celebrate those victories, we recognize there is still much work to be done. This pandemic has put a stronger spotlight on the inequalities impacting our people. From the economy to healthcare, our communities have been hit hard, and many have lost their jobs, homes, and loved ones. These have always been major issues, but the COVID-19 pandemic has exposed how decades of neglect and abuse exponen-tially worsen outcomes under crises of this magnitude. Our fight for the social, racial, and economic transformation of our communities will undoubtedly last for generations to come, but it is a vision and a world worth fighting for. As we say at LUCHA,"*¡Para mi gente, La LUCHA Sigue!*"[13]

Notes

1. Antonia Noori Farzan, "Racist History 101: When Arizona Blocked Spanish Speakers from Voting," *Phoenix New Times*, March 19, 2018.

2. SB 1070 required state law enforcement to ask people they suspected of being undocumented to present proof of legal immigration status during routine traffic stops. The law also made it a misdemeanor to be caught without those papers. It was the strictest anti-immigration legislation in the country at the time.

3. Randal C. Archibold, "Arizona Enacts Stringent Law on Immigration," *New York Times*, April 23, 2010.

4. An open air market or bazaar held on specific days of the week.

5. Uriel J. García, "New Mexico Job Woes Send Immigrants Back to Arizona," *Santa Fe New Mexican*, November 28, 2013.

6. Pema Levy, "The Secret to Beating Trump Lies with You and Your Friends," *Mother Jones*, October 6, 2020.

7. Yes for Phoenix was a campaign to pass a ballot measure that aimed to increase funding for our public school district.

8. Fight for $15/LUCHA por $15 was a campaign to raise the minimum wage in Phoenix to $15 per hour, and part of a national wave of campaigns to raise the minimum wage.

9. Proposition 206 was a ballot measure in which an affirmative vote supported raising the minimum wage to $10 an hour in 2017, and then incrementally to $12 by 2020, and creating a right to paid sick time off from employment.

10. BAZTA Arpaio was a campaign to block the re-election of notorious Maricopa County Sheriff Joe Arpaio.

11. US Census Bureau (2015), "Voting and Registration in the Election of November 2014," www.census.gov/data/.

12. US Census Bureau (2019), "Voting and Registration in the Election of 2018," www.census.gov/data/.

13. This translates to "For my people, the fight continues!"

4

New Virginia Majority: We Win by Expanding Democracy

Jon Liss

Virginia had huge voter turnout in 2020, with 69% of all eligible voters registered and 81% of registered voters casting ballots. Biden beat Trump by 10 percentage points—54% to 44%. Yet in terms of face-to-face voter contact, this was the worst year in New Virginia Majority's 14-year history. In 2020, because of the pandemic, we had to make do with phone calls, texts, e-blasts, direct mail, and social media ads. This ran contrary to our core approach to voter education and mobilization: identify a walkable universe of potential voters, find those with aligned politics, and then talk to them repeatedly to develop a "political" relationship and win them over to voting in the upcoming election.

In many ways, this year of very little direct person-to-person contact proved our concept, as the cumulative impact of our approach carried us through with a lighter, pandemic-safe touch. We still got good results. Nearly three-fourths of the voters of color we targeted turned out, as did just over two-thirds of the voters age 25 and under. For the 2020 election, we mixed in politically aligned women voters, but for the most part, these were the voters we'd focused on since our first election effort in 2008: infrequent or new voters of color, plus an overlay of newly registered voters in urban areas. Over our years of work, we have been in relationship and conversation with these voters and their communities. Many of them have become consistent, conscious, and aligned voters.

"What stands out the most for me is enlightening community members about the unique position we hold in this democracy as Virginians; a place where we do not take any second Tuesday in November off," said NVM Regional Organizer Nikki Duncan-Talley. "We remind our communities throughout the year of that year's coming election. We strategize with communities to try to ensure they have both economic and environmental justice (it is hard to remember to vote if you have no permanent address). We organize voter registration and community-led advocacy, and we mobilize our communities to go to the polls and to lobby for the change we need."

We are building a constituency that crosses geography, race, generations, nationality, and language. In 2019 and again in 2020 we saw the fruits of this patient labor. We're also gaining a deeper appreciation for some of the structural tensions in the work, and learning core lessons about the importance of strategic analysis and the power of transformative demands.

Virginia in flux

While demographics is not destiny, Virginia's changing demographics and political economy help to create the conditions in which our organizing has proven effective. The last 40 years have seen a wave of immigration—Latinx, Asian, and African—that has transformed the state. African Americans make up 19% of the population, and now another 17% is made up of other people of color. This population is concentrated in the urban crescent that runs from Norfolk through Richmond to Northern Virginia. Our success depends on organizing this base—with a particular focus on working-class women of color.

This is linked to the transformation of the Virginia economy. Industry, farming, mining, and fishing are on the decline. The public sector, semi–public sector (contracted public jobs), and high-tech jobs are expanding. Public investment in education, mass transit, and healthcare are aligned with the values and needs of this growing sector.

We have come a long way since we launched New Virginia Majority in 2007. Virginia was a bipartisan conservative state then. Democrat Tim Kaine was the governor. The House of Delegates was controlled 59–41 by Republicans. The State Senate had a narrow Democratic majority of 21–19. Over the following few election cycles, Republicans grew their majority to 67–33 in the House of Delegates.

The Jim Crow Constitution of 1902 still disenfranchised voters after a felony conviction, and Virginia had among the most restrictive voting rules in the entire nation. Under the guise of "truth in sentencing," the state had ended parole. Its top tax rate was set at $15,000.

Both parties ran Virginia with a business-first mindset. The legislature met for only 60 days during its "long session" and only 45 days during its short session. This was a state in which change was slow and limited, the bipartisan consensus conservative. State elections were held during odd years, which also tended to limit voter participation.[1]

Testing the limits of community organizing

The founding of New Virginia Majority in 2007 grew out of 20 years of community organizing in Alexandria, Arlington, and Fairfax by Tenants and Workers United (TWU).

TWU tried and still tries to learn lessons from the new and old left and from union organizing and fuse radical theory with building local direct-action campaigns that are centered on the leadership and demands of working-class communities of color. Seldom did this work cross the line and engage in electoral politics, and when it did it was almost always as a sidebar effort working for local candidates after hours or organizing Alexandria City Council candidates' forums.

A rapid sequence of events showed TWU the limitations of community organizing without an electoral strategy and also the possibilities of developing electoral work. Between 1996 and 1999 we were leading a battle to prevent the redevelopment and mass evictions of 900 mostly Latinx families from the Arna Valley Apartments complex. Over these years we built a tenants' organization that had a core of 30 leaders and an ability to consistently mobilize 300 residents to protests and Arlington County Board meetings and hearings. We had a coalition of 60 religious institutions and civic associations that supported our efforts.

In the end, we found the limits of local power and budgets in Virginia. Our call for cooperative resident ownership required at least $20 million in local funds. It required the county to use the powers of eminent domain to claim the affordable housing in the *public good*. Our last protest filled the County Board chambers. We shut it down with noisemakers. As the vote to approve redevelopment and mass eviction was becoming clear, we turned our backs on the board. One of our leaders, Reverend Roberto Morales, conducted an interfaith service and we marched out.

We had built a chapter within the TWU family, a powerful and deeply engaged tenants' organization. We had coalesced hundreds of middle-class institutional supporters—but still, we lost. We lost, in part, because the money needed to create a housing cooperative would have to be state (or federal) funds and the laws to protect tenants also had to be state laws, because Dillon's Rule severely restricted what localities could do.[2] The last of the Arna Valley tenants were moved out in December 1999. If our organization was to win future fights, we had to build state-level power!

Shortly thereafter, in May 2000, the city of Alexandria held its primary election. A close friend, Joyce Woodson, had recently been removed from the local housing authority board because she had called their redevelopment plans "ethnic cleansing." Her removal and commitment to affordable housing and working-class Black communities led her to launch a candidacy for city council.

We did several things for that election. We organized an election forum with 200 people where the main body of time was spent answering "yes" and "no" questions. The TWU had a Working People's Agenda, and we wanted to clarify which candidates were deeply aligned and which weren't. We did not want candidates to explain away or equivocate on their answers, so more than half of the forum consisted of simple yes or no questions. For example, "Do you support paying a 'living wage' for workers engaged in contracts with the city?"

Several of us were part of Joyce's "kitchen cabinet," working on policy and campaign strategy. In our spare time we recruited others and pushed a canvass program. When Joyce won her election, she became the first-ever Black woman on the Alexandria City Council. Importantly, lessons from her six years on the council shaped what was to become New Virginia Majority's inside/outside approach to struggling for governing power.

New Virginia Majority

After three years of research, analysis, and legal and corporate planning we launched New Virginia Majority (NVM) in 2007. We had many questions and few resources, and we knew that making the jump from good, even great, local organizing to state-level organizing was going to be a long and difficult process.

At first, we were a staff of two—I was the part-time executive director and Tram Nguyen was our first full-time employee, hired to run a citizenship program. We were trying to raise money to carry out a large-scale voter program during the fall of 2008. By September, we were all in on nonpartisan get-out-the-vote for the 2008 federal election cycle—but we were mostly running on financial fumes. The largest chunk of money was more than $100,000 from the Center for Community Change. As is often the case, this re-grant and work served multiple purposes. At a national level, for the first time since 1964 Virginia was (just barely) in play for the presidential election, with Barack Obama running against John McCain. Growing out of the work of Tenants and Workers United, we had a strong base in Northern Virginia and deep connections with the rapidly growing Latinx and immigrant populations.

There was no middle ground and no time to waste. We needed to educate and mobilize a universe of about 50,000 voters and we needed to do this between mid September and November 4. It was a bit like learning to fly while building the airport runway—but we gained great hands-on experience at doing large-scale nonpartisan voter mobilization. We were fortunate to have a foundation program officer, Adrianne Shropshire, who had previously been part of the senior leadership at Agenda/SCOPE. Agenda/SCOPE was a California-based voter mobilization organization whose founder, Anthony Thigpenn, had been one of the first organizers to take up large-scale voter engagement as a strategy toward building for governing power.

That first year, we ran a regional nonpartisan [section 501(c)(3) of the IRS code] program. We worked in Northern Virginia and we targeted low-propensity voters of color. As a nonpartisan campaign we educated voters about important issues "in play" as well as why we thought voting was important. For NVM that year was about immigration reform and healthcare access. If potential voters agreed with these issues, which were deeply aligned with our values and priorities, we would contact them several more times to make sure they got out to vote.

The first wave of potential voter outreach was geared to identifying voters who agreed with the statement, "Everyone should have access to healthcare including immigrants." While working the doors in Prince William County I remember having a great conversation on the door and I asked the voter if he supported healthcare for all including immigrants. He looked at me and said, "I'm in the military and we all have healthcare, shouldn't everyone?" I gave him info about where to vote and he asked me who our organization supported. I mumbled that this program was nonpartisan. He looked at me, made a big "O" (as in Obama) with both hands, and he said, "I gotcha." I could only smile back with a nonpartisan smile.

In November 2008 Obama carried Virginia with huge turnout, pushed by wide margins of support from voters of color—especially Black women. That first election was huge, and it set the stage for our next 14 years of work: patient and repeated voter outreach geared to turning working-class people of color into consistent and conscious voters. As we grew, we evolved our theory of change, which combined community organizing, policy advocacy, and voter mobilization.

Theory of Change / Teoria del Cambio

Community Organizing /
Organizacion
Comunitaria

Power / Poder

Voter Mobilization /
Movilización de Votantes

Policy Advocacy /
Abogacia

While there are many other aspects to our work including digital, earned media, fundraising, coalition-building, and administration, these generally support our primary activities.

Organizing, advocating, mobilizing

Community organizing: For NVM, this is the political heart of our organization. We situate working-class people of color—especially women—as the center of our organizing work. Over time our organizing has further refined our base by identifying geographically concentrated populations that are Black and/or immigrant. Many are formerly incarcerated people and many others are immigrants without permanent residency. Others are residents of public and private housing who are facing displacement and eviction. From this political center, we work to build local campaigns to both win concrete victories and to develop leaders who can help to move state-level legislative and administrative campaigns. Members and leaders from this work consult on statewide endorsements, participate in statewide issue campaigns, and actively engage with and lead campaigns that target local governments to resolve housing or other concerns. The hope is that member-leaders identified and developed by community organizing will also support large-scale voter education and mobilization.

Policy and advocacy: NVM's inside game of policy development and advocacy is unique among state power-building organizations. Led by co-executive director Tram Nguyen, over the last dozen years we have produced high-level policy and analysis and built deep relationships with elected and administrative officials. At our best, the mobilization of voters and energetic participation of community leaders is coordinated and narrowly targets the legislative votes or executive support needed to win real change that our members deeply and broadly need.

This policy work addresses the critique that says voting changes nothing—particularly with federal legislation often blocked or worse. In Virginia we've tried to connect voting more directly to changes in everyday people's everyday lives. Voting is a means to an end and to the extent that we can link our voting work to actual legislative wins and an improved life, it creates a positive feedback loop and reinforces the connection between voting and on-the-ground conditions.

Thus, connecting newly activated votes of color to legislative and local campaigns creates conditions and context which foster regular voting. Over the last four years NVM has led and/or contributed to campaigns that provided 600,000 people with healthcare through Medicaid expansion (2018), permitted undocumented immigrants to legally drive (2020), set aside $480 million for rent relief and eviction prevention (2020), and legalized less than an ounce of marijuana (2021). These, and local struggles and victories, are a self-reinforcing part of our theory of change. When voting is connected to local and state movement that results in legislation that improves people's lives, then voting truly matters and new voters become consistent voters.

Voter mobilization: NVM has learned that large-scale voter education and mobilization is both an art and a science. In practice it means identifying targets where our social base (working-class people of color and their allies) live in sufficient density to efficiently visit, with the end of increasing their voter turnout in support of candidates with shared values. For us, this is primarily done with paid canvassers who come from and are largely reflective of the voters we mobilize. This work is supplemented by volunteers who also visit voters at home, as well as text and call these voters. Our ability to do this effectively *at scale* shifts who is elected to local, state, and federal office, moves elected officials to support policies aligned with the needs and demands of working-class people of color, and creates a more aligned mass constituency for democracy, sustainability, and racial and social justice.

NVM has registered more than 200,000 voters since 2016. Over our history we have talked with more than 4 million voters. Thousands have been involved in legislative campaigns and local organizing. We are, year by year, creating a voting bloc that is aligned and engaged. As 2020 showed, one year with less-than-optimal voter contact doesn't stop these voters from voting. In many ways, our results were the cumulative product of 13 years of voter work. Although voter organizing is often measured as transactional and short-term, our approach is patient, and our results are cumulative.

Our ongoing efforts to restore voting rights to formerly incarcerated Virginians represent some of our most impactful and integrated work. The campaign to amend the state constitution arose directly out of conversations with hundreds of disenfranchised Black voters who we encountered in our early voter registration efforts. In working-class Black communities, more than one in four Black men were disenfranchised. Listening to members, we made changing the state constitution and establishing the right to vote a central campaign.

It is hard to measure the intensity of feelings around this issue. In 2016 we won administrative relief as then Governor Terry McAuliffe restored the voting rights of almost 40,000 formerly incarcerated voters.[3] By 2021, when various court challenges had been resolved, that number climbed to nearly 200,000.

"While restoration of my rights did not amend the harm and injury that racist white supremacy had knowingly inflicted, and still inflicts, upon me and thousands of others, it gave a degree of human dignity and power I never dreamed of knowing," NVM member Assadique Al Rahman said. We are currently gearing up for an expected constitutional referendum to establish the "right to vote" as a replacement for "felon disenfranchisement." In this case, our mass voter work fed directly into community organizing, then to executive policy, and now to legislative and electoral policy advocacy.

In 2017, Virginia's emerging new majority reduced the Republican House advantage from 66 seats to a narrow two-seat 51–49 advantage. In 2019, huge turnout flipped the state House to a 55–45 Democratic advantage. Democrat Ralph Northam won the governor's race, and the state Senate was narrowly (21–19) Democratically controlled. This trifecta allowed us to build on years of previous work and move a pro-democracy agenda.

The power we have built has resulted in changes which have removed obstacles to voting. Over the last two years Automatic Voter Registration has registered (and re-registered) about 1 million voters who interact with the Division of Motor Vehicles. No-fault absentee voting, mail-in and drop-off voting, and more have transformed Virginia from one of the most difficult (50th in 2015) to one of the easiest places to vote.[4] The collective impact of these changes resulted in an electorate that is largely reflective of Virginia's population (with the exception of noncitizen immigrant adults).[5]

2020 impacts

NVM's work of expanding the electorate, eliminating legal and administrative obstacles to voting, developing a conscious and consistent voting bloc, and connecting voting to social advances and a better life all contributed to Joe Biden's victory over Donald Trump in Virginia in 2020. Altogether the organization contacted 215,579 voters by phone, text, and email.

"After four years of Trumpism and in the wake of the brutal murders of George Floyd, and others, Election Day 2020 was on my calendar," Assadique Al Rahan said. "I predicted that it would be pivotal and historic. I knew I had help. So, I got almost 200 people to vote early, tens of whom I helped register. I drove most of them to the early voting precinct. On election day I drove Souls to Polls."

As good as NVM's work may have been in 2020, a range of other factors no doubt also shaped the election results. The white nationalism and overt misogyny and especially the inept management of the COVID-19 pandemic created a highly motivated voting base of white middle-income suburban residents of Northern Virginia and Richmond. When combined with voters of color in the urban crescent, they added up to the 10% victory margin.

Dynamic tensions

Within the three pillars of our work—organizing, advocating, mobilizing—there are structural tensions. Collectively we are building independent political power with a goal of winning some level of governing power. Focusing on state-level work there is an inherent tension with voter mobilization that seeks to win elections. We are not looking for symbolic wins but winning actual state House, Senate, and executive power. That means supporting a wide range of candidates who are cautious or even opposed to some of the far-reaching demands driven by members coming out of our community organizing base. This is often worked out through policy work that is constantly navigating the difference between what is possible versus what is needed or wanted. What is the balance of power between what we bring to the electoral or policy table versus the broader set of voters or elected officials needed to win an election or a legislative vote? Where are we in terms of our governing power? What is the actual racialized and class basis of power?

Another tension is reflected in the scale and velocity of voter mobilization versus community organizing. Community organizing, with few exceptions, is dedicated to one-on-one outreach by either a paid organizer or a recruited and trained member-leader. New outreach is not likely to exceed 15 new people for 40 hours of work in a given week. This takes into account the work of planning, training, internal meetings, etc. that is likely to take up the rest of the week. A full-time organizer may be adding a person or two a week to active membership. Early conversations and leadership development are measured in hours over weeks. Over the course of three months there may be four or five leaders who are co-building the work. Over time this work does build to a bigger scale, but even after several years organizing on a project or campaign, a core group of 20 leaders is what would be expected. Translating deep organizing into electoral mobilization is, again, patient work. At best this core group of leaders can generate four or five volunteers for a half-dozen weekends prior to an election to support voter mobilization.

Electoral or voter mobilization, on the other hand, needs to mobilize voters (mostly) in a two-and-a-half-month period between late August and early November. It must mobilize enough voters to win elections. In a typical state House election this can mean attempting to talk to 20,000 voters in a district with 80,000 voters. These conversations are short—maybe two to three minutes at most. On any given canvass, 80% to 85% of the target population are not home. This work is by nature repetitive and mass in scale. From our experience, neither texting nor phone banking has nearly as much impact as an actual on-the-door conversation. Conversations are geared to assessing a general agreement and then moving people to vote. In one two-month election cycle in one state House district there are likely to be more contacts and conversations than a full-time paid organizer has in four or five years. Furthermore, to date, only a small fraction, less than 1%, of the people we talk to about voting are going to become off-line involved with our state legislative or local organizing work. (NVM has two primary legal forms. As NVM we can endorse and work to elect local and state candidates; as the New Virginia Majority Education Fund, we can only encourage nonpartisan voter turnout through education and outreach.)

So, who are we accountable to in terms of policies, endorsements, and strategies? The 200,000 voters we attempt to talk to who also receive mail, texts, and phone calls during any given electoral cycle (and the 50,000 we actually talk with face-to-face),[6] or the 2,000 active members who are part of chapters, or the 300 leaders who are actively involved with us on a weekly basis? Holding both is a difficult balancing act given micro-differences within the class and race differences among, for example, Latinx low-income housing activists in affluent Loudoun County and working-class and middle-class homeowners in the same area. There is tremendous power in the organization of a militant but small minority. It is not primarily electoral power. Similarly, there is tremendous power in tens of thousands of mobilized and aligned voters, but the level of engagement mostly doesn't move past voting. At our best, there is a shared belief and interest in our policy or electoral work—for example, beating Donald Trump or amending the Jim Crow denial of voting rights to the formerly incarcerated—and both are *deeply and broadly felt.* At other times there can be both a disconnect on what we are fighting for and a misread of the actual power we have to effect change.

Embedded within this tension is identifying the "united front" or "voting bloc" needed to win elections, and then identifying the relationships among the different strata and peoples within that bloc. The Italian theorist Antonio Gramsci called this bringing together of different people in an historically constituted constellation a "historic bloc." For us this means constantly negotiating the relationship between Black power and rights with immigrant rights and power or workers' rights and power. Many times, there aren't differences, but moving an actual agenda means making choices and prioritizing some policies and geographies over others.

This dynamic tension requires leadership that can lean into and at times against either current in order to win elections, build, and motivate a strong working-class people-of-color base, and deliver real-life improvements.

Core lessons

Strategic planning and analysis are important prior to actions and on an ongoing basis as we build toward governing power. Who are the key sectors who are motors for change and racial and social justice within a given state? Where are these areas on a map? What are the demographic and political economic trends within a given state? Very specifically, which districts are in contention now and which will be in contention in three or five years? Can you build toward and support a Democratic trifecta (the executive branch, and House and Senate majorities)? Which areas and which candidates are likely to support your most far-reaching demands?

Data analysis is an important part of planning and evaluation. Where should we be putting in the long-term work of community organizing? While some knowledge is experiential, other knowledge, especially in a statewide project, requires data and research. Most importantly, where can mobilizing the broadest expression of our social base make an electoral difference? How is our work progressing? Even at a micro level—how well is our work going in a precinct or even with a particular canvasser? We are all stretched and often taking on more than it's possible to do, but data and planning allow us to be most impactful in our work.

What data and planning can't account for is the role of candidates—their effort, charisma, and capacity—in impacting our electoral work. Even with the best plans and deepest analysis it is hard to overcome a candidate who doesn't work hard, raise money, and have a reasonably aligned strategy and the ability to connect with voters. Candidate surveys are good for identifying formal positions, but there is often a need for fuzzy logic to back the right candidate in any given race.

Post-2020, let's take a step back and look at two other key lessons that are, or at least should, play out in strategies for 2022 and 2024.

In Virginia we have fought to expand democracy for our entire 14-year history. This key set of demands is both a demand on principle and a strategic demand whose realization further changes the power dynamic within the state. Simply put, the more the electorate reflects the state's actual population, the greater our ability to win and build power. Given Virginia's history as a Southern slave state the suppression of Black votes has been central to bipartisan white electoral power for much, if not all, of the last 150 years. As Bob Wing noted in the online journal *Organizing Upgrade*,[7] the United States was founded as a white republic.

And as the last five years have shown, revanchist white nationalism has recognized the centrality of rolling back any notion of widespread voting and democracy. The issue of democracy and all the anti-democratic obstacles in Virginia allowed us to mobilize and motivate thousands of voters. It allowed us to build the broadest front and bring out the most volunteers. Internally it has animated our work as we have built organizing, voter mobilization, and policy campaigns. The point here is that fighting for democracy against racist voter suppression allows us to build a broad front and it also will animate a Black (and Latinx/Chicano in, for example, Arizona) fightback.

This flows into perhaps the most important lesson with long-term national impact from our 14 years of work in Virginia. As the US economy and population changes, there is an opportunity to transform this country and address the built-in inequities and history of white Republicanism (nationalism) and white supremacy. As DuBois noted *last* century, "the problem of the twentieth century is the problem of the color line." Looking at the Southeast and Southwest it is possible to identify the contours of a "New South" by looking at regions with a historically rooted population of people of color, an influx of immigrants over the last 40 years, and a changed, modernizing economy (the GINI index is one indicator). In Virginia these layers of a *new majority* start with our Black Belt from Hampton Roads to Richmond, layers on a huge influx of immigrants from the Global South in Northern Virginia, and adds in white and people-of-color workers and contractors involved in government and technology. A similar dynamic or trend can be seen in North Carolina, Georgia, and Arizona, and in the not-too-distant future in Texas and Florida. In a reverse of the traditional conservative connotation of the "Solid South," this is the outline of a progressive and racially just Solid South that could be the generator of a sustainable economy that works for all.

Notes

1. Nancy MacLean, *Democracy in Chains: The Deep History of the Radical Right's Stealth Plan for America* (New York: Penguin-Random House, 2018).

2. The National League of Cities (NLC) explains, "Dillon's Rule is derived from the two court decisions issued by Judge John F. Dillon of Iowa in 1868. It affirms the previously held, narrow interpretation of a local government's authority, in which a substate government may engage in an activity only if it is specifically sanctioned by the state government." From NLC, "Cities 101," www.nlc.org/resource/cities-101-delegation-of-power/.

3. Various court cases blocked and delayed rights restoration. By summer 2021, nearly 200,000 people had their rights restored. See Brennan Center, "Voting Rights Restoration Efforts in Virginia," March 16, 2021, www.brennancenter.org/; also Margaret Barthel, "Nearly 200,000 Formerly Incarcerated Virginians Can Now Vote. Will They?" National Public Radio, November 5, 2019.

4. Reid J. Epstein and Nick Corasaniti, "Virginia, the Old Confederacy's Heart, Becomes a Voting Rights Bastion," *New York Times*, April 2, 2021.

5. Scotty Hendricks, "New Study Shows Which States Make It Harder (or Easier) to Vote," Big Think, October 29, 2020, https://bigthink.com/.

6. In the 2020 election cycle, New Virginia Majority contacted 215,579 voters by phone, text, and email.

7. Bob Wing, "The White Republic and the Struggle for Racial Justice," *Organizing Upgrade*, April 29, 2021, www.organizingupgrade.com.

5

Florida's Rising Majority Learns from Its Wins–and Its Opponents

Andrea Cristina Mercado

As the 2020 presidential election results trickled in during the days and weeks after November 3 and Arizona and Georgia surprised the country by going blue, many politicos were left asking, "What happened in Florida?"

They really meant, "How did the typical 1% GOP victory margin grow to 3% for Donald Trump?" But they missed plenty by only focusing on the top of the ticket. Voters won the first statewide $15 minimum wage in the South. We flipped Duval County, where Jacksonville is located, blue for the first time in a presidential election since Jimmy Carter and flipped Seminole County blue for the first time since 1948. Voters elected 95 of 132 local candidates endorsed by the statewide progressive coalition Florida for All. Voters sent Michelle Raynor as the first Black queer woman to the statehouse, and put Daniela Levine Cava, the first woman and first Jewish person, a former nonprofit leader, in the Miami-Dade mayor's office, which radically altered the politics and organizing terrain of Florida's largest county. We unseated county commissioners in Orange County, and it is now one of the largest county commissions completely run by women who are challenging corporate power.

Both sets of 2020 results are the outcome of determined, focused efforts worth studying.

Donald Trump won because the GOP made Florida a must-win last stand for the candidate and the party went all out. This included illegal maneuvers that are still under investigation, such as GOP operatives handpicking and bankrolling a candidate with the same last name as progressive champion José Javier Rodríguez in State Senate District 37; the progressive Rodríguez lost the race by 32 votes while the fake candidate garnered 6,000 votes. But an unprecedented collaboration of independent political organizations kept Trump's margin down and advanced scores of progressive candidates around the state. These gains came from years of organizing in communities of color and working-class communities, combined with a new level of shared vision and strategy that amplified the impact of our work.

Hot takes abound about which state gets to be "the next Georgia," shorthand for voters of color saving democracy against the odds and pundits' predictions. And while organizers in Florida are working day and night to do what our friends at the New Georgia Project, Fair Fight, Somos Georgia, and others have done, Florida is not the next anything, but itself.

Florida is not just a swing state. It is an all-out battleground.

Anatomy of the nation's third-largest state

Florida is the third largest state in the nation in terms of population, size, and economy: 23 million people, 67 counties, and 14 media markets. We are one of the most ethnically diverse states in the nation. Florida is home to the largest Haitian American, the largest Cuban American, and the largest Puerto Rican populations in the country. One in five Florida residents is an immigrant from another country. There is a constant influx of migrants from the Caribbean and Latin America. That number doesn't include the influx of transplants and primarily white retirees moving to Florida from the Midwest and the Northeast.

The state started as a "banana republic," and it is still run to benefit corporations. What was part of the Confederacy is now consolidated as the rearguard of the GOP with 20 years of unabashed Republican rule cementing institutional racism and widespread economic and educational disparities.

However, Florida is and has been the site of vibrant resistance. We are the home of the unconquered Seminoles, descendants of Indigenous people who eluded capture by the US army in the 19th century. Black Seminole rebellion resulted in one of the only formal emancipations of escaped enslaved people prior to the Civil War. In 1964, St. Augustine, Florida, launched its own part in the civil rights movement with the legendary wade-ins that desegregated its pools and beaches. In 2010 Organize Florida emerged from the ashes of ACORN,[1] and Florida New Majority was founded by the Miami Workers Center and Florida Immigrant Coalition to build independent political power centering Black and Brown communities. In 2013, Black youth took over the statehouse to seek justice for Trayvon Martin; Dream Defenders was born, and a seed for the Movement for Black Lives was sown. Several years later returning citizens would win the largest expansion of the franchise in America since women won the right to vote.

The right-wing voting bloc that elected Ron DeSantis and Donald Trump has a long history and an entrenched culture to draw on. Our forces, which include the people who saw their pay increased and themselves more reflected in many local governments in 2020, also have a legacy we build on.

A rising electorate starts making an impact

Over the past five years several organizations that were working on racial equity and economic justice campaigns to transform the state have been collaborating and shaping shared vision, and long-term goals that inform our electoral programs. We came together because we were frustrated by the pattern of resources pouring into Florida a few months before an election and then disappearing, how our electoral engagement wasn't serving our long-term organizing efforts, and the ways it often strained relationships among organizations. At the end of each election cycle—win or lose—progressive forces were no more powerful than before. Dream Defenders, Faith in Florida, the Florida Immigrant Coalition, Jobs with Justice, New Florida Majority, Organize Florida, and SEIU came together as the Statewide Alignment Group to change that. We invested in long-term visioning and relationship-building and were able to overcome distrust, with a shared purpose, and long-term plans. Our approach to electoral engagement was year-round, linked to local and state work on progressive policy campaigns to advance our long-term goals.

We had two aims: 1) break the back of Jim Crow by systematically challenging structural racism and reimagining public safety, and 2) advance nonpatriarchal co-governance by electing people who would go to bat for Black and Brown communities, often from within our ranks, and then create community–government partnerships to advance the policies, budgets, and representative democracy our communities deserve.

For context, in 2016 Donald Trump won Florida's 29 electoral votes by a margin of only 1%. His path to victory centered on decreasing Democratic support in key regions of Florida despite historic turnout and gains in Miami-Dade. Hillary Clinton won Miami-Dade by 287,214 votes, almost 79,000 more votes than Obama got in 2012. However, Democratic support in rural counties shifted almost 3% toward Republicans/Trump. This swing alone accounted for almost 128,000 more Republican votes, and Trump won by 112,000.

Going into 2016, Florida had nearly equal registration rates between people who registered as Democrats and Republicans, but we regularly experienced higher turnout rates among registered Republicans. On top of that, almost one-third of the state's voters register as independents with no party affiliation. At the end of the day, progressive voters turned out in 2016, but were eclipsed by voters animated by Trump. Progressive forces were shell-shocked that the unthinkable had happened: white supremacists had been emboldened and unleashed, and we were about to experience an all-out assault on gains made over decades, which would reshape the future.

Following the first year of a presidential administration that was focused on demonizing immigrants, undoing environmental regulations, undermining decades of civil rights policy, making unprecedented attacks on democracy, and fomenting global ire, the Statewide Alignment Group took our collaboration to the next level. We came together in 2017 to partner with the Florida Rights Restoration Coalition and collect the petitions necessary to put voting rights for people with felony convictions on the ballot. In 2018 we ran a scaled field program to win rights restoration with Amendment 4, and seized the opportunity to elect a bold progressive, Andrew Gillum, as governor. The campaign inspired millions. On Election Day we celebrated Amendment 4's landslide victory, but we lost the governor's race by less than half a percentage point. It was closer than any Democratic candidate had come in close to 20 years, and proof that a progressive Black candidate could win a statewide race. It also marked a notable shift in how our organizations were collaborating inside and outside of election cycles after years of strategic discussion and planning.

Like many places in the country, Florida Democrats experienced a rural and suburban rebound in 2018. Margins moved significantly back toward Democrats in most places, and urban areas were galvanized. We saw historic voter turnout for a midterm election, which usually has much lower turnout than a presidential election. Although 2018 turnout was 930,000 votes less than it was in the 2016 presidential cycle, Democrats only won 179,000 fewer votes in regions outside of Miami and Fort Myers. Overall turnout across the board ran approximately 12% higher than in the previous 2014 midterm cycle. Republicans had far outspent Democrats but were holding on by their fingernails. They used 2018 to test strategies to mobilize Cuban Americans that had stayed home in 2016, and saturated Spanish airwaves and the internet with attacks on Andrew Gillum as a socialist and a corrupt politician, repleat with dog-whistle racial politics. All told, the governor's race and the US Senate race both came close enough for a recount, but the GOP squeaked through.

While we celebrated the tremendous success of Amendment 4 to re-enfranchise people with felony convictions, we were also ringing an alarm bell. Outside the suburban rebound, there was a decrease in support for Democrats in Miami-Dade 15 times larger than the margin in Bill Nelson's Senate race and 4.5 times larger than the margin in Andrew Gillum's gubernatorial race. Democrats netted 220,000 fewer votes than in 2016, with a net loss of 152,000 votes from the 2016 margin. DeSantis ran as a mini Trump and the racially charged suspicions as "under FBI investigation" that DeSantis lobbed at Gillum (despite DeSantis's own House Ethics investigation), the communications channels the right invested in, and the constant visits to Florida by Trump and his cabinet members undoubtedly had an impact.

While the issues-based electoral organizing and cross-organization collaboration demonstrated our growing power and impact, the right's attacks and constant infrastructure-building and investment in long-term organizing pointed to the potential hazards.

Building on our shared work, the members of the Statewide Alignment Group launched "Florida for All" in 2020 as a long-term collaboration anchored by these state-based organizations working in multiple counties and committed to engaging communities of color inside and outside electoral cycles. As we had in 2018, we partnered with Win Justice, a national collaboration between Community Change Action, Color of Change Action, Planned Parenthood Action Fund, and SEIU.

We were clear that our 2020 program had to:

1. **Expand the electorate** by running large-scale voter registration programs.

2. **Increase turnout for voters of color** by establishing a deliberate and culturally competent civic engagement program to reach and engage Black and Brown voters in communities.

3. **Expand our geographic footprint** by working in counties with growing communities of color, outside of current community organizing epicenters in the largest urban areas.

4. **Move voters with persuasive messaging** online, in the media, and offline.
5. **Mobilize the base!** We knew we could not take voters of color for granted or simply assume that they would vote or cast ballots against Trumpism.
6. **Protect the electorate.** Critically important given the state's history of voter suppression, and tactics we witnessed in 2018 by Republicans specifically targeting early voting and vote-by-mail programs.

We knew that in order for Trump to repeat victory in 2020, he needed Florida. He had no path to the White House without it. And he specifically had to sustain his gains in Florida's urban areas like Miami and replicate his performance outside urban centers. So we had to expand our work to organizing in counties with growing populations of communities of color but less progressive infrastructure, while also continuing to engage people in places like Miami, Tampa, Jacksonville, Fort Lauderdale, and Orlando.

In Florida, elections are won on the margins time and time again, but the long-term strategizing and relationship-building we were doing were making a difference. We had a strong coalition, and we had the capacity to talk to voters on a massive scale. We had aligned on a plan earlier than ever, incorporating lessons learned in previous elections. We were putting all the pieces into place when we were hit with a global pandemic no one saw coming.

2020: Pandemics, police violence, and presidential elections

When the pandemic hit, we were in the midst of get-out-the-vote activities for the Florida presidential preference primary in March. Our offices closed, our canvasses shut down, and New Florida Majority transitioned our 200-person voter registration and canvass team into a remote phone banking operation within 48 hours. As we faced the health and financial impacts on our communities, with mass layoffs among hospitality and restaurant workers and disinformation on the virus spreading like wildfire, our team went to work conducting wellness calls. They contacted 1.2 million Floridians and had 52,000 conversations. And when resources became available for mutual aid, we distributed over $375,000 to the people who expressed financial hardship and sent teams of organizers to food distribution sites to hand out cash assistance and call on the governor to take action to protect public health.

Meanwhile, the state of Florida refused to adapt the March presidential primary to the pandemic conditions. It refused to create a way for people to vote by mail if they hadn't already requested a vote-by-mail ballot, a harbinger of what we knew to expect in the August state and local primary elections and the November general election. We worked with the Advancement Project, Demos, Dream Defenders, Organize Florida, and LatinoJustice to take the state to court to make sure voters would be protected.[2]

The resilience of organizers, canvassers, and our members cannot be overstated. As we pivoted to voter engagement strategies around the August Democratic primary, they continued to have the necessary people-first conversations that are rooted in our shared humanity. Our teams not only held it down on the volunteer phone- and textbanks, but also engaged our communities and constituencies with a multilingual Community Events Program and held popular education and leadership development courses with hundreds of people over Zoom. It was challenging to not have our in-person energy on the streets, especially when the Republican Party refused to take the health and safety of communities into account and continued to canvass and hold super-spreader political rallies. We got creative and partnered with graffiti artists and muralists to put up voter messages and held creative online events with musicians and movement elders. As the election neared, we hosted car caravans with decorated carnival floats and music, rooting our get-out-the-vote efforts in our diverse cultures.

Expanding the electorate

The Florida for All program focused on a universe of 3.8 million voters. Of these, 1.7 million were Black, 1.8 million were Latinx, 2.2 million were women, and 1.3 million were under the age of 35. The bulk of the work was focused on the infrequent voters in 10 counties that make up 80% of the Democratic vote share.

Our 2020 campaign had more than 1,240,415 conversations with voters over the phone and eventually on the doors, many of them the infrequent voters that both parties routinely ignore. Before the August 18 Democratic primary, we were talking about down-ballot candidates— the people we wanted to represent our communities in Congress, in the state legislature, or on county commissions. For the general election we focused on Biden/Harris, Amendment 2, which would establish a $15 minimum wage, and priority down-ballot races. We trained and engaged over 5,000 unique and amazing volunteers.

Many of the returning citizens who had collected petitions to put Amendment 4 on the 2018 ballot were hired to register voters, and then became election protection guardians of democracy. They held community barbecues with balloons, music, and ice cream at apartment buildings, and then stood watch at polling sites, monitoring the long lines over two weeks of early voting, handing out water, helping out people who looked confused or frustrated because their polling place had changed at the last minute, or who didn't want to be late to work. It was the first time we had executed election protection at key voting sites for every day of early voting, and innovated WhatsApp communications to report in quickly to a centralized group. Participation transformed people like Shacoya, now an organizer in Palm Beach helping families facing eviction, who said at first she just wanted a job, she'd never been into politics: "I learned so much and it's changed me. I never imagined how I would transform. My kids got involved and I'm so grateful. It was a hard year, but this work has been one of the best experiences for me." Or people like Cecil, who said, "I wasn't a political person, but I learned so much. I'm one of those Amendment 4 people, I learned how to canvass, how to register people to vote, how to phonebank, and get out the vote, be a poll monitor. It's for the cause."

Persuasive messaging

We invested over $1 million into a paid multimedia campaign to reach Black and Latinx voters in the 10 counties we concentrated on. We built out a Black leaders' coalition to engage the diversity of Black voters in English and Haitian Kreyol, and to test different messages with Black voters, including ones aimed at motivating them to volunteer. With Florida para Todos, we built working groups of Venezuelan, Cuban, Colombian, and Puerto Rican organizations and individuals to discuss and develop digital and radio content and spokespeople from distinct backgrounds, and leveraged Latinas en Marcha as a platform for Latinas to assert an unapologetic intersectional politics.

Program outcomes

In the August primary we saw the impact of our program, with 45 out of 55 candidates with a primary election opponent emerging victorious. Twenty-five of them had no serious challenger in November and won outright. We unseated corporate Democrats and elected champions from our communities—people like Angie Nixon, a longtime organizer and field director for our 2018 program, for state representative in Jacksonville; Omari Hardy, who unseated an anti-choice corporate Democrat in the state legislature in Palm Beach; Monique Worrell, who ran for state's attorney on a platform of criminal system reform and was down 30 points two months before the election; and Elizabeth Bonilla and Mayra Uribe, who won seats on the Orlando County Commission.

As we headed into the general, the pressure mounted. The resources that were scarce in June were now pouring into the state, and we decided to work with medical professionals and explore a door-to-door canvass. After speaking with several epidemiologists and public health experts, and connecting with labor unions and organizations that were on the doors, we developed our COVID canvass protocols and started our canvassing campaign with Somos Votantes. We knocked on over a million doors in a month, exceeding all expectations.

Reflecting on our program, post-election, despite the pandemic and the ruling party's voter suppression tactics, we met many of our goals, we made them fight for every inch, and the amount of time Trump had to focus in Florida made the White House victory possible. We increased voter turnout among voters of color. We expanded into more counties, we continued to deliver culturally appropriate and impactful messaging, and we innovated and updated election protection systems in our state. We have much to build upon as we continue our coordinated, year-round electoral work.

There is no break before the midterms

While liberal and progressive circles analyzed the elections for demographic trends and early predictions of the next state and civic organization to bet on, the GOP had one singular conclusion from 2020: we must be stopped.[2] In almost every state, the GOP introduced anti-voter bills to make it harder for people to participate in democracy. In Florida, Governor DeSantis took their efforts a step further to reduce people's access to the ballot and criminalize their participation in protests like those we saw in the wake of the murders of George Floyd and Breonna Taylor.

In a state where a record number of people voted by mail, jumping from almost 30% of voters to 44% of voters, Republicans are fearful of what that could mean for the 2022 election, given that 2.1 million Democrats requested vote by mail in 2020 compared to 1.5 million Republicans. So, the GOP statehouse pushed through a law to clear all vote-by-mail requests before 2022 and force voters to resubmit if they want to vote by mail every election cycle. Once again, we have sued the state to stop this anti-democratic ploy.

Meanwhile, after the election, two large civic engagement organizations in the state—New Florida Majority, which historically organized in Jacksonville and South Florida, and Organize Florida, which held down Central Florida's "I-4 corridor" from Orlando to Tampa Bay—joined forces to become Florida Rising, an aligned and coordinated statewide vehicle for what will become the largest organizing, voter registration, engagement, and turnout organization in the state. This wouldn't have occurred without the deep trust and relationships forged in the statewide alignment group.

Challenges, and change that doesn't happen overnight

The presidential margin in 2020 may have been 3%, but in the last midterms the races for governor and US senator were decided by less than half of one percent of the vote. If we are to overcome the GOP's move to create one-party rule by locking the majority of Floridians out of elections, we—the larger *we*—will need to learn hard lessons as we continue the momentum we've been building for the past decade.

Recognizing the unique right-wing Infrastructure in the state

There is a reason that Florida is the home to Roger Stone, Matt Gaetz, and now Donald Trump. Since the orchestrated theft of the 2000 election for George W. Bush, if not before, the GOP has sought to consolidate its power in the state. The result has been 20 years of GOP rule at the state level that has gutted our unemployment system and all public services. Nationally we've become an epicenter for disinformation that is deployed with a savviness that recognizes and speaks to the various nationalities and interests within the state. Content and strategies created and tested in Florida are deployed around the country, as we saw when communications and messaging from 2018 went national in 2020.

Rather than taking a reductionist approach to Latinx voters, they employ sustained multifaceted efforts. For example, current Governor Ron DeSantis chose a Cuban lieutenant governor as his running mate and launched his campaign from Miami's Calle Ocho. He and the other politicians who pass laws to repress protest and access to the ballot here are the same ones who most loudly rally for "democracy" on the island of Cuba. The Koch-funded Libre group was present at airports welcoming Puerto Ricans to Florida in the wake of Hurricane Maria, helping people find housing. Trump was outspending Biden two to one on Florida's Spanish radio outlets in June 2020. More broadly, a study our organization supported identified widespread instances of false information about the results of the 2020 election on local Spanish radio—including assertions that 200,000 more voters than residents voted in Pennsylvania, and that Black Lives Matter and antifa were behind the violent attempted takeover of the US Capitol on January 6, 2021.[4] In 2020 the majority of Latinos statewide voted definitively for Joe Biden, but conservative Cuban Americans mobilized in force in Miami-Dade and Latinos from other countries of origin joined them in voting for Trump. The GOP and its allied Libre initiative is actively courting Latino voters and contesting for their hearts and minds, and they are getting results.[5]

To organize in Florida is both to advance a people-first agenda and to counter-organize against the right's corporate and white supremacist program. Without the latter, the former will be nearly impossible to achieve.

Overcoming cynicism

The reach Florida civic institutions have built together is unprecedented. We can more quickly and directly connect with millions of voters than ever before. Yet especially for those of us seeking to expand the electorate by engaging new or infrequent voters, contact is not enough. We need to build a *relevancy* to the lives of working people and people of color that overcomes the entrenched cynicism that demobilizes and disengages.

Cynicism is complex and seeded by three things: the GOP's fomenting dissatisfaction with government overall, our own movements' critiques that don't also carry creative solutions, and a pattern of Democratic electeds who raise expectations in campaigns and seek to lower them in governance. As a result, there is a deep divide in our communities between those willing to participate in politics and those who have checked out of the process.

To engage or re-engage and effectively battle cynicism, it will take more than a new round of new candidates' smiling faces and another list of promises. In 2020, most of our organizations sought to leverage the presidential primary as a way to elevate progressive demands and ultimately ensure what we calculated to be the most viable platform and strategy to win the election. While that laid the groundwork for the massive relief bills and the child tax credit that Congress passed in 2021, it also disorganized and split movement forces across different camps and only engaged segments of the base that already believed in candidates in general. Meanwhile, ballot measures that are more relevant and have tangible, undeniable results, such as raising the state's minimum wage, are often overlooked.

We know that to win elections we need to win more of our people into the electoral process. This experience shows that doing that will require much more than candidate-based organizing—even the culturally relevant, technologically savvy, people-powered organizing we've been doing.

Year-round and local work

Florida, and any swing state, is familiar with a certain trend in each election cycle. We become, for a fleeting moment, the focus of all national attention. That attention takes two forms: replacement and reinforcements. In 2020, we saw both at play. On the one hand, national dollars and Beltway-driven formations took to the airwaves, hired canvassers, and parachuted into the state at times with little coordination or care for repetition. But the last cycle bore fruit with a different approach. Seed the Vote and the Unitarian Universalists' #UUtheVote campaign partnered with us to provide hundreds of volunteers from their bases and congregations to phonebank our lists with our scripts with results that fed into our data and follow-up apparatus.[6] We saw national programs work best when they were in amplification of and coordination with local organizations that are building connection, presence, and credibility year-round.

Credibility overcomes cynicism. It's built through relationships. That's probably why "relational organizing" was a buzzword and trend for 2020. But relational organizing that earns credibility takes more than apps and leveraging each others' fave fives. It's more than just believing your *tía*. It's about collective experiences that make us believe in each other and ultimately believe that change is possible. It takes a track record of being there, building people's individual and collective sense of power, and choosing fights that demonstrate that winning is possible—not just in an election cycle but when the election is over and the candidates are struggling to deliver. Local organizing and the infrastructure it both builds and requires—at the state, county, and city level—is the key to push through the successes that those same candidates will need to campaign on in the next cycle.

People facing eviction are more likely to entrust credibility about whether they should vote and who to vote for to the people who were there to protest the landlord and win rent relief. People whose relatives have been targeted by over-policing will be more ready to roll with the organization that rolled for them when their sister wasn't being given medical attention when she was locked up. And ultimately, we'll be more prepared and practiced for the campaigning it will take to win elections if we are engaging in it year-round to win on the issues and policies that will be up for debate in the next cycle.

After 20 years of rule and consolidation in the state, the GOP is hanging on tooth and nail, but we're just getting started. We're steadily deepening our community roots and expanding our geographic reach. Florida Rising now has monthly people's assemblies in almost a dozen counties, where community members participate in politics and democratic decision-making in real time. Faith in Florida ran a nationally recognized Souls to the Polls program in 2020, and has massively expanded their rural organizing program, and local tables are forming for organizations to come together to advance wins people can feel at the county level. We're tightening our collaboration and refining our strategy and message, leaning into frames that advance interdependence, representative democracy, and people and planet over profit. The laws they're passing and the stumbling blocks they're putting in our way are not insignificant, but they are obstacles that we are more poised than ever to overcome. The new majority coalition has arrived. It's only a matter of time before it is no longer ascendant, but holding the reins of power.

Notes

1. ACORN, the Association of Community Organizations for Reform Now, was founded in 1970 in Arkansas and grew to be a national and then international network of groups organizing in and advocating for low-income communities. It was one of the largest nonparty organizations registering voters in the US before a right-wing sting operation led to the dissolution of its US work in 2009. Statewide groups re-formed under other names.

2. New Florida Majority Education Fund, Organize Florida Education Fund, the Dream Defenders, Demos, LatinoJustice PRLDEF, and the Advancement Project National Office sued Florida Governor Ron DeSantis as well as the secretary of state in the US District Court for the Northern District of Florida. The suit was filed March 17, 2020, over the state's failure to make voting easier for the presidential primary. It was amended in April 2020 and settled in July 2020. For more information on Florida voting rights suits in 2020, see www.brennancenter.org.

3. Trevor Loudon, "A Democrat-Run Florida? The New Florida Majority's Plan to Turn the Sunshine State to Socialism," *Epoch TV*, July 21, 2021. The teaser copy asserts that "Mass voter registration drives are being organized in minority communities in key swing states across the American South in order to benefit the Democrats. Who's doing this? A network connected to the Chinese Communist Party (CCP)." https://www.theepochtimes.com/a-democrat-run-florida-the-new-florida-majoritys-plan-to-turn-the-sunshine-state-to-socialism_3898007.html.

4. Tim Padgett, "Report Spotlights 'Under-the-Radar' Spanish-Language Radio Disinformation in Miami," *WLRN-FM* Latin America Report, June 8, 2021, www.wlrn.org.

5. Marcela Valdes, "The Fight to Win Latino Voters for the GOP," *New York Times Magazine* online edition, November 23, 2020, www.nytimes.com.

6. UUtheVote is a nonpartisan program of the Unitarian Universalist Association. See https://www.uuthevote.org/.

6

Pennsylvania Stands Up: Stepping into the Whirlwind

Jacob Swenson-Lengyel and Jules Berkman-Hill

The streets were filled with dancing. In Philadelphia, the joyous resistance went on for days as Trump campaigners tried to stop election officials inside the convention center from counting the ballots. The party included balloons, speeches by movement electeds like Kendra Brooks and Nikil Saval, and even Gritty, the orange monster mascot of the Philly Flyers.

It wasn't just Philadelphia.

In Pittsburgh, community organizations hosted a parade, floats and all, as State Rep. Summer Lee addressed crowds demanding that the results of the election be respected. In Harrisburg, a dancer in full *carnival* attire, a Korean drum group, and a dad in a camo hunting hat and "Count Every Vote" t-shirt, with his two young daughters, stood shoulder to shoulder in the face of threats from right-wing militias. In Lancaster, the crowd of hundreds included clergy, military veterans, and huge banners painted like vote-by-mail envelopes proclaiming "Everyone Counts." In the Lehigh Valley, organizers brought donuts to poll workers after they stopped counting ballots overnight, to make sure they kept going the next morning.

These and other actions around the state capped an unusual and unrelenting election year, as people power at the ballot box and in the streets squeezed Donald Trump from office. They also spoke to long-term organizing efforts by Pennsylvania Stands Up and many other independent political organizations across the state.

Pennsylvania's political landscape

For those who only hear about Pennsylvania once every four years, there are some important things to know about our state's political terrain.

Pennsylvania sits at the intersection of several distinct geographic regions (an apt metaphor given the state's fondness for road trips and convenience stores). The northwest area of the state belongs to the American Midwest, both culturally and economically. Toward the southwest and southern border with West Virginia, the state melds into Appalachia. Northeast Pennsylvania (NEPA) is coal country and, like many other parts of the state, filled with post-industrial communities. Southeastern Pennsylvania belongs to the mid-Atlantic region and is home to Philadelphia, birthplace of American independence and a historic boundary between North and South.

These regional differences create distinct identities within the state, posing challenges for organizers looking to bridge diverse constituencies and build statewide power. Focus groups conducted in early 2020 revealed the lack of an overarching identity. Participants were far more likely to identify as residents of their local county than with the state as a whole.[1] Regional differences correlate with demographic differences and attendant voting patterns. About 75.0% of Pennsylvanians are white, 12.7% are Black, 8.1% are Latino, and 4.6% are Asian or Pacific Islanders. Philadelphia, however, has a people-of-color majority, as do several smaller cities located in majority white counties, such as Lancaster, Allentown, and Harrisburg.[2]

Despite being divided by racial and geographic identifications, Pennsylvanians across the state have experienced the devastating impact of neoliberalism. Deindustrialization has meant the disappearance of living-wage jobs in Pittsburgh, Erie, and many rural areas and small towns. Philadelphia is the poorest major city in the nation. As with the country as a whole, the rich have captured an ever-greater share of income since the 1970s.[3]

While Pennsylvanians have a shared stake in challenging the neoliberal status quo across race and place, neither the Democratic Party nor progressive organizations have had sufficient organizational infrastructure outside Philadelphia and Pittsburgh to reliably unite a multiracial working-class bloc. Republicans have controlled the state Senate every year since 1994, and the state House all but five of those years.[4] Choices by the Democratic National Committee have left local Democratic Party officials with less funding and staff, leaving them with a sense of being "alone in the wilderness." Organizers in rural communities also report the declining appeal of establishment Democratic candidates. Populist rage with political elites of all stripes has grown since the 2008 financial crisis. Many registered Democrats in these areas now regularly vote for Republican candidates.

Although the hollowing out of the Democratic machine presents opportunities for independent political organizations to become a driving force in Pennsylvania politics, progressive base-building organizations have been absent outside of Philadelphia and Pittsburgh in the last few decades. The overall ecosystem of progressive organizations is still relatively small. As in other states, these groups focus on different issues and constituencies, making coordination a challenge, given limited resources.

PA Stands Up: Building statewide independent political power

In recent years, however, a new wave of progressive energy across Pennsylvania has reversed these trends, leading to more organization and coordination statewide, particularly after former President Donald Trump carried the state by 44,292 votes in 2016. Our organization, PA Stands Up, is one notable example of this development.

PA Stands Up is a multiracial organization with 2,000 dues-paying members across nine local chapters. We held our launch conference in

March of 2020, but the three strands that make up our organizational DNA stretch back to 2016.

First, Sen. Bernie Sanders' historic 2016 presidential run energized progressives, including self-identified Independents, in Philadelphia and Pittsburgh, as well as more rural communities like York, Reading, and Lancaster. In Philadelphia, Amanda McIllmurray, Kelly Morton, and Lev Hirschhorn, a group of staff and volunteer alumni from the Sanders campaign, banded together to form Reclaim Philadelphia.

Second, in the days following the 2016 election, hundreds of resistance groups sprung up in all 67 counties. Several affiliated with Indivisible, including the ones created by Jane Palmer in Berks County and Alissa Packer in the Capital Region. These groups also received support from PA Together, a network co-founded by Hannah Laurison. Some retained their independence from national and local networks in order to build something new, like Lancaster Stands Up, which was formed by Jonathan Smucker, Becca Rast, Nick Martin, Rafael Diaz, Eliza Booth, and a few others following the 2016 election. Tying these central Pennsylvania groups together was a new populist approach to small-city organizing.

Third, progressives mounted a number of high-profile electoral challenges following the 2016 election. Reclaim Philadelphia powered civil rights lawyer Larry Krasner's groundbreaking election as district attorney in 2017. Lancaster Stands Up recruited Mennonite and community leader Jess King to run a progressive populist campaign for the US House of Representatives in 2018. The campaign knocked on almost 250,000 doors, making it the largest congressional field program in the country. The Rev. Dr. Greg Edwards also launched an insurgent campaign for US House in the Lehigh Valley. Although both King and Edwards lost their races, their campaigns transformed local organizing and political culture. Edwards' campaign manager, Carrie Santoro, and other volunteers, went on to form Lehigh Valley Stands Up. By laying the groundwork for Jess King's congressional race and running an independent field program, Lancaster Stands Up attracted new volunteers, members, and resources. York Stands Up, led by George Sanders, had formed by running candidates for municipal office in York County in 2017, and also expanded through the King campaign.

Recognizing the need for greater coordination and collaboration, these local organizations and candidates banded together to form PA Stands Up. Operating largely in southeast and central Pennsylvania, our organization is united by an aspiration to use local organizing to knit together a multiracial, urban-rural working-class bloc capable of winning statewide power.

It's up to us: Our plan to win in 2020

A Delegates Assembly of member-leaders from each chapter charts our organization's political direction. Over the summer, delegates ratified our general election strategy, although in many ways this simply formalized the work we had been doing from the start. Our strategy had four major components:

1. Support organizing to advance economic, racial, and social justice.

2. Pressure candidates to adopt progressive policies on our issues.

3. Elect progressive champions and flip the Pennsylvania legislature, particularly the state House.

4. Defeat Donald Trump in Pennsylvania by delivering the state for Joe Biden.

These goals guided the main areas of our work and resulted in a number of significant victories, although Republicans retained control of both chambers of our state legislature.

Crisis and opportunity: Stepping into the whirlwind

There were more social movement moments in 2020 than perhaps any election year since 1968. From the COVID-19 pandemic to the murder of George Floyd and Donald Trump's unprecedented attempt to steal the election, our election work took place alongside multiple, overlapping crises. From the very start, we looked to find the hidden opportunities in the midst of these devastating events: ways to step into the whirlwind by making collective meaning of the world around us, building our base, and winning on our issues.

Standing up for our neighbors

The pandemic shutdown happened the week after our founding convention. Rather than attempting to move forward with our plans, we pivoted our organizing to meet the moment.

Many of our local chapters initiated mutual aid efforts and campaigns to meet people's immediate needs. Along with Sunrise Movement and other local leaders in Reading, Celine Shrier and Jane Palmer of Berks Stands Up launched Berks Mutual Aid, delivering groceries and other essential goods to neighbors in need. Rick Krajewski, a Reclaim Philadelphia organizer and candidate for the state House, transformed his volunteer-driven campaign into a force for community support. Rick's campaign volunteers called hundreds of residents in the district each week and connected them to a local mutual aid network that had popped up. Nydea Graves, Rafael Diaz, and other leaders with Chester County Stands Up successfully forced the Chester County prison to release hundreds of incarcerated persons by echoing the national demand to "Free Them All." These efforts, and the pandemic more broadly, enabled us to push back against dominant narratives around rugged individualism as we centered an alternative vision of care and community.

As people lost their jobs and otherwise found themselves with more time on their hands, our chapters invited them to take active roles in the organization. A number of these unemployed workers, such as Eva Steinmetz and Neil Ren, became central leaders in our general election program.

We also took advantage of the virtual environment the pandemic forced us to operate within. A week into the quarantine, we held a virtual meeting for members across the state that drew 250 attendees. Union members, unemployed workers, healthcare workers, parents, and folks at high risk for COVID shared their stories about struggling through the first few days of isolation. Together, we felt less alone. We launched a political education forum called The Crisis and the Opportunity that regularly drew nearly 200 attendees from around the state.

Standing up for Black lives

Breonna Taylor. George Floyd. Ricardo Muñoz. Walter Wallace, Jr.
The week before the Pennsylvania primary, Minneapolis police brutally suffocated George Floyd to death, setting off the largest protest movement in US history. Pennsylvania was no exception. Indeed, a series of local incidents of police brutality, along with two heart-wrenching police murders, created a sustained movement in defense of Black lives. Both Ricardo Muñoz of Lancaster and Walter Wallace, Jr. were gunned down in the presence of family members who had contacted emergency services for support for mental health crises.

It's difficult to do justice to just how transformative this movement moment was—and to the courage that was shown. In July, 20-year-old Taylor Enterline led a Black Lives Matter march in pouring rain through Manheim, a borough of less than 5,000 residents that is 96% white. As Taylor and her friends marched, they were trailed by the armed Pennsylvania Light Foot Militia.[5] This was just one of dozens of protests in Lancaster County organized or supported by Lancaster Stands Up in June and July. Some of these small towns and rural communities had rarely, if ever, seen social justice marches and rallies. Even in larger cities, like Philadelphia, the crowds were unprecedented, offering new opportunities for organizing. A'Brianna Morgan, a mass liberation organizer with Reclaim Philadelphia, addressed a crowd of thousands, urging their support for campaign demands that predated the uprisings. In Allentown, organizer Ashleigh Strange used the movement moment to recruit dozens of new member-leaders to join Lehigh Valley Stands Up.

While the movement brought new leaders into our local chapters, it also prompted brutal crackdowns against those demanding justice. Taylor would later be arrested on trumped-up charges while participating in a protest after Ricardo Muñoz was murdered by Lancaster police. The district attorney set bail at $1 million. In Philadelphia, militarized police launched tear gas into a multiracial crowd of thousands that had been cornered on the side of I-676 with nowhere to go. Across the state countless videos showed officers kicking, beating, and gassing nonviolent demonstrators. In some places, such as Fishtown in Philadelphia, police allowed right-wing militias to intimidate or assault community members as well.

Despite these attacks, our organizers used these events to recruit and develop new leaders. In line with our organizing strategy, we sought to weave work on social justice issues together with our electoral efforts. For example, Morgan Tucker discovered Lehigh Valley Stands Up during the summer protests. Morgan went on to participate in our summer Fellows program and become a canvass captain, seeing the work to defeat Donald Trump as key to advancing racial justice. Other chapters experienced a similar influx of people looking to get involved.

Standing up for democracy

The final social movement moment took place on Election Day and in the weeks that followed. Pennsylvania Stands Up served as the in-state anchor organization for the national Fight Back Table and assembled a local network of dozens of faith, labor, and community organizations to stand up for democracy in Pennsylvania.

Democracy defenders had to move rapidly as the situation developed. In Philadelphia, organizers drowned out a press conference hosted by Trump's cronies with a dance party. In places like Lancaster and Allentown, pressure was applied to local officials who demanded a stop to the ballot count. In Montgomery County, Sue Caskey and other members of Progressive Montco gathered outside the courthouse where right-wing lawyers attempted to have ballots thrown out. In Harrisburg, demonstrators faced down elected officials like US Rep. Scott Perry and state legislator Doug Mastriano, who stood side by side with armed right-wing militias.

Dozens of vibrant local rallies and marches resisted the efforts to subvert the will of the voters. Together with our partners, we launched a robust and sophisticated effort that included mobilization, legal, communications, and logistics working groups.

"The effort to defend our democracy resulted in a generational level of focus," said Hannah Laurison, founding executive director of PA Stands Up. "It gave us a vision of what is possible when grassroots groups across the state come together for a unified effort."

Generative as these movement moments were, they also created challenges and contradictions that were hard to reconcile. The prospect of an all-out assault on democracy following the election forced a sharp trade-off between turning out voters to win the election and preparing to defend the integrity of the electoral process itself. When local police murders occurred weeks or even days before Election Day, it was difficult to translate the momentum in the streets into support for a candidate who was openly hostile to many movement demands.

How to beat a demagogue without a champion

Our chapters came together with an understanding of the unique threat that Donald Trump posed to our state and our nation, and we knew we couldn't trust the Democratic Party to meet the moment. We set out to build independent political power, meaning we would build a base across race and place that could operate both inside and outside the Democratic Party and the government. We hoped to speak to the disillusionment and abandonment people across Pennsylvania were feeling. Our experience since 2016 told us that we could move thousands of votes with an anti-establishment, progressive populist narrative and a bold candidate with an existing base of community support. When Joe Biden became the nominee, we faced a new challenge: how to beat a demagogue without a champion.

Although Biden grew up in Scranton, Pennsylvania, voters were skeptical that he would deliver what they needed. Among undecided voters, the most common response we got on the phone was doubt that things would be different with Biden as president. Our base was also skeptical of Biden's ability to deliver change, particularly after he assured rich donors that "nothing will fundamentally change" if he was elected. During the Black Lives Matter summer uprisings, we were frustrated with Biden's equivocal stance. While he promised to address violent policing, he also called for increased police funding and amplified right-wing narratives about isolated instances of property destruction.

Even though Biden wasn't the champion we hoped for, we knew we needed to defeat Trump, and that the massive investment in Pennsylvania during 2020 would support our growth as an organization. We met the challenge by designing a narrative strategy that could offer both the progressive base and swing voters a different way to think about politics.

Our narrative strategy: Not him, us

Acknowledging the alienation and isolation many swing voters feel, we focused on shared values, rather than partisan affiliation. We embraced the power of personal stories to connect with voters and activate a different framework—solidarity rather than scapegoating and scarcity. Talking to voters on the phone and communicating with our base and the public, we framed working for Biden as "Not him, us."

This approach built on many of the same strategies that Lancaster Stands Up pioneered. Since its founding in 2016, Lancaster Stands Up has placed a strong emphasis on integrating narrative strategy into every facet of the work, from conversations with voters at the door to member meetings and public communication efforts in the media and online. This came largely from Jonathan Smucker's use of narrative strategy in a rural context to harness populist energy and present a bold picture of change, while steering clear of messaging that would marginalize community members as "activists."

This strategy was also a centerpiece of Jess King's 2018 congressional campaign, where she adopted Lancaster Stands Up's motto, "America Is for All of Us," as her campaign slogan and wasn't shy about calling out corporate bosses and party elites of all stripes. While she didn't win her race, she significantly outperformed past candidates in a district with a 20-point-plus Republican advantage. This result was only possible because her campaign, along with Lancaster Stands Up as a whole, relied on inclusive populist rhetoric to flip Trump voters who were fed up with the status quo, but open to progressive political outsiders.

In 2020, PA Stands Up carried this approach forward in two ways. First, we aimed to build authentic connections with voters around shared values, but we didn't shy away from embracing voters' anger with the status quo. Instead, we promoted an inclusive populism that redirected voters' anger away from immigrants, protestors, and China, toward those who are actually to blame: big corporations and political elites who have sold out working-class people for decades. We de-emphasized political affiliations and asserted our independence from Democratic Party elites. This made it easier to persuade voters that we had shared values before ultimately getting them to a place where they felt comfortable voting for Joe Biden and our down-ballot candidates.

Second, we framed our work for Biden as part of the long struggle for social justice in America. Putting everyday Pennsylvanians at the center of our story about the presidential election made it possible to talk about the stakes in 2020 without pretending Biden was the magic formula. Our narrative strategy emphasized the ways in which social movements, rather than politicians, have been the drivers of change. Here's an example from our public messaging guide:

> Throughout our history, we've seen that when working people of all colors join forces, we've won big changes to make America work for all of us. The labor movement won a New Deal for American workers. The Civil Rights movement took on segregation and won the Voting Rights Act. Today, everyday working people are standing up for Black lives, fighting to raise the wage, and demanding healthcare and relief as our families confront the pandemic. But working people can't win big change unless we take control of Harrisburg and remove Donald Trump from the White House. We're under no illusions that change comes from Washington—or even from the state Capitol—but we

know that when our allies are in office, working people can make them do the right thing.

This approach also allowed us to recruit new members with an understanding that we would also hold Biden accountable and fight for what we deserve from his administration.[6] Since many of our members were disappointed by Biden's rhetoric and policy proposals, we focused on how a Biden victory would put us on better footing to struggle and win in the next four years, while keeping an eye on our long-term vision of transformative change.

Members responded to this message and persuadable voters did, too. With our partners at PA United, People's Action, the New Conversation Initiative, and Race Class Narrative Action, we designed a script and voter universe[7] that capitalized on our specific project of building independent political power, especially in rural areas and across race. The centerpiece of our program used a technique called "deep canvassing," which involves long, empathetic conversations (20 to 45 minutes) with conflicted voters. Several chapters had piloted deep canvassing, in Philadelphia as far back as 2017, and as part of a research experiment in Dauphin, York, and Lancaster in 2019. Our voter universe was designed to include voters who were more likely to be undecided and to respond positively to our canvass script.[8] We over-sampled women, Independents, people with incomes under $50k, and people of color—essential constituencies for our long-term power-building efforts in the state. Our script started by building rapport and talking about the unique moment that we were in with the pandemic, taking care to ask voters how they were doing. We would then share why we were supporting Biden and our stake in this election—a vulnerable story that also built trust with the voter—and asked what was at stake for them in this election. We finished by making the case, bringing in the race/class narrative messaging.

We had almost 50,000 deep canvass conversations using this script—more than half the 80,555-vote margin of victory in the state—and more than 40% of the undecided voters we spoke with reported being more likely to vote for Biden after our conversations.[9]

Make the Case

Thank you for sharing with me. Whether we are Black, White or Brown, we all want to make enough to live and have a safe place to raise our families. My concern is that Trump is more focused on blaming someone else [*immigrants, protestors, China*] than he is on taking responsibility and finding solutions.

What do you think about that? What kind of leader do you think we need at this time of crisis?

I believe this presidential election is about how we come together and care for each other. When I see Biden, I see a leader from a working class family who has lost his wife, daughter, and son, and because of his experiences will listen, build a great team, take responsibility, and find solutions that will work for all of us, not just the wealthy few.

AND recently I learned that _____ (*pick a talking point or fact relevant to your conversation*).

We also knew that to win Pennsylvania, we had to improve our margins in every county across the state, not just run up the score in one place. To widen our reach, we partnered with Pennsylvania United, which works in the western part of the state. Between us, we had hundreds of conversations with voters in every county. Our partnership with PA United was built on our collaboration in the Fellows Program, so our member-leaders were in relationship with people doing the same work in other counties. Our statewide Days of Action, led by members from Berks to Westmoreland, affirmed to all our members that we were doing what was needed to win the election.

Sending a Squad to Harrisburg

While our general election effort put us in the challenging position of doing work for a candidate whose values diverged significantly from our own, many down-ballot elections in 2020 enabled us to back progressive champions for local office, including our own members and staff.

Ahead of the primary, PA Stands Up volunteers made more than a half-million voter contact attempts, propelling several progressive challengers to victory. As a headline in the *Philadelphia Inquirer* put it: "Bernie Sanders may be done but his fans in Pennsylvania keep winning primaries." In Philadelphia, Nikil Saval, a founding member of Reclaim Philadelphia, self-identified democratic socialist, and co-editor of *N+1*, beat out a powerful incumbent for state Senate. Rick Krajewski, a Reclaim organizer, also defeated a long-time incumbent for state House. In the Philadelphia suburbs, Amanda Cappelletti defeated another senior Democrat. Other political outsiders defeated party favorites outside Philadelphia, including Shanna Danielson and Nicole Miller.

Many of these candidates were heavily involved in or recruited by our local chapter organizations. Shanna Danielson, for example, is a middle school band teacher who helped found Capital Region Stands Up. Some were actively recruited to run for office by our statewide political director, Lev Hirschhorn, and by Reclaim Philadelphia's political director, Amanda McIllmurray, who served as Nikil Saval's campaign manager. We offered training, coaching, and messaging resources for these candidates, and they also regularly attended and spoke at our public events.

We also set up a program, led by Shoshana Israel, to design and run voter engagement programs for our endorsed candidates. In a state where down-ballot candidates, particularly progressive insurgents, can't count on support from local Democratic Party committees, this represented a valuable resource. Pennsylvania Stands Up and our partners at Turn PA Blue launched a massive volunteer effort to support our endorsed candidates, along with other candidates running in key battleground districts. In total, we had more than 300,000 conversations with voters around the state using a distributed organizing model.

As in other states, our down-ballot candidates faced steep headwinds in the general election. We sent three champions—Rick Krajewski, Nikil Saval, and Amanda Cappelletti—to Harrisburg, where they joined a number of 2018 insurgents like Summer Lee, Elizabeth Fielder, and Danielle Otten. For the first time in decades, there is a real progressive squad at the state level. Nonetheless, while we succeeded in replacing several moderate Democrats, our goal of running progressive populist candidates to defeat Republican incumbents in conservative districts has remained elusive. The candidates who won key primaries outside Philadelphia all lost in the general election. That said, candidates like Tara Zrinski and Shanna Danielson closed the margin of difference in their districts, bringing new voters to the polls who were needed to defeat Trump, and they built strong volunteer bases that will continue to grow in coming years. In particular, Shanna Danielson's campaign increased Democratic voter turnout by over 10% in York County, and her district saw some of the biggest vote swings from Trump to Biden in the state.

The lessons we're carrying forward

Since the election, we've held a number of conversations with members, staff, and candidates to harvest some of the most important lessons we're carrying forward from the 2020 election. The analysis below represents our best effort to synthesize what we heard; however, we want to acknowledge that people had differing experiences and opinions depending on what chapter they belonged to and their role in our program.

Lesson 1: Always be developing leaders

Bringing about long-term change, both during and after election cycles, requires an intentional effort to develop community leaders. While the last six months of an electoral campaign are the most watched, the work of building leaderful organizations and developing a bench of powerful candidates requires years of work. During the 2020 election cycle, two capacity building programs laid a foundation for developing leaders in our local chapter organizations.

At the very beginning of the year, we launched the Fellows Program with our partners at Pennsylvania United. The Fellows Program was intended to use the presidential election as an opportunity to build power across the whole state both during and after the election, no matter who was at the top of the ticket. Over several months, almost 70 people were trained to do one-on-one meetings, draw on personal networks to build a base and recruit volunteers, tell their personal stories, and use persuasion techniques in everyday conversation.

These core organizing skills are essential to grow a local chapter; they're also key to running an effective voter engagement program. By May, our Fellows were already prepared to have deep canvassing conversations and to run canvass shifts in their home counties. Investing in local leaders early enabled us to begin work on the presidential election over the summer.

Our Narrative Squad took a parallel approach to building communications capacity at the chapter level. While field programs have relied on volunteers for years, communications have typically been the purview of paid staff. The Narrative Squad challenged that staff-driven model by recruiting more than a dozen local volunteer leaders to join a 10-week program to develop values-based communications skills. By equipping local volunteers to craft effective messaging, write their own op-eds and letters to the editor, manage social media, and use email to recruit volunteers and raise money, we expanded our overall impact on the narrative ecosystem. These volunteers worked with local organizers to manage more than two dozen social media channels and generate over 500 news stories, which would have been impossible for our communications staff to achieve alone.

Our field program built additional leadership development pipelines, notably in our deep canvassing program. Many campaigns start from the assumption that in order to turn out as many voters as possible, it's imperative to make it simple to volunteer and avoid asking volunteers to take on difficult tasks. But we knew that *voter persuasion, not just last-minute turnout,* was pivotal in Pennsylvania because of increased polarization and the razor-thin margin of votes that would decide the presidential election. Our persuasion approach involved moving two different kinds of swing voters: voters who are conflicted about who to vote for, as well as voters who are conflicted about whether or not to vote at all.

Training volunteers to persuade voters using the deep canvass method is difficult. Persuasion requires listening, empathy, and compassion. Volunteers must maintain a non-judgmental attitude and be vulnerable in sharing their own story. It can be incredibly challenging to share your own hardships with a stranger and maintain a nonjudgmental attitude when a voter shares beliefs you may find offensive. And yet, we knew that having thousands of these conversations would be necessary. So, we built a program where we asked volunteers to take on difficult, but incredibly meaningful work, trusting that with enough support people would rise to the challenge, and may even prefer the emotional connection of deep canvassing. Indeed, some deep canvassers formed such strong connections with the voters they spoke to that they received texts from those voters after they cast their ballot.

We offered volunteers opportunities to collectively process their experiences so they could give feedback, share challenges, and get ideas about how to improve future conversations. Some repeat volunteers became "pod leaders," and received training on how to facilitate canvass sessions, support other volunteers, and identify new leaders to grow the pool of volunteers. This enabled us to absorb an ever-increasing number of people into leadership roles and create a supportive culture for first-time volunteers.

These volunteer leaders have gone on to serve as campaign staff, build local chapters, and run for office themselves. Across the state, volunteers from our local chapters (and politically aligned efforts like the Bernie Sanders campaign) stepped up to manage state legislator campaigns. Nikil Saval's 2020 field director, Aileen Callaghan, started out as a volunteer on Bernie Sanders' campaign in 2016 and was a canvasser on Larry Krasner's 2017 campaign. Aileen knocked the doors in his neighborhood over and over again, building important relationships that he brought with him to Saval's campaign.

Maria Andrews had helped found NEPA for Bernie, then was the campaign manager for Tara Zrinski's race for state House. When we spoke with Maria about the ideal leadership development pipeline for campaign staff and candidates, Maria offered a diagram: She also pointed out that in rural

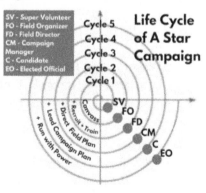

communities organizing jobs can be difficult to come by, simply because high-profile elections are less frequent and progressive infrastructure is sparse. Shanna Danielson, who ran for the state Senate, agreed: "I had to bring in a campaign manager from Iowa to find someone who was aligned with my values." This makes the pipeline from volunteer to campaign worker all the more important.

Since the election, Maria and other leaders have gone on to build NEPA for Change, a permanent organization coming out of the 2020 election cycle. This trajectory from electoral campaigning to permanent organizational infrastructure echoes our experiences from 2018 in the Lehigh Valley. We see a complementary relationship between developing skilled volunteer leaders, building a pipeline of campaign workers and candidates, and using elections to create robust organizations.

At every stage of leadership development, political education is also vital. Our first contact with new members is typically connected to a specific political struggle: an upcoming election, a mobilization after a police murder, or a campaign to protect tenants from eviction. People who are activated in the context of a particular campaign, movement, or election may not immediately see how the issue they care about connects to the broader picture. Nor may they immediately feel connected to other people across geography, gender, and race who are also struggling. Only sustained dialogue, engagement, and education can help each of us find the points where our stories connect and identify the ways in which the broader system of racial capitalism shapes each of our struggles despite the things that divide us.

Lesson 2: Local champions are key to building a local base

Every four years, swing states like Pennsylvania experience a tidal wave of out-of-state money and volunteers. This influx of resources is both a blessing and a challenge.

Dedicated volunteers who lived outside Pennsylvania were essential to helping us defeat Trump. More than half the volunteers in our field program came from outside the state through partners like People's

Action, Seed the Vote, Water for Grassroots, and Pod Save America. They also played a significant role in our down-ballot voter engagement program.

"There is a growing awareness," said Shoshanna Israel, who led our distributed organizing program for down-ballot candidates, "that local elections are really important and have a big impact on all of us, no matter where we live."

At the same time, these out-of-state volunteers weren't always aligned with our organization's overarching political vision. While we did significant training to familiarize all our volunteers with our script and approach to talking with voters, we knew that many of them were looking to volunteer with an organization—any organization—focused on electing Democrats. This presented us with an opportunity to shift politically active Democrats toward a progressive agenda, but that too required significant capacity.

"We had to make difficult decisions about how to direct leadership development resources between local and out-of-state volunteers," said Jana Korn, an organizer for the deep canvass program. "In retrospect, I think we could have been more intentional and selective in how we made those investments."

In a normal year, in-state volunteers would do their shifts in person. During the pandemic, we relied exclusively on phone-banking, which made it more challenging than usual to identify in-state and out-of-state volunteers. Indeed, we found that despite offering some advantages, operating in a virtual environment made building a local base through election work much more difficult.

We found that we were most successful using the election to build our local chapters in places where we had a strong local champion running in a down-ballot race. These candidates were more aligned with our overall mission and vision. They were themselves members of the local community. All of this meant that in many places, our existing base was more energized by local candidates' campaigns than by doing work for Joe Biden. It also meant that new local volunteers on these down-ballot campaigns were themselves more likely to share our progressive political orientation and thus become members of our chapters. Of course, because we always spoke with voters about the top of the ticket in addition to these down-ballot champions, there was also a trickle-up effect that ultimately supported the presidential election field program.

Lesson 3: We need to build statewide independent political power from the ground up

There's no question that independent political organizations were essential for Joe Biden's victory in Pennsylvania. PA Stands Up alone identified more than 53,324 Biden voters through our canvassing program. Our impact was even more evident at the county level. We improved Democrats' presidential vote share in 13 of the 14 counties where we have been working over the last four years, even flipping Northampton County.

Of course, PA Stands Up was just one among many groups talking to voters in Pennsylvania. Together with 58 other progressive organizations, the grassroots infrastructure moved roughly 282,000 votes for Biden, about 3.5 times his margin of victory in the state. With such a narrow win, every vote counts. Independent political organizations are making the difference.

A closer look at the results reveals some of the challenges we face for building statewide power in Pennsylvania. Following national trends, suburban counties saw the strongest gains, particularly the so-called "collar counties" surrounding Philadelphia. In more rural areas, Republicans retained a significant majority, even though the vote gains in those counties were key to Biden's win.

This helps account for our down-ballot losses outside Philadelphia and Pittsburgh. While progressives are winning governing power in major cities and suburbs, Republicans retain a strong advantage in most rural and small-town districts. Organizing investments in those areas are essential to winning statewide elections in the near-term, but electing local champions there is likely a long-term project.

"We did so much good work in 2020," said Shanna Danielson, who ran in State Senate District 31, where there are six registered Republican voters for every four registered Democrats.[10] "We were running a better race than many candidates in more competitive districts, but, flipping my home district is going to be a 10- to 12-year effort."

Danielson said running in such districts can take a toll on both candidates and volunteers, who are often demoralized and exhausted by the time the election is over. She suggested that a more fruitful strategy might focus on building power over a number of cycles in hyper-local races for school boards and city councils. After Jess King lost her US congressional campaign in 2018, Lancaster Stands Up has pursued just this approach. In 2019 and 2020, they focused on more local candidates, winning a number of municipal elections.

Even in Philadelphia, the process has taken time.

"Reclaim Philadelphia was only able to defeat powerful down-ballot incumbents as a result of a multiyear effort that involved building power at the neighborhood level," said Lev Hirschhorn, statewide political director.

Both Nikil Saval and Rick Krajewski door-knocked their districts repeatedly during elections between 2017 and 2020. Perhaps the most innovative effort was Reclaim's 2018 ward committee strategy, where they ran members like Nikil Saval for local Democratic Party committees in Philadelphia. While talk of taking over the Democratic Party has grown in recent years, this is a concrete model of how it can be done. Winning ward committee seats provided candidates like Saval with valuable experience, built a base that could be leveraged in future elections, and fractured the "political machine" powerful incumbents often rely on to win. Outside Philadelphia, many county-level committee seats remain vacant, providing an opportunity to lay the groundwork for future election cycles.

The work to build a Pennsylvania—and America—for all of us, continues

Our successes, and our setbacks, during the 2020 election have set the stage for ongoing work—and our approach will face a major test in the 2022 midterm elections.

With the retirement of Republican Senator Pat Toomey, Pennsylvania will have one of the most competitive US Senate races in the country, once again likely to be decided by a slim margin. Democratic Governor Tom Wolf will also be stepping down from office, another high-stakes race, where a Democratic loss would give Republicans another dangerous trifecta at the state level. Of course, both the governor's race and down-ballot contests for the state legislature also create a strong foothold for progressive gains and local base-building. As in 2020, our chapters will use issue campaigns on mass liberation, housing, and climate as a central power-building strategy, alongside our electoral efforts.

Through it all, our future success hinges on whether we can weave together a winning majority of working-class people across race and place, united behind a shared vision of a Pennsylvania—and an America—for all of us.

Notes

1.. "2020 Research Summary: Pennsylvania," Race Class Narrative Action, https://raceclassnarrativeaction.com/resources/.

2. US Census Bureau. "Race and Ethnicity in the United States: 2010 Census and 2020 Census," www.census.gov/library.

3. Elizabeth McNichol, Douglas Hall, David Cooper, and Vincent Palacios, "Pulling Apart: A State-by-State Analysis of Income Trends," Center on Budget and Policy Priorities, November 15, 2012, www.cbpp.org.

4. "Party Control of Pennsylvania State Government," Ballotpedia, https://ballotpedia.org.

5. This is one of two demonstrations Taylor and her friends led in Manheim. At the other, they were nearly hit by a car and passers-by spat at them and hurled racial slurs.

6. Indeed, following Biden's election victory, we pivoted quickly to produce a series of videos featuring our members to set the stage for holding his administration accountable. "We won this election because working-class people of all races

delivered for you," Sergio Cea, an organizer with Reclaim Philadelphia, proclaimed in the video. "Now it's time for you to deliver for working-class people," Nick Martin, a volunteer and co-founder of Lancaster Stands Up concluded.

7. A "voter universe" is a selection of registered voters that are identified by an organization for the purposes of voter engagement (phone calls, text messages, etc.) based on their past voting history.

8. The universe was based on an experiment run by our partners at PA United and People's Action. PA United contacted voters in Erie County using several iterations of the deep canvassing script. The experiment helped refine our script as well as our universe.

9. Since our deep canvass program focused on conflicted voters, this rate excludes people who identified themselves as extremely likely to vote for Trump or Biden early in the call, as we did not complete the script in those conversations. Note, too, that deep canvass conversations were only a portion of the 400,000 conversations our volunteers had through our presidential and state-level voter engagement programs.

10. "Voting & Election Statistics," Pennsylvania Department of State, www.dos. pa.gov.

7

States of Solidarity: How State Alignment Builds Multiracial Working-Class Power

María Poblet

I came of age politically at a time when California's electorate was majority white, older, and staunchly conservative. Two-term Republican governor Pete Wilson pushed to use the state government to screen migrants and systematically deny people social services based on immigration status (Proposition 187, approved by the voters in 1994, but halted in court), and signed three-strikes into law, mandating life sentences for third felony convictions and creating the conditions for the subsequent prison boom. Like many of my peers, I went from protesting Pete Wilson to getting deeply involved in community organizing and became part of a long-term project to change the political dynamics in our state.

Even though California is basically a foregone conclusion in national presidential elections, there is important work happening on the ground that can help us understand how elections relate to a much deeper and more long-term project of political transformation. Almost 30 years after we were protesting Pete Wilson, communities of color form a majority of California's electorate, which is now significantly more progressive. The Black, Latin American immigrant, and multiracial working-class communities I organized alongside at Causa Justa/Just Cause,[1] and represented as an elected Rent Board commissioner are no longer relegated to the sidelines of political debate. The very communities that have been historically taken for granted by traditional political parties proved decisive in 2020. The questions of housing affordability, criminalization, and democratic rights that were core to our community-based work 10 years ago are now in mainstream political and electoral discourse. These gains weren't made in one election by one organization, or the fight over one issue by a single community. Our advances were hard fought, are constantly under attack, and remain, as they began, a collective project.

This kind of long-term, movement-level work is not unique to California. California Calls, which played a pivotal role in aggregating grassroots power and helped launch the Million Voters Project, is an advanced model of work happening across the country. This groundbreaking work is a much-needed alternative to the traditional transactional Beltway approach to electoral politics. From Arizona to Pennsylvania, from Florida to Minnesota, progressive leaders are creating alliances that drive turnout among working-class voters of color. The breakthrough levels of voter engagement that state and local groups achieved in 2020 reflects 10 to 20 years of base-building, building solidarity across various constituencies, using integrated voter engagement and long-term strategy development.

State power-building groups amplify the political voices of communities who need transformational change the most—Black, Indigenous, Asian and Pacific Islander, Latin American, women and gender-oppressed people, disabled people, youth, workers, and more. State organizations are positioned to work more closely with communities. By organizing, supporting, and aligning the groups that represent these communities at the municipal and even neighborhood level, state power-building work is transforming low-propensity voters into politically conscious and active participants who are changing their states.

This chapter explores a model of long-term power building that organizations across the country are practicing. Its components include: 1) building new solidarities among and across historically marginalized communities; 2) challenging the transactional culture of elections; 3) forming an alignment to build governing power; and 4) developing long-term strategy.

Social blocs and new solidarities

Community-based work is built on relationships, and it runs deeper than the overtly political, drawing upon cultural competencies, understanding regional differences, and recognizing people's whole selves and webs of relationships to each other. The work happens all year long, not just in election season—through conversations door-to-door, in video meetings, in church basements, in school cafeterias, in hospital waiting rooms. To knit these organizing experiences into multiracial voting blocs, state power-building groups build levels of mutual trust and solidarity so that people from different demographic groups, regions, and communities see themselves as having a stake in the collective work.

Transformative power-building

Organizers at the state level readily recognize and relate to the complex dynamics of demographic and geographic differences, and they have taken on the overlapping challenges of both disaggregating and cohering progressive social blocs. This is often harder to do on a national scale in this political moment. Too often, we see evidence that the relationships and trust are not yet strong enough. National groups and leaders are operating in environments where even as the value of solidarity is held in common, the practice is compromised by dynamics that put an emphasis on differences, and too often result in fragmentation.

Transformative state power-building work builds new constituencies, new solidarities, and a new sense of power. People get in touch with the power of collective action through their experiences in community or labor organizing campaigns that relate to their everyday lives, and then join forces with other social groups to advance the broader political agendas they identify with. But it would be a mistake to assume that people will automatically recognize each other as allies, especially when they have no prior experiences of working together, or where their experience suggests that their concerns as a marginalized group with less power within a broader front will get pushed aside in the heat of battle.

And the broad demographic categories that traditional political parties use to formulate strategy don't always serve us. If our approach to engaging communities doesn't distinguish between a 20-year-old Black Dominican drag queen in Orlando and a 70-year-old white Cuban pastor in Boca Raton and puts them both in a category of "Hispanic," and therefore people we talk to in the same way, our electoral strategy will fail. And if our way of engaging communities treats a Salvadoran hotel housekeeping worker in Miami and a Black American nanny in Gainesville as if they have no political interests in common, our movement strategy will fail.

2020 offers many examples of how states can model the work of building new solidarities. For example, Georgia showed us what "intersectional politics" look like, with voter engagement led by Black and Brown working-class women. Florida Rising worked closely with Venezuelan, Cuban, Colombian, and Puerto Rican organizations to develop effective strategies for each of these communities. In Virginia, leaders across constituencies work to avoid having one community's needs pitted against another's, with leaders agreeing to advance different parts of their shared agenda by sequencing their focus—on one set of issues now, and another set later. LUCHA in Arizona was able to build upon their successes and base building for the last 10 years: recalling the state senator who was an architect of SB 1070 and ousting Sheriff Arpaio.[2] The strategies and relationships of solidarity that grassroots forces leveraged to win those campaigns at the county and state levels were exactly what was needed in the 2020 presidential race.

Learning the lessons of geography

In addition to race, gender, ethnicity, class, and national origin, state-level projects must contend with the effects of geography in their efforts to build governing power. As a report from the USC Program for Environmental and Regional Equity (PERE) notes, states need a geographic roadmap for their integrated voter engagement: "In the counties that usually vote in favor of progressive policies, what is needed is increased turnout among groups' base communities (low-income, immigrant, and young voters of color). In conservative regions of the state, new and infrequent voters need to both be moved to support progressive issues as well as be motivated to vote."[3]

Pennsylvania is among the states where regional differences pose challenges for organizers who seek to build statewide power. Pennsylvania Stands Up addresses this by working to create connections with leaders across regions while engaging communities in local politics. They harness the power of personal stories, moving the conversations away from partisan affiliation and toward a framework of solidarity.

From transactional to transformational electoral strategy

In 2020, aligned groups in several states were able to build on the deep and long-term relationships they have with their members and communities to reach low-propensity voters. This stands in contrast to traditional parties' practice of narrowing their focus on elusive "swing" voters.

Integrated voter engagement

Mass electoral mobilization aims for breadth, often at the expense of depth. Base-building groups must be more relational, as they target infrequent and persuadable voters. To address this tension between breadth and depth, state groups try to integrate voter engagement into their base-building and, in turn, deepen their relationships with their bases. This approach is called *integrated voter engagement* (IVE).

According to the USC Program for Environmental and Regional Equity, integrated voter engagement "connects the short-term, cyclical work of voter education, outreach, and mobilization to the year-round work of organizing communities, developing grassroots leadership, and waging campaigns."[4] With long-term IVE work, elections are treated as milestones in a movement-building strategy. IVE organizing thus engages new and infrequent voters in ways that motivate them to vote consistently, and to show up as well for local policy battles and other kinds of civic engagement.

Integrated voter engagement grew out of organizing in communities of color where leaders were frustrated by the ways traditional electoral campaigns would parachute in at election time and then disappear until the next cycle. IVE leverages the depth of relationships that community groups have among key constituencies and neighborhoods to reach unlikely, infrequent, and new voters. It represents a maturation of community organizing whose scope had too often been limited to the municipal or neighborhood scale. Its scope thus reaches beyond the short-termism of traditional electoral work, with notable results at particular moments in states like California and Virginia.

It is through integrated voter engagement that groups can break through the levels of cynicism that can be demobilizing in communities of color and for working-class people. By linking voting to issues that affect their daily lives, IVE makes voting more relevant to them. New Virginia Majority, for example, urges state leaders to always connect their victories in passing legislation to the voting power of new voters, showing them how their votes truly matter and turning them into more politically aligned and consistently engaged voters.

A tool like IVE works best in states where leaders do more than voter engagement. Getting millions of people to shift from non-voting to voting can be transformational, especially if those voters can find a political home within state and local groups after the election. When incorporated into a larger power-building strategy, the outcome of one election doesn't make or break the movements or stop their momentum.

Better national-state coordination

This transformational approach to power-building makes transformational change possible. Winning power in a battleground state isn't a short-term objective and can't be measured in a single election cycle. National organizing networks, labor unions, and other efforts that are leveraging the power of the states—whether they partner with someone in a state or built an organization there—are much better equipped to turn electoral work into long-term power-building with national impact.

In 2020 state power-building groups in several states were able to practice new models for coordinating with national groups. They shifted away from old patterns of repetition and competition. Groups in Florida, Arizona, Michigan, and Pennsylvania provided strategic perspective and grassroots volunteers, shaped the scripts for voter contact, and fed the energy and knowledge into their local follow-up apparatus and local elections.

The Washington Beltway problem

In contrast, the Washington, DC, Beltway voter mobilization groups tend to mirror the traditional parties' tactics and overlook the importance of base-building in motivating and holding onto low-propensity voters. As a result, their voter outreach is a transactional cycle of "lather, rinse, repeat" every two to four years. When grassroots state-level organizations are included in national strategy, too often they are brought in as junior partners to those large traditional electoral institutions, who use them only to outsource door-knocking in communities of color.

Beltway groups also tend to broker the distribution of a lot of the electoral funds that make their way to the grassroots. They may parachute people into a state, or pay state groups to hire new people, or "rent a base" in communities of color. This transactional approach to elections often pits grassroots leaders against each other in an unhelpful competition for funds. After the election, as the funds dry up and the extra people leave, the state and local groups must readjust to nonelectoral organizing conditions. This destabilizes the local groups that are building bases for the long haul. More powerfully aligned groups have intervened in this model, mediating the interactions with funders, working in solidarity with each other to ensure that they share resources and credit.

Aligning to build governing power

While the transactional approach to elections focuses only on change at the federal level, a transformational approach treats states as an important site to advance a progressive agenda.

States like Arizona and Georgia play a key role in determining the outcome of national elections. States like Florida and Virginia are on the frontlines of battling right-wing domination over state politics. States like New York and California are where progressive policies can be tested before moving to the federal level and can create a sense of the groundswell for change. Being able to leverage these opportunities takes planning, shared strategy development, and stronger alignment across progressive groups within a state.

Over the past ten years, we've seen a shift in statewide work away from individual organizational efforts and toward creating collaborative models where participating groups have developed alignment around the goal of gaining *governing power* in their states. While mainstream political parties and Beltway groups tend to develop their strategies squarely within the context of elections, state power-building groups are thinking more expansively. Governing power is the ability to win and then sustain power across a broad set of sites of governance to shift the power structure of governance and establish a new governing paradigm.

Rather than a limited view of governance that focuses on the most visible state elections or city council races, a broad view of sites of governance includes commissions and other government organizations that play roles like setting transportation fares, regulating rents, and determining school policies or climate disaster response plans. Too often, the combination of limited resources and a limited view of governance have led progressives either to overlook these less nationally visible sites of governance, or to focus on them to the exclusion of a broader strategy to shift politics at the national levels. There are experiments happening at the state level across the country that are attempting to bridge that divide and approach these questions from the perspective of pursuing governing power. For example, in 2020 the New York Working Families Party focused particular attention on state legislative races in and around Rochester, in western New York. The Assembly and State Senate seats in the area had long been held by a mix of Republicans and moderate Democrats. Working together with a set of allies, the New

York Working Families Party won competitive Democratic primaries and general elections with young, progressive candidates supportive of taxing the wealthy, in a way that changed the balance of power within the overall Democratic caucus in both houses of the state legislature.

To win governing power, state power-building groups need the capacities to design, drive demand for, legislate, enact, and defend agendas for progressive reforms that serve the needs of low-income, working-class, and historically marginalized communities. In doing so, these power-building groups will not only help hold electeds accountable through their terms in office, but fundamentally reshape the structure of the government itself, creating the conditions for more authentic and multiracial democracy.

Analysis of the current political moment suggests that the pathways to gaining governing power may be circuitous, with setbacks and side steps, as well as opportunities to make forward leaps, along the way. We will continue to oppose bad government policies, and to fight the advance of authoritarianism and white nationalism. We show up, mobilize our bases, and defend our communities. At the same time, we want to see ourselves as, and start acting like, we can run things, we can co-govern, and beyond this, we can ultimately reshape governance, in our communities, in our states, and in the nation.

With the goal of governing power as our compass, we use each arena of contestation as an opportunity to shift power, change the political climate, and take steps that get us closer to transforming governance. Electoral engagement is one of many arenas where we make these shifts, over time. This is the essence of what it means to build power in the states, through better aligned, coordinated work. This is what we're talking about when we talk about governing power.

No one organization can attain governing power. Only alignments of organizations can do this. This process of building practical solidarity across groups looks different in each state. Activate 48 is Arizona's first grassroots alignment process. It facilitated deeper trust and coordination among a set of organizations working in communities of color that were crucial to the presidential race in 2020, and that are setting goals for their state's governor's race, and beyond. To reduce the harm of the funding boom-and-bust cycle in their battleground state, Florida's Statewide Alignment Group created a set of values-based fundraising principles and protocols that unify groups and allow them to bargain collectively with philanthropy and political donors. These are elements of how we can reach beyond the short-term goal of winning elections, to pursue governing power.

While the framework of governing power is promising, it is nascent and not yet central to how progressives or even the left thinks about political strategy. We don't yet have examples of progressives holding stable, self-aware, intentional majorities with a coherent long-term agenda. What we have are opportunities to work together on campaigns, continuously reflecting upon and learning from collective experiences and repeatedly putting solidarity into practice.

Electoral engagement as part of long-term strategy

Building strategic alignment toward governing power doesn't always result in winning an immediate campaign. But it can help create a kind of durable infrastructure that can pivot from one battle to the next.

To illustrate the power of an electoral strategy that is part of a longer-term plan for governing power, we go back to California, a state that has made great progress in harnessing the power of the new multiracial working-class majority. California's reputation as the most progressive state in the nation rests upon the blossoming of community organizing in the early 1990s and the movement infrastructure we built with support from progressive allies in organized labor.

Heading into 2020, that infrastructure included the Million Voters Project (MVP), an alliance of seven community-driven state and regional networks: Alliance of Californians for Community Empowerment, Asian Pacific Islanders for Civic Empowerment, California Calls, the Coalition for Humane Immigrant Rights of California, Power California, PICO California, and the Orange County Civic Engagement

Table.[5] Collectively, these networks are some of the strongest power-building groups in California, and they represent the diverse geography of the state (urban and rural, northern and southern), as well as some of the constituencies that are most critical to moving a progressive agenda (including faith-based communities, Asian American and Pacific Islander communities, young people, immigrants and refugees, and Black Californians).

In 2019, Million Voters Project launched a process to develop a "Long-Term Agenda." At that time, MVP was gearing up for the culmination of two decades of work: advancing a ballot measure that would reform California's Proposition 13, taking on what has long been regarded as the "third rail" of California politics. Passed in 1978, Prop 13 rolled back most local real estate assessments to 1975 market value levels and limited property tax rate increases on both commercial and residential real estate. This had the net impact of severely reducing how much revenue local governments have available to cover basic services for residents, such as schools, hospitals, parks, and other amenities. It also required a two-thirds supermajority vote in the California legislature to pass new taxes. Over the decades, Prop 13 has hamstrung revenue options for governments at all levels. It has stymied the passage of new taxes, and it has increased the power of the fiscal conservative bloc in California state politics. Prop 13 was a harbinger of anti-taxation policies that spread across the nation.

Under the leadership of California Calls, community groups spent years building electoral infrastructure, evolving the assessment of what type of specific Prop 13 reforms to advance, and honing their analysis of exactly where, how, and with whom they would need to build power to win. They pinpointed how many voters they would need to mobilize to deliver a decisive margin that could overcome likely opposition to Prop 13 reform. They determined that they would need to mobilize 1 million new and infrequent voters. They came together under the banner of Million Voters Project, and spent a decade building their electoral muscle and deepening alignment across their respective networks.

Using the integrated voter engagement model, MVP ran a range of electoral programs that both built their base and tested whether conditions were right to advance reforms. MVP also built deep buy-in from the key partners who were necessary for such an ambitious fight, including labor unions. They developed a cross-sectoral campaign structure to hold together the broader front needed to pass the initiative. To appreciate these efforts, it is helpful to consider how ballot initiatives often are put forward with very little consultation among the forces that need to be allied. In many California election cycles, competing propositions end up splintering voters.

Knowing a presidential election year would have the highest turnout, MVP set their sights on 2020 to run a ballot initiative, which was run as Proposition 15, the Schools and Communities First Initiative. California Calls led the development of a broad coalition of 1,600 endorsers uniting diverse sectors—racial and social justice, labor, mainline organizations, elected officials and bodies, and more. The initiative was unique in that it was begun and co-led by community forces; for one of the first times, power-building racial and economic justice groups were setting the agenda and bringing labor on board, rather than stepping into an already-moving effort.

The campaign had record turnout, contacting 760,716 voters and identifying 592,862 Prop 15 supporters. Meanwhile, over $300 million in opposition funding poured into the campaign to defeat it. Due to the pandemic, the Schools and Communities First Initiative was unable to run a full field campaign, terrain where members are strongest. Schools and Communities First lost this time around, by 48% to 52%. The campaign planning included scenarios for how to carry forward the work if the initiative failed to pass, so that MVP and California Calls would be able to cultivate work and relationships built during the campaign.

Simultaneous to running the Prop 15 campaign, Million Voters Project launched a year-long process with leaders across the state to deepen strategic alignment within their networks. This included both strategic political education on key concepts, such as a multidimensional view of power, as well as the overall concept of structural reforms, and a Long-Term Agenda and why it is needed. The process included research into potential structural reforms for California and engagement with leaders to prioritize a set of three structural reforms for further campaign development.

The ongoing work to create a Long-Term Agenda is woven into field campaigns. Using the IVE model to advance a Long-Term Agenda strengthens the base and provides critical information on where voters and their communities are at on the issues. The fight for Schools and Communities First is now part of the Long-Term Agenda, and the two efforts together can guide the networks toward winning structural reforms over the next five to ten years.

As our social movement forces continue to align around shared narratives, shared strategic orientation, and a shared agenda for governing power, California will meet its social, economic, and environmental challenges, building a more just future for every community.

Conclusion

Long-term grassroots state power-building work may not factor into most standard summations of a high-profile national election, but these efforts were the axis of progressive change. Battleground states like Arizona, Florida, Georgia, Michigan, and Pennsylvania fight each election with the weight of national political outcomes on their shoulders. Their state power-building work is rooted in multiracial working-class organizing and building an alternative to short-term transactional approaches to elections. States like California, Minnesota, and New York advance a long-term strategy through each electoral cycle. Their state power-building work is building field-level alignment across organizations. These and other state power-building efforts are doing much more than contesting in elections: they are pursuing governing power.

While much about the future is uncertain, the political terrain in our country will be shaped by the solidarities we are able to articulate in our states.

Notes

1. See Causa Justa/Just Cause, at https://cjjc.org.

2. SB 1070 had such a galvanizing effect because it legalized racial profiling in Latino communities. SB 1070 cast suspicion on every Latino person in the state, subjecting them to profiling and requirements to show ID on demand.

3. May Lin, Jennifer Ito, Madeline Wander, and Manuel Pastor, *Vote, Organize, Transform, Engage: New Frontiers in Integrated Voter Engagement (IVE)*, PERE, October 2019, https://dornsife.usc.edu.

4. Lin, Ito, Wander, and Pastor, *Vote, Organize, Transform, Engage*.

5. See the Million Voters Project website, www.millionvotersproject.org.

Part 2

Communities of Color Drive the Win

8

Black Voters in 2020:
A Roundtable Conversation

Moderated by Karl Kumodzi, with:
Sendolo Diaminah, *Carolina Federation*
Arisha Hatch, *Color of Change PAC*
Thenjiwe McHarris, *Blackbird Action*
Mondale Robinson, *Black Male Voter Project*

The following is an amended version of transcripts of two separate conversations. They have been edited and slightly rearranged for clarity.

Karl Kumodzi (KK): 2020 was quite a year, to put things lightly. If events had progressed on the same trajectory as the three years before, it would have already been arguably the most consequential election in decades. When you throw in a deadly global pandemic, the uprisings spurred by the murder of George Floyd, the escalation in misinformation and voter suppression, and a host of other factors, it was historic—*nuts* is the political term. In the midst of all that, and perhaps because of all that, our movement showed up in unprecedented ways. Many of our folks who are usually pretty ambivalent about engaging in national elections not only showed up, but our collective efforts actually made a difference. We were able to unseat Trump and stop Republicans from keeping control of the Senate. There is so much to document from what we did, what we learned, and what we built. And we know that Black people, both organized and unorganized, were in many ways the difference makers in 2020. So we've brought you all here to dig into a conversation about why Black people were important, how our movements engaged and organized them, and what are the lessons that we can draw out of our experience in 2020 and apply to the larger work we're building. So without further ado, I want to go into some of the details. What did your organizations do? How did you engage folks? What strategies and tactics did you employ?

Sendolo Diaminah (SD): I can start, I think we're the little sibling in this. This was our first electoral cycle, quite an intense one for the first time. We started with a plan around door-to-door contact, and that got completely swept away. We ended up doing a phone-based program. And to be really honest, it undermined our capacity to work directly with Black people in the way that we wanted to. We're a multiracial organization and it's just so clear to us that in-person contact is our fundamental way of being in relationship with Black people. I mean, it's really the best way to be in relationship with anybody, but our folks in particular are like, "I'm gonna need to see your face and have a real conversation before I start taking action with you."

The second thing, though, we had a woman, Cheri Beasley, who was running for Supreme Court here in North Carolina. Incredible. Talking about her candidacy was the top thing that we did with our voters. We were like, "We want to talk to you about Cheri Beasley, both because she's talking about the pandemic and a moratorium on evictions, and because she's talking about the system of mass incarceration, and she is a Black woman running statewide." And that was the main person we talked about with all of our voters, so that we could have conversations about race and about economic justice. We put her face and her politics in front of every single voter. And we actually think that made us stronger, not weaker.

Mondale Robinson (MR): Since we're going in a little brother, middle brother, big sister situation—because Color of Change PAC is the largest civil rights org in this country—I'll go next. [Laughter] 2020 was the most expensive program year for us ever. Part of that was because we also recognized that sacrificing the door-to-door conversation does so much harm to the engagement of Black men, specifically those who don't normally vote, what the world calls sporadic voters. So in 2020, we saw what restaurants were doing with the little QR codes and copied that. Instead of cutting out our canvassing, we created a COVID-safe canvassing model. We put all of our canvassers in a hotel room and isolated them. We worked them less, paid them more, people got tested every day, and I'm proud to say that in 17 states we talked to all 6.2 million Black men registered to vote, with cell phones and everything. None of our canvassers were infected from COVID through our canvassing program. So that was powerful.

We also took some of our celebrities, some influencers—basketball players, football players, actors, head coaches from the NBA—and we got them to call people's cell phones, and leave a voicemail. They'd be like, "Yo, this is Doc Rivers calling on behalf of Black Male Voters Project, sorry I missed you." Then the brothers would hear the voicemail and be like, "Oh shit, Doc Rivers is on my voicemail. Is this true?" And then when my people called or texted they would be like, "Yo, Doc Rivers said he left a message for you." And people be like, "Oh, we were waiting on a call from you." So then it increased our interaction rate and cut our opt-out rate way down. Our opt-out rate in 2020 was lower than Bernie Sanders' was. We bragged about that all year.

We also had 4,000 conversations with Black men called Brothers Be Voting. No cameras, no women, no white people, just Black men in a room. We overpopulate the room with brothers who are gang members, drug dealers, and we invite a couple of people like us that are politically activated. And based on those conversations, we were able to build out our platform. We also created our BMEP Additory Approach,[1] which said, you don't talk to Black men two or three times in an election cycle. You talk to them fifteen times throughout a year. And when you do that, they're more likely to vote. So we saw a 20% increase in sporadic Black men voters in Georgia. And we know they voted for Democratic candidates because these brothers turned out in the primary. That's huge.

These are brothers who Barack Obama couldn't reach or turn out or motivate, but we were able to turn them out in the primary. We saw the same thing in Kentucky and Mississippi and also in other states that we were operating in. And the last thing that warmed my heart was we did a concert on the last day of early voting, and then we would tell whoever was the headliner that you had to stay and march the voters over to the polls.

Arisha Hatch (AH): I love that. It's so easy to just start with and talk about Black voters, but really what we care about is Black people. Our job is to be in deep relationship with our people, so that we can be powerful together. We want to talk to them three times before we even ask them to vote, and not feel like they're just voters that we're trying to mark. We started our PAC in late 2015, because we wanted to make a strategic intervention into district attorney races. At the time 90% were white males, 85% were running unopposed. It just so happened that Donald Trump entered the race at the same time, so it was hard not to talk to people about both things. Even within that work, we wanted to start with a brunch. We didn't want to start with knocking on people's doors or texting them. We wanted to invite people into community.

Prior to that, we were thought of as an online organizing entity. We always thought, our people don't want to go to marches or events, they just want to sign petitions and share things on social media. What we saw in 2016 was that we'd send out an email saying, come to a brunch, or a text-athon—sort of like a phonebank, but texting—and with very little organizing, 300 people would show up. And I'm like a community organizer, so when 300 people show up to an event, you're like, oh that's something, we should try that again. There was such a hunger for community and joy—because we were organizing amidst so much trauma, especially in those early days. We started building community through that. And so we got into 2020 and we were super hype, like this is going to be the year, it's all going to come together, these events are going to be amazing.

And then we were hit with the pandemic and had to lean back into our digital organizing roots. And yet community persisted. And I think that's the thing that I learned. I lost my father in the middle of the pandemic, early on when folks weren't getting together. And what I saw as I began to go visit our members was that these communities survived because of each other. There were stories of people who had met at a brunch four years ago who talked about, "I lost three loved ones, including one child during this time. It was my Houston squad that nursed me through it." And so that's what I was really proud of, that the program and the community continued to grow and support each other.

We had 25,000 grassroots volunteers making phone calls or sending text messages. We didn't knock on doors, but we did buy like 40,000 bags that said, *I'm Black and I vote*. They had masks in them and hand sanitizer. Our member leaders would hand them out and be like, "Hey, these are your three most important races on the ballot, and why we think you should vote for these sorts of people." Those were handed out in key states across the country. In addition to being forced back online, we were still able to have 700 safe events that were attended by tens of thousands of people.

Thenjiwe McHarris (TM): M4BL's Electoral Justice Project (EJP)—led by people like Jessica Byrd, Kayla Reed, Rukia Lumumba, and others—marshaled a cross-issue, national Black electoral justice force by building a network of local organizers and partners. EJP had a few pillars of work. The first is our Electoral Justice League, which invests in emerging and seasoned leaders to mobilize Black people and win at the polls. We give them resources to do the work and development from movement leaders. We've been doing that each year since EJP was formed.

Then there's the Black People Caucus Project, and the focus of that was to increase Black voter participation and focus on educating Black voters on the policy stances of leading candidates in the Democratic primary. The caucus project also targeted younger Black voters in the electoral process to demystify the presidential election process and created space for political debate around national policy while centering the

Vision for Black Lives, our policy platform. We really wanted to further position Black organizations as the messengers for the Black electorate, so we hosted a Black National Convention which was a live broadcast on August 28, 2020. It included a series of conversations, performances, and other activations geared toward engaging, informing, and mobilizing Black people. It was designed to advance our demands/agenda while also including sessions that focused on supporting local and regional power building, sharing interventions and civic engagement strategies, and ultimately demonstrating how we can build a Black political home for the movement.

KK: I have a couple of follow up questions. Sendolo, could you talk a little bit about how the work that you did in 2020 relates to the long-term vision and goals of the Carolina Federation?

SD: We build permanent chapters at the county level in the state of North Carolina, so we do electoral organizing as one moment in an overall rhythm of permanent organization. We start by building community, and that's through deep alignment training, which means we're building powerful relationships by being honest about our stakes, our pain, and our commitments. But it also means doing a deep dive around: what is politics and how do we understand it as something that comes out of the best of our traditions? And how do we understand the terrain that we're navigating? That's really, really essential. Then those folks identify issue fights that they want to take up. As much as I have opinions, the members are the ones who make those decisions, and they take up the issue fight that makes sense for their county.

I'll give an example. In Guilford County, they took up a fight around a school bond. The condition of schools was horrendous, from mold in the schools to kids having to wear their winter coats because the heat's out. The county commission in Guilford was controlled by Republicans, and they cut the school bond way, way down. It enraged our people. Then during the uprisings, thousands of our people came out. And our chapter in Guilford County was out there in the streets. So we used our digital infrastructure and our contact management database and our training around how you have one-on-one conversations to go out, collect the information of the people who are out, hold down facilitation for meetings for Greensboro Rising and then follow up with all those people.

So in the midst of the uprisings, our folks pivoted from the school bond campaign to support that with infrastructure around the uprisings. And then those new folks they brought in cycled into our electoral work and we defeated the Republican majority in Guilford County. We hired leaders out of that work into our field program. Our folks joined with the teachers union to push for a salary increase. At the local level, we pushed for the release of COVID-19 funding that had been constrained. So that's the cycle that was happening at the county level. And our people weren't just like, "Oh, yeah, we did an election, now we're going to go home." Our people were like, "We're more and more ambitious and audacious about what we think we can get, because we've been able to grow our power."

The long-term vision is for us to be doing that at the state level. With the politics and the numbers and the culture that's changing, we think it's possible for us to capture power at the state level and use that to transform things down to the local, and up to the federal. So our long-term vision is to take what we did in counties like Guilford all the way up to the state level. And our challenge is it's one thing to do that in Durham or in Guilford; it's a whole other thing to do it in the eastern part of the state. New Hanover County and the Southeast, for the first time in over a generation, went blue. And blue isn't enough, but that is a big deal. And we know that we have to have not just a different message, but a different way of building power with our people. We think North Carolina is actually a powerful bellwether of the country as a whole, and if we can move folks across the state of North Carolina, there's something to offer to other places. The last thing I'll say is we're very clear that corporate power is the problem. Until our people get enough power to change who owns wealth in this country, everything else is stuff around the edges. So our vision is to build enough political power to actually use government to change who has wealth. And we know we have to transform the electorate fundamentally with Black people at the center for that to be possible.

MR: I think it's telling that we know that Black people overwhelmingly vote for Democrats. And not just in this cycle, but 2016 as well, and the cycle before that, and the cycle before that. Eastern North Carolina is where a majority of the plantations were and it's where a majority of Black people are. That type of rural—where there's no hospital for a couple hundred miles, the water quality is horrible, the worst cancer cluster in this country, the electric bills are too high, and all of the other things that are plaguing these people. If we know that the majority of Black voters are there, why are so many Republicans continuing to win seats down there? It's because of a lack of investment from the Democratic Party.

So we forever blame voters for not turning out, and never blame the party. The party is responsible for putting investment in voters, which turns voters out. So they will claim credit for high-performance voters, call them super voters, and brag about these demographics. But if you're responsible for super voters, that means you've invested in them over and over and over to create that muscle within that community. Then you're also responsible for neglecting other communities. So the reason Black people in New Hanover and Halifax County and Pasquotank are not turning out is a problem of lack of investment.

Consider that the Democratic Party does not have a base in Iowa. Iowa will never be a Democratic stronghold. There's too many white folk, let's just call it what it is. But every four years they invest hundreds of millions of dollars into Iowa. And now Iowa has one of the best voting records probably in this country, because of the infrastructure built by holding their primaries there. Imagine if the Democratic Party in 2020 would have made Mississippi the first primary for the Democratic presidential candidates. Mississippi is the Blackest state in the union, where the Democrats have the strongest base. But the Democrats don't care about Black voters. They'd rather talk to the conservative-leaning white cousins and try to convince them to vote.

So the idea of New Hanover not voting for Democrats in a generation is not shocking when you consider that the state party and the national party has not invested in them ever. This is why I've moved from calling people low-propensity voters to calling them low-investment voters. And those that turn out all the time, call them high-investment voters. Because it shifts the blame from the voter to the party. And we saw that in 2020 as well, when we saw the Democratic Party spending a lot of resources on voters that are never going to vote for them. And it was organizations like Color of Change PAC, like the Carolina Federation, and my organization and so many others that said: we disagree with who the party is saying are priority voters, and we're focusing on our communities, those that are marginalized. And we saw those increases that we're responsible for and not the party.

SD: Preach.

KK: Arisha, in the last year there were two different paths that organizations took. Some explicitly endorsed Biden and told people to vote for him, and some did not endorse Biden, but framed their work around getting Trump out. Could you talk about what CoC did and what was the thinking behind that decision?

AH: Oh, yeah, we absolutely endorsed Biden. For us there was a clear choice, elections are about making real choices between real candidates. As an organization that's already confronted the idea that we're going to endorse a prosecutor—like someone who's gonna lock up Black people—I think we've gone through the mental process you have to go through to think about the ways in which you are positioning yourself to contend with and leverage power. So for us, there was no question in 2016 or 2020 about where we had the most power as an organization to leverage. We were slow to endorse, and that's because there was a set of conversations that we wanted to have with the Biden campaign. But we trailed our members. They had a deep sense of urgency. And for us, endorsement doesn't mean we agree with everything that you say. It's really important for us to be able to walk and talk with that sort of nuance. I know a lot of other people wrestled in a deeper way with that in a way that we didn't.

SD: I wanted to just add in to what Arisha was talking about with endorsements. We didn't do endorsements for every level. But we have offensive and we have defensive endorsements. And that was an explicit way that our people talked about stuff. Our offensive endorsements are people who our folks are lit about. People are like, [Clap] let's [Clap] go! And our defensive endorsements, we don't really *like* these people. But it is essential for us to elect them. And we had those honest conversations with people, and that built trust for our people because they didn't experience us as just saying any old thing. And it was our people who forced me to come up with some cute language to figure out how to do it. Because they were like, "Why are you trying to get me to be involved in these things?" And then when we had the conversation and they were like, "OK, I'm down if what we're doing is protecting our folks, *and* I want to have somebody I'm excited about." And that created a need to invest in candidate development because we have to have offensive endorsements that our people are excited about if we want to move folks.

KK: Let's dig in a bit. Broadly, what impact did Black voters have in 2020, and how did they show up differently than in 2016?

MR: I don't think Black people show up differently in elections at all. Since Black people have been able to vote in this country, we've seen them vote like nobody else votes: together. So much so that people begin to have conversations about the 10% to 12% of Black people that don't vote like the rest of us. We saw increases in millennial voters and the generation behind them at higher levels than ever in 2018, a midterm election. So it wasn't just 2020. What was wonderful for 2020, for me, was that every white person—meaning their political organizations, the parties, the pollsters, the news channels—all their political slips were showing. Especially as it pertains to Black men. They didn't know shit about shit. They literally said 20% of Black men were going to vote for Trump, Black men were not excited about the election, and that means that we were going to stay at home. And what we saw were the lies on display. There are no apolitical brothers in this country at all. There are brothers who don't care about the way we play politics, but that's different from apolitical. Every Black man I met and had a conversation with has a political position. Some of that does not translate to: I need to go vote for these whack-ass candidates. But they have positions.

And also there's no apathy in Black men. There's a level of antipathy that is grounded in 150 years of being the targets of voter suppression. We also saw that if we engage them not with the Barack Obama brothers with a suit and tie telling us to pull our pants up or stop getting tattoos on our faces, but if we engage them around issues that were important to them and show them how elections directly affect that, then you can move voting from that space of self-actualization, and brothers will see it as a tool to help them address some of the problems that they're plagued with on a day-to-day. So I was super excited to watch Black men in Georgia, brothers who were old enough to vote for Barack Obama in 2008 and 2012 but did not turn out, come out in 2020, and that's directly linked to the work that we were doing. They care about what's going on and they vote if you give them a reason to vote. And it can't be transactional because they see through that shit. So that idea of: this is the most important election or this candidate is going to change your life, does not work with Black men. Usually when you say it to brothers, you hear them say, "This shit don't make sense to me. My life ain't changed under any president." And it's true to some extent.

I also believe we are witnessing a younger voter—under 50—that will be forever more active than generations before them. If you go back and look at baby boomers when they were the age of millennials now, they weren't voting as much as these millennial voters are. I think millennials hit their peak way earlier, and they brought along the generation behind them. So I'm excited about these two fiery generations. Part of that is because we've never seen a generation that is as Black and Brown as millennials. So we're marking the first time that a generation is nearly 42% something other than white voters. And they're the largest voting block ever. So I think we're watching a shift in voter behavior in general.

TM: Black people did in 2020 what we have done historically—we organized in order to protect our people. Black lives have always been under attack and this in no way began with the election of Donald Trump. Many of our people understood that Trumpism marked an escalation, however, and the threat was not just about the election of Trump, but a far right-wing agenda led by radical right organizations with an eye toward specific policy priorities and conservative appointments. Trumpism serves their strategy as it fuels not only a growing appetite and demand for a "Trump" but also the popularization of a set of ideas and the building of a political base. Despite our victory, their agenda continues to advance in some ways and the threat continues, but many Black people understood that a second term was something that our people could not afford.

We have a history of organizing around elections as both a harm mitigation tactic and a strategy to impact local, state, and federal agendas. It has been used for the offensive and the defensive, like Sendolo mentioned, so it is not new, but we did see leaders who have a history of not engaging in electoral organizing understand that it was politically necessary. In the midst of a global pandemic, a recession, uprisings, repression, the targeting of our movement, massive voter suppression, intimidation, misinformation—Black people delivered the White House and the Senate. Turnout was historic for both the Republican and the Democratic Party with almost 70% of those eligible to vote turning out. The full spectrum of the right and the left understood 2020 to be an important battlefield. What this meant for Black voters in particular is in key states and in key cities from Atlanta to Philadelphia, and across the country, Black people had to use a variety of tactics to engage the Black electorate, while not ignoring the ways the Democratic Party has historically failed and betrayed our community. Much of what happened in 2020 was not only an uptick in organizing, but the result of years and decades of organizing—much of it taking place in the South. So really a combination of factors led to the wave of Black political activity that took place in 2020.

SD: I experienced the change less as what are all the Black voters doing, and more of what are all the different ways that Black people are grappling with things? And what are some of the new things that are on the horizon? I got to see our highly active volunteers and leaders really trying to figure out how we move from direct action and mobilization to electoral work to culture and communications, like the combination of those things. I remember listening to the presidential debates and listening to the way that reparations was being talked about, and in my lifetime, I had never seen anything like that. And I heard and talked to other Black folks about that. And the sense was, we are forcing a completely different conversation about what's happening in this country and what should be happening. And the development of a sense of political leadership by Black people, of the progressive bloc as a whole, is something that our people have been wrestling with. I really saw that. Some of our folks are like, "Yeah, people are supportive of Black lives right now, but they're not going to be supportive of us over the long term." Then somebody else will chime in from down the street, be like, "Nah, that's not true, this is different." So to me, I think it's really the range of political possibilities that our folks are wrestling with that feels different.

MR: Can I push back gently on that, brother? You're right, we definitely heard for the first time reparations become a topic. But it was brought up in a performative manner. It reminded me of when we saw the House Speaker and her caucus—Black ones included—put on Kente cloth and take a knee. And it was absolutely disgusting when they went right back to governing like they always govern. We saw different conversations around reparations in the primary, and didn't hear it at all in the general election. And then this administration is not talking about it at all again. So I think what frightens me is what happens to the Black people that came out because of the energy that you're talking about—those possibilities of what could happen with an administration that's willing to hear this conversation about reparations—but then nothing is delivered. We've had some stuff happen, but for those of us who knock on Black people's doors, they're going to say, we're still dealing with this, they didn't do this, they didn't do this. So I'm a little nervous about them using that language, then not giving us anything.

SD: I don't disagree with that at all. For me, there's a difference between them feeling like they have to even gesture in our direction versus ignoring us completely. That is nowhere near what our people need, let alone deserve, and so I'm in alignment with you about needing to push even further. *And* I think this is one of the things that is just the challenging work of being like, "What we got is what we had the power to get." How do we have a conversation with our people about the honest truth that we can't deliver things to folks that we don't have the power to get—and they're not going to give it to us. How do we not snatch defeat from the jaws of victories that we actually did win? I think there are stories that we tell to try to keep our folks mobilized—absolutely correct about what's not being done—but I think it can be demobilizing if we disappear all the things that we did, in fact, capture.

KK: This raises the question of social movements and all the work that's been done, especially over the past several years. What's your assessment of everything that's happened over the past seven years in Black movement—especially the uprisings last year post George Floyd—and how that impacted Black voters in November?

TM: Having reparations, the Green New Deal, and defunding the police take center stage during a presidential debate—while symbolic, immaterial, and performative—is still an indication that they have been forced to contend with our demands and either publicly appease or distance themselves from them. The fact that national coverage around the presidential election could not ignore these demands means these are no longer the demands of a few, but millions. And this has been felt at the national level.

AH: In the aftermath of the uprisings last summer, we experienced a lot of growth. Our membership went from less than 2 million members to more than ten million, many of whom were non-Black people. We kept saying racial justice is becoming a majoritarian issue in this country, politicians shouldn't run away from it. This is what people need to lean into. We saw people, despite the pandemic, come out of their homes and risk their lives to protest. And that was the preparation for getting out to vote and standing in long lines. Those that were allowed to couldn't continue to sit in their homes. And I think that was probably the best practice for what we would experience at the polls in November. And I think that show of outrage and power and mourning and joy powered the outcomes of this election.

SD: In the face of all of these things, being able to be in the streets together and in community with each other provides that capacity for joy. It's not lost on me that the stories and the history of Black people are the stories that are inspiring and moving the entire country through this transition. So many of the realizations and waking up that other people are going through draws from our people's history and stories. We ain't gonna say we told you so, but we're glad you finally got here! Right? Here's some tools. Some of those tools are joy. Some of those tools are resilience. Some of those tools are the fortitude that our folks come with. You said joy, Arisha, and I was like: Oh, yeah, Color of Change PAC was working with us in Durham in 2018 when we got Satana DeBerry elected as our district attorney, and they had these Black joy brunches. And sure, we haven't gotten somebody like Satana DeBerry or AOC into the president's office, but what we have done as a result of the swell of these movements and in combination with electoral work is that DAs are changing across the country.

We also got to change our sheriff. Color of Change PAC and the Working Families Party have been involved with that nationally. So there are already tens of thousands of people whose lives are being redirected away from mass incarceration. We haven't toppled the whole thing yet, but the things that we have changed are making real differences in people's lives. And I think that's also contributing and goes back to the joy piece, that more of our people get to be with their people because of the movements that we have been building and because we've linked that with electoral work. And that's the story that we try to tell to our folks. Literally there are thousands of people, this year and every single year, that as a result of our movements and our action are now free and are back home with their folks.

KK: I want to move us toward a close. What are the biggest lessons that you think the broader multiracial left can learn from the work that you all did? And how can we apply those lessons to building the kind of movement, winning the kind of world that we want?

MR: Data is important, but it is not people. Polls are stagnant and they're not true. The people that are responding to you are lying a lot of the time, or they're just trying to get off the phone with the pollsters. If you are organizing the communities, please be *of* community so you can make sure that you're speaking for that community in a way that's not distorted by people being bombarded with poll questions and they're just saying yay or nay and just hanging up the phone. 2020 showed me how three Black men—Lil Wayne, Ice Cube, and Kodak Black—can become stand-ins for what Black people are going to do, without any theory.[2] Then everybody started running these crazy polls about what Black men felt and did. And what we saw after the election was Black men voted where they always vote. Black people showed up like we always do. Even in the midst of a pandemic, we saw Black people vote like banshees. Which also tells me voting is a tool to help folks address their basic needs. 2020 taught me, of all the stuff that the Republicans are doing to prevent Black people from voting, none of it is more successful than starving Black people. Until we are talking about voting and hunger as a reason Black people don't go to the polls, then we're having a half conversation about what voter suppression is. And I think the lesson of 2020 is, we need to figure out how we provide services beyond a ballot for Black people, if we want them to vote for our candidates and issues.

TM: A lesson for me lies in the level of threat, and the scale of possibility. The far right's agenda and their ability to succeed in key arenas is clear. In addition, it is also clear how powerful the anti-racist, anti-capitalist left is. In the midst of a convergence of multiple crises it has never been more important to be clear about their strategy—while also visibilizing the alternative political, economic, and social reality we are hoping to build. The masses are hungry for something different. What is also clear is the role of Black leadership. Black leadership will be critical in building a mass multiracial working-class movement in the US.

SD: When we invest, there are results. It feels really clear that the number of leaders we have on the other side of this cycle is huge. We're a two-year-old organization, and we have hundreds of members now who have gone through this cycle and learned a whole range of skills and are embedded in a whole set of communities across our counties. And that is now infrastructure that wasn't there before. Resources were put there. Our people put in their time, their love, their care, and then also donors put in so that we can support our people in that process. And it just yielded results. We didn't win statewide in North Carolina, but we closed the gap [between the Republican and Democratic presidential candidates] by 100,000 votes, and that was while our opponents' [votes] were also growing. So we know that when investment happens, our people move. That feels like the biggest lesson to me, that we can innovate all kinds of stuff as long as we continue to get the resources to be able to engage with our folks.

This is another lesson. I didn't want to focus anything on white people till the very end, but I think one of the powerful things that our movements have been up to is actually dividing white people in a decisive way that hasn't happened since the Civil War. That really matters. It's true and it's powerful that we are building a majority people-of-color bloc in this country. And I think it's also really important that the bloc of white people—and whiteness as a project—has been falling apart. White folks who have been moved—by the Movement for Black Lives, the recession, the pandemic, the climate crisis—are looking at white people on the other side of the political divide, and saying, "I am less like you than I am like a Black person." That is a meaningful thing that our movements are accomplishing, and in my read, for the first time in the history of this country we have the cultural, social, material, and economic conditions to actually break apart whiteness as the majority bloc. The opportunities for us to transform what's going on in this country are really powerful. And I think Black people have been at the core of making that happen. Obviously it's been a long-run thing that our people have been up to, but I think we are realizing it in this generation.

KK: This has been a really rich conversation. I've learned a lot, and I want to thank you all again for your time, your brilliance, your work, and your humor. I hope our readers have learned a lot too. Thank you.

Notes

1. BMEP stands for Black Male Engagement Program, and Additory means "making an addition," thus the name explains BMVP's approach to engaging and adding Black men to the active voting demographic.
2. Ayesha Rascoe, "With Lil Wayne, Ice Cube and 50 Cent, Trump Makes Final Push for Black Voters," *NPR*, October 30, 2020, www.npr.org.

9

Lessons from Engaging AAPI Voters and Communities in 2020

Timmy Lu, featuring interviews with
Aisha Yaqoob Mahmood, *Asian American Advocacy Fund;* Laura Misumi, Rising Voices, *a project of Tides Advocacy;* Mohan Seshadri, *Asian Pacific Islander Political Alliance;* and Vivian Chang, *Asian Pacific American Labor Alliance, AFL-CIO*

The following chapter contains amended quotes from four separate conversations. They have been edited and rearranged for clarity.

In 2020, Asian American and Pacific Islander (AAPI) voters made a significant impact in the presidential election and in key races up and down the ballot across the country. This was the result of years of work done by grassroots organizers to engage their communities, while at the same time steadily building the relationships, capacity, and infrastructure to engage AAPI voters at scale. Electoral organizers engaging AAPI communities put in more effort than ever before in preparation for the 2020 elections, but also received more resources to do so than ever before—and it paid off. This chapter highlights the impact that AAPI voters had on the 2020 election season, and some of the organizing and infrastructure development that made it possible. There are many lessons to be drawn from this, but perhaps the biggest one is that AAPI communities are indispensable to building the type of multiracial progressive and left power needed to win elections, transform our communities, and transform the nation. This election shows us that in order to do that, there must be longer-term investments in advancing the type of AAPI-led organizing infrastructure that can continue to develop more politically conscious bases and leaders who can build solidarity across the diverse AAPI community and with other multiracial power-building groups.

Background

Asian Americans and Pacific Islanders are overall the fastest growing ethnic groups in the US, having almost tripled in the last three decades. This growing population is also becoming more diverse and complex: they have ancestors from more countries, more people identify as mixed-race, and there is more variation than ever across age, income, and other demographic categories. AAPIs are also a growing electoral force in more districts from the urban to suburban and rural.

Due to their increasing electoral power, AAPIs are being cultivated by both ends of the political spectrum. Between 2016 and 2020, Asian American voter turnout increased by 20%, or 11 points, and Pacific Islander voter turnout increased by 33%, or 14 points. Particularly important in 2020 were proportionally huge leaps in AAPI voter turn-out in key states such as Georgia (+84%), North Carolina, Florida, and Pennsylvania.[1] Aggregate national data has consistently shown that a majority of Asian Americans support Democratic candidates and progressive issues, including universal healthcare, gun control, progressive taxation, and immigration.

All of this data and increasing media coverage is encouraging, but it should not mask the differences in character and needs of specific Asian American and Pacific Islander subgroups, or the persistent challenges to solidifying a progressive majority among AAPI communities that vary widely in class status and access to power. While the AAPI label has offered a means to collective power for many communities,[2] it has also rendered invisible the complex and more marginalized lived experience of some Asian and Pacific Islander subgroups. Media coverage has tended to center a predominantly East Asian, more privileged subset of the Asian experience, perpetuating a model minority myth which says that Asian Americans are uniformly hardworking, have strong family values, are successful in school, and go on to have great careers. These broad stereotypes not only mask wide differences in wealth and other inequalities between AAPI subgroups, but are also used to dismiss anti-Asian racism, and anti-Black racism, and to blame other racial minorities for their collective struggles in the US. The only people who really benefit from these stereotypes and the model minority myth are those in power, who use it as proof that anyone can succeed under the status quo in the US.

Dominant narratives surrounding the rising Asian demographic also obscure how specific AAPI communities are being co-opted by conservative forces in the United States, which are being driven with increasing vigor by an emerging Asian American conservative right wing. These Asian American right-wing forces have had growing success organizing Asian Americans through misinformation, fear, and the model minority myth to support reactionary policies at the local, state, and national levels. In California, these forces have had significant wins recently by mobilizing Asian Americans to oppose affirmative action, comprehensive sexual health education, and affordable housing, often in direct opposition to Southeast Asians, Pacific Islanders, and working-class Asian Americans.

To truly build lasting political and ideological support for concrete progressive policy change, more needs to be done to empower and sustain AAPIs as a progressive force. Data shows that only 33% of Asian Americans reported being contacted through voter outreach in the 2016 election, compared to 46% of whites.[3] In addition, the majority of AAPI voter outreach is concentrated around late-stage, get-out-the-vote outreach, and does not take into account the diversity of AAPI communities. Data such as message research/polling focused on AAPI communities is similarly obtuse and under-resourced, and rarely disaggregates Pacific Islander voters. In this context of either political invisibility or aggressive right-wing targeting, AAPI-led grassroots organizations are showing that even new and emerging organizing projects can have a major impact in a short amount of time.

The organizations, landscape, and strategy

The organizations

Going into 2020, Asian American organizers were preparing to engage, persuade, and turn out voters in very different regional and political landscapes, and coming from different organizational trajectories. The leaders we spoke to and their 501(c)(4) organizations were relatively new, with the exception of Asian Pacific American Labor Alliance (APALA). The Asian American Advocacy Fund (AAAF) in Georgia was founded in 2018 and had an emerging electoral capacity and track record coming out of that year's midterms. The Asian Pacific Islander Political Alliance (API PA) in Pennsylvania officially launched only in July 2020. Although it is a constituency group of the AFL-CIO that was established in 1992, APALA had relatively small engagement in electoral organizing and had limited capacity prior to 2020.

As power-building organizations, they didn't spring into existence spontaneously, but rather emerged from years of grassroots Asian American community base-building and organizing by leaders, organizations, and other partners. API PA, for example, emerged from the efforts of two 501(c)(3)s. One was Asian Americans United, which has been organizing in Philadelphia's Chinatown for about 40 years around issues such as deportation, displacement, housing justice, language justice, and access to political power. The other was Vietlead, which has been building a base in the Vietnamese community in South Philadelphia and southern New Jersey over the last ten years, particularly around land justice, environmental justice, and anti-deportation.

Rising Voices was founded in Michigan only in 2019 as a fiscally sponsored[4] 501(c)(4) organization,[5] along with Rising Voices Fund—its 501(c)(3)[6] arm—so they had little name recognition or track record of organizing in the state before 2020. Rising Voices Executive Director

Laura Misumi noted that the close relationships and trust between a regional ecosystem of organizations and leaders in Southeast Michigan that cut across lines of issue and constituency were key to the organization's founding and its ability to leverage resources and move work successfully in 2020. These organizations included Detroit Action, where Laura worked, but also peer organizations such as 482 Forward and We the People Michigan.

LM: It was incredibly important to our formation and grounding … I'd already had the opportunity to kind of be plugged into a number of existing formations and coalitions that exist out here. The goal for us is to build and reinforce a strategic, multiracial organizing infrastructure and movement in Michigan because we know that's how we're going to win.

Despite being new organizations, the leaders had clear visions for what their roles were and the opportunities they needed to seize in 2020.

LM: Rising Voices came about because there is no organization that's focused primarily on developing the leadership and organizing capacity of Asian American women in Michigan. Our theory of change is that if you organize women into being the civic engagement messengers within Asian American communities, we will move forward.

Mohan Seshadri (MS): We are Pennsylvania's first and only statewide Asian American and Pacific Islander base-building and political and advocacy organization. We publicly launched in July of last year to get Trump out of office and make sure that our communities were turning out up and down the ballot for candidates who are going to actually listen to and fight for our people, rather than either just giving lip service, or worse, fear-mongering about our communities

Vivian Chang (VC): We have national staff and volunteer-run chapters. But for me, I think the purpose of a national group should always be about giving access and resources to local groups. So I think that's where I'm rethinking coalitions because the coalition is not about, "we're in DC and we tell you what to do and then you report to us." I think it should be people bringing in their different advantages and then supporting other groups.

There was an awareness among the leaders we interviewed that the mainstream political focus now included AAPI communities in ways that it hadn't before.

MS: Last year in battleground states like Georgia, Pennsylvania, and Michigan, Asians were finally on the map in the eyes of the political infrastructure outside our community. In many cases, they have never engaged with our community, had our interests in mind, or put in the legwork when it came to caring about power building. Our people were finally targets for turnout. So for the first time, we had a real opportunity to harness that desire for investment and channel it into year-round organizing and long-term power-building. If we didn't, it would go into short-term drop-in-drop-out field programs that might have an impact in the 2020 election, but would not actually build real deep, long-term grassroots governing power for our people.

The pandemic's tactical and strategic implications

As 2020 began, the leaders reflected on how the work on the ground started with well-laid plans, but the pandemic forced them to change and adapt. Organizations were already involved in 2020 Census outreach when COVID-19 erupted, and they had to then juggle mutual aid and prevention awareness along with electoral work. With door-to-door and other in-person outreach mostly out of the question, organizers had to shift strategy and embrace new tactics and tools.

LM: We know long term really leaning into developing a deep organizational infrastructure and building our base, that's what it's going to lead us to win. At the beginning of the year, we had this whole vision of how we wanted to really build relationships within local, very close, tight-knit communities by hosting potlucks in folks' homes, asking hosts to help recruit people and bring people in. We had three to start out with at the beginning of the year that were super successful and it really felt like this could be our thing. And so obviously, with the pandemic, we realized we couldn't do that.

AY: We had to quickly shift into phones and text messaging, and then reorganize our ground game virtually to support vote-by-mail, because COVID made it the easiest way to turn people out. With the increased focus on vote-by-mail, we had to focus our efforts more on voter support. We did endorsements and some political work later, but a big chunk of our work during the spring and summer was about vote-by-mail, like literally doing videos, workshops, talking to people virtually, and doing one-on-one trainings with people.

English proficiency has historically been tied to voter turnout. As AAAF's website points out, "20% of Georgia citizens speak a language other than English. Within AAPI communities, 80% speak a language other than English at home. Of the 80%, 43% speak English less than 'very well.'"[7] About 78% of Asians in Pennsylvania speak a language other than English at home. For organizers rapidly scaling up for 2020, assessing the landscape of language access needs in districts was of significant importance to planning outreach and capacity needs. Reaching multiple constituencies with in-language outreach was a critical strategy.

MS: Our first question on our script was, "We're API PA, an Asian American Pacific Islander political organization in Pennsylvania. Before we talk about the election, what language do you want to have this conversation in?" And then we offered 15 different languages for folks to choose from. It's not just are they able to have this conversation in English, it's are they comfortable having this conversation in English? Are they going to respond the same in a different language, things like that.

LM: What we have found through our digital ad data is that even for communities of non-limited English-proficient speakers who also speak another language at home, they're more likely to watch through to completion an ad that's in their other language because it's targeted to them and because it is acknowledging who they are as people and that they exist and that it's more likely to be shared. So for us, that's pretty significant because it highlights what we already know, which is that when you talk to people specifically and acknowledge who they are and the things that really make a difference, as opposed to flattening everyone's experience, that touch goes a long way.

Engaging Asian American communities with a vision for long-term power-building means that in-language outreach is not simply a tactic, but part of a continuing strategy to build a powerful and aligned base. That means grassroots organizers weren't just communicating Democratic talking points in Asian languages. They were getting to know their communities, meeting them where they are, and connecting with their needs, fears, and hopes.

VC: All these different groups had assumptions about AAPI voters. Usually, the first assumption is something like "We don't need to reach them because there's not enough of them and they're not going to vote." And the next assumption is "We just have to mention 'Asian' and then do the same exact outreach [as for non-Asian voters], you know, like putting an Asian face on the flyer."

MS: We know that Asian Pacific Islander voters broadly are fundamentally Democratic, want healthcare for all regardless of immigration status, want a stronger state and increased government investment in social services. They want a $15 minimum wage and a union. We score the highest of any community when it comes to environmental justice. And so when you have narratives around, "You need to talk to Asians about small business support or about immigration and education. And that's it," that misses the diversity of our communities and the fact that we're fundamentally progressive with an investment and outreach gap.

Interviewees noted that partnerships, relationships, networks, and alliances all played an important role in the 2020 work at the strategy and infrastructure level. As the phone and digital fieldwork began in earnest, connections and reaching out through community- based, relational and ethnic networks that could do this kind of personal organizing and engagement, was also marked as a distinct and powerful strategy.

AY: When I came on in 2019 and began to build the infrastructure, one of the goals that I set for myself was to strengthen our community relationships and build partnerships with other organizations. During the runoff, we were able to really activate these community leaders in this digital way where we hadn't before. We actually had them send out specific messages or specific content through their channels and what we called our digital activation squad.

LM: There is a really significant Burmese population [in the region], somewhere around 5,000 people. But when you look them up in the VAN,[8] there are like seven Burmese people in Michigan. One of my organizers, who we were able to hire through a partnership with APALA, is Tedim Chin, from one of the ethnic minorities of Burma, and we were able to build a partnership with the Burma Center in Battle Creek. And because of that relationship, because she is familiar with what the Burmese refugee population looks like and the different ethnicities, and so on, we're able to pilot a phonebank in four languages with them as well. And they made nearly a thousand hand-dialed calls, had over 90 conversations, and we would not have been able to talk to any of them had it not been for that connection.

The work generated momentum, as organizers gathered resources, allies, and confidence. As the election season got into full swing and organizations increased the scale of their outreach, they embraced national, local, and down-ballot elections in different ways. Although the presidential race was important, down-ballot races with close community impact were equally important.

AY: We endorsed in House and Senate races last year, but not in the presidential race. However, most of our communications, phonebanking, and textbanking were focused on county-level offices. It still was messaging on local issues, but it helped people understand why they needed to vote for Ossoff and Warnock. So we tried to stay away from some of the high-level politics of that election and focus on how they can help you here in Georgia.

MS: We helped get Biden elected. We helped get Trump out of office. We're really proud of that. But if we don't take state power, none of the things that we want to do is going to happen. If we don't flip the State House and the State Senate, none of the things that affect our folks' day-to-day experiences and living conditions are going to change. So we went into it with the mindset of winning the presidential election, the auditor general's election, HD 151, HD 18, CD 1, CD 7, and anywhere else we needed to build power and win justice for our people. And that's how things are going to change. Having that orientation at the state and the local levels is one of the areas where our program really demonstrated that no one ever bothered to talk to many of our people about elections in general, let alone about how to vote.

Impact

Amid rising participation from all ethnic communities, Asian Americans boosted their turnout higher than any other demographic, according to research published by the Census Bureau and Catalist, a Democratic voter-targeting organization.[9] Census data shows that no demographic group in recent years had boosted voter participation as much as AAPIs have between 2016 to 2020; not even Black voters surged as much from 2004 to Barack Obama's first election four years later. From 2010 to 2019, the Asian American population expanded by over 30%, representing more than 5 million people. Asian Americans' share of eligible voters has doubled, from 2.5% in 2000 to 5% in 2020, according to estimates from the Brookings Institute.[10]

Democratic political research firm TargetSmart reports that AAPI voter participation increased in every swing state. Asian Americans overwhelmingly backed President Biden in the battleground states of Georgia, Pennsylvania, Michigan, and Nevada.[11] Turnout in Michigan increased by 58%.[12] In Pennsylvania, almost 56,000 AAPIs voted early in 2020, up 4,719 percent from 2016.[13] During the general election in Pennsylvania, AAPI turnout doubled both in raw numbers—reaching 111,000—and vote share. By the time votes finished being counted, about

75% of registered AAPI voters in that state had turned out. In Georgia, another critical battleground state, approximately 62,000 more Asian Americans voted than did in 2016. Another Georgia study showed that about 59,000 AAPIs voted in Georgia.[14] In an email, TargetSmart noted that "considering that the Biden-Harris ticket carried Georgia by fewer than 12,000 votes, the AAPI surge was clearly decisive."[15]

This uptick reflects both long-term grassroots mobilization efforts, the imminent threat that so many Asian Americans saw from the rising tide of anti-Asian hate crimes,[16] local Census operations, multilingual phone banking and canvassing, and anti-disinformation outreach.[17]

The leaders we interviewed were appreciative of their role in bringing about this broad wave of impact.

LM: We know based on the numbers that Asian Americans are the margin of victory in a lot of these Obama>Trump counties[18] in Michigan. And that obviously the Dems were very much focusing their efforts on courting Obama>Trump white working-class voters at the expense of pretty much everybody else, all the other working-class voters in Michigan. There's not really huge infrastructure to do a significant amount of outreach in a range of languages with culturally competent messengers. And so for us, being able to create a layered program that tried to just talk to as many Asian Americans across the state was really important and ultimately very successful.

MS: What we did is we went out and we doubled the Asian American vote share in Pennsylvania and that doubling was half of Biden's margin of victory, which means that Biden's road to victory across the country to becoming president gets a lot less safe without the Asian American vote in Pennsylvania. And we did that by just building a massive program and running it in line with our values.

MS: We ended up having the largest Asian American electoral field program in US history. But that's not impressive to me. Obviously, we were splashed across all sorts of documents and presentations and things like that. But the base we built, the volunteers we recruited, the fact that we got to grow our staff from literally three people in a room in June 2020, two of whom were part-time and the other was me. By the end of the election, we had 75 folks on staff across the state, in some cases across the country, across every language that we needed to work in, across every community that we needed to work in.

Habits and agency around voting underwent a massive change, particularly with regard to vote-by-mail, which wasn't encouraged in 2016, since it had not previously been a very successful technique of getting the community out. The overall dramatic increase in turnout in 2020 is remarkable, but interviewees also spoke of a more nuanced shift toward being more comfortable with voting, voting by mail, and political education.

AY: By the time we got to Election Day, 85% of people who would vote had already voted. So we think the combination of early voting and vote-by-mail really helped to secure that turnout for our community. And I don't think that will shift. I think people really did like to vote by mail and we're going to keep doing our part to make sure that they can access that down the line.

MS: Despite suppression and challenges, Asians had the highest vote-by-mail signup rate of any community in the state. We had the second highest vote-by-mail return rate of any community in the state. And we were successful in having that turnout spiked to historic levels. But I also just think every day of how much more we could have done and how much more we could have pulled off if we didn't have that pandemic kind of riding on our shoulders at every turn.

LM: Research that we completed after the election showed that Asian Americans are particularly ready and persuadable to act and are really interested to be engaged civically. And that there was one test they did where they asked some questions at the beginning of the survey about the power of your vote and your voice to make change. And many people felt like, oh, it makes no difference, etc. After many other questions about civic engagement we ask the same questions again. In the end, there was a 30% increase in people's feelings that their vote counted and could make a difference in their day-to-day life. That says to me that our community is ready.

The new and exciting collaboration between Asian electoral organizations on a national scale, especially during the Georgia runoff, was apparent as a major place of impact, with exciting implications for the future of Asian electoral organizing. All of the leaders we interviewed agreed that the budding network—now officially launched as the Asian American Power Network—offered a crucial space to connect and share tactics and resources and that it catalyzed a major advance in their collective work, especially in the Georgia runoff elections.

LM: We couldn't have done it without being in an informal coalition with other Asian American 501(c)(4) organizations across the country. Asian American Midwest Progressives in Illinois, for example, helped us recruit 30 volunteers to help us with our program. We worked with API PA to coordinate volunteers to staff volunteer shifts in Michigan and Pennsylvania. The relationship we have with AAAF and APALA made volunteering in Georgia for the Senate runoffs seamless.

AY: We were just starting to build out our infrastructure and needed a place to connect, commiserate, ask questions, and get support and advice from others. When it came time to prepare for the runoff election, I was able to draw on the network of people we worked with and knew over the years. That network and those partnerships enabled us to do a lot of work that would not have been possible otherwise.

MS: We met multiple AAPI political organizations that were dealing with the same challenges and issues. So we started a series of calls to work it out, talk shop, do work, share resources. While our communities are fundamentally different across the board, in many ways, Indians in Texas shared issues and experiences with Indians in the Philadelphia suburbs. Chinese folks in Nevada have ties to Chinese in Georgia, but their histories and experiences are distinct. That's why we got together to develop and collate different messaging that would work for all of our communities, that was rooted in our values.

Challenges

The impact Asian American organizers had in 2020 was in the face of significant challenges. In a year with the overlapping crises of the COVID-19 pandemic and the economic fallout, Asian American communities also faced increased xenophobia and the fear of violence during a sustained wave of anti-Asian sentiment that was fomented by Donald Trump and his supporters.

MS: On the pandemic front, broadly, it was obviously a brutal year across the board. Our folks were failed top to bottom by government structures, by non-Asian health institutions, by everyone when it came to providing testing and treatment information in-language to our communities, when it came to providing that shut-down gap, the guidance in-language to our small businesses, when it came to providing vaccine outreach and engagement. We were trying to talk to our folks about an election and they were like, "This is important and we hate Trump and we're going to vote, but like this is not the thing that is currently top of our mind."

LM: We know that anxiety was incredibly high and people were feeling stressed and afraid to go outside, to go to the grocery store for fear of what might happen to them. What do you do with that sentiment? We connect our communities to mental health resources and acknowledge how much of a stigma it often is to talk about within our communities.

VC: One thing that's unique to AAPIs is that a lot of people, if they do receive some kind of community outreach in-cycle, it's through a nonprofit that does things like meetings in person, dinners, or they come to your building. So when they suddenly had to go virtual, they were like, "Whoa, we have none of these resources or these setups."

Voter suppression and misinformation were also major challenges to overcome.

AY: We're in Georgia. Our voters didn't understand that what they were facing was voter suppression. I think they internalized it as like, "Wow, I just don't know what I'm doing." We really took that opportunity to not just help them get the answers they needed, to walk them through the processes to request absentee ballots and all those things, but also to help them make the connections as to why some of these things were as difficult as they were and helping them to understand that the Republicans that were in charge were putting them in these really crazy circumstances where they were having to jump through these hoops to be able to cast a ballot.

As these were new organizations with most staff relatively green to large-scale electoral work, with a lot of traction but few resources and low capacity, scaling up to the level that these organizations did was challenging.

AY: There are no easy instructions on how to run a 501(c)(4) organization in terms of what kind of programs to do, what programs to run, how to organize your team and fundraise effectively, and how to plan your budget. So, in 2019, figuring out where to start and what we need to run a program in 2020 was a major challenge. Even before COVID came in and messed up the plans, we were trying to operationalize a plan in Georgia because no one expected Georgia to be where it was in November. That meant dollars didn't arrive in Georgia until late. So, until 2020, we had to operate on a shoestring budget. And not having the resources to hire senior-level staff with some of these skills that I later realized I really needed.

At a deeper level, the uncertainty around how to build an electoral program to scale reflected years of marginalization and low investment in AAPI voter engagement and organizing, and organizations have felt the strain of not having the infrastructure and resources that they need to grow their work. And there was a frustrating lack of understanding of Asian communities, on the part of some funders and national partners, that sapped capacity.

VC: There is some data stuff we did that we could have done better. As a small example, when we used Spoke for the first time,[19] we were learning it and using it in the same cycle. And then I did a lot of the uploads and I forgot to upload something, so then the data was wrong and we had to fix it manually on the back end. And that was my mistake because I thought it wasn't a problem, but I think if I were replaced with a data director that that wouldn't have happened. Right? It's interesting because that was a common mistake, but it's also kind of just indicative, again, of the fact that when groups like ours aren't plugged in we're going to make these super basic mistakes that take a lot of time.

MS: Both within and outside our ecosystem, the lack of belief and experience in all of this was just a massive challenge. As someone who has had to run around the state and the country since 2018 talking about the importance of building power in AAPI communities and investing in political organizing, one of the biggest challenges was that so many folks, especially outside our community, had never even thought about it before and so many folks inside our community just didn't think it was possible at the level that we needed.

AY: I had to educate funders and partners about how we do our work and what kind of resources, skills, and support we needed because Asian American outreach isn't always top of their minds. That was an investment, not just in translation, but in creating content and organizing for specific ethnic communities. That doesn't land with many people because other organizations and ethnic groups don't always have the same set of needs.

Lessons learned

We asked the leaders we interviewed to share the most salient lessons for their work in 2020 as they continued to organize their communities, and how they plan to bring those lessons forward to the 2022 and 2024 election cycles. Laura Misumi and the Rising Voices team strongly believes in investing in the leadership development of Asian American women.

They want to hire people who understand Asian languages and have cultural competency yet live in areas where they don't have a big presence.

LM: Trying to figure out how to do recruitment, because that feels core to a lot of other issues and challenges that we're facing, including how we do base-building, and how we introduce ourselves to the Asian American communities of Michigan.

Hiring was also an important need and lesson learned for Aisha of Asian American Advocacy Fund, with a specific focus on building their bench of mid-level organizers (a challenge reflected by all of our interviewees):

AY: I think we did what we could with the resources we had. So hiring some entry level folks was all we could do at the very early stages. But I would definitely make sure that we're investing in some more seasoned organizers and some seasoned senior staff whot can help really build out the programs

Aisha also stressed the importance of grounding their work in the ongoing needs of the community, beyond the focus of the elections:

AY: I love the emphasis that we placed on not just being there to help voters understand candidates and issues, but just kind of being there as support for elections. Our in-language hotline was very successful because we didn't just run it on Election Day. We had it going year-round, people were calling us in the middle of the summer asking us random questions about the election. We'll definitely keep things like that because it helps us stay grounded in the community.

Vivian took away the need for innovation and nimbleness in their orientation to future work and the ongoing need for the mainstream to understand the diversity of Asian American and Pacific Islander communities and what is needed to empower them.

VC: So I think obviously the big, big lesson of 2020 is just innovation, pivoting, being willing to meet the need rather than continue with your established plans. But I feel like another big lesson was definitely to look for the people where they are, don't just assume. We're not a monolith. There are so many assumptions made by mainstream political organizations or media about the AAPI vote. That means that there wasn't an investment where there needed to be, or it was always the same thing. So the success that we saw was through folks being like, "Let's go back to the drawing board. Let's actually find out what people care about."

Mohan reflected that practice, tactics, and tools they developed doing deep, in-language, culturally proficient outreach and organizing that was done in 2020 was very valuable and that sustaining and sharing it will be critical to winning in future elections.

MS: We spent a week or two phonebanking Vietnamese-to-Vietnamese, Chinese-to-Chinese, and South Asian-to-South Asian, specifically to have these longer persuasive organizing conversations—not only to win this election but also to build our understanding and muscle of dedicated persuasion tactics for low-English-proficiency and elder voters in our communities. Because this is not a 2020 issue. This is not a 2022 issue. We won't be able to build the power and win the shit we need to win unless we meet our people where they are and specifically counter right-wing messaging both within and from outside our communities.

Mohan also strongly stated the need for robust, sustained investment in long-term organizing infrastructure in Asian American communities.

MS: I do want folks to know—and to be clear, like the folks in Georgia, the folks in Michigan, etc.,—that we made history. We ran first-of-its-kind programs. And we made do frankly, with less than longer-term political infrastructure and 501(c)(4)s and PACs and organizations that had not been around for longer than one or two years and we'd never seen that kind of investing before. And if folks want us to do it again, if we want Asian Americans in Georgia and Michigan and Pennsylvania to turn out the way we did last year in those incredibly important gubernatorial races, Senate races, state races in 2022, we have to see that same level of investment.

Conclusion

AAPI communities are tremendously diverse, and the specific skills and tactics needed to mobilize them are as distinct and nuanced as their places of origin. The strategy to solidify AAPIs as a progressive bloc, however, can be remarkably simple. Every leader highlighted in this chapter spoke to the need to invest in year-round base-building and voter engagement on down-ballot and major federal races. While these organizations had tremendous successes in mobilizing AAPI voters against Trump in 2020, they did so in spite of the boom-bust cycles that parachute resources into swing states while leaving these organizations to fend for themselves in off-years or in critical local and statewide races.

These are also very young organizations still building their programs and internal leadership. The leaders interviewed were working, in 2020, without a clear playbook, but with a deep desire to build for the long term and do so in community with other AAPI organizers. It's this orientation that has led them to form the new Asian American Power Network, a national organization of state-based Asian American-led 501(c)(4) organizations committed to building a progressive bloc of AAPI voters (alongside other communities of color) necessary to transform the US. The network is helping to bring together the essential components for this bloc: investing in organizing outside of just the presidential election cycle so that organizations can win concrete benefits for their communities, developing the leadership pathways necessary to train a whole new generation of AAPI political organizers, and crafting a national strategy for advancing a transformative AAPI politics. These leaders are showing that it is possible to organize AAPIs into a progressive bloc and making the case that such a bloc is necessary to win advances in battleground states.

This chapter couldn't have been completed without the contributions of Will Buford, Marian Jones, and Lia Dun who assisted with drafting and editing. Thank you.

Notes

1. For a comprehensive analysis of Asian American and AAPI demographic data on voter engagement, we recommend AAPI Data and their recent 2020 media guide.

2. The term *Asian American* was first coined by Chinese American, Filipino American, and Japanese American students in the San Francisco Bay Area in the 1960s as a strategic, unifying political identity for Asian ethnic groups to use as they resisted both US imperialism in Southeast Asia, and white Americans' use of *Oriental* as a derogatory term for Asians in the United States. By the 1980s, the US Census Bureau, pressed by Asian and Pacific Islander activists demanding visibility and recognition, grouped persons of Asian, Native Hawaiian, and Pacific Islander ancestry together and created the category "Asian Pacific Islander," which continued in the 1990s Census. In the 2000 census, "Asian" and "Pacific Islander" became two separate racial categories. Throughout this text, we tried to use only *AAPI* if we are specifically including Pacific Islanders as well, as most people use the *AAPI* as shorthand even when they're not talking about Pacific Islanders.

3. Aastha Uprety, "5 Ways to Increase Asian American Voter Turnout," Center for American Progress," May 7, 2018, www.americanprogress.org.

4. Fiscal sponsorship is an arrangement where for a percentage fee of incoming funds, the fiscal sponsor assumes legal responsibility for the project. Rising Voices receives accounting, compliance, operational, and programmatic support and dedicated staff to support its back-end work from Tides Advocacy, so that Rising Voices can focus on programmatic work.

5. A 501(c)(4) is a nonprofit organization that can endorse political candidates in addition to conducting advocacy and outreach—this is one key difference between the 501(c)(3) and 501(c)(4). The other is that while these organizations are exempt from taxes, charitable donations to them are not considered tax-deductible

6. A 501(c)(3) is a "charitable" tax-exempt nonprofit organization. Nonprofits in this classification are limited to the kinds of political activity or advocacy work they can undertake. Donations to these organizations are tax-deductible.

7. "AAPIs in Georgia," Asian American Advocacy Fund, www.asianamericanadvocacyfund.org.

8. NGP VAN, Inc., is a privately owned voter database and web hosting service provider used by the Democratic Party and other nonprofit organizations. It is used by political and social campaigns for fundraising, campaign finance compliance, field organizing, and digital organizing. It was formerly known as Voter Activation Network, Inc. (VAN).

9. Catalist: Progressive Data, https://catalist.us/.

10. Ronald Brownstein, "Don't Sleep on Asian American Voters," *Atlantic*, May 20, 2021.

11. Alexandra Hutzler, "Asian Voter Turnout Hit All-Time High in 2020 Presidential Race, Census Bureau Finds," *Newsweek*, April 29, 2021.

12. Nicholas Reimann, "Asian-American Voter Turnout Soared over 45% In 2020 Election, Study Finds—and That's Probably an Undercount," *Forbes*, April 21, 2021.

13. "AAPI Voters Turn Out in Historic Numbers in PA," API PA, April 5, 2021, https://apipennsylvania.org.

14. Catalist: Progressive Data.

15. Brownstein, "Don't Sleep on Asian American Voters."

16. AAPI Data and 2020 media guide.

17. Catalist: Progressive Data.

18. Counties that voted for Obama in 2012, but went to Trump in 2016.

19. Spoke is an online tool developed by MoveOn that allows volunteers to reach potential voters through SMS messaging.

10

Stepping into Indigenous Political Power: The Resurgence of the Native Vote in 2020

Lycia Maddocks (Quechan Indian Tribe)

In 2020, not only did we take to the streets, we committed to meet one another at the ballot box. Social justice and equity groups across the US determined to leverage our voter blocs to convey a strong message: that Americans must stand united, ensuring that our local and national political culture and representation promotes the common good and reflects our collective voices.

Among the voters who were a prominent presence in making this commitment were American Indian and Alaska Native (AI/AN) people, dismissed in past years as statistically insignificant on the national front. According to the 2010 Census, AI/AN people experienced the greatest undercount at 4.9%, nearly double that of the next most undercounted population group. AI/AN people are generally missing from data, a tactic that is embedded in federal policies adopted to remove, erase, and oppress Native people. Truth be told, because the United States has yet to reckon with its past of Native genocide—physical and political—the effects remain in place in the modern form of chronically underfunded tribal and Native communities, erasure of Native people from the education system, and ongoing battles over land and natural resources.

Nonetheless, through the perseverance and advocacy of Native leaders and allies, 574 federally recognized tribal nations and dozens of state-recognized and tribal nations without federal recognition are thriving. Despite broken promises, broken treaties, and continual erasure from education, policies, and narratives, momentum is building. Some have called it a resurgence, but regardless of label, 2020 proved to be the year when Indian Country reminded itself and the federal government of its political power—its *sovereign* political power. As nations within a nation, Native people and tribal nations reminded their communities about the laws, agreements (or treaties), and protections that federal Indian law reinforces. More importantly, it was time to raise our profile both through political representation on local and national levels and in the culture more broadly, in order to assert and make manifest the responsibility the US has to its Indigenous people.

Over the past decade, moves toward equity and inclusion in broader governmental policies and public narratives have offered glimmers of hope to AI/AN people. The Obama administration took promising steps toward true government-to-government relationships and solutions, and Native people became more vocal in demanding stronger, more effective policies that advance the self-determination of tribal communities, required funding appropriations that align with the treaty and trust obligations to tribal nations, and consent over consultation. The goal for Native communities in relation to any government entity is to secure and strengthen rights to continue to practice culture, traditions, and land stewardship without unjust restrictions.

Many government bodies, elected officials, policy makers, and court systems are woefully behind in understanding the obligations of the US to its Indigenous people, and yet this ignorance did not stop Native people from organizing in 2020 to get out the Native vote. Grassroots advocates like Native Organizers Alliance, National Congress of American Indians, NDN Collective, Four Directions, Inc. and many more ensured that Native people organized and prepared their communities to show up on Election Day 2020. By taking the time to tell their stories and educate urban and rural Natives, as well as garner support from ally communities for an Indian Country political agenda and community needs, these supportive, trusted groups set the foundation. Native voters showed up at the ballot box and even ran for office. These efforts created a groundswell of hope and determination, fostering the will to press forward toward a new era of Indigenous power and policy.

Narrative change and storytelling: Identity and the power of creative resistance

When Native people go unseen in the mainstream media, in K–12 education, or in policymaking spaces, our voices and needs are minimized. Invisibility perpetuates the continued harm that Indigenous communities have faced since colonial contact. We are forced to confront stereotypes, false narratives about US history, and the real impact of government policies that undermine tribes' unique cultures, traditions, and well-being.

If Native people are not engaged in the political process our traditional lifeways will remain at the mercy of policymakers who are likely to place their own interests over ours. Policies that fail to adequately protect our cultures, land, and resource rights are a perfect storm for invisibility. Native people are already omitted from data, and tribes are seldom consulted on decisions over land and natural resources where tribal communities have strong cultural ties. These practices leave unacknowledged an entire population of people who nonetheless still exist and have basic human rights. The resulting invisibility also fosters ignoring the obligation to enforce laws that tribal nations negotiated, as sovereign nations, in exchange for land and resources. The federal government has often studied the effects of our invisibility. Reports from the US Commission on Civil Rights include *A Quiet Crisis: Federal Funding and Unmet Needs in Indian Country* (2010, updated in 2016) and *Broken Promises: Continuing Federal Funding Shortfall for Native Americans* (2018). Both illustrate the effects of invisibility on healthcare, housing, education, and so many more issues that plague Native communities.

Understanding these dynamics, IllumiNative, an Indigenous-led narrative-changing nonprofit organization, took on the task of ensuring that Native people are no longer missing from data, from stories, and from the public eye. IllumiNative's goal of encouraging narratives that engender pride about their identity among Native people was not its only focus. In fact, IllumiNative knew that for the narrative regarding Native people and their needs to change, research was essential. From 2016 through 2020, IllumiNative undertook three studies: 1) to analyze societal narratives around Native people, 2) to understand how education systems could bring high quality content about Native people into US classrooms, and 3) to understand how identity and the 2020 political landscape could fuel civic participation, particularly in the 2020 elections.

Complementing the narrative work, IllumiNative, Native Organizers Alliance, and the Center for Native American Youth recognized the need for greater understanding of modern Native and Indigenous populations and designed plans with the next seven generations in mind. Again, with Native people generally missing from the data, this group wanted to know more about what would make Native people feel "valued, seen, and safe." The group launched the Indigenous Futures Project and hosted a survey to collect data to better understand the needs and concerns of Native and Indigenous communities. This partnership yielded the Indigenous Futures Survey (IFS), "the largest research project ever conducted in Indian Country with participation from over 6,400 Native peoples from across the country, representing 401 tribes and from all 50 states." Survey questions were designed to capture a snapshot in time. The group hoped to elicit an accurate reflection of personal identity and examine voter sentiment, in order to uncover what would ensure that Native voters—especially the young—would flex their voting power.

The survey found that 96% of Native American participants reported that being Native was an important part of their identity (p. 10), but 87% felt that the average American did not care about Native people's experiences (p. 52). The report revealed a profound feeling of underrepresentation and invisibility among modern US Indigenous populations. Paired with the Reclaiming Native Truth Survey of 2018, the IFS Survey gave Indian Country an unprecedented opportunity—its first in modern history—to communicate with Native voters in a deep and comprehensive way.

As 2020 unfolded, Leah Salgado (Pascua Yaqui), deputy director at IllumiNative, could see the potential for this long-needed research to create a uniquely different political environment—one where Native people could be informed and inspired and would show up to the polls as never before. "Throughout our research, a couple of common themes occurred," said Leah. "First, we saw that Native people are actively looking for visibility—we want to be seen. And we want inclusion in education, politics, and the movement conversations happening around us. But we also realized that these were clear spaces where we are being left out of polling, data collection, and messaging." A solution to these concerns was to leverage the research data from each of their Reclaiming Native Truth and Indigenous Futures Survey reports and 2020's national conversation about racial equality to fuel a bold conversation about how Native people are consistently, and sometimes blatantly, missing from societal narratives.

Even more fundamentally, it was past time to do away with images of Native people as relics of the past and even as caricatures and cartoon mascots. IllumiNative saw this as a moment—the biggest opportunity in modern history—of maximum pressure on schools, national sports teams, and brands to evaluate their content and their stories. As the world saw "corporate social responsibility" and "diversity, equity, and inclusion" statements roll out daily in the wake of a heightened focus on social justice and equality, the time had come to move beyond superficial gestures to protect brand reputation and take concrete action. The results? The Washington football team, the Cleveland major league baseball team, and countless high schools across the country changed their racist team names and mascots. The momentum was catching on and now it was time to dig a little deeper to ensure safe, inclusive futures for Native people.

To ensure that Native people felt a sense of connection to events happening around them, IllumiNative focused next on storytelling through art—what many in Indian Country would call "creative resistance."

"We saw that a lot of political messaging by non-Native groups just wasn't going to work for Native people," said Leah, "and what we learned from our research is that Native people still carry traditional values with them, meaning the way that Native people think about their role in the world is one that's community based—it's not about the individual."

This knowledge helped inform the effort to engage Native communities through art that presented graphic representations of Indigenous realities. Partnering with 32 Indigenous artists, IllumiNative built a campaign of messages and imagery that would resonate with Native voters, using social media, radio, billboards, and even eye-catching murals in urban and rural areas where the local Indigenous population would glimpse culture combined with messages on the power of voting, all in a single magnificent piece of art.

"Our strategy went beyond wanting Natives to feel included," said Leah. "We knew that non-Native organizations were using their data to nail down their messaging and the Native perspective simply wasn't present in their results. Our research and data-gathering identified these fundamental issues and we saw Native people show up to vote."

And then IllumiNative moved on to another strategy: turning voting, the most basic stage of political power, into a more all-encompassing form of power that will end for all time the invisibility not only of Native people but of their sovereign governments.

Large-scale organizing: Training indigenous leaders and supporting trusted messengers

The 2016 fight against the Dakota Access Pipeline brought together tribal nations and a broad range of allies in a historic gathering. Judith Le Blanc (Caddo Nation), director of Native Organizers Alliance (NOA), described Standing Rock as galvanizing a "new normal" of collective action in the face of something egregious. From this historic show of solidarity, NOA knew Indian Country, with support from allies, had to continue applying pressure. It cultivated leaders across Indian Country who would continue the momentum, resulting in issue-based, 21st-century organizing. A NOA-built ecosystem of "mocs on the ground" equipped Indigenous people to mobilize their communities for social change on demand.

Implementing this strategy, NOA, Four Directions, Inc., and the National Congress of American Indians began outreach and education to Native voters well ahead of the 2020 campaign season. Reaching Native voters required unprecedented on-the-ground efforts. The organizations hosted two Native American Presidential Forums at which candidates were invited to share the stage with tribal leaders, grassroots advocates, and traditionalists from around Indian Country, marking some of the first instances of direct dialogue and exchange of ideas between candidates and Native community advocates and tribal leadership. As a result, presidential candidates including Senators Bernie Sanders and Julián Castro, and former Vice President Joe Biden, each crafted priorities for Indian Country, including strengthened government-to-government relations, addressing the effects of racism and inequities, and resolving overdue financial obligations that could fund housing, education, healthcare, and environmental and lands issues.

The events garnered audiences of more than 300,000 real-time viewers and attendees, with more than 1 million viewers of broadcast replays. Participants left with the truth of each others' struggles affirmed and information about the importance of the 2020 Census and election to relay to their communities. "We didn't need to convince anyone that this was the time to get involved," said Judith LeBlanc. "But we had work to do to develop the logistics and the structures for our organizers to speak up, speak out, and take action." Recalling the extraordinary energy of Standing Rock, Judith notes that "people became savvy to the importance of modern organizing and issue-based voting. After 2016, we educated our Indigenous communities to pay attention to which candidates supported our causes or ignored them." This generation of Native people was being prepared for the biggest year for civic engagement, and many looked forward to the promise of visibility and a voice in national narratives through the power of their votes and participation in the 2020 Census.

In 2020, *Indian Country Today* (ICT), the largest and most widely recognized Indigenous news source in the US, reported tracking a record number of Indigenous candidates: "In all, 114 Indigenous candidates ran for public office, with 72 of those candidates successfully elected. Of the total candidates, 67 were women." Amid the excitement, Congresswoman Deb Haaland had the rumor mill buzzing across Indian Country. Would one of the first Native American women to serve in Congress consider the position of secretary of the interior, assuming responsibility for interfacing with and upholding the federal government's responsibility to tribal nations? The question remained open as the impact of the Native vote became apparent.

All voting is local: Getting out the Native vote and Indigenous participation in the voting process

Heading into 2020, Native communities were feeling empowered and educated. Many eligible voters were committed to resetting political relationships with government at all levels to create change and move toward equity for Native people. As a result, candidates vied for the Native vote and sought to learn more about why that vote can be so significant. Actually getting out the Native vote, however, came with unique challenges. Up until now, lack of data exacerbated Indian Country's challenges and even diminished tribal nations' voting power. Historically, government at all levels has pursued intentionally restrictive policies that limited Native communities' voting rights. In fact, two of the most prominent national Native organizations, Native American Rights Fund (NARF) and National Congress of American Indians (NCAI), were founded to resist such policies. Looking ahead to 2020, these organizations partnered to analyze modern voter suppression. In 2019, NARF released *Obstacles at Every Turn: Barriers to Political Participation Faced by*

Native American Voters, a report that outlined modern challenges facing Native voters and their root causes. Among these obstacles were distance to polls and post offices, lack of resources such as transportation and funds for transportation to polling places or to obtain ballot boxes, the digital divide and access to technology, atypical mailing addresses, voter identification requirements, and out-and-out racism.

Not only are Native people geographically dispersed, many by forced relocation, but they are chronically undercounted and underrepresented in both urban and rural communities. Lack of internet service and mail infrastructure magnify these issues, making it harder for Native people to cast ballots and to keep up with changing voter registration requirements. These and multiple other factors contributed to outdated Native voter files. In 2020, these barriers to outreach, voter education, and voter support all became apparent, and Native people had to navigate around the barriers in county election offices and even the courtroom. With the added challenge of the COVID-19 pandemic and momentum from the presidential forums, the prospect of a year of setting the tone for visibility and being heard was daunting.

Jaynie Parrish (Dine/Navajo), executive director for Northeast Arizona Native Democrats (NEAZND), watched as COVID-19 cases saturated her community. She faced a pivotal career decision: should she stay in Washington, DC, in the immensely supportive learning environment at Emily's List? Or should she return to her community, the Navajo Nation in Arizona, the largest tribal nation in the country? She chose to return home. "Like many other communities, Native organizers took on the responsibility of becoming community aid groups. Above all else, Native communities needed groups that could move resources and aid while tribal leaders leaned into their federal partners to gain access to personal protective equipment (PPE) and other medical support. We let our people know we were here to help and spent a lot of time relationship-building by supporting our communities the way they needed us the most," says Parrish. NEAZND participated in food and PPE distribution, even making deliveries to their most rural relatives. "Going out into our communities regularly helped us to see that we had a good base of politically engaged citizens, and in some Arizona counties, we had community members that were seasoned enough in the political landscape and ready to do outreach work, as well as cultivate newer, younger organizers."

Despite the pandemic, Jaynie and her organizers knew they still had a mission—to ensure that their community outreach would yield enough Native voters so their candidates would prevail. Now that her team had built a rapport and identified other local trusted messengers, it was time to design a strategy to help communities see the importance of voicing their concerns about how chronic underfunding in key areas had limited Native people's capacity to respond to the pandemic. NEAZND hoped this analysis would underscore the importance of representation that would address the needs of tribal communities and further encourage Native people to exercise their right to vote.

In addition to the impact of the pandemic, Jaynie also realized that in Arizona, barriers that Native voters face—access to ballot boxes and polling places, ongoing threats to purge permanent early voter lists, transportation, and even translation of ballots and educational materials—would certainly come into play. First, she and her team learned that under-resourced county election offices had no money for additional ballot boxes and limited funds for staff. Securing and placing ballot boxes, and planning for voter outreach, especially in extremely rural locations, had to be addressed quickly. NEAZND secured grant funding to ensure that Arizona voters in five counties had access to ballot boxes, within a reasonable distance, and hired local citizens, at $15 per hour to conduct outreach.

The next big effort would be to develop an outreach strategy that would overcome communications barriers such as lack of current contact information, the digital divide, and delivering accurate information to tribal communities that had no local news source. "We really stepped up our outreach tactics and utilized tribal radio, social media, and phone banking. Texting proved to be our campaign lifeline," says Jaynie. She also mentioned that due to the unique state and tribal borders, some northeastern Arizona voters could view news only on the nearest New Mexico stations. "Many voters weren't getting the latest information on elections and ballot measures, so we had to think quickly about other options to keep them educated and informed. Some may believe that postcards are a thing of the past, but it worked for us!" After these strategies proved successful, Jaynie and her team moved toward hosting community meetings at which they provided more education on voting, important dates for the upcoming elections, and information about what was on the ballot. So that voters knew exactly how they would get to and from polls, the team helped them make Election Day voting plans. To ensure that every Native vote counted, the team also helped to confirm that each ballot was filled out properly.

Like many community-based organizations, NEAZND took on the tall order of ensuring fair and equal access to the polls and voter education. Most important, in a moment when people across the globe were prioritizing health and safety, navigating social unrest, and balancing their commitment to change, NEAZND delivered true community support. Despite the adversity, Arizona responded by showing up. "We increased voter registration by 21,000 new voters, saw nearly 50% in early voter turnout, and saw between 82% and 85% overall turnout. That's a 30% increase for us over the last general election," said Jaynie. The NCAI Policy Research Center reported a record-breaking number of votes cast and measured the strong potential impact of the Native vote in key battleground states such as Arizona, Georgia, Nevada, North Carolina, and Wisconsin by taking the Native voter population and comparing it against the margin of victory. It seemed that the mixture of messaging and meeting the needs of the Native communities proved to be effective.

Speaking of messaging strategies, looking back at 2016 is a prerequisite to continuing to move forward. Theresa Sheldon, the Native American political director of the Democratic National Committee, took a few lessons, especially around social media messaging, into her 2020 strategy. "The Obama administration said that Native Americans were the second highest group on social media," explained Theresa. "As you can imagine, we went heavy on Facebook messaging for the Obama campaign and saw a great voter turnout. But if we look at the 2016 election, we saw that social media was used differently to reach voters. The facts show us that social media was used to spread disinformation. This hurt voter turnout and we needed to figure out a way to turn that around in 2020."

In the age of unmediated digital information, voters were forced to filter good information from bad and were left on their own to make the best candidate selections. Theresa further explained how, at the national level, we were confronting problems of ethics and access. "We had to recognize that Native voters are politically diverse, so it was important that building trust with our Native voter base meant really focusing on the local issues." Theresa knew her messaging needed to reach the average person, the one just working hard to get kids to school with barely enough time to get to a polling place, or the voter without enough money or a working vehicle to travel the long distance to the polls. She realized that many Native voters still faced voter intimidation and problems having their tribal IDs accepted as government-issued ID. Theresa said, "We needed to talk about and confront why these policies were in place and develop messaging as a tool that would help Native people vote responsibly."

While Theresa and many others around Indian Country witnessed voter suppression laws being introduced in 48 states, she also realized that sending out-of-state organizers was not the best way to educate and inform Native voters. "Native voters deserve consistency and relationships. That's how trust is built," she explained. In states like Arizona, Michigan, Wisconsin, and Washington, the strongest messages focused on who was willing to advance and reinforce the rights of Native people. More importantly, Native people were seeking candidates committed to solving the unique issues that matter most to tribal communities.

"Party association can make us buy into a lot of things that are not inherently good for us," Theresa said, "but challenging voters to understand which Native issues the candidate was willing to take on really made voters pay attention." By understanding how power shifts occur, Native people began thinking about how to leverage this power to address land and climate issues. She saw Native caucus groups in Washington State begin to form and use their political power to pass resolutions that would later become part of the Democratic Party platform. "Native issues were moving from controversial to under consideration status," Theresa said, "but the real power will come when we have solid voter turnout in midterm elections." While the Native vote strongly influenced the national elections, local elections are at least as important if not more so. "Imagine having someone from your tribal community on the county board, or sitting as a judge. Imagine active participation and representation from tribal communities in county races. Proper representation can change the way that entity behaves toward tribes," said Theresa.

The Deb Haaland strategy

The story of the Native voter turnout in 2020 would be incomplete without noting the year-end announcement by President-Elect Joe Biden that not only reflected and responded to the massive participation of Native voters but transformed the US government's engagement with Native people. The announcement ultimately led to the highest form of representation ever from Indian Country. Enter the Deb Haaland strategy. Many called the nomination of Laguna Pueblo citizen and then Congresswoman Deb Haaland (NM-1) as secretary of the Department of the Interior (DOI) a down payment on the Biden administration's commitment to creating a true government-to-government relationship between tribal nations and the US. "Having Haaland as the secretary of DOI and a member of Biden's cabinet would serve as a constant reminder of the inclusion of Native people at the highest level in our country," said Leah Salgado of IllumiNative's reasoning for helping to design a public campaign to support Haaland. "We believed her nomination and confirmation would further normalize our existence and would fundamentally change how we are seen. Native people must be seen as leaders." Haaland's nomination, another first for her, also meant that tribal nations could begin to see DOI actualize its mission to "honor its trust responsibilities or special commitments to American Indians, Alaska Natives, and affiliated Island Communities …" Not only did she serve as one of the first two Native women in the US Congress; she was now on the road to becoming the first Native American person to serve as head of a department that could fundamentally change the way tribal homelands, resources, and wildlife are managed.

So support poured out from IllumiNative, Native Organizers Alliance, the National Congress of American Indians, NDN Collective, hundreds of tribal nations, and dozens of Native-led organizations to ensure that Deb Haaland was confirmed as a member of the Biden cabinet. These determined advocates also engaged other organizations, especially those with an interest in public lands and environmental protections, and began educating the general public about why this nomination and subsequent confirmation would be so important to Americans as a whole. The strategy group worked tirelessly to publicize Haaland's willingness to work across the aisle for common-sense policies as well as her competency in key areas, making her a perfect fit for the role of DOI secretary. All these efforts paid off. On March 15, 2021, Deb Haaland was confirmed, by a vote of 51 to 40 in the US Senate, to serve as the 54th United States secretary of the interior.

What's next for the Native vote

Several lessons can be learned from the 2020 Native vote: lessons about increased power and representation in key offices and the impact of historic federal funding support. But the bigger story is about Indigenous futurism—the idea that Indigenous people, our knowledge, and our traditional lifeways can pave the way for humanity's future. Moreover, this concept emphasizes the key role that Indigenous leaders must play and debunks false narratives from US history, including the eradication of Indigenous people as relics of the past. Native people have been waiting for a moment when we truly are visible and heard.

Native people are also operating on an understanding that we have allies among like-minded social justice partners who are willing to take on the responsibility of recognizing and reinforcing us as active members of society. As is evident from the remarkable participation of tribal nations and Native people in the economy, government, education, television, sports, and more, Native people are far from gone. We are still here. We stand ready to support a future in which traditional and cultural knowledge are respected as a form of science and spirituality. Moreover, Native people recognize the value of Native and non-Native allies in the fight to protect the land, natural resources, and wildlife of the territories we steward. When we were invisible, our land was overrun. Now that we cannot be ignored, we want to steward the land again.

As we prepare for the 2022 midterm elections and the 2024 national elections, we are also preparing for unprecedented numbers of Native candidates and policy platforms that we expect will be included in any race in which candidates who prevail will oversee areas occupied by Native and Indigenous people. If 2020 proved nothing else, it made local and national audiences aware of Native people's demand to be included, our refusal to tolerate erasure, our determination to stand up for our land, resources, and lifeways. We will continue showing up to the polls so that we are never again invisible.

Notes

1. Indigenous Futures Project, "From Protest to the Ballot Box, and Beyond: Building Indigenous Power," 2020, http://indigenousfutures.illuminatives.org.
2. Aliyah Chavez, "Indigenous Candidates Made History in 2020," *Indian Country Today*, online edition, December 28, 2020, https://indiancountrytoday.com.
3. Native American Rights Fund, "Comprehensive Field Hearing Report 2020," https://vote.narf.org.
4. National Congress of American Indians Policy Research Center, "Native Vote Report: 2020 Election Results," December 15, 2020, www.ncai.org.
5. US Department of Interior, 2021, www.doi.gov/about.

11

No One Is Coming to Save Us: Self-Organizing in Latinx Communities for Political Power

Rafael Návar

Introduction

In places where year-round grassroots organizing is strong and directly connected to electoral work, 2020 saw significant increases in Latino voter turnout. In most battleground states, Latino voters were decisive in defeating Trump. The key to engaging with these voters is grassroots/electoral organizing paired with national support that follows grassroots leaders, not episodic voter turnout.

2020 also reminded us that Latino voters have not fully aligned themselves with either party. Latino communities are contested electoral terrain. Populism from the left has traction, but so too does right-wing authoritarianism. Nothing should be taken for granted as the ranks of Latino voters continue to grow.

Much of the mainstream post-2020 analysis has focused on concerns about a rightward shift among Latino voters. These analysts tend to downplay or outright ignore Latino support for Bernie during the Democratic primaries. To make sense of these trends, I offer historical and cultural context for the election, beyond the fog of the pundits, national consultants, and corporate Latino media analysts.

The contexts we need to consider as we make sense of the electoral math include the impact of the 2008 financial crash, the recent and ongoing pandemic, and the project of forming a shared Latinx identity out of our multiple experiences and histories. I look at the organizing and movement-building in four states—most of it independent of the Democratic Party—that enabled a historic increase in Latino voter participation. The pillars that support success in these states include strong local organizing, support from national political formations, and expanded access to voting.

Deciphering the Latino vote in 2020

According to the Latino Policy and Politics Initiative report,[1] the Latino vote increased by 30.9% over 2016. This was the single largest four-year increase. The report summary continues:

1. Latino voters supported Biden over Trump by a nearly 3-to-1 margin in key counties in Arizona, California, Colorado, Illinois, New Mexico, Nevada, New York, Pennsylvania, and Wisconsin.

2. Latinos supported Biden over Trump with a 2-to-1 margin or larger in the several counties in Texas, Georgia, Washington, and in Florida outside of Miami-Dade.

3. In Arizona, the size of the Latino electorate and their overwhelming support for Joe Biden flipped the state from Republican to Democrat for the first time since 1996.

4. In Georgia and Wisconsin, where the difference between the winning and the losing candidate was roughly 12,000 and 21,000 votes, Latino voters' strong support for Biden and growth in votes cast helped tip these states in favor of Biden.

Credit for the historic increases in Latino votes should go to the organizations on the ground. The self-organizing capacity of our communities enables us to grow this arm of our political power. Mijente, formed in 2015, draws attention to the need for more political organization in Latinx communities that operates year-round to promote economic, racial, gender, and climate justice. We work to support political organizing that is independent from establishment Democrats and corporate interests.

Prior organizing and progressive infrastructure made the difference in states like Arizona and Georgia, and in parts of Florida, Colorado, and Nevada. Still, Trump did make gains where left organizing is weak or not directly linked to electoral fights, such as the much-talked-about Rio Grande Valley in South Texas.

While Latinos were a critical component of President Biden's victory, there is much concern post-2020 about the inroads Trump made from 2016. In states like Texas and Florida Trump made gains of 9% and 14%, respectively, from 2016 according to Catalist.[2] How could one of the most overtly racist presidents make these kinds of gains with the Latino vote?

Absent analysis of neoliberalism and its impact on Latino communities, and both parties' failures to address these conditions (especially after the financial crash in 2008), mainstream and liberal pundits are at a loss to explain increased support for Trump among Latino voters in 2020. They mostly ignore Latino voters' enthusiasm for Bernie.

Bernie's gains during the primaries in California, Texas, and elsewhere suggest that his campaign represents the politics we must expand upon for a future where an active and aligned Latinx bloc of voters wields real political power.

Latinos and US realignment: From the financial crisis to the pandemic

It is in the context of the recession that began in 2008 that we can understand the rise of both Trump and Bernie. Each in his way appeals to those who felt left behind. Both parties' failures to address the crisis and offer solutions sharpen the appeal of an authoritarian demagogue like Trump. But also, these failures can make people more receptive to the democratic socialist populism of someone like Bernie. We saw these dynamics at play in 2016 and 2020.

The fallout from the 2008 Recession (and the "Great Theft" wherein our people bailed out Wall Street while we lost our homes and much of our community wealth) continues, and it was manifest in the voting patterns of 2016 and 2020. A crisis of this proportion that exploded a 40+ year increase of income inequality precipitates a realignment of social and political forces. For Latino voters, this realignment makes many of us susceptible to overtly anti-elitist appeals. And, too often, it is a right-wing version of this critique that speaks to working-class Latinos, especially in communities without progressive organizing that provides an alternative framework and struggles for making sense of neoliberal devastation wrought in our communities.

When the big banks and financiers crashed the economy in 2008, instead of being held to account, they were rewarded with a massive bailout. This exposed the hypocrisies of "free market" rhetoric. While they got billions, homeowners caught in the crisis lost everything. Generations of family wealth in Latino and Black communities were wiped out. Those who had been targeted by predatory lenders were then blamed for the ensuing wave of foreclosures. In the face of massive bailouts for the financial industry, "individual responsibility" was a cruel joke. Clearly, there was a different set of rules for the 1% and for everyone else. To a growing number of people, it was clear that, in America, rules don't matter. Everything is about power.

The absence of left-leaning community organizing and meaning-making has people on the left struggling to make sense of what happened to them in 2008 and in subsequent years.

Both Bernie and Trump offered a politics that would disrupt the status quo preserved by the political managerial class. While Bernie focused on the corporate and financial power center behind the DC operatives, Trump's attacks focused on government itself and this managerial political class.[3] Bernie's proposals would redistribute economic and political power to the majority. Trump's politics wanted to transfer power from the political class to himself and further increase the economic and political power of the 1%. Since 2008, income inequality has only increased from an already dire state.

Then came a pandemic that would sacrifice Latinos at the altar of capital at the highest rates of any ethnic group in America.[4] Latinos are well-represented among the ranks of the disposable workers who had to put themselves at risk so that corporate giants could add to their profits even as the rest of us experienced yet another recession—lost income, more foreclosures and evictions, no childcare and too little healthcare. Being acknowledged as "essential" workers did not change the fact that Latino communities experienced some of the highest death rates in the country.

The instabilities wrought by the economic crisis and pandemic will be disruptive for years to come and will only further expand these political openings with Latinos who already have a weak allegiance to either party. To solidify a left base within our communities that can repel rightwing appeals, we must organize year-round and in elections with a clear critique of neoliberal politics, linked with racial, gender, and LGBTQ lenses. Absent this foundational work, larger sections of our communities may be peeled off either into inaction or into the clutches of the GOP.

Part of our project, as left organizers, is to provide a common framework, with analysis and meaning-making, connected to proposals that speak directly to the concerns of our communities. Critical to this project of creating a more progressive political understanding is the formation of a shared identity: a Latinx identity, out of our many, varied experiences, ethnicities, and histories.

Latinx: A people in formation

Por toda nuestra América empieza a demostrarse el deseo—como si ya hubiese comenzado a cuajar el alma continental—de conocer, por su raíces y desarrollo, la composición de los pueblos americanos.

—José Martí

Much has been written about the term *Latinx*, a lot of it focused on how well the term polls among Latinos.[5] Polling is a peculiar tool—it can tell you where the consciousness of a people is at that very moment, but not where it is going. Forging new identities of consciousness is the task of an organizer, not a pollster. New terminology takes hold when it helps make sense of the struggles a group of people are in together. For example, a term like *Black Power* was not popular with most Black people at first, until good organizing and the struggles for racial justice created a shared consciousness that became encoded into the terminology.

Latinos in America have a more difficult task in forging a collective identity, given that we have arrived in the US with distinct histories. As a mix of newly arrived migrants as well as people that preceded the colonial US state, we are a group that possesses significant heterogeneity within our uniformity. Even the concept of "Latinos" as an identity is in formation. Given the myriad stories of how we got here, and how we interact with the dominant cultures in the US, Latinos are not a singular, homogenous group.

And yet there are deep common threads of history that we share: experiences with indigeneity, Blackness, or a mix of the two with European colonization, and, in most cases, a shared language. The historic process of colonization and our resistance to it unites us as people who have migrated and/or had to negotiate in the heart of the US Empire, and who must deal with the continued legacy of colonization in our respective countries of origin.

We are a people in formation, and this historic process has a major impact on our current voting dynamics. We need a term that reflects this "in formation" status. *Latinx* is a good candidate because it is explicitly anti-colonial, pro-Black, pro-women, pro-LGBTQ, with a working-class identity and sense of shared power.

Struggle is one core component that forges a community. Its leaders, and the fights that have led to greater freedoms, can form the bedrock of a people's identity. For example, the Mexican Revolution is a fundamental event that forged the Mexican identity. We have not had a similarly seminal event that brings together Latinx peoples in the US.

Till this day the major driving force of identity for Latinos has been regional or within our own specific Latino subgroup. These fractured political developments have brought each of our respective groups to the Democratic Party on similar yet distinctive roads. Those struggles have seen the Democratic Party as a vehicle to move forward our specific demands, sometimes alongside of our own political formations like the Raza Unida Party or the more radical Young Lords.

We formed Mijente in 2015 precisely to organize and orient Latino communities in a politics that is rooted in pro-Black, pro-LGBTQ, pro-woman and pro-working-class values. Since Mijente's inception, it has been clear to us that we need more spaces that unify Latinx people in the US to move forward a left Latinx politics.

What we can build upon in the states

The regions that saw both increased Latino voter turnout and increased support for Democratic candidates were the ones where we had the largest on-the-ground organizational capacity—Arizona and Georgia. In each of these states and regions, organizers built upon three pillars:[6]

1. Local left Latino organizations building political power year-round that pivoted to explicitly electoral engagement, and providing state-wide leadership for progressives

2. National support—resources, funding, expertise, coordinated efforts

3. The expansion of voting accessibility, through voter-friendly laws

Meanwhile, areas in states where little to no progressive infrastructure exists saw an increase in Latino votes for Trump. According to the Catalist report,[7] Nevada and Texas both moved 9% in favor of Trump from 2016. Within Texas it was precisely the areas with no left electoral infrastructure like the Rio Grande Valley that drove statewide totals into the Trump column.[8]

Arizona: It takes all three pillars

The passage of SB 1070 in 2010 would lead to an "explosion" of Latino organizing in the state in defense of our communities that 10 years later would not only stop Trump in his tracks—delivering the state to a Democratic presidential candidate for the first time since 1996—but help to elect two Democratic senators as well.[9]

SB 1070 had such a galvanizing effect because it legalized racial profiling in Latino communities. SB 1070 cast suspicion on every Latino person in the state, subjecting them to profiling and requirements to show ID on demand.[10]

Organizations on the ground like Puente and LUCHA were organizing for over 10 years to defend and improve our communities. They laid the groundwork for the results we saw in 2020, building up the three pillars: local organizing, national support, and better voting laws. They took on strategic targets, starting with the architect of SB 1070, State Senator Russell Pierce. In November 2011, after a coordinated campaign led by Latino community organizers, Russell was recalled.

In 2016 these same forces would succeed in defeating Sheriff Arpaio, with national support. One of Mijente's first electoral projects was supporting the efforts on the ground in Arizona to defeat Arpaio. Working with Mijente and as the National Political Director of the Communications Workers of America (CWA) at the time, I was able to provide resources along with other national partners to the multiple efforts that would lead to Arpaio's defeat. These fights in defense of our community offered immediate relief to many of our loved ones and helped to crystalize the power dynamics within the state, which inevitably helped to build a stronger affiliation with the Democratic Party, especially since most of the attacks against our communities were coming from the GOP.

As Latinos were being politicized by these fights, more inclusive voting laws were creating more entry points to voting, which in turn, increased Latino voter turnout. The passage of these laws was achieved through the efforts of in-state organizations, with support from national organizations as well.

In Arizona, the places where Latinos had the largest movement toward Trump were in areas with less than 5% Latino density.[11] These places lack significant left Latino organizational capacity that engages voters politically. Absent deeper organizing in their areas, it is doubtful that any amount of persuasion would have moved voters to support progressive or Democratic candidates.

Georgia: Making the impossible possible

Ade Nichols began organizing in Georgia's Latino communities 20 years ago to fight against deportations. Over those 20 years she built up organizing capacity in both the densely Latino urban centers like Gwinnet County and in less dense rural areas as well. Her organization, the Georgia Latino Alliance for Human Rights (GLAHR) was also one of the founding organizations (along with Puente in Arizona) for Mijente. In 2018 Mijente partnered with the GLAHR Action Network[12] for their first foray into electoral politics in support of Stacey Abrams' bid for governor of the state of Georgia. Mijente provided resources, technical capacity, and expertise, including sending senior staff into the state.

This would be the first time any Latino organization in the state would directly support a candidate. Their work resulted in an impressive increase in the Latino vote and though Abrams' bid was unsuccessful—mostly due to questionable election processes—this electoral work was significant in laying the groundwork for the 2020 election results.

Having developed best practices and new leaders and skills in 2018 GLAHR Action Network and Mijente ramped up their work in 2020 for the presidential and two US Senate races at a time when very few organizations were making significant investments in the state of Georgia for Latino electoral work. Their efforts, along with the much larger efforts led by Abrams in the Black community, led to a Biden victory and forced a runoff for both Senate races. Though other organizations would come into the state for the runoff to help with Latino turnout, it was GLAHR and Mijente who led the massive door-knocking efforts. As a result, every single Latino door in the state was knocked on. They had over 200 organizers focused solely on the Latino vote-making over 1 million contacts. By Election Day Latinos would "shatter runoff-turnout records."[13]

In addition to helping deliver the vote for the Senate and White House, GLAHR Action Network was also able to defeat two anti-immigrant sheriffs in Gwinnet and Cobb County. After years of fighting these local offices' participation in federal deportation they were able to end it completely with the elections of two new sheriffs that ended the 287(g) programs in the two counties.[14]

This increase in Latino voter turnout echoes the winning formula in Arizona: building a base, getting national support, and improving access to voting. Without Ade Nichols' work over 20 years to build a real organizing base in the state, along with the national support from Mijente (and other national funders) to increase capacity in 2018, it is doubtful that the 2020 success would have taken place in the Latino community and therefore the victories in the presidential and US Senate races.

Texas: A close primary

It is no surprise that Rio Grande Valley is where Trump made the largest inroads with Latinos, given the lack of investment and attention on the part of the Democratic Party in this area of south Texas. While many pundits have puzzled over Trump's gains there, they tend to overlook or ignore the fact that, during the Texas primary, Bernie won these same districts. Trump gained on the margins. Bernie won majorities. Despite massive opposition from corporate media and most Latino elected leadership in the state (including the faux Latino Francis O'Rourke), Bernie won the Latino vote in the Rio Grande Valley based mostly on his message.

With better resources early on, and an infrastructure half the size of what the Bernie campaign built in California, Bernie could have won the Texas primary. Bernie's campaign represented the politics we must expand on.

In other less-dense areas with Latino populations, voting participation is low.[15] The Democratic Party does not invest in these areas. It is up to progressive organizations like the Texas Organizing Project (TOP), Texas CWA, and Workers Defense to engage with these voters, and these organizations' resources are limited by their own heavy investments in urban centers.

Discussions are now being held among leaders in the state on how to ensure they can build real lasting organization in all the major Latino areas. This will help counter the right-wing incursions in the Rio Grande Valley and elsewhere, which include the opening of a second "Hispanic Community Center" in Texas by the National Republican Committee in McAllen.[16] Mijente is also looking to support these organizing efforts by engaging our members and bringing additional national capacity in heavily Latino communities across the state.

California: Nuestro gallo es Bernie Sanders

A Democratic socialist won the Democratic primary in the fifth largest economy in the world, with the largest population in any state. He did so despite being outspent by Bloomberg 6 to 1, and if you include the other candidates—Steyer, Buttigieg, Warren, Biden—he was outspent 14 to 1. Latino voters were the driver of Bernie's victory. They voted for an unabashed progressive candidate who spoke to the real living conditions of Latinos and working people in the state of California. Bernie named who was responsible for these conditions. Latinos delivered for Bernie despite the efforts of establishment Latino Democrats, pundits, and consultants who tried to downplay or dismiss voters' enthusiasm for Bernie and discredit left proposals. During the primary campaign, these entities were more of a challenge to the Bernie campaign's efforts than overt right-wing attacks, given their significance in the Latino community.

The campaign knew it had to take on cash-flushed opponents, elite Latino operatives, and a corporate media structure. We were able to build a field program in California that tapped into already existing progressive organizing capacity on the ground, hiring organizers from the communities, recreating a modified version of the local organizing pillar that is so critical for electoral success. Of course, we had significant national support from the campaign. Over the years, California has passed a series of laws that facilitate voting as well. We targeted heavily Latino districts across the state and won all 19 of them, and the top 34 Latino districts in the state. In total Bernie won all but 6 of the 53 congressional districts in the heavily Latino state, taking losses in the least dense districts.

Even in this deep blue state, Democrats cannot afford to take Latino voters for granted. The recent recall election offers a cautionary tale. Early on, polls showed a majority of Latino voters supporting the recall of Democratic governor Gavin Newsom, sending shockwaves through the Latino Democratic establishment in California. Undoubtedly, many of these voters are the same ones who supported Bernie Sanders. Though in the end the majority of Latinos voted against the recall for many it was a defensive strategy decision.[17] Better to stay with the devil we knew rather than the ones running Texas and Florida. And yet exit polls demonstrated a drop in Latino support of 6 points from Newsom's vote in the 2018 election.[18]

What these operatives are unable or unwilling to reckon with is that the Democratic Party, like so many other center-left parties around the world, is losing support from its diverse working-class base. Latino antagonism with Newsom, or the Democratic Party, is rooted in massive frustration with the political and economic elite in the US and over 40 years of neoliberal crises of the working class in the US that has been aggravated by the pandemic. Even now a major infrastructure reconciliation bill is being held up by two Democrats in the US Senate, one of whom owes her historic win in Arizona to Latino support.

Latinos have borne the brunt of the pandemic. Politicians who claim to respect essential workers, asking them to risk their lives to make a living and to spend their downtime in cramped living spaces will lose the respect of Latino working-class voters when they get caught dining at an exclusive restaurant with their wealthy donors during a lockdown. Having won the recall on the backs of Latinos, Newsom vetoed a farmworker bill facilitating the right to organize within a mostly Latino industry.[19]

As more articles get written to demonstrate that Latinos are becoming more conservative, they will have the "California Bernie problem" to contend with, and since they can't, they will try to ignore it.[20]

As this overview of four states affirms, we need more self-organizing in all Latino communities, independent of the Democratic Party establishment, its liberal Latino operatives, and corporate interests.

Building political power for the long term

Leading up to 2020, we knew that we needed to use our collective political power to push Democrats leftward while joining forces with others to halt the spread of racist right-wing authoritarianism. Going forward, we need to contend with three interrelated problems that can drive Latino voters into apathy or worse, toward the right.

1. Our tenuous relationship with the Democratic Party
2. The corporate media targeting Latino communities
3. The demobilizing effects of Latino elite operatives

The Democratic Party. Progressive and left Latinx organizers understand that the Democratic Party, nationally and in most of our states, is the more viable vehicle, at this time, through which to pursue our policy goals, compared to the extremely antagonistic Republican Party. We also understand that it is not our party. It does not defend our communities. It is not our ally.

Latinos are an emergent power base in America that has not fully aligned itself with the Democratic Party. It is clear in most postmortems and analyses that Democrats cannot treat us as a pure turnout base.[21] Latino voters are more fractured and persuadable.

We do not have a history of struggle where the party sided with us, and we don't have nostalgia for the New Deal, or the Great Society. Instead, we are more likely to feel ignored by the party much of the time, and/or disappointed as party leaders like President Obama, who failed to deliver on promises like comprehensive immigration reform and instead facilitated the bank bailouts.

This stands in contrast with Black Americans' historic relationship with, and solid support for, the Democratic Party. From Black leaders' participation in the New Deal coalition through the civil rights movement, Black voters have forged an affiliation with the Democratic Party. Black voters consistently support Democratic candidates at or above 90%. Latinos rarely break 70% levels, and according to the Catalist report were at 63% in 2020.[22]

Even within the Black community the historic allegiance with the Democratic Party is facing a threat for similar reasons. As the generation of leaders from the civil rights era who entered Democratic Party politics like John Lewis begin to pass on, the stalwarts of the historic allegiance are no longer there to help preserve it.

In the wake of the 2020 elections the Democratic Party should take note that Latino communities are: A) Looking for alternatives to the (non)solutions that are being offered by elected officials of either party; B) are extremely receptive to policies and candidates that propose left economic proposals that include racial, gender, and LGBTQ lenses. This is especially true for Latinos under 30.[23]

Increased spending on electoral outreach may allow for marginal short-term improvements in Democratic Party support. But without real local organizations on the ground building the shared analysis, the political consciousness, and the power to get behind candidates who support more transformative change, we could see increasing movement of Latinos toward either greater apathy or right-wing candidates. Either way, the Democratic Party, and the whole progressive project will suffer.

Corporate media. Any discussion about Latino voters must acknowledge the power of the corporate media infrastructure that is aimed at Latinos. It is a critical force that shapes voting habits, lends support for or criticisms against progressive policy proposals, and assaults Latinx consciousness daily.

The media infrastructure that is the primary source of information, analysis, and meaning-making in America is center-right on most of the issues impacting our communities. Even Univision and Telemundo broadcasts on the issue of immigration are full of anti-immigrant alarmism against those immigrants who are not already here. It plays upon fear and draws out the worst impulses within our communities: anti-Black, anti-immigrant, anti-poor, transphobic, etc.

While most organizations are struggling to fund the creation of simple communications materials, the airwaves and social media offer up a daily barrage of right-wing-infused media messaging. To compound the problem, right-wing disinformation runs rampant online as well as on the airwaves. This becomes part of the ecosystem that any Latino organizer must contend with when walking into the community. It is the common air we breathe when having political and economic discussions with the unorganized and unaffiliated in our communities. It creates a significant barrier against raising a critical consciousness and getting people engaged.

Latino operatives, within and outside of the Democratic Party. The disconnect between the mostly working-class base of Latinos versus the managerial/elite class of Latino operatives that have access to decision-makers is stark. Staff and operatives that work directly for elected representatives or the groups that lobby them often curtail left policy solutions. This makes it harder for organizers and activists to convince working-class voters to support a party that appears unable or unwilling to confront increasing crises with bold measures. In these ways, Latino operatives play a role in pushing working-class Latino voters farther away from the Democratic Party.

In addition to limiting what is possible in DC, many of these operatives and institutions limit what is possible in our communities. They tend to be the gatekeepers for who is allowed to run for election and be properly resourced to win. Though there is a fledgling ecosystem of left organizations trying to support left candidates, the funding challenge is massive.

Conclusion

In the absence of a Democratic Party that is defending our communities, the necessity for self-organization has become the mechanism for building Latinx political power. We are seeing significant growth in the Latino vote in those places where we have built our own political power. This is where hope for our communities lies, within our own capacity to organize and build our own power. No one is coming to save us.

For Latinx organizers who want to confront the rising fascist threats in the years to come and build radical alternatives to the current socio-economic order, it is paramount that we build organizing infrastructure that is linked to national action in the heavily Latino areas that are currently unorganized.

We need to pay attention to Latinx communities everywhere, not just in the well-resourced urban areas that are solidly Democratic. There are many "islands" of Latinos that can be organized, politicized, and even radicalized, as support for Bernie during the primaries indicates. As organizers, we can foster distinct visions for America's political, economic, and social future. These islands of consciousness and their daily struggles must be connected nationally through shared campaigns and demands that will begin to forge the Latinx identity in America that is inclusive and provides dignity for all our people.

Notes

1. Rodrigo Domínguez-Villegas et al., "Vote Choice of Latino Voters in the 2020 Presidential Election, Latino Policy and Politics Initiative," https://latino.ucla.edu.

2. Y. G. Robinson, Catalist, 2021, "What Happened in 2020," https://catalist.us/wh-national/.

3. Jerome Karabel, "Trumpism Lives On," *Le Monde Diplomatique* podcast, December 2020, https://mondediplo.com.

4. Kiara Alfonseca, "High COVID-19 Death Rate among Hispanics May Be Linked to Work," ABC News, May 6, 2021, https://abcnews.go.com.

5. Leah Asmelash, "Just 4% of Hispanic or Latino People Prefer the Term 'Latinx,' New Gallop Poll Finds," CNN, August 5, 2021, https://edition.cnn.com.

6. This third pillar is under attack in most Republican-led states, with deliberate speed in states that went for Biden, like Arizona and Georgia, as well the major battlegrounds, like Texas and Florida.

7. Y. G. Robinson, "What Happened in 2020."

8. M. Hennessy-Fiske, "We've Only Started: How Latino Support for Trump Grew in the Texas Borderlands," *Los Angeles Times*, November 12, 2020.

9. For a detailed summary of SB1070, see www.ncsl.org/research/immigration/analysis-of-arizonas-immigration-law.aspx#Summary_of_SB1070_and_HB2162.

10. Although parts of the law were struck down by the US Supreme Court, it inspired similarly racist profiling laws around the country and emboldened nativists to attack Arizona's bilingual education and prohibit teaching Latino history in public schools.

11. Rodrigo Domínguez-Villegas, 2021, p. 10.

12. GLAHR Action Network is a 501(c)(4).

13. Suzanne Gamboa, "In Georgia, Latinos Shatter Runoff Turnout Record as Groups Make Last Push for Voters," NBC News, January 5, 2021.

14. These agreements allow certain local law enforcement officials to act as federal immigration enforcement officials. For more information, see www.aclu.org.

15. Nadia Galindo, "Voter Turnout Low in Rio Grande Valley," local NBC News, February 28, 2014, www.valleycentral.com.

16. Suzanne Gamboa, "Republicans Target Latino Voters for 2022 with Community Centers," NBC News, October 4, 2021, www.nbcnews.com.

17. Maanvi Singh, "'It Was Never about Saving Newsom': How Latino Voters Played a Major Role in California," *Guardian*, September 25, 2021.

18. León Krauze, "Latinos Showed Up for Newsom, but Some Latino Men Tilted Right. Democrats Need to Pay Attention," *Washington Post*, September 15, 2021.

19. Jeremy B. White, "Newsom Faces Backlash after Attending French Laundry Dinner Party," Politico, November 13, 2020, www.politico.com.

20. Christian Paz, "The Voters Who Could Turn California Red," *Atlantic*, August 4, 2021, www.theatlantic.com.

21. Equis Research, "2021 Post-Mortem (Part One): Portrait of a Persuadable Latino," Equis Research, April 12, 2021, https://equisresearch.medium.com.

22. Y. G. Robinson, "What Happened in 2020."

23. Gus Bova, "A Democratic Socialist Damn Near Won the Texas Primary," *Texas Observer*, March 4, 2020, www.texasobserver.org.

Part 3

Workers on the Doors

12

UNITE HERE: Drawing On Our Knowledge, Fighting for Our Future

Marcy Rein interviews Mario Yedidia, Stephanie Greenlea, and Diana Valles

When the COVID-19 pandemic threw 98% of the UNITE HERE members who work in hotels, restaurants, airports, and casinos out of work, the union went all in on the 2020 election. UNITE HERE hit the doors earliest, hardest, and longest of any organization on the progressive side of politics. Some 1,700 members knocked on 3 million doors as part of the union's comprehensive campaign. Then 1,000 laid-off UNITE HERE hospitality workers joined the team that turned Georgia blue, knocking on another 1.5 million doors. The effort stretched the union and everyone who took part. It affirmed some organizing lessons and helped tip the presidential election in critical states and deliver come-from-behind wins in the January 2021 Georgia Senate runoffs. In this interview, three people who were in the thick of this effort talk about what it meant and how they did it. Mario Yedidia is the Western Regional Political Director for the UNITE HERE International Union. Stephanie Greenlea is assistant to the secretary-treasurer of the UNITE HERE International Union, and a member of the union's Black Leadership Group. Diana Valles is the internal organizing director for Culinary Workers Union Local 226 in Las Vegas, Nevada.

How did the union come to the decision to jump in as deep as it did?

Stephanie Greenlea (SG): Way before the pandemic, UNITE HERE had a plan to go all in on the 2020 cycle, because we knew that another four years of a Trump administration, the racist policies and the immigration and all of this, was going to be hard.

But then the pandemic happened. It was not only that we might not survive another four years of Trump. It was also like our people might not survive, tomorrow. We were scrambling to do food banks and food relief, and working with employers about retention and recall, just trying to hang on to jobs, and they were kicking people off of healthcare. It became a very immediate fight for our lives.

Hospitality workers who never stopped working or were quickly back in the shop during the first wave of the pandemic were too often working in unsafe conditions, without sufficient PPE, social distancing, ventilation or mask mandates. At the outset of the pandemic, we saw the industry almost immediately move to take advantage of the crisis as a way to slash labor costs under the guise of "public health"—something they have continued to press up to now. Hotels, for example, have seen COVID-19 as an opportunity to end daily housekeeping.

Ninety-eight percent laid off means a real hit in resources for a labor union, and our executive committee was really grappling with how to allocate those mostly disappeared resources in a time of crisis. And making the decision that we got to go, and we got to go big, and we got to go now, and really digging deep because of the desperate situation our members were in.

Our members' response to that desperate situation was to want to mobilize, and so we had no problem recruiting at all.

Diana Valles (DV): We are a union of immigrants and people of color. We come from 178 countries. We speak 40 different languages. We thought it was going to be hard, but people were ready to go because everything that was going on in that minute was affecting us directly, and our families too. The suppressing at the borders. The immigration issues. Everything. Almost everybody has somebody undocumented, at least here in Las Vegas. That was a big trip for them, people were so scared.

The members said, "Let's do this." From the local that I represent, Local 226, we got 500 rank-and-file members ready to do the job. I believe that is the biggest number we ever had. We are always doing political campaigns, but this time was humongous. People were raising their hand to say, "I'll do it," despite the fear.

When we had to go to Georgia, we said, "Here is another step. Now you're going to have to travel, leave your family for months, and you're going to be there doing the same thing that you did here [in Nevada]. And they were ready. They were like, "We have to win this too," and they just packed their stuff and left, to totally different weather, a different time zone, with no family. These were their holidays too, and they did it again because they I think our union did a great job of making them understand that everything we were fighting for was there. Either you go and fight for it or you're going to lose everything.

Mario Yedidia (MY): The affiliate unions of UNITE HERE—the Culinary Workers Union Local 226 in Las Vegas, for example, UNITE HERE Local 11 in Los Angeles and Arizona, or the Hotel Trades Council Local 6 in New York City—have spent decades building political power, and so the decision of where to go started with the work that the local unions have done for many years. And then we overlaid that with a basic political calculus about where the Electoral College votes were going to need to come from.

In the end, the 2020 presidential margin was 34,000 votes in Nevada. It was 10,000 votes in Arizona. It was 13,000 votes in Georgia, and 80,000 votes in Pennsylvania, but that was just 1%. These are four examples. We knew it was going to be that close, and that's why we waged door-to-door work at scale in those places.

We identified 440,000 infrequent voters to vote for Biden. Trump lost by 32,000 votes in Nevada. In Nevada we moved 42,000 infrequent voters, right? Trump lost by 10,000 votes in Arizona. We moved 48,000 infrequent ones. So it was that kind of anticipation of how close the election would be and the way that moving infrequent voters could contribute in a decisive way that led us to choose Florida, Arizona and Nevada, Pennsylvania, and ultimately, the runoff work in Georgia.

Can you talk more about the impact of COVID on your members?

SG: There's no way to overstate how hard this context was for doing this kind of door-to-door campaigning, and our people did it. COVID wasn't just a thing out there that people were afraid of. If you think about who we are and who our people are, there was real and frequent and really close-to-home death all the time. People were losing people all the time, not able to bury people—and it was really racialized. When I'd be on calls with majority white folks, the fear was real, but abstract. When I was on calls with a majority people of color, almost every person knew somebody who had just gotten sick or just gone on the vent, whatever. And that was piled on top of all the other things, from the fires to the heat to the police violence to the racism on the doors to the just straight-up fatigue of being out there.

How did your experience dealing with COVID at work inform your organizing?

MY: A number of our members were essential workers, people who never stopped working, and others worked in sub-industries like gaming where people came back to work very quickly. So, familiarizing ourselves with how the virus spreads and the basic epidemiological information about the virus was what we all had to do in March and April. Local 11 and their training academy developed a series of protocols.

At the same time, in other places like Las Vegas and across parts of California, for example, we were fighting for local laws and language and contracts that would protect workers from the virus, so we had 11 pages of bargaining and statutory language specific to different classifications in the hospitality industry, for cooks, for environmental services workers, etc.—about PPE, social distancing and so on, that would allow people to work and stay safe, and that was a fight that workers dealt with in every shop and that we were trying to deal with too politically. We took that language and those practical experiences with the virus in workplaces and put protocols in place to keep people safe during canvassing.

Can you talk a bit about the responses that canvassers got on the doors?

SG: On the Zooms with the canvassers, the report backs were all over the place. Really hard stuff, from encountering racism on the doors or guns being drawn, or homeowners' associations or cops or whatever chasing our people around, to the most beautiful stuff you've ever heard. An 80-year-old first-time voter in Georgia, or connections about people who know people from around the way. Transformational stories that came back like moving people from "no" to "yes," and the hope that brought back to the rest of the team. It really was all over the place: blood, sweat and tears and laughter and joy and pain and anger and all of that stuff, eight hours a day, six days a week.

DV: We went through a lot, good and bad. My role was to canvass in the last weeks and it was a beautiful thing to see that you can connect with people because you're talking to people like you. When you talk from your heart, you really can connect. If you find somebody from your country, for example, you can start talking to them. "Remember when we first got here? What were our dreams, why we got here in this in this country in the first place? They are trying to take that away from us."

Even though they are afraid to open the door to you, when you start talking, they want to invite you into their house and we couldn't do it, right? We were supposed to be talking at the door and observing social distancing and asking them to wear a mask. If they didn't want to wear a mask, we couldn't talk to them.

And before we used to be able to put people in our car and take them to vote. Not anymore. Now we have to organize them and trust them that they're going to go and vote. And I personally have the experience of or one or two of them calling me after that, very happy. "OK, I did it. I just voted and it was only me, but I did it." Everybody was getting those calls.

Of course, you are also dealing with racism. You find people that are Trump voters and they treat you really, really bad when you go to those doors. Me, personally, I'm from Mexico, I'm Latina. I don't speak good English, but when I go there and they hear my accent they're like, "We don't speak Spanish here, is she speaking English?"

But the overall experience was really, really motivating. After going and knocking on doors and walking all day long, our canvassers were so energized at the end of the day.

MY: Just to add on to both of Diana and Stephanie's points: How was it every day? It was historically hot, because working-class communities of color are bearing the brunt of climate change, and we felt that in Las Vegas every day. It was historically smoky in Reno, Nevada. The air quality was such that we weren't supposed to be walking, and we lost a number of canvass days and switched to phone-banking because of the historic smoke in Northern Nevada from the fires in California.

The other thing that it was: people sharing their story on every door, so having the courage to put themselves out there. The core of our work is telling our stories to one another on the doors. In Atlanta, you had 1,000 people doing that every day. Trying to do that on 50,000 doors.

And doing it! The other point is that we were talking to a historic amount of people. The contact rate was 30% on the first pass. It's never higher than 22% on a political canvass, but because of COVID, and because we were talking to working-class voters, especially in Nevada where the unemployment rate reached the highest in the country over the summer during the pandemic, people were home, and people were wanting in general to talk to us.

So, there's all the hard work, but there's also an organizing culture. You're talking to people who disagree with you every day, and you're still moving people to action. And so the platitudes about, "No, these voters don't talk to us," or "All Trump voters are like this"—you cut through all that when you're having a lot of actual organizing conversations every day.

SG: We were on the doors in West Philadelphia when Walter Wallace Jr. was murdered by the police. Some of our canvassers heard the gunshots. Some of our canvassers had grown up in that neighborhood and were food service workers in Philadelphia who had come out to try to transform the vote in that city and with it the state and the country.

The canvass meetings after Walter was murdered were obviously, really, really, really, really hard. A lot of tears, a lot of things that had to be worked through, a lot of fear.

And people were saying, "Yep. I'm knocking for my life and if I'm not knocking for mine, I'm knocking for yours, so we're going." And people went back out there.

And there was all this nervousness about whether the city was going to explode that night. But people went back out on the doors and their commitment to staying on the doors and continuing to talk to other people about what was at stake and about what difference they could make in it—I'll never forget it as long as I live, in that particular context of COVID, anti-Black violence, and the economic suffering in Philadelphia, one of the poorest cities in the country.

We then decided to take a little more time off the doors, and we went to Love Park in Philadelphia and arranged a concert with our partners. It was in the middle of the night, and it was joyous and beautiful and again, a multiracial picture of workers. And the absolute best of what this country and our communities can be, right, on the eve of the struggle. I think that was October 26, just days before the election. And it was just such a hopeful thing that it got turned into, led by working people.

A lot of times the administrative side of organizing gets overlooked, but it scaffolds all the rest. What were some of the particular challenges you faced in this effort?

SG: We had to do all sorts of things administratively that we wouldn't have otherwise done. We usually double up in hotel rooms on long campaigns like this or share vehicles to ride to turf and we couldn't do any of that. We had to figure out food distribution in a completely COVID-safe way, and we had to figure out expense reimbursements that couldn't really be done in person—and some people don't have bank accounts.

We had to transfer everything we did to a digital environment. Getting your walk sheets—we had to use the app, so no more clipboards, right? We had to train everybody on tablets.

We had to figure out logistics and spaces. We had to figure out how to safely go visit these spaces and map them out. And we had to calculate square footage to be able to socially distance seriously. We had to go research ventilation and the buildings that we were going to use in turfs. And we had to make real decisions about field offices. How to distribute lit? How to distribute food? How to keep people hydrated?

How to help people have safe housing? So many residents in some of these cities had precarious housing, so the extended stay–type hotels that we would use to house canvassers became really chaotic. In many cases they weren't safe for our canvassers to be there, and so we had to figure out the next hotel that would have the right drive time to the turf so we could still hit the door number goal. And somebody had to go research that or you're going to get stuck in traffic.

But again, the beautiful thing is there were so many people who saw what we were trying to do and were blown away by it. I remember calling various hotels or various vendors and being like, "We need 300 sandwiches tomorrow. What can you do for me?" They'd ask why and we would tell them why, and they would say, "Oh, I really want to try to figure this out because I want to help you guys." And so we had all these people join in with us; we had travel agents on the phone with us at two and three in the morning. We had people just trying to help us make it happen in this really incredible way …

The Pennsylvania operation on the presidential was the fastest thing we've ever stood up. It was the largest canvass we had ever stood up at that point (Georgia was bigger), and it was the shortest amount of lead time. It was something like 500 people and we got everybody there in something like 10 days because we got funded late. It was unbelievable, and really hard administratively.

How did this work build on your union's history, and build the union for the future?

MY: The strike at the Frontier Casino in Las Vegas, Nevada—six years, four months, and 10 days long—was transformational in the history of the Culinary Workers Local 226. We had a first-time canvasser, Rocha, who works at the Strat hotel. Rocha knocked the door of this Frontier striker, Louise Toston, and the photographs that they took together were nothing short of revelatory for both the young people who've never been engaged in their union before, and especially old timers who were able to recall that struggle. I remember the president of our union, D Taylor, talking about the food, collard greens in particular, that Miss Toston made on the Frontier picket line and shared with the strikers. That moment of connection of this very concrete, very Las Vegas working-class struggle.

DV: That's who we are. I think that picture reflects who we are. The roots of the union and the future of our union, right there together. Thanks to the Frontier strikers, we built this town, Las Vegas. They were so strong and determined for six years, four months, and 10 days. No matter what happened, they would be there in the street until they got their new contract.

As soon as they knocked on her door, she went and got this plaque they gave all the Frontier strikers at the end. It was a confirmation: "I'm one of you guys, I was fighting for you probably before you were born."

SG: We were really intentional about leadership development on these campaigns, really purposeful about that and having people go from being a canvasser in the presidential to being a lead in the Senate runoff, or being a lead in the one and becoming a director in the next one.

We were very intentional about developing leadership of color in particular. Really on purpose, and we did it by identifying people, holding on to them, really taking the time and the directors meeting to talk about how are they doing, what do they need help with? With the goal being to expand capacity and real skills. How do we get this person to be able to lead their own team, and hang on to another group of canvassers, to start to think like a director? We were really intentional on not just doing that on the field side, but on all sorts of sides that are relevant to a campaign. So we were training people on data, how to think about campaign data in a different way. We were training people on comms in a different way and creating opportunities for people to level up who had never done it before or never done it at that level before. We were doing it on admin, right? Taking people who had never had to think about how to get a room block or whatever and teaching them how to do it. And we did grow our capacity.

And people are going back to work. That's where they came from and how we recruited them. A lot of these folks were shop stewards or they're union committee people in their shops, so they're already learning to organize right in their shops, and that's where they go back to after these political campaigns, to keep them in motion and keep building power.

DV: Some of the people who we recruited to be canvassers are in training now to be organizers. Some of our staff too, like one who was a lead organizer is now one of the directors running one of the biggest card checks in our union right now, with 3,000 workers. She's leading that, she is great. Another organizer who was one of the greatest organizers on last year's political campaign now has a group of organizers who he oversees.

In all levels—shop stewards, committees, organizer, lead organizer, they came back being another person. Their growth was immense. When you look at them, it's like "Where is this coming from?" They're great people and then through the struggles they completely bloom. They take more responsibilities. If they were shy and quiet before, they now want to talk. They now think that everything is possible. You want to try to tell them, "OK, we now need to do this," and they say, "No, no, I did it." They take the initiative. It's amazing what these campaigns do to our people.

SG: And people want to keep going. It was pretty clear on election night that we had lost Florida. I was on Zoom with the Florida team

and they're all in the hotel rooms watching the returns together virtually, and it was just getting clearer and clearer. And there was some real
disappointment and some real anger that we couldn't make the difference there. But people were celebratory about the things they had won,
like the $15.00 an hour minimum wage. Then somebody comes off of
mute and says, "Alright, cool, so we didn't win Florida, but what's good?
We're going for DeSantis or what?" It was 11:00 o'clock at night and the
person was like, "OK, so what's next?" I will read that as what we are
doing right.

And the last thing I'd say is that people really came to love each
other on these teams. If we said we got a shot to get back with your
squad—"We're going again on the midterms, for this or that" people
would be like, "Oh yeah, where's my crew? We're going, right?" They love
it because of the sense of power and team and community. In a moment
where otherwise everything was trying to tell you not to trust a single
other soul, we did something really different by bringing people together
to fight for each other. That will survive it, I think.

MY: The other thing that I don't want to lose is just the basics of the
organizing. Every day when you do a house visit or when you knock on
the door of a voter, you do four things. You share your story. You connect
with the voter and ask questions and listen.

You make an assessment of where that person is at and you try
to bring them to some action. Then you're going to assess afterwards
whether they were really with you or they were just trying to get rid of
us or whatever.

So in Georgia we were hitting 80 doors a day, and talking to 30%
of the people, so you were doing it close to 20 times a day. That builds
one's ability to do that in the shop and elsewhere. Finally, in terms of
leadership development and growth, to run a meeting you have to lay out
goals for a group of people. In our world you have to actually role-play
the conversation. And you have to manage your time. Because of the way
that we run the political canvass, we're doing that at least twice a day. The
role-playing usually only happens in the mornings, but the other parts

of it, the motivation, the reviewing of goals and managing time, that's something that happens every day. So you get practice.

The moment made conversations about race essential—but so often our organizing sidesteps them, because they can be volatile. What did you learn about having these conversations?

SG: It was really important that we made space to talk about racism explicitly and frequently, and to think about the skill of talking about race and racism as a skill that you can train on.

We spent a lot of time trying to do that in a way that was rooted in place. In the valley we were talking about the Bracero Program and immigration. In Georgia we were talking about the history of slavery and the civil rights movement and of that together and what it meant for today.

We started with the leads and directors and we really tried to talk about racism as a system of power, and how we have to be clear about how that system of power works if we're going to take it on, and if we're going to win. We were trying to make it less sensational and meet people where they were, with their experiences of it every day, and just give some common language, some tools, and some space. So, we spent some time in small groups, and the teams after trainings would spend some time talking one-on-one and together to start to build that muscle about how to organize through that, because we know there's no going around race, right? Not in this political moment. We can query whether you can go around it ever, but certainly not now. And you have to go through it. And you have to scale up and learn how to be organizer-ly and leader-ly in building power that can actually confront racism.

MY: I have one thought about non-Black leadership in our union and racism. The universe that we targeted in Fulton County, in the heart of Atlanta, was 91% African American. All of our canvassers were largely talking to Black folks every day. And they were talking to voters in a context where a lot of the noise about Warnock and Ossoff that we could hear was obviously white supremacist. For much of our non-Black membership, understanding how to talk about race, anti-Blackness, and the context in which we were operating in 2020 in Georgia required seeing ourselves as part of a long struggle for freedom for Black people in our country. The way in which those things are connected was really clear for many of us non-Black people. In a way that was transformative.

What else did you learn that will be helpful going forward to 2022, 2024, and beyond?

MY: The main lesson that many of us took away from it in our union is that the core way that we organize works—telling our stories and sharing in a face-to-face way what matters to us, and bringing other people to collective action through face-to-face conversation.

We can't overstate the need for door-to-door canvassing to be fully resourced in low-margin, high-turnout elections. In every state that I'm aware of where we got up on the doors in the summer of 2020, Trump was already up – and that campaign was talking to our voters, to working-class people, to people of color and immigrants. And they never stopped, because they understand power, and I think part of why the margins were so close and part of why our margin in the House is only four House members at the moment is because we didn't do enough canvassing.

We need the fifth-best midterm elections since the Civil War to hold Congress next year. And I don't think we'll be able to do it unless we make sure that door-to-door canvassing is a piece of it. It's not a romantic attachment to canvassing. No, no. Fully resourced canvassing when we know that the margin will be close. It is both a science and an art to calculate that.

SG: If there were an easier way to do it that was this effective, perhaps we'd propose it. It's not like mobilizing like we did is always convenient or cheap. But I know that working people have to lead any plan that we have for rebuilding this country. Unions and progressive organizations just have to clear the way and provide the support for them to lead.

What UNITE HERE hospitality workers demonstrated is the only thing that will save us: commitment to each other, and to a vision. Nothing different.

We made a decision to get on the doors, to draw on the strength of our knowledge about in-person organizing early, to stay out there, to stay connected to the voters, because so much was at stake. And we did it as a multiracial grassroots force of workers at a time when there was—and still is in a lot of ways—extreme polarization. We did it by people deciding across race and across the country to choose each other and to do it together. And with people being laid off the way they were, it ended up being the people with the least who decided to do the most in service of a vision of democracy that includes all of us.

13

Gulf Coast Area Labor Federation: Steps on the Road to a New Texas

Hany Khalil and Jay Malone

Outside of Texas, Americans across the political spectrum tend to think of Texas as a solid red state. In fact, our population is rapidly growing, urbanizing, and becoming more diverse, creating new potential to organize a progressive political base and change the electoral landscape. Texas is so large and holds so much weight in Congress and the Electoral College that when it flips, American politics will change for a generation. Knowing this, Republicans have aggressively used gerrymandering, voter suppression laws more restrictive than nearly anywhere else in the country, and racist cultural battles to hold onto power.

To take advantage of the opportunities that shifting demographics and economic growth create, we need a better-resourced progressive infrastructure that can reach every community. The labor movement plays a vital role in building the kind of year-round voter engagement that can start to transform the state.

At the Texas Gulf Coast Area Labor Federation, AFL-CIO (TGCALF), we are expanding our capacities to run effective electoral programs. In 2018 we were instrumental in electing labor allies to additional Texas House, congressional, and county seats. Building on that success, in 2020 we dramatically increased turnout among union members in the Houston region and helped narrow Donald Trump's margin in Texas. Though we ultimately failed to flip the additional Texas House seats we had targeted, the narrow loss margins show that we can win in Texas with additional capacity. With more resources, long-term capacity-building, political education, and new electoral vehicles that reach beyond our members, the labor movement can continue to play a pivotal role in building the road to a new Texas and, with it, a new America.

Shifting population, fluid politics

Texas is now home to 38 congressional districts, having gained 2 in the latest census, and the Houston region has been the center of the population growth and demographic change sweeping Texas. With 2.3 million residents, the city of Houston is the center of this vast megalopolis and the fourth-largest city in the country, just behind Chicago; 4.7 million people live in Harris County, home to Houston, making it the third-largest county in the country.

Texas became a majority minority state in 2004, but this has long been the case in the Houston region. Latinos make up 44% of Harris County's population—the second largest concentration of Latinos in the country behind Los Angeles County—with whites making up 29%, African Americans 20%, and Asians 7%. Rapidly suburbanizing Fort Bend County, which borders Harris to the southwest, is now roughly divided between African Americans, whites, Latinos, and Asians.

Texas Republicans have maintained control over all branches of our state government since 2002. Since they took power, they've used it aggressively to entrench their control over the state. In 2003, the new GOP majority redrew congressional district maps. Although the new district lines were later overturned as racial gerrymandering by the Supreme Court, they served their purpose, leading to the unseating of five Democratic incumbents in 2004.

Democrats nearly won the Texas House back in the 2008 Obama wave, clinching 74 of 150 seats, but when Obama was next on the ballot in 2012, Democrats in Texas were trying to break a Republican supermajority in the Texas House after massive GOP gains in 2010. In 2014, Wendy Davis raised hopes for a Democratic comeback, but lost to GOP standard-bearer Greg Abbott by a historic margin. The first real sign of hope in over a decade came in 2018 with Beto O'Rourke's run against US Senator Ted Cruz, which also saw Democrats pick up 12 seats in the Texas House, just nine seats away from a majority, and two seats in the Texas Senate.

Texas' urban counties are the seat of rapid blue growth. In 2018 Harris County elected Democrat Lina Hidalgo, a 28-year-old immigrant of Colombian descent, to head the county government, while Fort Bend County elected an Indian immigrant as its county judge.

With the wind in our sails after big gains in the 2018 cycle, we headed into 2020 with substantial optimism. The national climate and shifting voting patterns in the Gulf Coast region made the Houston region a focal point for efforts to flip the statehouse, expand the Democratic majority in Congress, and build local political power, while helping to move Texas into the swing state category for President Biden.

The political shift in our state has been driven by demographic shifts, but demographics are *not* destiny. Each sector needs to be organized. Every constituency has to be fought for. This was most clear in South Texas. For decades the Democratic Party has taken the vote for granted in the traditionally blue and heavily Latino Rio Grande Valley. Republicans, who ran an aggressive door-to-door program, were able to expand their margins in key South Texas counties, flip county-level seats, and pad Trump's statewide margin.

Labor reorganization drives a large-scale, effective electoral program

Recognizing the importance and potential of both Texas and the Houston region for the national labor movement, in 2015 the AFL-CIO merged five central labor councils into a regional labor federation. By reorganizing and combining resources, the new federation has subsequently made strides in the effort to build a stronger labor movement on the Gulf Coast.

The Gulf Coast Area Labor Federation now brings together 92 unions representing 58,000 members in 13 Houston-area counties. The bulk of our members work in the transportation trades (aviation, shipping, public transit, etc.), the building and construction trades, the public sector, manufacturing (heavily petrochemical), and retail. Union density in the service sector is low but growing with aggressive and creative organizing in hospitality, building services, and entertainment.

Moving into the 2020 elections, the TGCALF had been on a trajectory of modernizing our political work, deepening our investment and engagement. We identified our priority races using data to match opportunity with capacity and need. We asked four questions:

1. Is the office essential to accomplishing our policy goals?
2. Is the race competitive, and does our endorsed candidate have a strong chance of winning?
3. Can we have an impact on the outcome of the race?
4. Does organizing on behalf of our endorsed candidate contribute to long-term power-building? What does that look like?

If the answer to all four questions was yes, then we prioritized that race in our first tier. Our Tier 1 goals included protecting our allies in Texas House Districts 132 and 135 and picking up Texas House Districts 26, 134, and 138. Our Tier 2 goals included protecting the competitive Congressional District 7, picking up three additional congressional districts and county seats in Harris and Fort Bend Counties. Our Tier 3 goals were to contribute to cutting margins by which Trump and Senator John Cornyn were likely to win.

Because the TGCALF did not have an active state or federal political action committee and our program was funded by member dues, federal labor laws limited us to member-to-member communication. Our total universe included more than 300,000 union members and members of their households.

When we started planning our Labor 2020 program, we thought we would be able to do in-person outreach. Our program for the primaries finished in March just as COVID-19 hit. We rethought our approach and introduced as many layered elements as possible to make up for the lack of in-person contact. We recognized by May that the odds of direct voter contact being safe were low, so we upped our digital outreach, running targeted ads on Facebook and Google and hiring a graphic designer to help make the ads more appealing. We also ran a large mail program, with pieces tailored to each county and congressional district. All this ensured that every member got multiple contacts: mailers, calls, text messages, and varied digital impressions.

Our program engaged affiliates and members across our federation. It was driven by union release staff, members who are freed/assigned to work on electoral work full time with support from their international unions. Our largest contingents came from the United Steelworkers, who released eight members to us full time starting in August. The Brotherhood of Maintenance and Way Employees, Teamsters who work on railroads, followed with another six release staff, and the International Alliance of Theatrical and Stage Employees (IATSE) released two local members from their stagehand and stitcher unions, both of whom lost their jobs due to COVID and were highly motivated to hold government officials who had botched the response accountable. The American Federation of Government Employees (AFGE) District 10 released two members from their NASA local to us full time. The Insulators Local 22, AFSCME HOPE Local 123, and Transport Workers Union Local 260 all released staff part time to phonebank and reach out to members on worksites.

Although not every affiliate released staff to us, 42 affiliates designated local union political coordinators who participated in our weekly calls, and 32 affiliates completed at least one volunteer shift. In total, we made 200,000 calls and distributed 25,000 worksite flyers. Our digital ads were viewed 3 million times, and we sent 120,000 pieces of mail to union households.

We managed our entire direct mail program in house, with 55 unique pieces going to union households, each with a unique slate. An unemployed stitcher from IATSE Local 896, who was released to us by her international union, was integral to the success of the program. She suggested asking members to send us pictures of their slate cards, and we were inundated with pictures of proud union voters from the beginning of early voting.

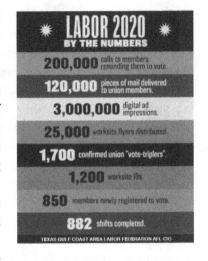

One of the components we're most proud of is that we scaled up and strengthened a coordinated worksite program. The AFL-CIO has developed a new organizing tool called ActionBuilder to support workplace organizing. We became one of the first labor councils to adapt ActionBuilder for electoral use. ActionBuilder allows unions to track political conversations their people have in the workplace just as they would in an organizing drive. Conversations with co-workers at the workplace are much more effective than traditional persuasion and direct voter outreach tactics because they draw upon pre-existing relationships. However, they require significantly more organizing resources at the outset. Volunteers need to be trained to have the conversations and use the tool.

Three of our affiliates decided to join the experiment with Action-Builder: Transport Workers Union (TWU) Local 260, representing Houston public transit workers; International Union of Painters and Allied Trades (IUPAT) District Council 88, and IATSE Local 51. Their volunteers and organizers had large numbers of structured conversations, which they tracked and followed up as if they were trying to help a new group of workers form a union. The TWU talked to members at bus interchanges. IUPAT went out to construction sites. IATSE's members, being in entertainment, were mostly laid off. The union had already been doing outreach on COVID relief, so they incorporated the electoral conversations there.

Building on common interests

During our direct voter outreach, we were careful to drive engagement based on interests, not on partisanship. Though nearly all of our endorsements were Democrats, in all these conversations we led with the issues, not the party.

We had a standard approach: First, we introduced ourselves as union volunteers. We saw a big difference just from doing that. We didn't frontload the conversation with our perspective. Instead, we started by asking the member what issues were most important to them. The most common responses were COVID, education, jobs, the economy, infrastructure, and healthcare. We had a conversation tree that was built off those responses. If someone said jobs were most important, for example, we would explain how voting for our endorsed candidates would advance policies that would lead to job growth, particularly union jobs.

Most of our members are essential workers in industries that did not experience closures or major drops in output, so, with a few exceptions like building trades members who saw slowdowns in work, they've worked through the pandemic. Members in the entertainment and hospitality industries were some of the few who experienced massive layoffs. If we were calling an IBEW member, we knew they were probably working. If we were calling a UNITE HERE member, we knew they probably were not. We had bigger goals than just electing individual candidates—we wanted to win a pro-worker majority in the Texas House, protect a pro-worker majority in Congress, and elect a pro-worker president—so we talked about how a candidate would help advance those policy goals.

A big difference between labor and other movement organizations that do electoral work is that we're organized around our places of work, so people aren't self-selected by their political beliefs, as is the case in community organizing, Democratic clubs, etc. The same workplace can include supporters of both Bernie Sanders and Donald Trump. This makes our electoral work more challenging. But we do have an understanding of the value of common interests and banding with people who share those interests to improve your own life. This opens different ways to have conversations.

Instead of talking about issues on their own terms, we put them in the context of larger issues that should be unifying. We might not agree on some things, but we know that the more we're divided, the less we can accomplish. Understanding that can be a lesson for folks in many areas. You need to develop that sense of unity, solidarity, before you can convince people to rally around a candidate or issue. One of the reasons we were trying to incorporate more union organizing tactics into our program was that a lot of the voter contact approaches we usually use aren't as effective at leveraging that sense of common interests.

For example, in a state where tons of workers hunt game, gun safety is a challenging issue for us. Some of our members and leaders are still talking about the time that Beto O'Rourke got up on a table and said, "Hell, yes, we're going to take your AR-15, your AK-47." That played into destructive frames about what Democratic elected officials are trying to accomplish, and let Republicans leverage the issue in a divisive way. This type of political messaging works by separating us from our common interests. You might benefit from electing candidates who will vote to tax the rich and expand social programs and union jobs, but you vote against those candidates because you've been persuaded that you should be more afraid of that candidate taking your guns.

If we do the conversation right, we talk about workers' common interests. We don't try to convince anyone that they're wrong, unless they have extreme views—believe in Q-Anon or are outright white supremacists or militant anti-vaxxers—but we try to shift the conversation toward which candidate will make our lives better and our community stronger, and talk about it in a holistic way that doesn't allow individual negative issues to take away from the bigger picture.

One of the most invigorating parts of the campaign was the response we got at the bus interchanges. In the Houston metro system, there are key interchanges where all the bus routes come together, and our organizers from TWU Local 260 were going to those interchanges and talking to members. One Local 260 bus driver said he wasn't going to vote, because it didn't matter. The organizer kept talking with him over a period of weeks. Eventually there was a breakthrough, and this driver said he was going to show up and talk to everyone on his route, all of the engineers and mechanics and other drivers. He saw how much it mattered to the organizer and they had built a relationship. There's an important lesson there about what motivates union members. Part of it is issues, part of it is relationships with your union brothers and sisters. The people around you do care about you. Voting is that important to them that they're willing to brave the heat and keep coming back to talk with you about it.

Historic turnout, mixed results

Our work paid off in historic turnout: over 90% of our members voted. Texas in general had a big turnout, but turnout among our members was over 25% higher than the general public, and 14% higher in our targeted House districts. Early turnout was so high that we ran out of people to call on the day before the election. We made four passes through our list.

We contributed to cutting Trump's statewide margin from 9% in 2016 to 5.6%, the narrowest for a Republican since 1996. By comparison, that's 2 points less than Trump's 2020 margin of victory in Ohio—making Texas unquestionably a battleground state.

Ultimately, although we succeeded in driving member engagement and ran a large, effective program, we failed to achieve most of our priority electoral goals. We did contribute to a sweep of countywide offices in both Harris and Fort Bend Counties, a Tier 2 goal. But overall less than half (48%) of our endorsed candidates won, and we won only three of nine Tier 1 and 2 legislative races (HD134, HD135, and CD 7). Statewide, Texas labor made no progress toward our goal of flipping nine Texas House seats, leaving redistricting in the hands of our opponents and us on the defense again in the 2021 legislative session. This failure to make significant gains in the Gulf Coast reflected the pattern statewide and across the nation, with the exception of electing Biden-Harris.

In part, this had to do with the broader political environment over which we had little control. We underestimated the right-wing electoral mobilization. Trump motivated his base and they came out in higher numbers, balancing the enthusiasm our members showed.

The pandemic hurt, too. Had we moved to face-to-face work earlier, we could have done more. If we had followed UNITE HERE's lead in figuring out how to knock on doors safely, our outcome would have been better.

A close look at the data shows that more gains were possible. We saw up to 10 points between the top and the bottom of the ticket. Biden won almost all of our competitive state House districts and we lost all but one. But the margin between winning and losing all of those districts was 16,000 votes, spread across 14 state House districts. Each district has about 180,000 voters. You're talking about tiny margins to flip the statehouse. In campaigns we call a margin that small a "field margin," and if you lose by a field margin, that says you did not knock on enough doors to win. That was clearly the case in this election. There's no way we as a federation could have done more given our resources—but more could have been done overall to flip these seats.

In the spring of 2020, international unions and allied organizations had signaled that they would invest in Texas at a much greater scale than they ever had, and the Biden campaign stated publicly that they considered Texas a swing state and would invest. Those investments came, but not at the scale necessary to flip Texas. The investment in the Texas AFL-CIO's PAC was the largest in Texas history but would have needed to be an order of magnitude larger.

Texas is uniquely challenging because we have 32 media markets; and only little over 25% of them are in the big metro areas of Houston, Dallas, San Antonio, and Austin. Statewide there also needed to be a big focus in the Rio Grande Valley, but that didn't happen.

To maximize the electoral potential here, we need investment, and we also need a different kind of organizational vehicle. Our low union density—the percentage of workers organized into unions—poses a challenge in the newly competitive districts. The density in our member universes in our targeted House districts range from a low of less than 1% in one district we won to a high of 2.5% in HD135. These numbers increase when households and Working America members are included. But even with the most effective member-to-member program, these are not sufficient numbers to drive outcomes in key districts when our opponents are effective at turning out their base, as was especially the case in 2020. Our assessment is that we need to build a political action committee that will enable us to reach out beyond our membership.

With whatever resources we can bring to bear, we also need to change the way people think about politics. Many Texans approach voting decisions with a limited understanding of how policy is made. We need to do more education on what majorities mean, especially for voters in swing districts. We saw lots of votes for split government, GOP candidates at the state level and Biden at the top of the ticket. When you vote for a Republican in the legislature, nothing will get done. Majorities are the only way something gets done.

We were making our case based on pro-worker positions. But so much of Americans' perceptions of politics is based on personalities, based on individuals, not based on movements or majorities. Electing a specific member of the Texas House or of Congress doesn't do all that much. We need majorities to accomplish the big things that are going to get our country back on track, and we didn't talk about that enough. We need to educate voters about how we accomplish policy. It's not only what we're for, but how we accomplish them.

The labor movement's role in the progressive ecosystem

It's important that we look at 2020 in context. The Texas labor movement plays a critical role in a whole ecosystem of groups that are changing the nature of politics in the state. Our experience is that when workers organize in unions, there is the deepest opportunity for people's experience of power on the job to build solidarity across racial lines and for people to develop leadership skills to use for long-term change.

But our path isn't linear. We've seen some setbacks and some advances in the last 20 years, but we've been steadily eroding the Republican presidential margin. That's what the right wing is afraid of, which is why we're seeing the aggressive attack on voting rights and levels of gerrymandering reminiscent of the Jim Crow era. But if we continue to train our members, increase the scale of workers with whom we can talk, build out our community networks, and increase investment over time, we can turn the state and finally go on the offense for working families in a big way.

Notes

1. Working America, the community affiliate of the AFL-CIO, is an organization for working people who don't have a union on the job. See www.workingamerica.org/about.

14

'There's a Purpose in This': Domestic Workers Enter the Electoral Arena

Linda Burnham and Ai-jen Poo

Domestic workers exercised more muscle in electoral politics between 2017 and 2020 than they had since the dawn of domestic worker organizing in the late 19th century. This did not happen by chance. More than two decades of organizing for better wages and working conditions convinced movement leaders that it was time to project the interests of domestic workers in key electoral contests.

Domestic workers mobilized voters in Stacey Abrams' gubernatorial campaign in Georgia, in the 2019 elections that flipped the Virginia state legislature from a Republican to a Democratic majority, and in the 2020 presidential election. They demonstrated the capacity of working-class women of color to turn out "low-propensity"/highpotential voters and to impact electoral outcomes. And they forged the link between the distinct processes of ongoing base-building, electoral campaigning, and advocating for policies to improve conditions in the domestic work industry.

The decision to engage in electoral organizing should be understood in the context of the movement's broader goal: to develop sufficient political power to win the rights, respect, and recognition that domestic workers deserve.

The current iteration of domestic worker organizing began to take shape in the 1990s. Women who cleaned houses and took care of infants, children, and elders began to do battle against wage theft and insist on the most basic labor rights. Led by immigrants from Latin America, the Caribbean, the Philippines, and South Asia, domestic workers formed worker centers, cooperatives, and support groups across the country to gather and wield their collective power.

Thirteen of these organizations came together at the US Social Forum in 2007 to found the National Domestic Workers Alliance (NDWA). Together they shared lessons from more than a decade of local organizing. They also began to develop strategies aimed at increasing the capacity of the domestic worker movement to improve the conditions of the workforce. Working women who had long been considered "unorganizable" got busy organizing themselves.

One of the central challenges of the domestic worker movement is the disaggregated character of the industry. It is a labor market of millions of workers and millions of employers. Though there are some industry norms in terms of wages and expectations, each worker ultimately comes to a unique agreement with an individual employer. There is no bargaining unit or human resources department. Often enough, there is no written agreement or contract. Because the work takes place behind the doors of private homes, many workers are subject to levels of abuse that are rare in more formalized sectors of the economy. And, because these private homes function at the same time as millions of distinct work sites, the mechanisms to stop abuse and raise standards cannot be the potentially powerful collective action of hundreds or thousands of workers against a single employer.

In addition to the challenge of a radically dispersed workforce, domestic workers are burdened with outright exclusion from many of the legal protections afforded other workers. Core labor rights won by workers in the 1930s, and codified in the National Labor Relations Act, are explicitly denied to agricultural workers and domestic workers—the result of invidious and racist compromises with Southern legislators. The

Fair Labor Standards Act still excludes live-in domestic workers from its overtime provisions. Domestic workers also face explicit or de facto exclusion from many labor protections enacted at the state level.

In addition to these exclusions, the composition of the workforce is itself an expression of profound inequalities related to gender, race, and citizenship status. Domestic workers are, disproportionately, Black women, immigrant women, and undocumented residents. Given these conditions and characteristics, resolving the challenge of how to focus the organized power of domestic workers to improve working conditions is far from a straightforward proposition.

Over the past two and a half decades, domestic workers have approached the problem of how to aggregate and exercise their power from many different angles. They have waged successful campaigns to win Domestic Worker Bills of Rights in eleven states and three cities. These legislative wins, among the principal achievements of the movement, were designed to create enforceable rights and protections for the labor force, including rights to meal and rest breaks, paid time off, overtime, and notice of termination. NDWA's Bill of Rights strategy is a work-around for two problems: the absence of federal and state-level labor protections, and the challenge of holding millions of individual employers accountable to a baseline of labor rights.

The Bill of Rights strategy compelled NDWA to confront how power is exercised over the lives of domestic workers through policy decisions (or inaction) that rest in the hands of elected representatives. Domestic workers became skilled at telling the story of their lives and their industry. They learned to fortify their own power by forging relationships with those who had more organizational and political clout. Strong ties to organized labor proved to be especially important as domestic workers learned to navigate their way around city halls and state capitols to influence elected officials and the legislative process.

But it wasn't until the 2016 presidential campaign that the power to influence the outcome of an election forced its way onto the domestic workers' agenda. Obviously, the stakes were high. Trump spouted anti-immigrant venom as he rolled down his wretched escalator to announce his candidacy. He didn't disguise his love for the billionaire class and his disdain for workers. His intention to use his campaign platform to propagate anti-Black racism across the nation (it had long been his calling card in New York City) was clear from the outset. The unapologetic vulgarity of his strutting brand of male supremacy was both bracing and distressing. Women of color, Black women, and immigrant women (categories which obviously overlap) are the predominant demographic in the domestic work sector. Trump's candidacy, with its promise of regression on multiple fronts simultaneously, embodied the most concentrated threat in generations to the well-being of domestic workers, their families, and their communities.

In 2016, leaders of the domestic workers movement scrambled to sort out what to do about that threat. Domestic workers had no organizational vehicle that lent itself to electoral campaigning, or to unite workers to support a particular candidate. or mobilize them based on their broader identities as concerned citizens and residents with an investment in democracy.

NDWA decided that it was critical to galvanize and marshal the power of women of color to engage in the elections and make their voices heard. To project collective visibility and articulate the interests of women who are typically ignored, NDWA teamed up with other organizations to launch the nonpartisan coalition We Won't Wait. Organizers held 3 million kitchen table conversations with working-class women and women of color about their experiences in the economy and their hopes for the future. A September 2016 summit in Washington, DC, brought thousands of women together to discuss their top-line issues and build momentum for the get-out-the-vote sprint. The hotel ballroom crackled with the energy of women seeing themselves in each other and recognizing their potential to affect the forces that shape their lives. Nearly everyone in the room—like nearly everyone in the nation—believed they were about to witness the historic election of the first female president.

Then, Trump.

Shellacked and shocked by the 2016 election results, leaders in the domestic workers movement were also highly motivated to ensure that domestic workers would never again be peripheral to the pivot point of national politics. With Trump's ascent to power, the movement was forced into a radical reckoning with what it meant to have been caught flat-footed in the face of an election of such consequence to domestic workers. The domestic workers movement was not alone in this reckoning. Social justice groups across the country scrambled to figure out how to bring on the talent and resources to help make sense of an unfamiliar terrain.

In the case of domestic workers, that meant creating the organizational infrastructure to contain and direct the electoral aspirations of the women of color at the heart of the movement; raising prodigious amounts of 501(c)(4) money to support that infrastructure; and creating a team of organizers ready to go deep on the nuts and bolts of electoral engagement. It also meant opening up new kinds of conversations with domestic workers about candidates and their platforms to determine which ones were worthy of support.

First up: Georgia

Jess Morales Rocketto was brought on to build and lead Care in Action (CiA) the new "policy and advocacy home" for the domestic workers movement. Jess, a force field of fast-talking intensity who had headed Hillary Clinton's 2016 digital organizing campaign, was charged with standing up a credible operation that could impact electoral outcomes while also embodying the goals and values of the domestic worker movement. It was 2017, an off year. Jess and a hastily assembled staff had to determine where to throw down, and what the movement's unique contributions could be and to map out the best places to experiment to build this nascent electoral muscle. As it turned out, Georgia was a blinking neon sign.

Stacey Abrams' campaign for governor of Georgia was shaping up to be a heroic battle. It pitted a highly accomplished, ambitious, and respected liberal state legislator—the first Black woman to run for governor in Georgia (or to receive a major party's nomination anywhere in the country)—against the Republican secretary of state, Brian Kemp. The choice could not have been starker. Abrams stood for expanding Medicaid to meet the healthcare needs of poor Georgians; widening and protecting access to the ballot for all of Georgia's citizens; and supporting public education "from cradle to career." She was known for her willingness to negotiate with Republicans—who controlled the Georgia Assembly and the governorship—to reach reasonable compromises.

Even more to the point, Abrams had carved out a credible path to victory, garnered the support of both the Black political establishment and white liberals, and spent years building a grassroots vehicle to expand the electorate, the New Georgia Project. Hers was not a symbolic campaign. She was playing to win. And she was playing to win in a national political context that contained the possibility of Georgia shifting from red to blue in the 2020 presidential campaign—for the first time since Bill Clinton's win in 1992.

Brian Kemp's bid for the governorship offered voters a blunt contrast. The pickup truck for rounding up "illegals" and the guns featured in his campaign ads were props that distracted from his main talent. As Georgia's secretary of state, Kemp presided over a deliberate and multipronged approach to voter suppression. He investigated organizations that were highly successful in registering new voters. He oversaw the aggressive removal of inactive voters from the rolls. The number of inactive voters nearly doubled while he was in office, from 714,000 in 2012 to 1.3 million in 2018. More than twice as many voters were purged from the rolls between 2012 and 2016 as had been between 2008 and 2012. While Georgia's population grew by more than half a million people from 2012 to 2018, the number of registered voters dropped. An academic expert on the finer points of voter suppression called Kemp a master of the art, "practiced and steeped in the nuances of disfranchisement."

As absurd as it may seem—and as contrary to the most basic tenets of voting rights—the man who oversaw a radical narrowing of the Georgia franchise in ways that disproportionately suppressed the Black vote, advantaged Republicans, and propped up their control of the state and their representation in Congress was now in charge of an election in which he himself stood for governor. People, in what world are we living?

The domestic workers movement had already made a long-term commitment to organizing in Georgia. The Atlanta chapter of NDWA was launched in 2013. The chapter anchors a statewide network of domestic workers which meets regularly to provide mutual support and to strategize and advocate for domestic workers' rights. Workers develop their outreach and leadership skills by building their chapter, campaigning for better wages and benefits, building support for Medicaid expansion, and creating a presence for domestic worker issues in progressive circles and among elected officials. We Dream in Black (WeDiB), an NDWA initiative, connects members of the Georgia chapter with Black domestic workers across the country.

Beyond contemporary politics, Georgia holds a special place in domestic worker history. The founding of NDWA at the 2007 World Social Forum in Atlanta brought 21st-century domestic worker organizing to national scale, but the historic connections stretch much further back. In the 1880s, in one of the first recorded labor actions by domestic workers, Atlanta washerwomen held out for higher rates by refusing to take in laundry. And in the 1960s, Dorothy Bolden, one of the heroines of domestic worker organizing, led the National Domestic Workers Union of America. Standing up for Stacey Abrams felt like a natural extension of this rich history.

Finally, putting together an electoral operation in Georgia seemed to be within reach. Care in Action was a fledgling operation with only about $250,000 in the bank. Not exactly nothing, but for a serious ground operation, close enough to it. There was no way to imagine having an impact in larger states—Texas, New York, Florida, California—without exponentially greater resources. But Jess Morales Rocketto figured that something could be launched in Georgia on a very tight budget, with the possibility of more to come.

So Georgia it was. Care in Action brought on Nikema Williams, then a state senator who, at the time, represented Georgia's 39th district. (Williams now represents Georgia's 5th Congressional District as a US Representative, filling the seat held by the legendary John Lewis for nearly 35 years, until his death in 2020.) The Georgia General Assembly, by law, meets for no more than 40 days per year. For the rest of the year, legislators run businesses, write romance novels, brush up on voter suppression tactics, or find other employment. Williams happened to be looking for work at precisely the time CiA was looking to hire.

It was a brilliant match. Williams knew her way around Georgia politics, had worked closely with Abrams in the legislature, deeply understood the stakes in the race for governor and was ready to go all-in on a grassroots campaign. There was no path to an Abrams victory without mobilizing people who had never been inspired to vote before. Williams was ready to join domestic workers in figuring out how to produce a record turnout of infrequent, or "low-propensity voters"—voters who, with the right investment of time and resources, had the potential to provide the margin of victory.

It may have been a brilliant match, but that is not to say that starting a new electoral operation was entirely without tension. First, of course, there was the matter of endorsing the candidate. A delegation of domestic workers and organizers met with Abrams in October 2017. Abrams answered their questions and talked extensively about her commitments to the health and welfare of all Georgians. She satisfied the workers that her candidacy represented a new day for the state and a historic advance for Black women in politics. The last question was from a Georgia domestic worker: "What do you need to win?" Abrams replied, "I need you to show up and to get involved." The unanimous response: "We're in."

The endorsement process was a baseline lesson in electoral organizing. One hundred percent alignment with a candidate is a rarity, especially since progressives have only recently begun to systematically groom and field candidates. The Abrams candidacy was deemed worthy of enthusiastic support despite any questions about her position on one issue or another.

Electoral work is data- and metrics-driven with a hard end date: Election Day. What constitutes a win is completely unambiguous: either your candidate triumphs or she loses. Community-based organizing operates on a looser model. Relationships are established and tended to; leadership capacities are built over the course of long-term, often multi-year campaigns. The pace of door-knocking and phone-banking for CiA's Abrams campaign was rigorous. Each canvasser was assigned a set number of doors to knock on her shift. But the canvassers were mostly poor people, domestic workers and others from the community hired to get on the doors. What happens when a canvasser's compromised health gets in the way of her ability to do the job? How to handle the logistics of getting canvassers who were reliant on an inadequate public transportation system out into the communities they were supposed to cover? How to support the canvasser in distress, having just lost her housing, or one of her three jobs? Poor folks' problems.

CiA put together solutions to those problems and a whole lot more. It helped enormously that dealing with poor folks' problems is in the DNA of the domestic worker movement. Every aspect of domestic worker organizing—from campaign development to organization building to leadership development—has to take into account the ways in which systems built to provide healthcare, transportation, housing, education, and adequate nutrition consistently fail low-income workers. Solving for unforeseen emergencies is business as usual.

Care in Action knocked on 76,965 doors, made 272,609 calls, and sent 1,460,101 text messages. Their work contributed to a historic election. From 2016 to 2020, Black Georgians increased their voter registration by 25% and more Georgians voted in 2020 than in any previous election. Georgians broke records for early voting and for runoff turnout.

Domestic workers' electoral efforts were substantive enough to earn a shout-out from former President Barack Obama. Ex-presidents give a lot of speeches, but each speech is a limited resource. There are a finite number of people and organizations who can be name-checked. Besides, name checks are boring, except to the people being checked. On November 2, 2018, four days before the gubernatorial election, President Obama gave an hour-long speech on behalf of Abrams' bid for the governorship. By that time he had put in months of campaigning for Democratic candidates in the midterm elections. His voice was hoarse, but his energy rose to meet the passion of Abrams' supporters packed into Forbes Arena at Morehouse College. His speech was interrupted every couple of sentences with shouts of approval and chants of "Vote! Vote! Vote!" Nearing the end of the rally Obama said, "I've heard about the domestic workers right here in Georgia, mobilizing for Stacey like never before … If they're not too tired to vote, you better not be."

Something had shifted in the course of the year domestic workers spent campaigning for Stacey Abrams. The campaign became an expression of the power of Black womanhood; the role of Black womanhood in the defense of democracy and voting rights. Georgia gained national—if not worldwide—attention as a nodal point in the contest between those prepared to butcher the democratic franchise in order to keep Black voters from the polls and those dedicated to expanding the electorate and its ready access to this most basic citizenship right. Domestic workers, out on the doors every day in their orange t-shirts, came to embody the resistance of Black working-class women to historical and contemporary infringements on their rights and their lives. Wielding a combination of moral authority and an effective voter mobilization operation, they became avatars of a hard-nosed determination to get Abrams into office and keep open the democratic space.

And yet, despite all this, Abrams lost the race. It was close. When they finished the ballot count in the three-way race that included a Libertarian, Kemp had 50.2% of the vote and Stacey had 48.8%. In the days following the election, Stacey declined to concede. It's one thing to be beaten by your run-of-the-mill good ol' boy. It's another to lose to a master of voter suppression. Abrams demanded that the race not be called until all provisional and absentee ballots had been counted. In light of the history of Republican trickery, and the fox minding the henhouse of democracy, she demanded a recount. A runoff election between the two top vote getters would have been triggered had Kemp's numbers fallen below 50%. A small blizzard of lawsuits and countersuits were filed.

Domestic workers continued to stand tall for Abrams in the aftermath of the election. On November 13 they showed up at a "Count Every Vote" rally at the capitol rotunda organized by Southerners on New Ground and Georgia Latino Alliance for Human Rights, two progressive organizations with deep roots in Georgia and the South. Nikema Williams, who had so ably led the mobilization of domestic workers as canvassers and voters, was back at the Capitol for a special session of the legislature. In a bright red blazer, four strands of pearls, a flower-print dress and high heels, Williams was dressed for her role as a state senator, not for a protest rally. Yet she recognized some of her constituents and joined them in calling for a recount. She and 15 others, including NDWA and CiA staff, were arrested and jailed. Williams could have been out in 10 minutes, but she refused to be let go before the other protestors were released. The protest, and the news conference that followed, made the national news and placed the recount demand squarely in Black Atlanta's civil rights tradition.

But the numbers refused to add up. A few days later, on November 16, Abrams suspended her campaign. Without formally conceding, she allowed that the contest had reached an end point and vowed to continue to resist voter suppression.

On broader terrain

CiA interpreted its work on the Abrams campaign and the recount as "proof of concept" that domestic workers could be mobilized both as organizers and as voters in critical electoral races, and that their role in mobilizing women of color voters like them was essential. It was time to scale up what CiA had learned in Georgia. There was no race more critical than the upcoming one for the White House. In early 2019, CiA decided to carry forward the baseline principles developed during the Abrams campaign and to expand their interventions to several states. Four main principles frame CiA's approach to electoral work:

- Focus on mobilizing the voting power of "low-propensity"/ high-potential women of color voters.
- Commit to states where domestic workers can be mobilized, both as canvassers and as voters.
- Build state-level infrastructure and invest in the leadership of local women of color leaders and organizers who know the electoral terrain.
- Endorse women of color candidates who will promote an agenda that includes support for the rights and dignity of domestic workers and building support for caregiving across the lifespan.

CiA had to make decisions about where to experiment with applying these principles, decisions that were not easy. First, there were financial considerations. As in 2017–2018, the states with the largest numbers of domestic workers—Florida, Texas, New York, and California—were too expensive to operate in effectively. A data-driven approach to decision making also forced other considerations to the fore: How many women of color in a given state are eligible to vote? How many of them are registered? How many of those who are registered actually vote? What proportion of the voting age population do women of color voters constitute, and how decisive would it be to maximize their exercise of the franchise?

The composition of the state legislatures was also part of the calculus. Were there candidates running for the legislature who were worthy of domestic workers' endorsement and commitment to hard campaigning? Would a win by such a candidate help shift legislative power in a more progressive direction? And, of course, in the context of an unfolding presidential race that was rapidly accumulating Democratic primary contenders, the potential role of the state in determining the outcome of the 2020 general election was a weighty factor in the decision-making process.

It was a complex matrix. After months of research, debate, and discussions across teams, CiA decided to operate in seven states: Georgia, North Carolina, South Carolina, Virginia, Arizona, Nevada, and Michigan. In each state, they set up listening sessions designed to build relationships on the ground; identified values-aligned local leaders who knew the electoral landscape; figured out which lanes were already occupied and which could use more energy and resources; and determined which candidates deserved domestic workers' support. In several of these states, NDWA had chapters or local affiliates already well-integrated into the ecosystem conducting nonpartisan GOTV and voter registration work.

As CiA built infrastructure in the states for 2020, the politics of Virginia loomed large. Several women of color were running for the Virginia General Assembly in 2019 and the balance of power between the two major parties was in contention. The State Senate had been in Republican hands for more than 20 years. They also controlled the House of Delegates for most of that time. The long-term work of organizations such as New Virginia Majority, SEIU, and Planned Parenthood Action Fund, among others, had opened up the possibility of flipping the legislature from Republican to Democratic control. And Virginia was projected to be a battleground state in the presidential election.

And so, CiA endorsed and worked for several Virginia candidates in 2019, including Jennifer McClellan. McClellan, an incumbent who won her bid to keep her state Senate seat, went on to sponsor legislation that eliminated the exclusion of domestic workers from Virginia's minimum wage protections. In the 2021 legislative session she sponsored the Domestic Worker Bill of Rights in Virginia. McClellan reflected on her personal connection to the work: "As the daughter, granddaughter, and great granddaughter of domestic workers, I know how essential domestic workers are to the economy and how poorly mistreated they've been for generations. Today, the Virginia General Assembly took action to reverse Jim Crow–era laws and expand protections for domestic workers."

Virginia became the first southern state since slavery time to legislate an expansion of labor rights for domestic workers. The domestic worker movement demonstrated its capacity to create a reinforcing loop between candidate endorsement, electoral organizing, and the passage of progressive public policy. And, in concert with a strong progressive alliance, the movement contributed to the election of Democratic majorities to both houses of the Virginia General Assembly for the first time in 25 years.

2020

Meanwhile, the Republican and Democratic primaries were well underway. The domestic worker movement had never before engaged in a presidential endorsement process. The Democratic primary contenders were invited to a gathering of domestic workers in Las Vegas, Nevada, in February 2020. Elizabeth Warren and Tom Steyer addressed 400 workers and Bernie Sanders sent a video message. In presidential primaries, political currency consists in making a clear choice relatively early on, and being prepared to defend that choice in a highly contentious political environment.

But there was no established process to determine whom the majority of domestic workers supported, and there were significant differences of opinion among leaders in the domestic workers movement and CiA staff. Some on staff were very strong supporters of particular candidates and vehement opponents of other candidates. Others were skeptical of, or opposed to, endorsing any Democrat at all. As relative newcomers to electoral politics, the domestic worker movement was not quite prepared to negotiate these conflicting pressures and to settle on an endorsement that could win the enthusiastic support of the movement as a whole.

But once Biden secured the nomination and selected Senator Kamala Harris as his running mate, the ticket attracted backing across a very broad spectrum—from those desperate to elect anyone prepared to oppose white supremacist authoritarianism to ardent Biden advocates.

Harris was already on record as a strong supporter of domestic workers rights. She had introduced legislation in 2019—a federal Domestic Workers Bill of Rights—to extend minimum wage, overtime, and paid time off protections to workers in the industry. Domestic workers gave the Biden-Harris ticket their endorsement and proceeded to manifest that support in the only real coinage of the electoral realm: contacting voters and getting them to the polls.

CiA established operations in each of the seven targeted states. And then COVID-19 scrambled even the most thoughtful planning. Instead of getting on the doors in massive canvassing operations, most domestic workers and others pivoted to phone banking and texting. The conversations started with wellness checks. "How are you and your family doing during this pandemic?" Not well. Phone bankers took in the pain points—fear of contagion, how to keep food on the table, job loss, how to handle kids stuck at home all day long. They listened with empathy and eased into "Do you know how to vote safely? Do you plan to vote? Do you know what's at stake in this election?"

Melanie Jackson stayed on the doors, with extensive COVID safety protocols in place. Jackson is an extrovert; she will happily strike up a conversation with the person standing behind her in the supermarket checkout line. Jackson is also a caregiver on weekend night shifts for an individual with a severe disability. She is in the work because she loves the work, having been inspired to become a caregiver by the stellar team that took care of her elderly parents in the years before their deaths.

When someone at her church encouraged Jackson to become a canvasser for Reverend Raphael Warnock, she didn't hesitate. She was so good at door-knocking that she was promoted to supervisor in CiA's canvassing operation. Hundreds of canvassers rallied at 9:15 every morning in the parking lot of the Cascade Skating Rink in Metro Atlanta. Jackson was in charge of a crew of about 25 canvassers—Team Get It Done. She gave out assignments, kept them motivated, baked cookies for the team, and solved problems. She loved being on the doors herself and knows she made a difference. One conversation in particular stands out. Jackson knocked on the door of a Black man, a registered Democrat who said he probably wasn't going to vote. Jackson looked him dead in the eye – steady eye contact being one of her superpowers. "You're really going to pass up the opportunity to send the first Black man to the Senate from this state since Reconstruction?" He looked right back and said, "You know what, sister, since you said that, I'm going to do it. I'm going to vote for your guy."

Asked what she learned from her work on the doors, Jackson had two things to say. First, "There's a purpose in this." And second, "We as a profession have power in our numbers."

Election math is brutal. It can take dozens of attempts to actually reach a potential voter. Of those reached, only some fraction of them will go on to vote. Across the seven states, including the two Senate races in Georgia, the general election, and the senatorial runoff, the domestic workers movement made nearly 35 million outreach attempts, primarily focused on women of color potential voters. Eight million of those attempts succeeded in reaching potential voters. Of the 2.7 million unique potential voters contacted, 55% of them went on to vote, nearly 1.5 million people. Many of these voters had not gone to the polls in 2012 or 2016. They were, in fact, low-propensity/high-potential voters.

Multitudes line up to lay claim to victory, while failure has no friends. In every election there are many actors on the ground, sometimes collaborating, sometimes competing. A tangled complexity of factors influences every outcome. Nonetheless, the numbers do tell a story. CiA and the domestic worker movement contributed substantially to 2020's unprecedented voter turnout. Domestic workers also played a significant role in the Senatorial victories of Raphael Warnock and Jon Ossoff in Georgia. CiA endorsed and worked for 76 women of color candidates running for statewide and local office. Seventy percent of them won their races.

The Care Agenda

Of course, the interests of domestic workers reach well beyond the election of any particular candidate to local, statewide, or national office. A policy agenda designed to protect labor rights and raise standards for workers has, over the years, expanded to include support for the care needs of individuals and families. In close collaboration with Caring Across Generations and Hand in Hand (a network of "high road" employers who advocate for change in the domestic work industry), the domestic workers movement developed an approach to public policy that links families' care needs to the needs of the care workforce. Our nation is notoriously poor at ensuring that children, elders, and people with disabilities have access to the high-quality, affordable support they need to thrive. NDWA spent years nurturing an alignment of interests between those who receive care, those who provide it, and the family caregivers in between.

In the 2020 elections, organizations representing this broad constituency intensified their advocacy for a substantial expansion of federal support for caregiving. The pandemic had thrown many social tensions into sharp relief, including the outsized burden for caregiving that women carry and the essential nature of the work of paid caregivers. Candidates were quizzed about their positions on care and encouraged to support concrete legislative measures to expand both access to care and the quality of care jobs.

It is not by accident that a narrative about care as an integral part of infrastructure emerged in 2021. The narrative built on at least a decade's work. The challenge was to turn narrative and anecdote and good ideas into concrete proposals for policy change that could be incorporated into proposed legislation. More than a dozen organizations joined with NDWA and Caring Across Generations to assert that infrastructure is more than bridges, roads, the electric grid, and internet access. The Care Can't Wait coalition worked closely with economists and policy experts and pushed for a robust investment in care infrastructure, including:

- Equitable access to affordable, high-quality childcare and preschool
- Decent wages and benefits for early childhood educators
- More than $400 billion in new Medicaid funding for a radical expansion in access to and eligibility for long-term support services
- Improved wages, benefits, and training for homecare workers
- 12 weeks of paid family and medical leave, with comprehensive coverage and an inclusive definition of family

The Biden administration included an unprecedented expansion of federal support for family leave, caregiving, and the care workforce into its budget. The incorporation of a care agenda into this administration's core policy goals underscores the mutually reinforcing dynamics among grassroots organizing, policy campaigns, and electoral work.

Organizing and transformation

There is debate within the social justice left about whether electoral organizing is "transformative" or not. The logic of ongoing issue-based and constituency-based organizing is very different from that of electoral organizing. Building a base of members, organizers, leaders, and supporters requires sustained, in-depth relationship-building over an extended timeframe. The aim is to transform marginal interest—or even disinterest—into deep engagement, active participation, and long-term commitment. When done well, it engenders a transformation in consciousness from apathy to concern about particular grievances to an understanding of the dynamics of broader social and economic inequities. Grassroots organizing also encourages and enables individuals' transition from passivity to collective action. In social justice organizing there are many ways to count wins and losses: members recruited, lessons learned, skills acquired, relationships built, credibility established. The work has no end date.

Elections are time-bound and unambiguous. Just show up and vote. No complex, drawn out transformation of consciousness required. Get to scale as quickly as possible and hit the numbers. Go broad, not deep. Either you win or you lose, there is no middle ground.

But to get millions to flip the switch from non-voting to voting—isn't that transformative? The domestic worker movement mobilized thousands of canvassers and phone bankers in active defense of democracy. For many it was their first experience with mobilizing voters to impact the political landscape. Each came away from the experience with new sets of skills, along with the texture and content of hundreds of conversations with their fellow citizens. Their work centered the political power of women of color in a system designed to minimize and negate that power. The rhythm and metrics and subjective feel of the work are different from grassroots organizing. But that too can be transformative.

From 2018 to 2020, the domestic worker movement threw down in the electoral arena in ways it never had before. That work has changed the way domestic workers and their allies exercise their collective power. Electoral engagement will no doubt be an important component of the domestic worker movement going forward. Integrating distinct forms and methods of organizing will be an ongoing challenge. Lessons learned in meeting that challenge will inform the work of NDWA and CiA in the 2022 and 2024 electoral cycles.

The defeat of Trump was a win for low-income workers and for all women whose lives are constricted by race and gender inequities. But Trump's defeat, while crucial, left standing the systems and politics and institutions that devalue domestic workers' lives. Domestic workers have taken their place as an important element of a progressive ecosystem determined to maximize—in the immediate and over the long haul—its influence on the political direction of the nation.

Our gratitude to Melanie Dawson Jackson, Auntionette Jenkins, Jess Morales Rocketto, and Mariana Viturro for sharing their insights about mobilizing domestic workers for the 2020 elections.

Part 4

Bernie, Democratic Socialism, and the Primary Battles

15

Bernie 2020: 'Not Me, Us'

A roundtable discussion led by Alex Han, Executive Editor, *Convergence* Magazine, with Yong Jung Cho, National Field Director, Green New Deal Network, and Neidi Dominguez, Executive Director, Unemployed Workers United

Introduction

At the end of April 2015, in an email to supporters, Bernie Sanders announced his campaign for the 2016 Democratic Party nomination for president. In the 24 hours that followed, this nascent campaign raised over $1.5 million—more than any other contender for the presidency, Republican or Democrat, had ever raised on their first day. That launch, and the grassroots movement that grew in its wake, has fundamentally transformed what is possible in American politics. Through the 2016 campaign, the four years of Trumpism that followed, and into his 2020 run and beyond, Bernie has played a lead role in the leftward shift of the Democratic Party and forced democratic socialism into the lexicon of modern power politics. While neither campaign ended in victory, his current seat at the helm of the Senate Budget Committee, along with the growing ranks of democratic socialists and progressive allies in the House continue to keep alive the "political revolution," and the hope of necessary change to come. What follows is a conversation with senior staff from the Bernie 2020 campaign, on the possibilities that exist, the challenges we face, and lessons to learn from this critical juncture.

What was your role in Bernie 2020?

Yong Jung Cho (YJC): I was the national constituency organizing director. I spent about half of my time working directly with field directors in the states and state leadership teams, helping strategize on the overall field plans. In places where there were constituency organizing programs and staff in the state, I worked directly with those deputy field directors on building out specific constituency programs, whether it was labor, student programs, Black, AAPI, Muslim, or Latino voters, in each of the states. I would spend the other half of my time working with our national staff on the organizing team, building our distributed organizing programs within key priority constituency groups.[1]

Neidi Dominguez (ND): My role was national deputy director of states. And what that ended up being really was supporting some of the state directors in the primary states in thinking through their partnerships and allies on the ground. And a lot of work on operations! We had so many volunteers everywhere, but if there was a large group of volunteers coming into one or several places, our team was also thinking through all the operational and logistical needs. Making sure that the state directors were getting what they needed in terms of resources and capacity and extra support. I think our team was like the command center—when directors needed to get through an urgent matter with the communications team or the political team or the organizing team, or up the chain of command to Chuck [Rocha] or [Jeff] Weaver.[2]

Alex Han (AH): I came in to coordinate politics in the Super Tuesday states, but I ended up playing the role of Midwest political director, and as part of the national political team working a lot with labor unions and progressive organizations nationally. Our team was the point of contact for elected officials, and especially in states where we didn't yet have a state director, I was responsible for outreach to electeds, unions, political organizations, the state and local Democratic Party organizations, you name it.

What is your overall assessment of what the impact of the Bernie 2020 campaign has been so far, and could be going forward?

YJC: I don't think it's a coincidence now that the Green New Deal is in public discourse, along with a $15 minimum wage and having a good union job, taking strong action on climate, Medicare for All, healthcare as a human right. These are values that Bernie campaigned on in 2016 and the work the campaign did in 2020 has played a big role in shifting the political window of what is possible now. You know, there was a week after the Nevada caucus where I thought that a democratic socialist was going to be president and it felt more real than it ever had before. And I think that scared the political establishment—it showed organizers on the left what was possible, but then it also showed the establishment that it was possible as well.

So there were political impacts, and then there was a ton of organizing impact. I think one of the biggest values around organizing a presidential campaign is that millions of people who have never engaged in politics before will become engaged for the first time. The mobilizing and organizing of new volunteers—the stories that we would hear from new volunteers saying, "I've never done this before, but I'm going to make phone calls or I'm going to go knock on doors" was hugely motivating. And then the Bernie 2020 organizing department was the best distributed-organizing campaign anywhere up until that point. Which became critical in March of 2020—we already had the staff and the knowledge and the tools for running distributed campaigns before COVID-19.

Beginning in early March, there was a solid month or two where we were doing millions of voter contacts by text messages and phone calls, having virtual one-on-one organizing meetings at scale, and a lot of progressive organizations were learning about Zoom for the first time. So the skills that we had developed were being shared across institutions, and I saw Bernie alums, after the campaign, go on to support a ton of organizing projects from the critical organizing work post–George Floyd. Lots of work on the general election, union campaigns like the

Emergency Workplace Organizing Committee (EWOC)—initiated by Bernie 2020 staff and now a joint project of the United Electrical Workers and DSA—came out of the Bernie staff. Some members went into the Sunrise Movement to build on the momentum that came from the constituency program. So, I feel like there was both a political impact and a huge organizing impact because we knew how to run distributed campaigns.

ND: I think the biggest impact was shifting the possibility that we can have things like universal healthcare—it popularized the idea that the government is in fact responsible for providing some of these basic human rights to its people. It sounds very simple, but we all know that these ideas aren't necessarily popular in a lot of progressive spaces, if we're honest, right? People can be totally down with "economic justice," but they're not necessarily down with socializing healthcare or a guaranteed income. They're down for "good jobs," but they're not necessarily down for actually socializing a lot of these benefits and turning them into public goods.

Honestly, that was one of the main reasons I came to work for the 2020 Bernie campaign. Living under Trump, working at the Painters Union, it was a moment of true reckoning, of thinking, "What are we really going to have to do in this country to win for poor and working-class people?" I've worked with non-union car wash workers, and with day laborers, then I went to work with the AFL-CIO—a whole other experience—then I went to a union that represents construction workers. What I saw from the Obama years into the Trump years was the immediate retreat of the labor movement. For traditional unions there were a lot of internal political challenges. For other worker organizations like worker centers, their capacity was overwhelmed.

We were so swamped under all the attacks of Trump that what we were doing was day-to-day defending our people from being deported. And that's as much as you can do when you're under that kind of attack. We made some advances, but they were so small compared to everything else that was happening. Being at the Painters Union, we were doing amazing work in the South and I was still finding myself at times trying to convince organizing directors around the country that they should be organizing immigrant workers, that doing that was a key part of their survival. And I felt like sometimes I was having these split-personality moments where at times I was just so angry that I had to still make this argument and just feeling like, "This is why we can't have nice things."

YJC: Another thing that was really powerful was the amazing work coming out of our media department. The short-form videos around issues got millions and millions of views and were a way to articulate Bernie's values and policy priorities and what the campaign meant. It was powerful and important, from an organizing perspective—the videos helped do persuasion and got people who were already activated even more committed.

AH: There are impacts on how we run campaigns, which I think are in large part about the amazing distributed organizing program we had, the organizing and field work in places like Iowa, Nevada, and California just to name a few, the ways in which we used the creation of our own media to advance both narrative and our volunteer effort, and the way we were in the vanguard of digital organizing with the BERN app and online tools.[3]

What are the lessons from the campaign that can guide us into the midterms and the elections beyond?

ND: One of the main lessons is that institutions do not alone dictate how members of those institutions are going to fall. This was made most clear in Nevada, with what happened on the Las Vegas Strip when the Culinary Workers Union's leadership refused to endorse Bernie and then sent out messages claiming his healthcare reforms would "end culinary healthcare."[4] Many of the union's members voted for Bernie anyway. That seems like a very basic lesson, but I think it's something for our movements to really think about, given how much we tend to silo ourselves. When it comes to a presidential campaign, or another political campaign, people are still people, and whoever wins the minds and hearts of those people wins. Of course, it matters what they're going to be hearing from the institutions, unions, or organizations that they trust, but they still have autonomy. It seems like a very basic lesson, but it's a question I've definitely been sitting with: "How do we move people to our side as a whole of who they are, not just with the institutions that they're part of or not part of?"

Another one of the lessons that I'm taking away is the ways we can use distributed organizing for mass base-building. Organizers will say, "We want to do base building," and you just use digital tools to get to more people online. But what I saw in the campaign was, yes, you use tech tools and digital tools to get to more people, but it matters how you set it up, what you do with them once they are engaged, and most critically how you actually move them to take action, even if it's virtually. In the campaign, being able to do it to scale where people themselves can volunteer and self-manage their stuff like that was a huge thing for me. I feel like in the unions and worker centers that I work with, everything is either all-volunteer or all staff-run. And when you get to the point where you have staff, you forget about how to build a volunteer base and have volunteers run things. And the scale was just ... I've never seen a scale like that!

Another lesson learned is that we live in a country where there are extreme differences in the ideas and visions of what this country should be. I'm probably not going to articulate it very well, but I've been sitting with thoughts about the people that voted for Trump in 2016 but who then voted for Bernie in 2020. There's something there, and we can't just pretend that didn't happen, you know? The mass mobilization of young voters of color for Bernie, I mean, he's an old white man! They didn't vote for him because of what he looks like, or because they have a lot in common. But the thing that brought us to him was his values and what he's for. I think people underestimated how popular he was going to be with young people of color, even though he's an old white man, but it's because young people of color in this country want the things that he wants.

YJC: Where to even start? The easiest lesson is this: you know who Bernie is, he is honest and has always been honest about what the problems are and what the solutions are. That resonates with people because we all understand that there's massive inequality and that there's a handful of people who are controlling the wealth and therefore have politicians in their pockets. So being able to name that and say exactly what something is, and to lay out what is possible when millions of us come together and organize together, that's something that everybody can understand and I think it is incredibly mobilizing. We should be looking for candidates that are going to be honest about what the problems are, the crisis we face, and what it's going to take to fix them.

It's even more compelling when we say that we want the whole thing. We don't need to compromise away our "we want it all" vision, even if we have to take incrementalist steps to get there. I think politically the lessons from 2016 and 2020 are the same on that front.

You know, the goal of a presidential campaign is pretty simple, which is to win the most votes, win the most delegates, and so from an organizing perspective, you identify voters, convince voters, then turn those people out to vote. We used traditional organizing tactics to do that, but through things like the BERN app we were identifying people that we weren't reaching in any other method of traditional campaign work. The BERN app was our best tool to develop a relational organizing program at scale—it enabled supporters to easily talk to everyone in their phonebook about our campaign and track that data in an easy-to-use way.[5]

I would say the biggest lesson for me personally is that our institutions in the progressive movement are weak. It's not because of our inability to organize, it's because of a decades-long right-wing campaign to break down our unions, break down institutions, and destroy our social safety net. And it was within a week of the Nevada caucus where I thought, "Oh, our institutions are really weak" as we watched the political establishment, the whole structure, as all these former candidates came out and endorsed Biden. It was clear that the establishment was able to move quickly and cohere quickly—which gives them strength.

That's why I'm in the Green New Deal Network now, because we really need to be investing in organizations engaged in long-term power-shifting. Eight years from now, if we have a candidate that sparks the imagination of the American people, we need to have institutions that can support a candidate like that in addition to a campaign that has strong organizing and strong mobilizing capacity. That lesson was reaffirmed when Georgia happened. The run-off election in Georgia was not just a reflection of the zeitgeist: people wanting to elect two Democratic senators and to have an opportunity at a full Democratic trifecta. It was because of the hard work of years of institution-building and leadership development that led to that happening. So, a real focus on institution-building is my personal biggest lesson from 2020.

What were the key challenges or pivotal moments in the campaign?

YJC: I do think that a strong organizational and movement ecosystem is really important for a progressive to win the presidency. It's not to say that there weren't organizations running independent expenditure campaigns and doing turnout and making endorsements and doing the work in the field,[6] but in our movements and the organizations that have come out of those movements, there's still a long way to go in terms of membership, in terms of infrastructure.

AH: The campaign itself dwarfed in size any other campaign, PAC, or independent expenditure committee. Those things existed, but the scale of the campaign created a different set of needs. What did we need from movement infrastructure? I think being able to articulate that more clearly, earlier in the campaign, would have been helpful. So many great organizations jumped in to support and put their own resources into mobilizing in their own ways, which was fantastic and at times a real shot in the arm for those who'd been plugging away, whether they were staff or some of our thousands upon thousands of volunteers.

ND: One question that I've always sat with was, what else could we have done if we'd had a more comprehensive labor strategy? In part because I think that it lived in different places—with the national political team and the different state teams—that were not fully connected. And I do think we had the potential to have a much bigger scale. Just like we ended up doing this kind of ad hoc, interdepartmental team doing the Latinx outreach work on all fronts, I wonder if we could have done the same for labor. I think that was one thing where we had all the ingredients, but we were all doing so much.

YJC: It feels like so long ago, but the pivotal moment of the Bernie campaign was the endorsement from AOC, then the endorsements from Rashida Tlaib and Ilhan Omar. Obviously, these endorsements were important because of the health issues Bernie had in September of 2019, and the summer of 2019 was hard because of a split in progressive forces. In 2016 it was simple and clear because it was Clinton versus Sanders, but the field was much bigger in 2020. The Warren versus Sanders dynamic was challenging to say the least for both campaigns. It's a dynamic that deserves deeper examination.

AH: You could point to a lot of challenges, but I do think the points where it became "Warren versus Bernie" were some of the most painful for many of us on the team. The campaign itself was very disciplined in how we talked about and frankly thought about those questions, but no campaign can control things outside of it—or how they are perceived, and those perceptions can be really damaging, particularly if the media is primed to misinterpret things. We had the deck stacked against us with the mainstream media and a huge swath of the Democratic Party establishment in a way that no other Democratic candidate has since Jesse Jackson, and there are certainly parallels you can see in how our campaigns were treated. Real differences on policy and politics were turned into at best an intra-progressive slap fight, and at worst the bad behavior of a tiny sliver of internet users was magnified into the top political story of the week.

ND: I'll be really frank. This campaign at its center created the opportunity to speak to a broad national audience very clearly about a set of really important issues—economic inequality, the skyrocketing cost of housing, our broken healthcare system—among them, and yet we never talked as clearly about race. I think Bernie did much better talking about immigration than he did about race, frankly. I heard him speak about his own connection as being from an immigrant family, and I think that's why it comes across as authentic and real from him.

AH: Any candidate for president is going to have challenges talking about race—especially with the complex ways that race, class, and gender exist together—and Bernie is no different. We don't have a shared language that can be used effectively at a national level without flattening or oversimplifying that complexity. While that's not a satisfactory answer, and it would be a cop-out to leave it there, it's also all true. On the left, we have work to do that can't possibly be worked out in the middle of a very public presidential campaign. At the same time, I think we never found our footing to talk about race in a personal way. In any campaign there are moments you can jump on and make a leap forward. I think Bernie's call for a moratorium on deportations was one of those leaps that continues to bear fruit to this day, and I'm sure there were other opportunities that we missed. There are challenges stacked on other challenges—staffing, resource allocation, the time and energy and brain-space of the campaign leadership. As big as our campaign was, these things are finite.

What was accomplished that couldn't have happened in another form of organizing? And what are the limits that a presidential campaign puts on the kind of movement-building organizing that you think is important?

ND: Mijente wouldn't have endorsed Bernie if he hadn't said, "I will stop deportations of people, as soon as I become president." That alone will forever change the DNA of how we at Mijente think of our role in a presidential campaign. It's a clear example of when his positions on issues made organizations like ours for the first time ever feel like we had to lean in, and also to feel the excitement of leaning in because this was someone that we could actually roll with and didn't have to compromise. It has opened up this door where you think, "He can't be the only one, there must be more," and I think that's right.

In 2016, Mijente had this realization right after we won in Phoenix to get rid of Arpaio. And then that same night we lost the entire country to Trump. And the next morning, those of us in Arizona, because we were there on the ground, we said to ourselves, "We should have leaned into this presidential campaign. We should have done whatever we needed to do." And we decided we're not going to repeat the same mistake. And then Bernie made it where it was exciting to actually do it.

YJC: More and more, politics is becoming nationalized. A presidential election is the most visible thing in politics for someone who isn't an organizer. And for someone who isn't an organizer, elections are one of the easiest ways of getting involved around issues and the presidential election is the most visible. You are just operating and organizing on a different scale in a presidential election than in any other kind of campaign. So, for instance, if you are doing political education, if that's a part of your campaign, you are doing political education training for people at a scale that you probably have never organized before. Also, the narrative work, doing the persuasion work at that scale is really hard to do in any other kind of movement formation.

AH: The timeline of a presidential primary is not conducive to movement-building. You have these intensive organizing operations focused on a small handful of states for months and months, and then, all of a sudden, you are off and running across dozens of states with millions of voters in a very compressed amount of time. At the same time, you have a ton of attention which cuts in multiple ways—it's hard to aim that attention in the right place and time.

But if you think about movement building more broadly, we were able to create moments of real inspiration. I think of the town halls the campaign did across Iowa on Medicare for All—no one had articulated on a national stage the needs of real everyday people who are hurting, and we were able to give a platform and attention to so many people who were able to talk about their pain and invite others to collectively work toward a solution. We can do town halls all day long outside of the context of a presidential campaign and do very good work but have only limited impact. And I think it's important for us to keep in mind how we are building a movement that lets mass numbers of people share an experience—whether that's the exhilaration of winning a primary or caucus, or the grief that is just below the surface of the policies that we are fighting for.

YJC: There are things that are both challenges and positives, like having a clear end date, and a campaign that's large enough for people to see it as their political home. Once it ends, there aren't really easy places that people can identify as their new political family or community, particularly for a campaign like the Bernie campaign, where some contingent of folks were drawn to Bernie because the Democratic Party in its current form didn't represent them. They were drawn to a vision of a new party or pushing the party to adopt a lot of the policies and values that Bernie was campaigning on. I do think it's important to note that in Nevada after the 2020 election, the Nevada Democratic Party leadership shifted to the point where it is now run by a Bernie supporter, who won her election by beating another Bernie supporter who was a bit closer to the political establishment.

Parties in the US are weak compared to parties in other countries, and we learned that you can help shift the party and what the party stands for a lot through the primary system and also by getting elected into the party infrastructure. And one of the challenges or limitations is that there isn't an easy place for people to plug into long-term—elections are by their nature meant to be short-term organizing vehicles.

Right now, we are seeing a shift in the Democratic Party. One form of that shift is the Congressional Progressive Caucus redefining what it means to be a Democrat. AOC has talked about this a lot, about rooting ourselves in the values of the Democratic Party as a party for working people, and in fighting for working families. So, I think there are opportunities as we continue to organize on this broader vision of an economy and society that works for all of us. Given the current political system, one way to do that is by electing more leaders who are aligned with this broader vision.

Summary

Bernie 2020, like the 2016 campaign that came before it, made clear the value of contesting for power at the highest levels. A national campaign that shows its viability can reach tens of millions, and be a critical lever to push left ideas and programs into the mainstream. A presidential campaign can and should also be a vehicle for recruiting people by the thousands into the ongoing work of movement building. In order to accomplish this, the left and our progressive allies in the labor and community organizing movements need to think creatively about infrastructure. Our organizations, unions, and coalitions can maximize impact and growth by building structures that can bring in new recruits and also help continuously lay the groundwork for the next campaign—including ways to engage with and recruit candidates on the front end, while laying out clear rules of engagement where necessary.

What the 2016 campaign started, the 2020 campaign honed as a model a way of bringing movement energy into a large-scale national political campaign. It developed and advanced organizing methods that have both scale and depth, and it created a political space for activists who are not inclined to participate in electoral politics through the established vehicles. Community and labor-based organizations and networks could benefit from both the organizing methods and the experiences of those who were drawn to left politics through the Bernie campaigns.

Both the 2016 and 2020 campaigns succeeded in surfacing and building on a progressive force both inside and outside the Democratic Party, pushing the center of the party leftward while at the same time helping build forces outside the party willing to work in coalition. Programs like a Green New Deal, a $15 minimum wage, and Medicare for

All have shown their traction with wide swaths of voters, Democrat and independent alike.

There is a lot of talk about who might be "the next Bernie," but that's a construction that manages to be unfair to both Bernie and the next standard bearer for the left/progressive alignment that challenges for the presidency. We'll never again have a candidate of his era, shaped by the New Deal and the civil rights movement, a lone democratic socialist in Congress during the long death of neoliberalism. The movements we are building, the advances these campaigns have helped us to make, and the moment we're in are what will shape the next fight, and the next candidate who can model the slogan: "Not Me, Us."

Notes

The interviews have been edited for clarity.

1. Distributed organizing harnesses the collective energy of geographically dispersed volunteers, using technology, toolkits, and trust to connect people and build relationships at a national campaign scale. According to Tim Ellis, "When volunteers can use technology to quickly plug into a campaign from anywhere and begin meaningfully contributing to the campaign's goal, that's distributed organizing." "The Nuts and Bolts of Distributed Organizing," *Monitor*, June 1, 2021, https://monitormag.ca.

2. Chuck Rocha and Jeff Weaver were senior advisors to the Bernie 2020 campaign.

3. Peter Marks, "Developing BERN, the App That Powered the Largest Relational Organizing In History," Medium, May 25, 2020, https://petermarks.medium.com.

4. Walter Peric, "Nevada's Culinary Union, Bernie Sanders, and Labor's Missed Opportunity," *Nation*, February 18, 2020; Nidhi Prakash, "Members of Nevada's Largest Union Defied Their Leadership to Support Bernie Sanders," Buzzfeed News, February 22, 2020, www.buzzfeednews.com.

5. Peter Marks, "Developing BERN."

6. FEC, "Understanding Independent Expenditures," www.fec.gov.

16

Our Revolution: Everything Depends on Local Organizing

Larry Cohen

Members of the Will County Progressives—the Our Revolution (OR) group in Joliet, Illinois—had gathered at The Drunken Donut to await the results of the March 17, 2020, Democratic primary. The polls had just closed. Our Revolution–endorsed Marie Newman was trailing eight-term incumbent US Rep. Dan Lipinski. But Cook County OR members texted Suzanna Ibarra to let her know that "Marie was just standing there with her arms folded and a big smile on her face," said Ibarra, a member of the Joliet group and co-chair of Our Illinois Revolution. "She knew that Will County had worked our butts off for her, and we had her back." Newman ended up winning by nearly 3,000 votes. "It was 1,000% an upset," Ibarra said. Newman was one of nearly 500 candidates that Our Revolution endorsed in the 2020 election cycle; 76% of them won. OR candidates prevailed in races for everything from school board and highway commission to Congress.

At the national level, through its work for Bernie Sanders, OR helped continue reforms critical to democratizing the Democratic Party. By turning out its voters and cooperating with other groups OR helped defeat President Donald Trump's bid for re-election.

But on the downside, OR and other Sanders supporters couldn't sustain the momentum of his presidential campaign. Some hard-fought local races were lost, like Texas civil rights attorney Mike Siegel's congressional bid.

Beyond the W's and L's, Our Revolution defines success as building sustainable capacity for electoral work and issue campaigns and rebuilding the Democratic Party. Nearly all the nearly 500 endorsements in 2020 began with local or state groups. When we look back at those endorsements, we ask: In how many cases, win or lose, did these groups grow stronger? Conversely, where, and why did local organizations fail after the elections?

As OR Executive Director Joseph Geevarghese said, "OR always evaluates issue and political campaigns first on the likelihood that we can build stronger local powerhouses if we engage." In other words, are these local powerhouses more likely to build capacity for the next campaign if they engage in this one?

We also need to look at how we are building capacity at the state and national level to challenge the rules in our eighteenth-century democracy. It's the rules, not just the rulers, that prevent the US Senate from acting on the $15 minimum wage or voting rights. It's the rules on voting rights and voter registration that hold down turnout in primary and general elections.

Our Revolution history and theory of change

Our Revolution grew out of the local groups that were the backbone of Bernie Sanders' 2016 campaign. Bernie initially lacked the funds for state staffing, and groups of active volunteers preceded the campaign in most states. These groups built turnout for huge events in state after state throughout 2015. As primaries and caucuses approached, campaign staff helped direct the volunteers who canvassed, called, and sent personal text messages. They built support around core issues like Medicare and college for all, criminal justice reform, decent work and a new foreign policy based on human rights. Our Revolution was launched by Bernie in August 2016 in a national video stream to hundreds of locations across the country. Many of the local groups from the campaign, and new ones, formed the basis of the organization. Although we have a board with some high-profile members, the center of gravity is issue work in the local groups.

We're in this to change our lives and be happier, and that happens through the work on issues. They could be local, state, or national. Obviously, we can make more progress on local issues, but national issues have bigger consequences.

We're heavily involved in primary elections, but also general elections and referendums. The third aspect of our work is party-building. That's what we call building and transforming the 57 Democratic Parties and the Democratic National Committee. People think there's one party. There are 57 state and territorial parties, 3,000 county parties, and in some cases, municipal parties. The national Democratic Party exists only at conventions and through the Democratic National Committee.

Local groups are the building blocks of our organization. If they don't thrive, the organization won't—just like a strong union depends on strong locals. If shop stewards are not meeting and mobilizing members of the local, there is no real union there. There might be a union contract, but it's more like a vending machine contract. Similarly, in OR the local group is where members meet, even if on Zoom during COVID. You have friends. You get a pizza, have a coffee, walk a neighborhood, build connections.

The biggest change in OR capacity since 2016 has been the build-out of state hubs. Initially the focus was on a more elaborate state structure in several states—Massachusetts, Maryland, Texas, and Wisconsin. The relatively small national staff, led by Executive Director Joseph Geevarghese, has built hubs of local groups and organizers in 27 states over the last four years. These groups have made a real difference in issue and electoral work and at times in state party change.

We support our state and local work by holding national organizing meetings every Monday evening on Zoom. Typically, 5,000 people attend, some on video and some calling in. Coupled with the weekly OR email newsletter, members get a real sense of organizing across the US.

OR's 2020 electoral work occurred in several phases. First, the presidential and other primaries. Then, mobilizing convention delegates around rules and platform, and finally, turnout for November 3 and the Georgia US Senate runoff elections.

National elections: mobilizing for Bernie

Our Revolution's support for Sanders 2020 was overwhelming once Bernie decided to run in March 2019. We carried out our work in the primaries independent of the Sanders campaign, as legally required for a membership-based organization. We focused on mobilizing our several million supporters. We had our own lists and volunteers and hired additional staff for several of the key primaries.

Preparing for the February 3 Iowa caucuses, we focused on the deindustrialized counties on the east side of the state along the Mississippi River, including Davenport and Bettendorf and Burlington. We worked out of union halls, and had volunteers calling our members and knocking on doors to build turnout. Manufacturing job loss has hit the area hard, and Bernie had a convincing record on fighting for jobs and against bad trade deals for decades. He emerged with more votes than any other candidate in the caucuses, but because of the way Iowa allocates delegates, he won slightly fewer than Pete Buttigieg.

Most of OR's work on the New Hampshire primary was done on the phones, by calling and texting. We were only aiming to turn out our people, and texting was actually more effective and less intrusive. Bernie won with 25.6%, just ahead of Pete Buttigieg with 24.3%.

OR viewed the February 29 South Carolina primary mostly as an opportunity to mobilize our supporters and strengthen the local organization. We did this by leading with Medicare for All. Nina Turner spent a lot of time in the state for the Bernie campaign, but the Democratic Party machine turned out the Biden vote. In the end, the difference was Biden compared to all the other candidates. He ended up with 48.65% of the vote, and Bernie came in second with 19.77%. No one else got any delegates.

After South Carolina, we saw the hand of Barack Obama. He was instrumental in getting Buttigieg and Klobuchar to drop out just before Super Tuesday. Some people thought Biden would be better at beating Trump, and some didn't want Bernie no matter what. And there was the whole dynamic of Bernie and Elizabeth Warren. The only way either of them would have been nominated is if they collaborated, and that never happened.

Still, Bernie came within 13 delegates of winning Texas. "It's painful how close we were," said Kristi Lara, a national organizer for OR based in Texas. Bernie's message resonated in the state with its populist tradition. "LBJ, Sam Rayburn, Jim Hightower, all ran on populist ideals. In 2016 we were seeing a lot of positive response. People trusted Bernie. We were hoping to build on that in 2020." Two polls taken close to the election showed him ahead.[1]

But the Sanders campaign had lagged on sending staff into Texas. OR took up phone banking and block walking, as did other groups like the Sunrise Movement and the Democratic Socialists of America. The campaign, when it did arrive, held major rallies after the deadline for voter registration had passed. Only registered voters can vote in the Texas Democratic primary, and they must complete registration by 30 days prior to the election to be eligible to vote.

Bernie toured Texas less than two weeks before the primary, drawing large and enthusiastic crowds—but missed the opportunity to sign up new voters. This was also true of the Biden campaign, but by Super Tuesday President Obama and most of the major candidates had united behind the former vice president. For example, on election eve former candidate Beto O'Rourke was by Biden's side when he campaigned in Texas.

"Our message is a winning message," Lara said. "It does cross the lines as far as traditional political belief systems. It invigorates and encourages young voters. It's powerful in and of itself, but we have to be strategic. We have to understand the structures that are in place that are trying to stop us."

In the primaries through Wisconsin, we mobilized our people to show up and vote for Bernie. Wisconsin has a large Our Revolution supporter list. In the chaotic April 7 primary, Bernie won about 32% of the vote, compared to 63% for Biden.

Bernie's April 8 decision to suspend his campaign marked a low point for morale in OR. But even after the withdrawal, we continued to campaign for Bernie. Primaries determine the selection of convention delegates, and have consequences for the internal dynamics of the state parties. Both are important to the work of building a popular, movement-based Democratic Party.

It was obviously much harder to turn out Bernie voters without Bernie. The pandemic meant that only phones, email, and text were available to mobilize our voters. OR did not raise money for mailers or paid media. Convention delegates are only awarded to candidates who get at least 15% of the votes in a state. Once that threshold is met, delegates are proportional. We failed the 15% threshold in Maryland, even though it is a big Our Revolution state. We missed it by a fraction in Rhode Island. We hit it in New York, even though Gov. Andrew Cuomo tried to cancel the primary.

Delegate numbers were important, since without one-third of the delegates we could not bring issues on the party's rules or platform to the floor. In 2016 Bernie had more than one-third. This led to a process of reforming party rules, which included limiting the role of so-called "superdelegates" in the nominating process. (Superdelegates are not bound to follow the voters' will. They are governors and members of Congress, members of the Democratic National Committee, or other notable party members.)

In 2020, despite OR's continuing efforts, Bernie finished with about 1,100 delegates, shy of the one-third needed to ensure a decisive role on platform and rules, but enough to negotiate. As a Rules Committee member, I was able to help negotiate the only resolution passed by the convention. Resolution 1 provided for a continuation in 2024 of the reforms adopted in 2020. Bernie delegates on the Platform Committee were able to reach agreement on healthcare reforms that fell short of Medicare for All but included sharp cuts in pharma prices and lowering the age on Medicare. Similar proposals on the environment, a $15 minimum wage, and cutting student debt all continue to provide the basis for federal reform efforts in the Congress despite narrow Democratic majorities.

Defeating Trump

OR messaging in the general election was all about defeating the lying Donald Trump. While the 2020 Democratic Party platform was a compromise with many positions from the Sanders campaign, unity was based on preventing four more years of Trump. We focused on the industrial swing states of Wisconsin, Michigan, Iowa, and Pennsylvania. Within those states, we zeroed in on heavily working-class counties. Most of our work was focused on turnout of our own supporters and their families. Because of COVID-19, most of the volunteers did computer assisted calling and personal texting. We held state-based Zoom calls to build the volunteer lists.

OR emphasized Trump's lies on jobs, particularly in industrial states where Trump promised to keep plants open—from Lordstown to Carrier—and then did little or nothing. We weren't the Biden campaign, so we could focus on Trump lies. We had people show up at Trump-Pence events with signs reading "Trump lied about our jobs." We had an event at a Siemens factory in Burlington, Iowa, where Trump had gone in 2016 and said, 'Don't worry about your jobs,' and then the plant had shut down. Laid-off workers from GM's Lordstown, Ohio, factory attended events, saying Trump had told them not to sell their houses and now they were out of work. In Indianapolis, the Carrier plant was a focus. During the 2016 campaign, Trump promised to save jobs at the plant; after the election, he made a deal with the company that was supposed to stop offshoring, but only a fraction of the plant is still operating.

Fighting plant closings and organizing for a $15 minimum wage have always been major OR issues. While we probably didn't change a lot of voters' minds, we did help boost turnout. Particularly in Michigan, where the outcome was so close, that focus did matter. Obviously we didn't flip Ohio, so we have to be clear about scale in a presidential election. It's very hard to impact swing voters, but organizing can impact turnout. And in places that were going for Trump, organizing can make a difference in local elections. In the general election, OR concentrated on state and local races.

State and local elections

In 2020, Our Revolution made endorsements in nearly 500 state and local races across 30 states. We won more than three-fourths of those. Some of those victories came at the city level. For example, Baltimore elected a member of an OR group to the city council and picked the OR-endorsed candidates for mayor and comptroller. Ann Arbor, Michigan, elected an OR candidate to its school board. OR-endorsed candidates carried numerous state legislative contests, including 37 in Connecticut, 18 in Illinois, 20 in Minnesota, and 7 in South Carolina. OR-backed state ballot measures won in several states, including a Colorado initiative favoring paid family leave, Florida's $15 minimum wage, and drug law reforms in Montana, Oregon, New Jersey, and Washington, DC. We also backed several successful candidates for Congress, including first-timers Rep. Cori Bush from St. Louis and Rep. Marie Newman from Illinois.

We owe our success to smart targeting and hard work by staff and volunteers. Most of the local groups aren't interested in insane missions. We say there's no point in doing elections if we don't have a 50% chance of winning. We can build the group without getting suckered into an election where we get slaughtered.

If local groups want national OR endorsements, they have to show that the campaign will build the group, and commit to getting volunteers to work on the campaign. Most do, because with the national endorsement they get tools for phone calls and mass texts, materials, and access to a sizable email list. And where we do get involved, we can make a difference in who the Democrats are as a party. Will County was a case in point.

In Will County, Illinois, Suzanna Ibarra, Richard Rodriguez, and the other OR members had been building their chapter since 2016. Both the local work and statewide organizing support helped elect Marie Newman to Congress from Illinois District 3.

Newman had given Dan Lipinski the toughest fight of his political career in 2018, but she lost. "As hard as you think you're working, it takes 100 times more effort. It's not for the faint of heart," Ibarra said. OR set their sights on 2020.

Lipinski had held the seat for 8 terms, his father before him for 11. He was a DINO—"Democrat in Name Only"—opposed to women's right to choose and LGBTQ people's right to marry, to the Affordable Care Act and the Deferred Action for Childhood Arrivals (DACA) program.

Still, unseating him took a combination of relentless door-knocking and direct action to expose some of his more extreme positions. In January 2020, for example, the congressman signed on to a Republican-sponsored amicus brief asking the Supreme Court to uphold Louisiana's strict anti-abortion laws. OR organized a petition signed by members of 48 groups representing a half-million women in Illinois—and a sit-in at the rotunda of the building where Lipinski had his Lockport office. They raised a ruckus until he committed to answering to them about his views.

That same month, the state OR hub had formed at a summit that also included members of other progressive groups, among them the Democratic Socialists of America, the Progressive Democrats of Illinois (PDA), and Black Lives Matter of Will County. "Our different local groups are like fingers on a hand," Ibarra said. "The state group is like an arm. We're stronger together." This proved especially true in Newman's race, because the congressional district spills over three counties.

Newman's primary win pitted her against a Trump Republican in the general election, so OR switched strategies. They put aside the political theater and focused on what Ibarra called "kitchen table topics, like being strong on unions and transportation and infrastructure." With a crew of 30 to 50 volunteers, they concentrated on visiting, calling, and texting to turn out the reliable Democratic voters.

Texas, on the other hand, showed us a much more mixed picture. Texas is another strong Our Revolution state. OR endorsed 37 candidates in state and local races, and 17 won. Several of the people we backed helped lead the Democrats in walking out of the state legislature to block attacks on voting rights in 2021. Newly elected Jasmine Crockett was among them.

Crockett's Dallas district was both a stronghold for Black Lives Matter and a strong Bernie district. A team of about 10 people called a list of about 1,000 OR supporters and Bernie voters three times. In smaller races, Bernie voters can make a difference, because they can be independents and infrequent voters. "If we build relationships with them, they will vote," Kristi Lara said. "We explain that this person is part of the progressive movement, can we count on you?"

But in general, not being able to do the kind of intense door-to-door work that powered Marie Newman's win hurt the Texas efforts. "We saw a 'red wave' in the South, and Texas in particular. Voter turnout increased for their side," Lara said. Concern about spreading COVID -19 led many Democrats to opt out of door-knocking. "You could see the recipe for loss. As Democrats, populists, progressives, if we intend to win, we have to have a field program that includes canvassing. I hate that we have to keep learning this."

Congressional candidate Mike Siegel was among those burned by the lack of direct voter contact. The civil rights attorney lost by a wider margin than he had in his 2018 campaign. Structural obstacles affected both his races. Texas "has a horrific history of gerrymandering," Lara commented. CD 10, where Siegel ran, stretches from the west side of Austin through deep-red rural areas to the western suburbs of Houston—a drive of more than two and a half hours, taking in parts of nine counties.

Such obstacles only reinforce the need to master the mechanics of elections. OR is a new organization. We're learning. In Texas, Lara said,

"OR candidates are running in a party without a culture of mobilizing. And the lists that they're using aren't accurate. Canvassers are being sent to doors with Trump flags flying. Every time you turn out the opposition there's a problem. The data isn't just wrong, it's foul. It sets up first-time and rural candidates to fail. But we are becoming more sophisticated. We can tell from campaigns. Our candidates that barely lost were running strategic campaigns."

In the Georgia US Senate runoff elections, we mobilized our list of 30,000 OR supporters statewide, working with state and national volunteers, and strong local groups in suburban Atlanta and Savannah. Organizing mechanics were well practiced. We helped voters follow through with the three-step process they had to navigate to vote by mail: request a ballot, fill it out, and mail it back.

Reflections on 2020

The 2020 cycle nationalized much of OR local election activity. Starting with the Iowa caucus, we promoted turnout not only with local groups but also national volunteers. Unlike many other organizations, we had no paid callers. Our calls went out to the large OR supporter lists in most key primary states. Supporter lists were built from prior electoral and issue work. This is the strength of OR electoral work—a strong base of volunteers is calling virtually all supporters and focusing just on turnout. This makes a huge difference, since turnout is so low in most US elections.

Since the 2020 election, OR's congressional strategy has depended on the Congressional Progressive Caucus. Chair Pramila Jayapal (D-WA) has led the effort to adopt tougher caucus rules, and now membership requires compliance with caucus positions on at least two-thirds of the issues. There are 94 caucus members, a significant percentage of the 222 Democrats in the Congress. OR groups are willing to challenge Democratic incumbents in primaries who do not support the Progressive Caucus positions. Most Democrats are elected in districts where the primary is potentially the only real contest. This takes the connection of electoral and issue work to a much higher level. With our allies we work with the caucus on positions that then define the basis of support in future congressional elections.

At the state and local government levels, OR groups and state networks are similarly linking issues and electoral work. Replicating the strategy of the Congressional Progressive Caucus in a state legislature or city council may not be formalized, but similar scorecards on key issues will drive future electoral work. The challenge is sustaining political activity beyond an election. Can we build a movement that is about governing? Not talking, not just policy, but governing and living happier lives? One of the reasons why elections aren't more successful in our country is that people don't see their happiness increasing by their political activity, even if their political activity is limited to voting. We've got a long way to go to figure out what politics is in a meaningful way. We have more elections than anywhere else, and it's not clear that they're helping us build anything, beyond the ego and esteem of the candidates.

Candidate addiction is in part real and in part driven by the difficulty in sustaining organizing on a volunteer basis. Money in politics in the US is a real sewer, and it drives far too many outcomes in both parties, but sustaining volunteer activity is not an easy alternative. OR continues to look for new ways to sustain our work, like the weekly Monday night national Zoom calls with an average of 5,000 attending and a great mix of candidates, electeds, issue leaders, and organizers presenting. Replicating these calls on a state basis requires a mix of good presenters and organizers for the Zoom and an effective state action program. State activity ebbs and flows, unless charged by a big issue campaign or a candidate like Nina Turner for Congress.

For Our Revolution, the 2020 election was significant, not only in defeating Trump, but also in building a more resilient and better prepared OR for the years ahead. There was a feeling of electoral success, some movement on issues, and a continuing emphasis on party reform. These are key elements in building a popular democratic movement, while recognizing that these changes can be reversed unless organizing can continue to increase supporters, create new allies, and inspire us all to move forward.

Marcy Rein contributed writing and reporting to this chapter.

Notes

1. Patrick Svitek, "A Confident Bernie Sanders Barnstorms Texas with Burst of Momentum," *Texas Tribune,* February 23, 2020.

17

Democratic Socialists and the US Presidency in the Neoliberal Era

David Duhalde

DSA in 2020: From the thick of it to the sidelines

Thousands of Democratic Socialists of America members poured tens of thousands of hours into electoral work in 2020, and their collective efforts were an important factor in Bernie Sanders' bid for the presidency. DSA members also contributed—in some cases decisively—to the victories won by progressive and socialist candidates running for local and state office, and several seats in the House of Representatives. During the course of these efforts the organization continued the explosive growth it experienced beginning in 2016, reaching over 87,000 members by the end of 2020.

When it came to the main event however—the fight to deny Donald Trump and the racist authoritarian bloc behind him a second term in the White House—DSA as an organization officially sat on the sidelines. As the largest and fastest growing socialist organization in the United States, the decision to sit out of one of the most consequential presidential elections in decades had reverberations throughout the left, as well as within its own ranks.

It caused confusion, led to criticism, and provided no clear direction to thousands of potential volunteers. It may also have created tensions with other parts of the left. It meant DSA did not connect itself to any of the formal anti-Trump coalitions or informal alignments that involved the overwhelming bulk of progressive groups and individuals—especially in the labor movement and communities of color. While some of those formations gained influence and credibility among working-class people and communities of color who joined the effort to defeat Trump, DSA squandered the opportunity to do the same. Only some of that damage was mitigated by the decision to take part in the US Senate runoff election in Georgia in January 2021.

The reasons for the decision to not endorse and help elect Biden are not simple. It did not flow from the organization or its leadership being united on a particular view about how US-based socialists relate to electoral politics and mass movements. The reality behind DSA's decision lies in a wider series of external events confronting a group facing unprecedented membership growth and untested internal processes. The decision must also be contextualized within the history of how DSA has handled White House candidacies since 1980, and in the political evolution of the organization's membership. Especially important are the ways that internal decisions leading up to the organizational endorsement of Sanders during the primary race run set the conditions for a "Bernie or Bust" resolution without proper consideration of the possible consequences.

In the fraught period ahead, neither DSA nor the broader left can afford to repeat these kinds of mistakes. Although the decision was a political error, the events that unfolded afterwards offer lessons that will serve DSA and the left. This article is my attempt to tell that story and draw out those lessons.[1]

DSA and presidential elections, 1980-2012
The evolution of DSA's presidential endorsements since 1980 informed how the group landed at a nonendorsement in the 2020 general presidential election. Regardless of what those who support and critique DSA's 2020 decision say, both sides exaggerate how much a nonendorsement strayed from DSA's previous stances. Still, the choice in 2019 to pre-empt

any possible endorsement of a Democrat other than Sanders later down the line was unprecedented for DSA and its predecessor organizations.

DSA was birthed in 1982, out of the merging of two socialist organizations—the Democratic Socialist Organizing Committee (DSOC) and the New American Movement (NAM).[2] Leading up to the 1980 presidential election, DSOC led a coalition project dubbed the "Democratic Agenda" that brought together labor and other mass organizations. Their goal was to curtail rising neoliberalism and defend a New Deal coalition on its last legs by backing Senator Ted Kennedy in his bid to wrest the Democratic nomination from incumbent President Jimmy Carter. They were unsuccessful, and after President Carter secured the party nomination, he went on to lose to Ronald Reagan. DSOC—much as DSA would do 40 years later—did not endorse a candidate for the general election after Kennedy lost the nomination.

DSA went in nearly the opposite direction in 1984 and endorsed the consensus pick of Walter Mondale—Carter's former vice president and running mate in 1980—in the general election after making no endorsement in the primary.[3] Jesse Jackson ran in the primaries that year, and the decision to not endorse the progressive movement candidate was reflective of some demographic traits and political choices of early 1980s DSA. The organization remained heavily white and with a large Jewish membership that prioritized relationships with labor leaders. Jesse Jackson's sympathies for Palestinians and reported anti-Semitic comments did not help him, but neither did a DSA leadership generally unconnected to Black and other people of color–led social movements.

When Jesse Jackson ran again in 1988 at the tail end of Reagan's presidency, DSA enthusiastically joined his campaign efforts along with many other progressives, socialists, and communists. He won three times as many delegates as in 1984, and the relative success of his campaign and the Rainbow Coalition gave hope to many that a multiracial national movement could spring from his campaign. However, the lack of a democratic Rainbow organization, Jackson's own personal agenda, and other factors dampened hopes about a new democratic alliance against racial capitalism.[4] Jackson would go on to lose the Democratic nomination, and Reagan's vice president, George H.W. Bush, would go on to win the 1988 presidential race.

The fortunes of DSA and the broader left steadily declined from the Reagan era into the Bill Clinton administration. In 1992, Clinton became the first Democratic president since Carter, and rose to power championing a "Third Way" politics that blended socially liberal and fiscally conservative policies, reflecting the rightward shift in the country and growing neoliberal hegemony.[5] DSA's influence, already waning from the mid-1980s, further sank through the 1990s and early 2000s. During this entire period, DSA did not endorse presidential candidates, partly because of the lack of major presidential candidates that challenged neoliberal hegemony in the White House.

In 2000, Ralph Nader's candidacy for president on the progressive Green Party ticket inspired millions of votes. However, DSA did not endorse him either. The organization lacked unity and many members thought that Al Gore—Bill Clinton's vice president and Democratic nominee for the presidential race—would obviously prevail. George Bush Jr.'s victory was a wake-up call to many that conditions could get even worse.

Four years later in 2004, after DSA membership was largely divided between Howard Dean or Dennis Kucinich in the Democratic primaries, John Kerry won the nomination and DSA promptly endorsed him in the general election. It was the organization's first presidential endorsement in 16 years. Although Kerry was hardly progressive, DSA believed that he was the only candidate who could defeat Bush in the general election, and that was top priority. Many members went to work to elect Kerry or to unseat Bush.[6] Hardly any members actively supported Ralph Nader's independent run that year, drawing lessons from 2000, when many believed that Nader split Democratic votes and was partially responsible for Bush's victory. This experience is important because it mirrors the conditions in 2020 in some important ways, and a much smaller and very different DSA chose a different path than they would 16 years later.

Kerry lost that election, but after making our first endorsement since 1988, DSA would take some critical steps to modernize its electoral structures including getting a political action committee (PAC) so it could spend money on federal races.

After an eight-year Bush presidency that launched endless wars, DSA and other left formations threw their weight behind Barack Obama's historic campaign. Although Obama was masterful at using social movement rhetoric and building a multiracial electoral coalition, his time in power did not break with neoliberalism and DSA declined to re-endorse him in 2012. DSA did however publicly state that his re-election would be better than the victory of his Republican challenger, Mitt Romney.[7]

The 2016 election and the Sanders era

At the end of Obama's two-term presidency, DSA still had not endorsed a presidential contender in the primaries since 1988. Bernie Sanders would soon change that. Once the senator from Vermont began sending out feelers to test his viability as a candidate, groups like DSA and the Progressive Democrats of America (PDA) began circulating petitions urging him to run for president. While on the surface, the self-described democratic socialist seemed like an obvious candidate for DSA to rally behind, there were a few other factors that led to our support.

First, even before Sanders' run, there was a renewed and growing interest in socialism across the country. The devastation brought on by the 2008 financial crisis, growing inequality, the increasing inability of neoliberal policies to meet the material needs of people, and the far distant memory of the Cold War and anti-Soviet propaganda were among many factors that contributed to a growing openness to alternatives to capitalism, especially among younger people. In addition, eight years of right-wing attacks and labeling of Obama as a socialist not only had zero detrimental effect on his reelection, but those attacks arguably backfired as his moderate policies defanged the foreign specter of "socialism" in the eyes of many, especially with the working-class people of color who supported him and were the target of socialist organizations like DSA.

Lastly, campaign finance laws had changed significantly since DSA's first major support of Sanders' Senate run in 2007. The Supreme Court ruling in *Citizens United*[8] greatly expanded the ability of nonprofit organizations with a 501(c)(4) designation such as DSA to spend money supporting specific candidates during campaign season.[9] This gave DSA more freedom to independently support a candidate in whatever way and with whatever messaging we chose than if we coordinated with the candidate's official campaign.

DSA launched a supportive independent expenditure operation called "We Need Bernie" that engaged chapters and brought in new members throughout 2015 and 2016.[10] The decision to do that was brought forward by DSA's National Political Committee (NPC), and won widespread approval at the 2015 national convention. This was partly because of Sanders' political stances, but also because of his prior relationship with DSA since our support of his 2006 Senate race.[11]

While Sanders' 2006 US Senate candidacy brought some press coverage and helped slightly grow the membership, DSA continued to be of only very limited political relevance. For several years, DSA hardly broke 6,000 dues-paying members. After Bernie lost the primary election in 2016, DSA unsurprisingly declined to endorse Clinton by name but embraced the "Dump Trump" effort.[12] Few of us imagined he would win, but correctly saw his authoritarian streak and attacks on the voting rights of communities of color, among other threats, as extremely dangerous. His surprise Electoral College victory shocked the progressive world to its core, and his presidency quickly proved to be just as scary and dangerous as his campaign was. This horror sparked thousands of new activists, especially millennials, to join organizations like DSA, PDA, and new formations like Our Revolution and Indivisible in droves.[13] This crowd of new socialists and radicals transformed DSA. After the inauguration and the Women's March in January 2017, it was clear that progressives were mobilizing at an unprecedented scale.

The next few years would see DSA's numbers swell into the tens of thousands, but what was more important was how the character of

DSA changed with this influx of new members. The influx ranged from experienced leftists coming from other anti-capitalist formations to the newly introduced to socialism who lacked any background in the left movement and its history. This change in the size and character of DSA is crucial to understanding how the "Bernie or Bust" resolution came to pass, and how we eventually declined to throw the full weight of the organization into the 2020 general election.

It is important to note that after 2016's loss, while Sanders and organizations like Our Revolution focused a lot of their work on efforts to reform Democratic Party structures and processes—especially after controversy around the party's 2016 presidential primaries and super-delegates—DSA remained absent from these struggles. After our 2017 convention, we began shifting away from our legacy of intra-Democratic Party work to begin supporting the formation of a new workers party. This dynamic is critical to understand as it was a harbinger of how DSA could appear much more in lockstep with Bernie than was actually true.

The road to 'Bernie or Bust'

The broader history of DSA endorsements laid out up to this point makes it clear that DSA has not consistently endorsed presidential candidates in primary or general elections. Sometimes we did the former and a few more times we did the latter, but most often we endorsed no one at all. People on all sides of the debate surrounding our 2020 nonendorsement of Biden have falsely made it seem like DSA had a long history of either formally endorsing or informally backing the Democratic nominee. This misunderstanding inaccurately colored the debate throughout 2020.

DSA's ultimate backing of Sanders' second presidential run started in 2018 when the national organization and its chapters began having discussions about an endorsement. Although the external perception might have been that DSA was fully behind the race before Sanders declared, this was not the case. The hesitation from DSA members to re-endorse Sanders were multifaceted, but all were rooted in the fact that this organization was different from the one that had backed him in 2016.

Some members felt that throwing down in the presidential elections would overextend DSA's capacity, and that new formations like Our Revolution could handle it on their own, especially since many DSA members would volunteer as individuals anyway. Others felt that Sanders had missed the mark on sex worker rights by voting for the anti-sex-trafficking legislation SESTA-FOSTA and disliked his foreign policy positions.[14] Sanders' consistently poor showing with African American voters and disconnect from surging Black social movements also caused some supporters in DSA to wonder if he had learned anything from 2016.

We also knew that Sanders could not win without his grassroots base, which DSA was a very important part of, and DSA would have been marginalized if we didn't endorse his campaign. If we supported Sanders, we had to figure out how to do so while being clear about the differences between his social democratic program and our democratic socialist vision.[15] We did not have unity around how to demarcate that difference while still supporting him.

Organizationally, the new DSA also lacked any consensus on how to select a presidential campaign to get behind. Historically, only the National Political Committee (NPC) would determine a handful of national endorsements. By 2016, DSA had developed an internal culture and process where major endorsements came from local chapters, so that endorsements were more democratic and had local buy-in.[16] After local chapters vetted and nominated candidates, a National Electoral Committee made up of volunteers from around the country would analyze the races further, and eventually the National Political Committee would decide whether to endorse the candidate. Chapters could only nominate candidates running in their jurisdiction, which was determined by assigning zip codes to every chapter. Notably, under this new process, DSA's Vermont chapter did not submit Bernie Sanders' 2018 US Senate race for an endorsement and the National Political Committee quietly acquiesced.

However, this process applied only to local and state races, and we still lacked a formal method for endorsing national candidates. For decades, the de facto practice was that the NPC would make presidential endorsements without any clear process that incorporated chapter input. In 2015, the convention resoundingly reaffirmed that body's decision to back Sanders. However, three years later when we started having discussions about backing Sanders' 2020 run, DSA had grown and changed. Members were more accustomed to having input in endorsements, and had practice through the local endorsement process outlined above. Leadership understood this, and had to balance these new expectations and culture with a tight timeline.

DSA's national convention is where the decision to endorse Sanders was supposed to happen, but that was slated for August 2019, less than a year before the primary elections would take place. If a decision wasn't made until then, DSA would miss valuable time needed to prepare for its independent expenditure operation. Given how slow things moved in the volunteer-led and short-staffed organization, the desire to endorse before the convention made sense. A compromise was reached that DSA would send a poll to all members asking if we should endorse Sanders. The results of this poll would inform the NPC in their decision-making process.

At a late January 2019 NPC meeting, they voted 10 to 3 to form an exploratory committee to begin the process to endorse Sanders. They told the membership:

> Included in this announcement will be a political rationale for why we are considering Bernie Sanders and no other candidate in the Democratic primaries. This rationale will make clear that we are not rubber-stamping Sanders, but instead that we have high demands on him politically, and that we will push Sanders towards our positions as much as possible.[17]

A few days later, the poll went out via email and about a quarter of DSA's then roughly 53,000 members voted. Nearly 75% of the voters supported backing Sanders. The NPC interpreted this as buy-in to back Bernie ahead of the upcoming biennial convention. While the NPC had promised that the upcoming preconvention gatherings would still debate backing Sanders, they voted to endorse before all those gatherings could be completed. The fact that the poll offered no alternative to Sanders alongside the endorsement being made before the debates at the preconvention gatherings could take place left a sour taste in some members' mouths.

So much of this situation was unprecedented. The scale of our decision-making process and expectations around engagement from DSA membership in 2019 had no parallel in our organization's history. At the time this was taking place, I was the political director at Our Revolution, and we endorsed Sanders almost immediately after he announced his candidacy. I stayed away from commenting on DSA's process because of my role at Our Revolution, but privately, I thought the process chosen was a poor one. I have since contended that DSA should have built an endorsement process that incorporated its rules for a special convention as outlined in our constitution. In that scenario, chapters representing a certain percentage of the membership can call for a national gathering to address whatever issue they deem important. It would have been better to encourage chapters to nominate presidential candidates for the NPC to consider. It is hard to imagine such a mass of chapters or members not choosing Bernie, but they would have had the option between him and other candidates inside and outside the Democratic Party.

By the time that DSA's August 2019 convention rolled around, the NPC had already endorsed Sanders and we had already launched our independent expenditure operation under the banner of "DSA for Bernie". The "Bernie or Bust" resolution—formally called the "In the Event of a Sanders Loss" resolution—began circulating ahead of the convention. Some DSA members in swing states signed a letter against it. A handful of members, including myself, also spoke on the floor against it. We argued that it would prematurely tie the organization's hands in the event of complex scenarios such as Sanders getting a vice presidential nod. Supporters of the resolution contended that we should aim high and that planning for these other scenarios meant we were giving up ahead of time. On all sides of the debate, we could not overcome the resounding feelings that the only endorsement a socialist organization could make would be for Bernie Sanders.

The resolution overwhelmingly passed at the convention. This vote outcome formally meant that DSA would only back one Democrat in the primary or general election: Bernie Sanders. Many of the supporters of the proposal would not realize its far-reaching effects until much later. It hurt DSA's ability to work with other mass organizations during the general election, and paralyzed the organization around the general presidential election as the COVID-19 pandemic, surging mobilizations against police violence, and growing right-wing violence changed the political landscape in unforeseeable ways.

'DSA for Bernie' and the general election

Once the NPC made the decision to endorse Sanders back in March 2019, DSA launched an independent expenditure operation in its support of Sanders' 2020 run under the banner of "DSA for Bernie." The independent expenditure was a distinct legal body that was technically separate from DSA, but obviously connected and coordinated.

In order to carry out this massive independent electoral effort, DSA would have to spend serious resources. The proposal to spend $100,000 on access to voter databases and staffing for "DSA for Bernie" proved controversial because we have limited resources as a smaller, nonprofit organization, and our members have strong and opposing opinions about how that money should be spent. One of the selling points was that DSA could keep data on volunteers and voters in order to plug them into our longer-term work after the election. This investment of DSA resources could then help the organization expand its reach both in the short and long term, especially in areas where the Sanders campaign didn't have a physical presence. In the end, after much deliberation and discussion, "DSA for Bernie" got the fiscal support it needed from the organization.

The nature of the presidential primaries made it so that the first few states to vote required nearly all the Sanders campaign's attention. This provided an opportunity for DSA to be one of the main mobilizers of Bernie supporters in states where the campaign could not dedicate much of its early time, such as California, Texas, and Massachusetts. DSA, maybe more than any other non-union group, led Sanders volunteers on canvasses and phonebanks in those places. In the end, "DSA for Bernie" had huge metric success, although we felt that we didn't do enough to support building power with local organizations in the places we operated. Overall, "DSA for Bernie" engaged with 91 out of 199 chapters to knock on 576,000 doors, identified 40,000 Bernie supporters, and gained over 15,000 members during the campaign.[18]

DSA's investment in internal infrastructure and the independent campaign helped Sanders' showing in the primaries and helped our organization grow. DSA did not just work alone, but also collaborated with the coalition People Power for Bernie.[19] This alliance was made up of some of the movement nonprofits that backed Sanders in 2016 and new additions such as Sunrise Movement, Our Revolution, and Dream Defenders. The formation stayed together after the primary, although DSA exited once Bernie lost.

In April 2020, Bernie Sanders lost the Democratic primary elections for the second time in four years. This time, however, he was much more ready to enthusiastically endorse his opponent, partially because the stakes were so much higher. Donald Trump was mishandling the COVID-19 pandemic by denying basic science and allowing countless deaths; emboldening and encouraging right-wing violence, and showing no commitment to respecting the democratic will of voters in November should he lose. These and other compounding crises gave massive pressure for groups to rally behind the Democratic nominee despite their hesitations over Joe Biden.

Biden was a deeply flawed candidate for the left to rally around under normal circumstances. He was frozen in time, and was steadfast against the issues that were dearest to Bernie supporters, such as Medicare for

All and student debt cancellation. Like his Democratic predecessor Barack Obama, Biden also seemed uninterested in courting the Left's vote, and was happy to leave that work to Sanders and other prominent progressives.

DSA was very influential, and big, so there was lots of outside pressure to break with our resolution and endorse Biden. I knew that the National Political Committee would not overturn the will of the convention. One important consideration that was missing from all sides of the debate was that Joe Biden did not want a DSA endorsement. Both the DSA members who did not want to endorse him and the comrades who did seemed to avoid the assessment that an endorsement might actually hurt him. Biden was interested in appealing to the center, not the left, and a socialist stamp of approval could have undermined his campaign strategy. The degree to which the debates around an endorsement avoided this led me to believe the debates were much more about public posturing than actual political assessments.

The essential point was that once Bernie dropped out of the race and endorsed Biden, DSA did little—if anything—to mobilize against a Trump presidency. In public statements, DSA was critical of both Biden and Trump while admitting that Trump was worse,[20] but the NPC lacked any mandate or consensus to overturn the resolution. DSA then declined to stay on the People Power for Bernie coalition as it rebranded to the United Against Trump coalition, even as they hired former Sanders 2020 labor coordinator and prominent DSA member Jonah Furman to staff the alliance. In May, the NPC voted down board members of the Socialist Majority Caucus (which I was a part of) in their effort to push chapters in swing states to consider discussions about voting for Biden.[21] Jennifer Bolen, an NPC member, summed up the majority stance when she wrote that the effort "violated the spirit" of the "Bernie or Bust" resolution and "sound[ed] like an endorsement" of Biden.[22] So while the rest of the left and progressives began struggling with the real choice between Trump and Biden, DSA was frozen. DSA even abstained from efforts framed only around defeating Trump because many argued that those efforts were de facto pro-Biden, since he was the only candidate that could beat Trump.

It was one thing for DSA not to endorse Biden. That was predictable and consistent with previous actions. Declining to do anything related to the general presidential election had dire consequences and was the wrong decision.

On April 12, 2020, DSA tweeted "We are not endorsing Joe Biden."[23] It went viral, amassing over 16,000 retweets and 90,000 likes. Our Revolution, on the other hand, also did not endorse Joe Biden but made no such public proclamation about their decision. Providing no information of what the organization would actually do besides not backing Biden left DSA open to criticism from other leftists and from moderate and right-wing critics. DSA's poor messaging alienated its allies and sowed tensions within the membership, especially less active members who were not plugged into the endorsement process. It was difficult for them to understand exactly what had gone into the decision making, and this gave space for leftists to criticize DSA's inaction on platforms as prominent as the *New York Times*.[24] Whether this was done with the hopes of actually influencing DSA to change the decision or not, it allowed its critics to shame DSA and hurt its reputation. DSA eventually did send out guidance on how to approach the 2020 elections, but it was in September and sent privately to chapter leaders. No public clarity was offered as the uprising of the summer swept the country and the threat of political violence increased.

As the political situation grew worse going into the fall, some members felt the lack of a position was unsustainable even if changing DSA's stance was impossible. To address this, I joined with others in October to publish a letter expressing our concerns with a possible Trump victory.[25] We avoided mentioning Biden. We asked others to sign on and sought to create a vehicle for members to openly express their concerns. We also sought to provide organizing opportunities for members who wanted to do electoral work to plug into as individuals. These opportunities were focused on down-ballot races with the aim of turning out Democratic voters key to defeating Trump. We viewed this not just about messaging but about organizing, and we strove to be different from the previous open letters and articles, which seemed more focused on demonstrating righteousness to others[26] than influencing DSA to change their stance.

Our effort was greeted both with praise and scorn. Those primarily concerned with removing Trump from the White House were more sympathetic. Many of those who had voted enthusiastically for the "Bernie or Bust" resolution were less happy. Some members even lied and said we were pushing DSA members to campaign for Biden, which was objectively false. There was a feeling that we were trying to get around the convention resolution and that using our DSA titles implied an endorsement. This argument rang hollow to me, because the resolution just prevented endorsing a Democrat besides Sanders, and did not bar individual DSA members from doing electoral work. Most active DSA members, even those who were against our letter, believed that the resolution closed off any possible presidential endorsement, but the author of the resolution said that it left the door open for the endorsement of a third-party candidate.

People inside and outside of DSA understood that the only choices were Biden or Trump. The Green Party received 75% fewer presidential votes between 2016 and 2020, despite higher turnout, and only two DSA chapters endorsed Howie Hawkins' race. They were both promptly chastised for doing so outside of a formal national process. Our national formation should have owned that there were two choices and the majority of working people were picking Biden.[27] We should have not shied away from publicly and significantly helping to defeat Trump, even if that meant electing Biden, because those were the only two real choices facing working-class voters.

Although DSA and Sanders' rise had coincided, this relationship grew more distant and awkward as time went on. While prominent democratic socialist elected officials such as Sanders, Rashida Tlaib, Alexandria Ocasio-Cortez, and Jamaal Bowman pushed turnout for Biden, their own organization was absent. A few days before the election, Sanders, Tlaib, Ocasio-Cortez, and Bowman joined with many other liberal-left mass groups for an online turnout rally in support of Joe Biden. DSA, whose rise paralleled many of their careers and had helped elect many of them, was not at the event. Our absence was glaring and hard to forget.

After November

Thanks to the tireless work of progressive and left organizations, Joe Biden defeated Donald Trump without DSA's help in the November general election. In doing so, he flipped the state of Georgia, which had not been won by a Democrat since Bill Clinton's win in 1992. The turnout that propelled Biden's victory there also pushed the two US Senate races into runoff elections, since no single candidate received the majority of votes. With the "Bernie or Bust" resolution no longer holding DSA back, the organization mobilized against the GOP incumbent senators. DSA deployed volunteers in the runoff elections and contributed to the successful effort to stop Republicans from gaining those two seats, all without ever making an endorsement.

This shift demonstrated to me that DSA was willing to be part of the type of coalition politics needed to defeat the far right. DSA matured through our experience of 2020, and we have learned through democratic struggle how to make better political interventions and plan for different scenarios. Even beyond the election, as of August 2021, DSA has continued its foray into mass politics and electoral engagement through logging over a million phone calls to swing-state US senators in support of the labor law reform PRO Act.[28] This kind of coalition work highlights that DSA is ready to be part of broader social movements.

Conclusion

At the August 2021 DSA convention, two years after our fateful gathering where the "Bernie or Bust" resolution passed, we faced no hard questions about presidential endorsements. However, over 1,000 delegates in attendance debated electoral strategy more broadly and struggled over the question of how DSA should relate to elected officials we champion who in turn endorse corporate Democrats in other elections. To my pleasant surprise, an amendment to the electoral strategy resolution calling for DSA to discourage our electeds from doing this only got 40% approval and failed.[29]

This demonstrates that DSA members understand that elected officials play a different role than our organization in defeating the far right, and that we need to employ a multitude of tactics on a variety of fronts in order to do that. We need to provide flexibility for officeholders such as Cori Bush—a socialist in a purple state—to work to defeat the far right by working with whomever they deem necessary, and that calculus changes based on time, place, and conditions. Socialists should avoid solutions and blanket decisions that are devoid of an analysis of the particular conditions and scenarios at play. The willingness of delegates at our 2021 convention to move away from pre-emptive rules and resolutions is a healthy sign of a maturing democratic socialist movement.

Since 2019, I have not encountered anyone who voted against the "Bernie or Bust" resolution and regretted it. I have, however, encountered plenty of people who did vote for it and later admitted that it was an error. DSA's involvement in the Georgia runoffs and the results of this most recent 2021 convention are positive signs of a move away from sectarianism and toward a more popular front understanding. I am glad to see this shift and look forward to a stronger DSA ready to tackle a far right that shows no sign of abating in 2022.

Notes

1. This chapter was written by David Duhalde, a longtime member and leader within DSA. It does not represent organizational views.
2. Joseph Schwartz, "A History of the Democratic Socialists of America: 1971–2017," www.dsausa.org/about-us/history/.
3. Schwartz, "History of the Democratic Socialists of America."
4. Bill Fletcher, "Governing Socialism," in *We Own the Future,* ed. Kate Aronoff, Peter Dreier, and Michael Kazin (New York: New Press, 2020), p. 98.

5. Paul Heideman, "The Third Way Is the Past: Socialism Is the Future," *Jacobin*, July 9, 2021, www.jacobinmag.com.

6. Democratic Socialists of America Political Action Committee," DSAPAC Statement on 2004 Elections," *Democratic Left* (Summer 2004), p. 2.

7. DSA National Political Committee, "After the Election: Keep Fighting," *Democratic Left* (Winter 2012), pp. 4–5.

8. *Citizens United v. FEC* was decided January 21, 2010. For details about the decision, see www.fec.gov/legal-resources/court-cases/citizens-united-v-fec/.

9. A 501(c)(4) is a type of nonprofit that can endorse candidates. Donations to a 501(c)(4) are not tax-deductible. Groups like DSA, Our Revolution, Center for Popular Democracy Action, People's Action, and Organize for Justice are 501(c) (4)'s.

10. An independent expenditure is money spent on political advertising that expressly advocates for the election or defeat of a clearly identified candidate and which is not made in coordination with any candidate's campaign. Individuals, corporations, labor organizations, and political committees may support (or oppose) candidates by making independent expenditures, and they are not contributions, so are not subject to any contribution limits.

11. Elizabeth Henderson. "All Out for Bernie," *Democratic Left* (Winter 2015), pp. 5–7.

12. DSA National Political Committee, "Dump the Racist Trump; Continue the Political Revolution Down-Ballot; Build Multiracial Coalitions and Socialist Organization for Long-Term Change," August 16, 2016, www.dsausa.org/statements/election2016/.

13. Our Revolution is a political action organization that sprang from the 2016 Sanders campaign email list, and had a board hand-picked by him. The organization has since grown more independent of Sanders. Indivisible started as an online publication by Democratic congressional staffers looking for ways to peacefully resist the incoming Trump administration, and its co-founders Leah Greenberg and Ezra Levin have since turned it into a chapter-based membership advocacy organization.

14. Eoin Higgins, "The DSA Isn't 100 Percent Sure about Hopping on the Bernie Bus," *Vice*, March 14, 2019, www.vice.com.

15. This distinction is similar to the socialist tradition of minimum versus maximum program. Sanders' agenda was the minimum of what democratic socialists should advocate for, but our long-term visions (that is, our maximum program) would strive for a rupture with capitalism.

16. David Duhalde, "DSA Chapters: Propose National Candidate Endorsements by June 1," May 24, 2017, www.dsausa.org.

17. DSA Exploratory Committee, "Report from the Exploratory Committee for the 2020 Presidential Primary," January 18, 2019.

18. Meagan Svoboda and Alec Ramsey-Smith, "DSA for Bernie: Building Power through Class Struggle Campaigns," June 7, 2020, https://medium.com.

19. Alex Seitz-Wald, "Progressive Groups Unite to Boost Bernie Sanders as Democratic Attacks on Him Mount," NBC News, January 30, 2020, www.nbcnews.com.

20. DSA National Political Committee, "Beyond Bernie," May 12, 2020, www.dsausa.org/statements /.

21. Andrew Sernatinger, "Tail Can't Wag the Dog: The DSA NPC Vote on Swing States and the Questions for Democracy," *New Politics,* June 9, 2020, https://newpol.org.

22. Jennifer Bolen, Twitter post, May 5, 2020, 7:03 p.m. https://twitter.com/irockgnomes.

23. Democratic Socialists of America, Twitter post, April 12, 2020, 11:00 a.m. https://twitter.com/DemSocialists.

24. Mitchell Abidor, "These Young Socialists Think They Have Courage. They Don't," *New York Times,* May, 13, 2020.

25. "DSA Members Organizing Against Trump," https://docs.google.com/forms/d/e/1FAIpQLSeLowxXwuJhiRNznw057xOiRpY05AeY1-WeKWkDxj-9DrfyVxg/viewform.

26. Paul Heideman, "Stop Trying to Shame Socialists into Voting for Joe Biden. It's Not Going to Work," *Jacobin,* May 14, 2020.

27. Matt Karp, "The Politics of the Second Gilded Age," *Jacobin,* February 17, 2021, https://jacobinmag.com.

28. The Protecting the Right to Organize Act, or PRO Act, is a proposed federal law that would expand the ability of employees in various industries to collectively bargain in the workplace. It would also weaken "right-to-work" laws in 27 states.

29. Metro DC DSA, *Washington Socialist,* https://washingtonsocialist.mdcdsa.org.

Part 5

Mobilizing Voters Across the Country

18

Protest, Politics, and (Electoral) Power

Maurice Mitchell, Working Families Party

From turning out the vote to defeat Trump to championing progressive candidates up and down the ballot in key races, the Working Families Party (WFP) played a decisive role in 2020. We did this in close coordination with many allies in community, labor, and other social movement groups. We saw this work as part of a larger, more long-term strategy to build the multiracial democracy that we deserve, one that reflects a commitment to racial and economic justice. To get and keep that democracy, we at WFP understood that we needed to do more than defeat Trump and get a few progressive Democrats elected down-ballot. We aimed to use electoral work in 2018 and 2020 as part of our efforts to gain governing power for our communities, especially those communities that have been historically marginalized. By "governing power," we mean communities having the power to shape and move an agenda that transforms our society.

In the weeks before Election Day, hundreds of WFP volunteers and organizers along with The Frontline, a multiracial campaign of state and national organizations, took to the streets of Philadelphia with black T-shirts that said "VOTE TODAY PA." They staffed early vote centers, directed voters to new early voting places, answered voters' questions, and distributed face masks, water, and sanitizer to voters. At the same time, roving flatbed trucks with musical acts toured the city to entertain folks waiting in hours-long lines to vote. One video clip of voters dancing to the "Cha-Cha-Slide" went viral and garnered tens of millions of views online.

It was an unprecedented turnout operation to meet an unprecedented moment. We were in the middle of a global pandemic, a crippling recession, and facing what I had been telling audiences for more than a year was the single most important election of our lifetime.

And it worked. We didn't win everything we wanted, but the intervention of organizers, activists, and social movements in key states like Pennsylvania, Wisconsin, Georgia, and Arizona literally saved the country—at least, temporarily—from right-wing authoritarianism. There's so much more we need beyond averting disaster, but reflecting upon the lessons from that intervention may help us move from defense to offense and build the nation we deserve.

That moment and many others in 2020 cannot be properly understood without some context.

White backlash and Trump's rise to power

The 2020 cycle can't be divorced from the 2014 murder of Michael Brown Jr. in Ferguson, Missouri, and the movements that grew from that catalytic moment. Like many at that time, I decided I couldn't sit on the sidelines as history unfolded before me. I took a leave from my job, traveled to St. Louis, and embedded with local Black-led organizations that had requested support. Within months, through the labor of local community members and organizers across the country, we built the Movement for Black Lives. I played a behind-the-scenes role, co-founding a project called Blackbird, which provided capacity and strategic support to organizations and organizers within the movement, developed frameworks for coordination and direction, and helped the movement become an international force.

But as I later learned in 2016, the movement that had built so much momentum was about to meet the gale-force wind of white backlash in the form of misogyny and Trumpism. The 2016 election was supposed to be a mere formality. While not thrilled with the prospects, many thought the first woman president in Secretary Hillary Clinton was a foregone conclusion. We had very real, substantive issues with the former New York senator and First Lady. Few thought the country would elect the failed businessman, reality TV star, and boorish buffoon, Donald Trump. In fact, so much of our power analysis was built around a mirage of inevitability.

The ascendance of Donald Trump to the highest office in the land laid bare a bitter truth: social movements that lack governing power would always be subject to the organizing of other, often more resourced and consolidated, forces. Social movements pose questions, surface contradictions, and sometimes topple powerful interests. Questions require answers, contradictions call for resolution, and power vacuums inevitably get filled. With the ascendance of Trump, white nationalists filled the vacuums.

To be clear, the Movement for Black Lives and the ubiquity of "Black Lives Matter" changed the national conversation. We'd gotten the ear of elected officials from the statehouse to the White House. But Trump heading to the White House meant that we were about to encounter a wannabe strongman leader who was openly hostile to the movement and now had all the instruments of the federal government at his disposal. Under Trump, we understood that social movement power was essential but insufficient on its own. The change we sought required the complementary ability to answer questions through policy and fill power vacuums via co-governance, where communities are in direct conversations with their elected officials to influence policy decisions. It was in this context that some of us began to experiment with strategies and vehicles that allowed us not simply to call the question but to advance policies that are informed by social movements.

The Working Families Party

In 2018, I was tapped to become the second national director of the Working Families Party. Over the years, WFP had established a track record of electing progressive champions in municipal elections nation-wide. As protest movements captured the nation's imagination, building progressive electoral coalitions that are multigenerational and multiracial, bringing together labor unions, social movements, people's organizations, and everyday working-class voters became a necessity. With 2020 looming, WFP felt like the perfect vehicle for expanding this model of pairing social movement energy with electoral power. By leaning into a more intersectional politics, we would center leadership from communities that have been traditionally at the margins. Going forward, we would place more emphasis on base-building, and on developing leaders through political education, so that this intersectional, electorally focused coalition would hold together for the long haul, building and exercising grassroots governing power.

We would build this coalition from the grassroots up, starting with key local races with national strategic importance, gearing up for the mission-critical 2020 presidential election. First up, Philadelphia.

For years, Philadelphia's Democratic machine has maintained an iron grip on the city and its institutions. Many of these Democratic council members were closer to the Chamber of Commerce than they were to their own constituents. So we decided to do something about it. There are ten districts in the county, each represented by a member, along with seven at-large seats. City rules mandate that at least two slots go to a minority party—for decades that had been the Republicans. The WFP saw an opportunity to make the central contest in Philadelphia not between Democrats and Republicans, but between Democrats and progressives.

In 2019, the WFP ran two candidates for those at-large seats: Kendra Brooks and Nicolas O'Rourke. Despite some threats from the Democratic Party establishment and spending from the Chamber of Commerce, the formidable pair put together a coalition of working-class Black and Brown voters and progressive activists, along with the backing of local organized labor and endorsements from progressive elected officials within and outside the state.

When the dust settled, Brooks finished sixth with 60,000 votes, becoming the first minor party candidate to win a spot on the council in a century. The Kendra Brooks coalition proved to be a winner. But this win wasn't just about changing Philadelphia. It was also about building a base of WFP voters we could mobilize in future election cycles—including 2020. Kendra's vote total was 15,000 votes more than the margin of victory for Trump in 2016. We knew that if the coalition turned out again, it would make the difference in a close election. Outside of Pennsylvania, we invested heavily in states that were essential to turning the tide in 2018, 2020, and beyond. Our plan called for engaging new and infrequent voters in Wisconsin, Georgia, and Arizona—all states where we had been building relationships on the ground in the years preceding the election. The bottom-up, grassroots base we had been building was about to take center stage.

The Democratic Party primary and our endorsement

In 2019, Democratic hopefuls across the ideological spectrum lined up to take on Donald Trump in the upcoming 2020 election. Everyone left of center knew the stakes if Trump was allowed another four-year term— this time without the constraints of having to run again. The WFP was no different.

The opportunity ahead of us was historic. Making Trump a one-term president was a lofty mission, but one that would be incomplete. Trump needed to be defeated, but we also needed the most progressive president possible to right the wrongs of the last four years and address centuries of systemic racism, economic inequality due to corporate greed, and the growing threat of climate change.

At first glance, it may sound odd for a third party to endorse another political party's candidates, but our definition of "party" differs from conventional wisdom. A lot of people think of a party as just a ballot line. We see it differently. For us, a party has four major components, none of which are constrained to a ballot line: 1) a group of people who 2) share a common ideology, 3) a platform of policies informed by that ideology, and who 4) work to make change through elections. That's it. That's a party—and the WFP is the political home to thousands of Americans whether we have a ballot line or not.

In 2016, we supported the charge to draft Massachusetts Senator Elizabeth Warren to run for president. Four years later, she threw her hat in the ring for 2020. We also had Senator Bernie Sanders, who WFP had supported enthusiastically in 2016. We were among his first national endorsements. Both Sanders and Warren were giants of the progressive movement. Also, former HUD Secretary Julián Castro was in the race and made issues like police violence and homelessness hallmarks of the campaign. With multiple progressive contenders, the 2020 WFP endorsement would be both coveted and competitive. There were deep wells of support for both Sanders and Warren within WFP, and so we knew that no decision we made would make everyone happy. Still, it felt important to get engaged and build momentum for a progressive candidate in the context of a wide-open race.

Our endorsement was decided via a ranked-choice vote, following in-depth interviews with five Democratic candidates. The process included our grassroots members and online supporters, as well as the WFP National Committee, which includes delegates casting votes on behalf of WFP's state chapters, which themselves conducted their own local deliberative processes. When the dust settled, Senator Warren was our pick.

The most persuasive arguments for Senator Warren included her potential to forge a new winning primary coalition that brought together ideological progressives with newly activated voters shocked into action after Trump's election; the way Senator Warren was bringing new, transformational ideas into the public discourse like universal childcare and a wealth tax; and her commitment to movement building, demonstrated by brave endorsements for several of our down-ballot candidates like Jessica Cisneros in Texas and Kendra Brooks in Pennsylvania.

After the choice was made, we went all-in to elect her, first announcing our endorsement at a rally attended by more than 15,000 in New

York's Washington Square Park. The staff and I crisscrossed the country on the campaign trail, organizing voters around the senator's policy-based, structural change approach to transforming the US economy and democracy. The Warren campaign made key interventions and offered popular ideas like the wealth tax, abolishing the Jim Crow filibuster, universal childcare, and dramatic anti-corporate reforms to government corruption. Despite an early surge following the WFP endorsement, by January, the Warren campaign had lost steam and come up short in key primary fights. When she dropped out of the race, we immediately and enthusiastically endorsed Bernie Sanders, who was the second-place finisher in our ranked-choice process.

Up and down the ballot

Having a Democratic president—of whatever ideological stripe—only takes us so far. Progressives needed victories in Congress and on the state level to have a share of real governing power. In Obama's first two years, corporate-backed "moderates" in the House and Senate dithered and negotiated with Republicans and were predictably routed by the Tea Party wave in the midterms. After that, the Obama presidency was hobbled by a GOP-controlled Congress and statehouses that cherry-picked their voters through gerrymandering, allowing them to scuttle as much federal legislation as they could.

Our mandate was clear: work with a dual electoral strategy. Be in coalition with Democrats to win majorities, while also electing more progressive champions who will fight hard for a robust agenda, often against the Democratic Party establishment. With that in mind, we launched a massive effort to elect progressive candidates up and down the ballot across the country.

Our biggest win of the primary was in New York's 16th Congressional District. The incumbent, Eliot Engel, had been in office for more than three decades and hadn't faced a competitive, credible challenger in years. Running to Engel's left was the Justice Democrats–backed Jamaal Bowman, a 43-year-old principal and New York native. Jamaal was a father of three and the founder of one of the most successful middle schools in the city. Along with a strong record of community advocacy regarding education, he also ran to Engel's left on police reform and healthcare.

Following our allies at Justice Democrats, the Working Families Party endorsed and invested in Jamaal's campaign early. He was the right candidate with the right message at the right time. Combined with a robust campaign infrastructure, we knew he would be a formidable challenger to Engel. A key factor in defeating Engel was expanding the electorate and meeting regular and new voters where they were. It was less about getting people to vote *against* the incumbent, and more about getting them to vote *for* Jamaal.

During a rare trip back to the district to attend a rally about police brutality, Engel was caught on a hot mic saying the quiet part out loud: "If I didn't have a primary, I wouldn't care."[1] To supplement the campaign's well-organized ground game, which found Jamaal introducing himself on street corners and subways throughout the district, WFP partnered with the Justice Democrats on a massive independent expenditure.[2] While highlighting Jamaal's platform, we also seized on Engel's hot mic gaffe, highlighting his absence in the district and disregard for his constituents, who knew all too well what police misconduct looked like up close. Despite the pandemic, the Bowman campaign dramatically expanded the map. The 2018 Democratic primary in the same congressional district drew a little more than 30,000 voters. When every vote was tallied in 2020, more than 89,000 New Yorkers in Congressional District 16 cast a ballot. Jamaal garnered 55% of the vote, upending the establishment and proving the viability of a well-organized, people-powered campaign.

Meanwhile, in neighboring Rockland County and upper Westchester, WFP-endorsed Mondaire Jones won a crowded primary in the state's 17th Congressional District, beating out several well-funded figures from the establishment to become one of two gay Black men to enter the halls of US Congress.

Even where we came up short, we showed that progressives can be competitive everywhere. We endorsed Jessica Cisneros in Texas' 28th Congressional District. The immigration attorney lost to long-serving incumbent Henry Cuellar by less than 3,000 votes. There are rarely moral victories in politics, but giving a scare to a representative who earned the nickname "Trump's favorite Democrat" was a balm to soothe an otherwise stinging loss.[3] In districts where conventional wisdom said progressives had no chance, the Cisneros campaign defied the odds and laid the foundation for more work to come.

We also made significant gains on the state level, electing a new class of organizers, activists, and working-class candidates to office. The Rhode Island WFP and a constellation of progressive organizations drove a wave of victories for progressive challengers and incumbents. Ten out of 11 of the WFP slate won their primaries. One standout is Leonela Felix, an attorney and progressive policy advocate who beat 10-year incumbent Raymond Johnston Jr., a retired police officer backed by Right to Life. Meanwhile, Brandon Potter, whose experience with Rhode Island's broken healthcare system inspired him to run for office, ousted incumbent Rep. Chris Millea, an NRA-backed establishment Democrat and close ally of the scandal-embroiled House Speaker. The successes built off four years of work by progressives to organize against the conservative Democratic establishment and paved the way for major progressive victories on a $15 minimum wage and equal pay legislation.

In New York, we won 33 state legislative primaries across the state this cycle, including three new WFP challengers who unseated Democratic incumbents—Jessica González-Rojas, Marcela Mitaynes, and Amanda Septimo. Eleven more new WFP-endorsed candidates who won in open Democratic primaries and 17 WFP progressive incumbents won against challenges from the right. It made for the most progressive legislature in a generation, which in turn played a key role in the undoing of New York's famously anti-progressive governor, Andrew Cuomo.

In New Mexico, a group of progressive women backed by the New Mexico WFP under the banner of "No Corporate Dems" shook the New

Mexico Democratic establishment. Siah Hemphill Correa and Carrie Hamblen unseated some of the most powerful elected officials in the state, while WFP-backed former educator Leo Jaramillo ran a successful primary against incumbent Sen. Richard Martinez in District 5. These victories led to real material benefits to the people. Funding for public education became law as a concession from the bruised Democratic leadership.

Finally, in Delaware, a diverse and progressive WFP slate—including Black, LGBTQ, and Muslim candidates—ousted five white male members of the Delaware State House and Senate, including the Senate Pro Tem.[4] They effectively challenged the "Delaware Way" of bipartisan, corporate-friendly governance that has dominated modern politics in the state and since being elected, have led a successful charge for a $15 minimum wage in famously pro-business Delaware.

We made similar interventions in the criminal justice system. In 2019, we established a national criminal justice initiative to recruit and elect progressive prosecutors. Communities of color have long been concerned about mass incarceration. But to date, most of the attention has been focused on legislative solutions. While all of these are worthy and necessary fights in their own right, WFP focused on changing the decision makers in district attorney offices. The country's biggest cities and counties often take center stage when it comes to criminal justice policy, but our criminal justice team found excellent candidates ready and willing to run on decarceral platforms from coast to coast. In an analysis of prosecutor races across 10 states from 1996 to 2006, Wake Forest law school professor Ronald Wright found that 85% of incumbents faced no challenger. WFP was part of a group of forces including Color of Change and Real Justice PAC that had decided that it was time to change that and give voters real choices. Because of our work in 2020, WFP-endorsed prosecutors won races in major counties in Texas, Michigan, Florida, and Colorado.

The presidential election: 'A door, not a destination'

Even though Democratic voters were in support of progressive ideas, a number of factors led to the defeat of the progressive candidates in the presidential race. Teasing out those myriad factors fully would require a separate book, but identity, prejudice, and skepticism around the American electorate's appetite to elect a transformational "first" was also in the mix. The beat-Trump ethos made many skittish about nominating another woman or a Jewish socialist. Even moderates drawn to Mayor Pete Buttigieg were cautious about nominating an openly gay, married man. Despite the most diverse Democratic field in history, we were colliding with the reality that having the first-anything in 2020 might be enough to derail any candidate who didn't fit the old mold of being older, male, straight, and white. Additionally, the forces of moderation within the Democratic Party worked very hard and effectively at ensuring the ascendancy of Biden.

Neither of the progressive candidates won the Democratic presidential primary, but we were clear-eyed going into the general election. Joe Biden became the standard-bearer and pick to take on Trump, and progressives knew we had to push the Democratic nominee as far to the left as possible. Donald Trump was an existential threat, a global leader of the far right, and we had to defeat him at all costs. The campaigns run by Elizabeth Warren and Bernie Sanders were instrumental in injecting progressive ideas into mainstream discourse. Canceling student debt, a wealth tax, and healthcare for all were no longer fringe ideas. Even candidates closer to the center were talking about the need for transformative changes. Our picks were not victorious, but our policies were front and center.

"Making Donald Trump a one-term president is our moral mandate and a necessary step to building the world we want to see," I told the *Nation* in August 2021. "Our plan is to beat Trump while organizing a multiracial movement powerful enough to turn our demands into policy. Electing Joe Biden is a door, not a destination."[5] This was less an assessment of Biden in particular and more a statement on the overall conditions we found ourselves in. We are fighting a long, protracted battle for our lives. "A door, not a destination" would be something I repeated often in the months leading up to the general and the months after. These were effectively our marching orders.

Following our autumn endorsement of Biden, the WFP also unveiled an ambitious policy platform called the People's Charter to give progressives a powerful and inspiring agenda to fight for—a roadmap out of crisis. It could serve as a rallying point for progressives and a north star for our organizing in what we hoped would be a Biden Administration. The People's Charter was the outcome of months of internal debate and study, polling, and collaboration with a number of movements. A number of progressive organizations, thousands of people, and a dozen members of Congress signed on. From organized labor to community organizers, we galvanized the left behind a uniform set of demands. This was multiracial, multigenerational movement-building in action.

We also caught the attention of the right. Fox News wrote a stunningly even-handed article with the not-so-subtle headline "Progressives, including 'Squad,' Release Agenda to Push Biden to the Left."[6] The TV segment on the charter said that we were pushing the "real agenda," as the screen read off our allegedly nefarious, yet wildly popular policy demands of a $15 minimum wage, healthcare for all, affordable housing, and canceling student debt. With Trump's approval rating underwater, the people already had a villain to vote against. Projects like The Frontline and the visionary demands like the People's Charter gave the nation a vision to vote *for*.

Ordinary people leading us through extraordinary times

We found ourselves at a crossroads unlike any this generation had seen. The lives claimed by COVID were ticking upwards every day with no end in sight. Police violence, reform, and abolition were front and center in everyday conversation. Communities stepped in where governments failed to provide mutual aid for neighbors. And there was the ever-looming threat of white nationalist violence, thanks to a lawless president who traded dog whistles for bullhorns to communicate with his base. As daunting as these crises were, it was the perfect opportunity for us to show that we didn't need superheroes or saviors to get us out of this mess; we just needed ordinary people willing to give a little more to produce extraordinary gains.

The Frontline ethos was simple: everyone had a role to play. You could be a protester, a poll watcher, a worker willing to strike, a social media influencer, a wealthy funder, or a mutual aid organizer. This was bigger than an election and we had to do something seldom done in electoral organizing: cater to the whole person. We created a map that amplified mutual aid resources across the country and provided information on where people could get connected to services for mental health, immigration, housing, healthcare, and more. We also realized that Biden's centrist campaign left some voters unenthused.

Our work became deeply collaborative, channeling the energy and power of social movements into electoral might. After the uprising against the brutal police murder of George Floyd in June, I took a month away from the WFP to help the Movement for Black Lives organize the largest protest mobilizations in US history.[7] And then we brought that power and passion to the polls. The Working Families Party teamed with the Movement for Black Lives Electoral Justice Project, United We Dream Action, and dozens of local groups to build a campaign and network called the Frontline. Our goal was to channel the energy and momentum we saw in the streets following the murders of George Floyd and Breonna Taylor into electoral power. We recruited tens of thousands of volunteers to send millions of texts and engage in deep relational organizing in their communities. As most of the nation was homebound, this method of organizing involved giving all our efforts a personal touch: volunteers were explicitly engaging people already in their networks.

Joy to the Polls/election planning
The shadow of white nationalist violence, voter suppression, and COVID-19 loomed large as the calendar crept closer to Election Day 2020. If there

was no access to the ballot or voters were too afraid to vote, the most ambitious, inspirational agenda wouldn't matter.

Voter intimidation and misinformation is a well-worn tool of the right. Our political enemies directly challenged voters at the polls, sent mailers with fake polling locations or the wrong election date, and employed a variety of other tactics. Additionally, because of the importance of this election, longer lines were expected on Election Day. Long lines and machine shortages are forms of voter suppression all their own. To counter this, Nelini Stamp, the Working Families Party's director of strategy and partnership, was tasked with heading Joy to the Polls/Election Defenders, a massive nonpartisan organizing effort in collaboration with the Frontline that trained organizers to keep an eye out for conflicts at the polls while making the process of voting as pleasurable as possible.

This involved a two-pronged approach. First, we conducted a series of digital and in-person trainings for volunteers across the country that focused on de-escalation tactics. We also equipped volunteers with PPE and water for voters at the polls. The second phase involved cultural organizing. We engaged a number of artists with ties to the cities where we'd be operating who agreed to perform short concerts at various polling locations. And truthfully, is there a better way to de-escalate potential conflicts than through music and culture? "On election day there will be two-, three-, four-hour lines. So we want there to be an act that comes around and performs for 20 minutes and gives the voters something to look forward to," Nelini Stamp told the *Guardian*.[8] The concerts went over well, but a viral video of volunteers from the Resistance Revival Chorus and voters doing the Electric Slide in Philadelphia exploded on social media, which got the eye of mainstream media. The increased attention allowed us to bring increased interest to Joy to the Polls, election security, and voting in general.

Joy to the Polls was an undisputed win, but our work was far from over. For years, there was chatter about Trump either refusing to accept the results of an election he lost, attempting to steal the election outright, or simply refusing to leave office. Behind the scenes, a coalition of organized labor, business, political strategists, and progressive organizations coordinated to ensure that Election Day (which turned into Election Week) went as smoothly as possible and to prevent Trump from throwing the country into chaos.

In our organizing efforts, we focused more on the security of our election systems, got out information on how to vote by mail, how to find polling places, and of course, bringing Joy to the Polls. For health reasons, there was limited in-person canvassing. WFP significantly ramped up our phone- and textbank operations, teaming with a number of partner organizations to phone and text voters in swing states around the clock. We recruited 30,000 volunteers who made 2 million voter contact attempts and held 630,000 conversations with voters.

By the time polls closed on Election Day, I knew we had left it all on the field. The waiting game was set to begin.

The big day and defending the people's vote

Despite a few disruptions and threats, Election Day was surprisingly, but welcomingly quiet. However, the four days between Election Day on Tuesday and the Saturday when results rolled in felt like months. Donald Trump did his best to cast doubt on the incoming election results and to stir his base into angry and violent protest in what amounted to a preview of the violence we would see unfold at the Capitol on January 6, 2021. But the progressive grassroots were ready.

In Philadelphia, the WFP and its allies staged a multiday street party with music, dancing, giant puppet displays, and more. When Trump's lawyers staged a press conference downtown to spread disinformation about the vote counting, WFP Organizing Director Nicolas O'Rourke played DJ and drowned out the lawyers with a blast of Beyoncé. The next time Trump's team held an event, they avoided downtown and chose instead to hold their event in the suburban parking lot of Four Seasons Total Landscaping, a local small business.

We fought hate and fear with love, and it worked. When the final tally was counted, Joe Biden triumphed over Donald Trump. This wasn't merely a victory for Biden, or even the Democrats, who also took back the House and would later reclaim the Senate after a runoff in Georgia. Popularly, beating Trump had the air of toppling a corrupt authoritarian regime. Across the country, celebrations rang out in the streets. A certain song from YG and the late rapper Nipsey Hussle saw a more than 400% increase in streams (if you know, you know). It was jubilant, and, for a brief moment, many of us were able to exhale.

If this were Hollywood, the defeat of the bad guy would be the perfect end to the movie. And maybe one day, the 2020 election season will make for a harrowing limited TV series. However, our work continued in the days, weeks, and months after the election was decided for Joe Biden.

Lessons learned about voter turnout

The 2020 election season provided some lessons for a lifetime. I took a few things away from the year about how we motivate people not only to vote, but to stay engaged. Here are some lessons that will stay with me moving forward.

First, it was crucial to give people something to vote *for*. Voter anger is weaponized cycle after cycle, but we cannot and should not count on rage to win elections. Donald Trump and his cronies were cartoonishly evil, but we didn't rest on the idea that voters would be motivated to go to the polls solely to vote him out. Across the country, we ran progressive champions up and down the ballot that put forth a vision for a country that truly allows everyone to thrive. As a result, voters hit the polls in record numbers and rewarded these visionaries with their trust and their ballots.

Next, it was essential for us to tell people what we wanted them to do in plain language. A significant amount of our organizing focused on three things: introducing voters to the candidates and their platforms, letting voters know how to register to vote and find their polling place, and when they could vote. After we did those things, we asked for their votes.

Lastly, we must meet voters where they are. In 2020, the pandemic forced us to do just that. We knocked on doors where it was safe. But we also invested massive resources in digital ads that carefully targeted voters on social media, as well as phone- and textbanking. After George Floyd's murder sparked the largest protest movement in American history, we registered people to vote at the protests. Campaigns did outreach outside of subway stations and bus stops. In a move that proved the 2020 election was truly an all-hands-on-deck effort, the Black Male Voter Project helped create Get Your Booty to the Poll, a public service campaign aimed at Black men who patronize strip clubs. The takeaway here is simple: wherever people are is where voters are.

Conclusion: The road ahead

The 2020 election proved to be the most important election of our lives, but with so much uncertainty in the world, the 2022 and 2024 elections are sure to be as important. Trump was defeated, yet his movement has completed its takeover of the Republican Party and grown more extremist than ever. The biggest takeaway from the year is that there is always the next election, always a new battle to fight, and always more people to organize. Proximal losses and victories are mere battles in efforts to win the long-arc struggle.

We saw record turnout in 2020, with more than 158 million voters heading to the polls. Joe Biden got the most votes of any presidential candidate in the history of American presidential elections. Donald Trump, an unrepentant bigot, misogynist, and one of the most inept presidents in our short history, received the second most votes ever. After four years of near-unspeakable levels of corruption, more than 74 million people went to the polls and essentially said, "I'd like more of that."

If we take our eye off the ball for even a moment, we'll be right back here with the next Trump. And the next Trump will likely be a smarter and more charismatic figure (as I write this, the 2024 Republican hopefuls are already filled with such characters). The violent insurrection on

January 6 and continued attempts by Republicans to gerrymander and suppress votes on their way to a permanent majority prove how tentative any political victory can be, and all that we're still up against. Trump is no longer president, but Trumpism remains. The "Big Lie," as we've come to know it, has captured the imagination of the Republican Party and completed their transition to an authoritarian cult, unified around white supremacy, voter suppression, blocking legislation that helps people, etc. This is the version of the party we will have to contend with for some time to come.

Electing Joe Biden and Kamala Harris is the door, not the destination to the world we say we want to live in. We voted for large-scale, transformative relief. We used our voting power to push the Democratic Party in a more progressive direction. Even the "establishment" Biden-Harris ticket moved leftward. As a result, we are bringing on the pressure to get Congress to pass more relief, a bold infrastructure bill that includes support for care work, and to keep pushing for healthcare, debt relief, climate justice, etc. To get out ahead, we have to vote people in and then immediately hold them accountable every step of the way, 365 days of the year.

With our democracy under constant attack, we must stay organized and ready to mobilize. Trying to engage with our elected officials as individuals leaves us feeling isolated and powerless. We all need a political home. We think the WFP can provide that home to millions of people, as individual members and as part of other social movement groups, working in solidarity to build a multiracial movement to transform America and make it finally live up to its promise.

Notes

1. Jason Silverstein, "New York Congressman Caught on Hot Mic at Protest Event: 'If I Didn't Have a Primary, I Wouldn't Care.'" CBS News, June 4, 2020, www.cbsnews.com.

2. An independent expenditure is money spent on political advertising that expressly advocates for the election or defeat of a clearly identified candidate and which is not made in coordination with any candidate's campaign.

3. Patrick Svitek, "Jessica Cisneros Will Again Challenge US Rep. Henry Cuellar in Democratic Primary for Congressional Seat," *Texas Tribune*, August 5, 2021.

4. In Delaware, the Senate President Pro Tempore is the chief leadership position in the Senate. They are elected by the majority party and confirmed by the entire Senate.

5. John Nichols, "The Working Families Party Endorses Biden and Harris," *Nation*, August 14, 2020.

6. Marisa Schultz, "Progressives, Including 'Squad,' Release Agenda to Push Biden to the Left," Fox News Network, October 8, 2020, www.foxnews.com.

7. Larry Buchanan, Quoctrung Bui, and Jugal K. Patel, "Black Lives Matter May Be the Largest Movement in US History," *New York Times*, July 3, 2020.

8. Poppy Noor, "Joy to the Polls: The Group Performing for Americans as They Line Up to Vote," *Guardian*, October 26, 2020.

19

People's Action: Building 'Movement Politics'

Ryan Greenwood

September 21, 2019. Des Moines, Iowa. A band of organizers and rank-and-file members from Iowa Citizens for Community Improvement Action and Iowa Student Action started filling the Iowa Events Center (home of the Iowa Wild hockey team) at 7 a.m. Members of People's Action groups from Colorado to Illinois streamed in to join them. We were there to do a different type of presidential forum. No canned stump speeches. No millionaire TV presenters with blow-dried hair. No letting candidates off the hook. We organized 3,000 people to attend, and the *Guardian* was there to livestream. To top it off we organized our rank-and-file leaders to present, tell their stories, and ask tough questions of the candidates. We paired leaders of Iowa CCI Action with Central American refugees and union organizers to talk about how the same global corporate agriculture systems are attacking workers in the Global South and family farmers in Iowa. When Pete Buttigieg stated opposition for Free College for All, we pushed back.

This was the high point to date of our practice of Movement Politics—our effort to build political organization centered on people in the multiracial working class, and our path to power, not the business-as-usual politics of the consultant class and candidates whose primary motivation was to work their way up the career ladder. Our work throughout the 2020 cycle gave us the chance to deepen our understanding of that practice—and contribute to the defeat of Donald Trump, buying us valuable time to keep organizing.

Twenty years ago, if you'd told us we'd be putting candidates on stage with our members, endorsing one, and helping elect them, our organizers would have said, "Nope, not what we do, not possible."

National People's Action—the main predecessor to People's Action—spent decades doing awesome community organizing. We helped lead the fight to pass the Community Reinvestment Act,[1] and we bird-dogged its implementation.[2] We organized people from Chicago to Los Angeles and Des Moines to hold banks and bankers accountable. We recruited leaders and led creative direct actions targeting corporate evildoers from Omaha to Ohio, even once dressing up as Robin Hoods and building a bridge over the moat that surrounds the headquarters of Chase Bank.

We won victories that moved over a $1 billion deposited in banks back into community control. We taught tens of thousands of people to confront their oppressors directly, to step on the grass and always ask "why" when someone tells you, "You can't do that." Many laws don't exist to improve the lives of us in the multiracial working class. They are there to prevent us from holding the powerful to account.

All that helped alleviate suffering and improve people's lives. We brought some small measure of power and liberation to ourselves and people who needed it.

One thing we did not do was electoral politics. We saw politicians as targets. The people we'd put up in front of a crowd and shout "yes or no!" at if they gave some long-winded answer that dodged one of our demands. They weren't us. Politics were dirty. Power corrupts. We were the people organizing against the politicians. They could take care of getting themselves elected: we'd hold them accountable once they got there.

But even as we organized and built and won, our lives and those of people we loved and organized got harder by most measures. From the 1980s to today unions got crushed. The wealth gap between the multiracial poor and working class and the rich grew. Gentrification pushed people out of their long-term communities. Corporate agriculture and profit-before-people, and planet extraction decimated our communities. White supremacy and nationalism metastasized after the civil rights victories of the 1960s and 1970s. A generation of Black and Brown people were locked up. In many ways we in the multiracial working class had less power and agency in the mid 2000s than we had 30 years earlier.

So, we started to ask how we got here. After the victories from the 1930s to the 1970s, how had the right reclaimed hegemonic political power in the country? How had they grabbed economic wealth and made life harder for the rest of us? There are multiple answers to that question, of course. The right had a strategic direction and a long-term vision. They used racism as a strategic weapon to divide Black, Brown, and white working class and poor people. And they used politics every step of the way. They ran right-wing movement candidates, like Barry Goldwater for president in 1964 who, even as they lost, trained generations of activists. They took over school boards and city councils. They built political organizations to sustain this work.

The right wing learned a key lesson: government is not the problem, it's the prize. Government could advance liberation or oppression. It could break unions, or it could help people form them. It could concentrate wealth in the hands of billionaires or keep it in the hands of the multiracial working class who made it. If the right controlled the government, they could spend hundreds of billions of dollars over decades to lock up millions of Black and Brown people while collapsing systems of public education and public health. The right used election campaigns, the largest public conversation we have about our country and where it's going, to dramatically shift the terms of debate in their favor. The lesson for us: if the right could win governing power, we could too. For all their flaws, elections point to our asymmetric advantage: organized people can beat concentrated wealth.

But we did not want to do business-as-usual politics. We did not want to run around to people with money selling slices of the electorate to push a milquetoast Democrat just past ever crazier Republicans. We didn't want to show up at people's doors selling the next politician looking for a better job as the solution to all their problems. We didn't want to build campaign offices as hubs of community action, only to tear them down the day after the election. Electing a Democrat, without an organization to move a postelection agenda, held limited possibilities to really improve our lives.

We began to envision a people-centered Movement Politics. With Movement Politics we would focus on building permanent people-powered political organizations, so once candidates became elected officials, we could back them up to create real changes in laws that made our lives better and hold them accountable if they did not. We would lean into tactics and strategies that were built on people power, not money. We would listen to and elevate the voices of local people, not for-profit consultants. We'd highlight the need for dramatic change, not centrist messaging. We would center race in all our organizing, not dodge it when there were white people around. We understood that talking about racism was a key part of winning both the election and the policy changes we wanted. Finally, we decided to not treat politicians as the other. We didn't want a seat at the table of governance. We wanted to run the table. To do that we had to *be* the politicians. We had to start running our own for school boards and city councils from Lewiston, Maine, to Los Angeles, California.[3]

Building Movement Politics

We started small. Organizations that had been founded with political work in their bloodstream like TakeAction Minnesota and Maine People's Alliance joined us in 2009. And we built new arms of our organizations capable of doing politics. In Chicago in 2013 the Illinois & Indiana Regional Organizing Network (IIRON) founded the People's Lobby (a 501(c)(4) organization capable of advocating for or against legislation full time, and backing candidates, and then, in conjunction with National Nurses United, formed a political action committee (PAC) called Reclaim Chicago. Sunflower Community Action built out Kansas People's Action and challenged Kansas Secretary of State Kris Kobach on his anti-immigrant stances and voter suppression in 2013 and 2014. Iowa CCI built out Iowa CCI Action, which famously bird-dogged Mitt Romney at the state fair during his 2012 presidential run. When they pushed him on corporate taxes, he proffered the memorable reply: "Corporations are people too, my friend!"

Increasingly we elected our own to public office. People like Crystal Murillo from Colorado People's Action now served on the Aurora City Council. Andre Vasquez, a DJ and Reclaim Chicago leader, was elected to the Chicago City Council. Robert Peters, the political director for The People's Lobby, won the Illinois State Senate seat in the same district that President Obama once represented. TakeAction Minnesota's anti–mass incarceration organizer Nelsie Yang became the first Hmong woman and youngest person ever elected to the St. Paul City Council. Our Philadelphia organization, Reclaim Philadelphia, elected their mass liberation organizer Rick Krajewski to the Pennsylvania State House. He defeated a 30-year-plus incumbent. Over five years we elected more than 360 of our member-leaders to public office.

And yet it wasn't enough. Donald Trump's electoral college win in the 2016 presidential election caused incredible fear among our base. He reshaped the American electorate, motivating right-wing voters who helped defeat many of our state and local candidates, changing the terms of the debate at all levels. We could no longer just focus on our states and cities. The incredible power of the federal government could be used to loot wealth created by the multiracial working class and put it in the hands of billionaires, and it could be used to round up our undocumented members and put them in private detention centers. We would need to play big at the federal level as well.

Community organizing as a sector had engaged federally for many years, especially since the 2004 elections. However, it played powerlessly. Democratic Party structures and funders determined their candidate for the presidency and the issues they'd run on. They realized that community organizations had better capacity and authenticity to reach out to communities of color. They funded Latinx organizations to talk to

Latinx people and turn them out to vote, Native organizations to turn out Native voters, Black organizations to turn out Black voters, Asian organizations to turnout Asian voters, and so on.

While building race-and ethnicity-based people's organizations can build power, this top-down strategy viewed community organizations exclusively as a tool to reach certain groups of voters. Those voters were also tools to be used to elect Democratic Party candidates. Left behind? Any strategy to build real political power for people who'd been disenfranchised over generations; any real desire to listen to them and treat them as individual human beings with intersectional concerns. The result: hardening cynicism. We needed to build Movement Politics to change this model.

Five organizations joined together to create People's Action in 2016. We used this process to recommit to internal democracy. For too long progressive nonprofits hid the ball. They claimed a base and accountability to people in the multiracial working class while they were actually run by wealthy people, foundation officers, and elites. We believe in what Justin Vest, the director of Hometown Action in Alabama and a People's Action board member, calls "ground-truthing." To deliver on power and liberation for people in the multiracial working class in a specific geography, we have to be run by them. What is true in a specific state is true nationally as well. Not only does this model undermine funder capture (a process where the people writing the checks make all the real decisions in an organization based on their self-interest), but we build more real power by supporting people's agency within our organization. This agency builds commitment and leadership. This is the sweat-equity necessary to build a people's organization and impact the public sphere.

In our by-laws, we established a Delegates Assembly to control the organization. Made up of two members from each state/local member organization—from OneAmerica Votes in Washington State to Neighbor to Neighbor Action in Massachusetts—this Delegates Assembly would be the genesis of power in the organization. It would determine our major strategies and endorsements, and elect people to our Board of Directors. As a result, an overwhelming majority of our Board of Directors, the people who ultimately control our money, determine our budget, and hire and fire our staff director, are leaders or directors of our member organizations..

In spring 2018, the Delegates Assembly convened in Chicago to determine our strategies for the coming years. After substantial advance conversations, and much debate in the meeting, delegates ultimately voted 54 to 5 to make a People's Presidential Campaign our lead Movement Politics strategy in the coming years.[4] This campaign's strategic goals were to build our organizations through our political work (rather than leaving them depleted), put our concerns in the center of the debate (rather than having possibilities for change defined by the DC consultocracy),[5] advance an aligned candidate to the presidency, and ultimately defeat Trump.

Our plan had several phases: form a platform to run on (developed through meetings with the leadership of our member organizations, and ultimately ratified by 1,000 attendees at our convention); engage the candidates in private and public forums on the platform; endorse a candidate well in advance of the primaries/caucuses; advocate for that candidate, and then meet with the staff for a new president to advance movement co-governing.[6]

The People's Presidential Forums

After we built our platform, we started planning for presidential forums in Durham, New Hampshire,[7] Des Moines, Iowa, and Las Vegas, Nevada. Ultimately, we engaged in different ways with Vice-President Biden, Senator Harris, Mayor Buttigieg, Senator Sanders, Senator Warren, Secretary Castro, and Andrew Yang. (We had lighter levels of engagement with other candidates.) *How* those candidates engaged was illustrative and determinative for us. Our endorsement and engagement criteria were about the issues, but not exclusively. We wanted candidates who were with us on our policy agenda and agreed with our worldview but also had the life experience backing that up: they weren't "Johnny come latelies" to our movement.

And we didn't just want rhetoric about what they would do for the multiracial working class. They needed to run more Movement Politics campaigns and throw out the business-as-usual political tactics. Less accountability to for-profit consultants, more to people's organizations. More time with people who are most impacted by the crisis of racism, the climate emergency, and massive inequality; less with well-heeled donors. We wanted candidates who understood they couldn't do it alone. Why? To move a transformational agenda a president needs to have an understanding of how to engage in movement co-governing—advancing an inside-outside strategy. Finally, we wanted candidates who would motivate our membership to put in their time and money behind our organizing for them.

How did the candidates stack up? Vice President Biden tried to ghost us. His campaign sent us ever-changing staffers and refused to have their candidate even meet with our members. Iowa CCI Action called him out on his opposition to Medicare for All in newspaper ads, ultimately implementing civil disobedience at his office to get a response. His senior staff did engage, but ultimately they were driven by the heads-down/don't-engage-the-voters/avoid-all-possibilities-of-mistakes strategy that lost them Iowa, New Hampshire, and Nevada so overwhelmingly.

Senator Harris similarly engaged at the staff level but not with our members. The campaign at least showed the respect of applying for our endorsement and completing our questionnaire. Run by a for-profit consulting firm, the campaign was either intentionally not engaging or just disorganized in the weeks we were inviting them to our events—we couldn't tell which.

Andrew Yang showed up to the Las Vegas People's Presidential Forum led by our amazing local group PLAN Action. In front of hundreds of primarily Black and Brown residents, the entire press corps of Nevada, and an international audience live streamed by the *Guardian*, he lectured renters on his ideas for dealing with the housing crisis. If you can't afford the rent, double up! If you don't like your landlord, move and get a new one! We'd painstakingly prepped Yang's staff and they told us he didn't even read the briefing packet for the event. He got booed off the stage.

Mayor Pete Buttigieg was a puzzle. His campaign showed discipline in engaging with us. They nailed meetings and follow-up. At our Iowa People's Presidential Forum, Buttigieg engaged in tense conversations with our members about his refusal to support Free College for All and his poor record around policing in South Bend. Driven by neoliberal ideology, the campaign was unable to bend and respond to real human concerns that didn't match an Ivy League policy platform. To their credit, however, they were tenacious. After his rough showing at our forum, Buttigieg still turned in an endorsement questionnaire. After being informed that he lost in our endorsement vote, his campaign replied within minutes to set up a debrief call to learn from the experience. We in the progressive movement could take a lesson from this. We can learn from those we disagree with.

Secretary Julián Castro rose in the estimation of our members through the campaign. He came in third in our endorsement vote. He anchored his campaign in the key racial justice fights of our time, from Puerto Rico to the border to policing. This was a revelation for our members, who were sick of being told that talking about race was "divisive" and not a winning strategy. And Castro engaged again and again. Case in point: the Las Vegas People's Presidential Forum. The forum occurred when his campaign was losing steam. Staff were holed up in San Antonio to raise money and pulled out of the forum. We pushed back. Our argument: the people attending the Las Vegas People's Presidential Forum were the exact people his candidacy was designed to uplift. So he hopped on a plane and showed up when doing that was hard. This is the sort of accountability we want from political leaders: to engage with us not just when it's convenient, but to do so when it's tough.

So why didn't we endorse him? On some issues, like Medicare for All, he opposed us. And his past was a hang-up, notably his mid-career actions at the federal Department of Housing and Urban Development. However, Secretary Castro's candidacy raised a challenge for us as a progressive movement: how do we treat elected leaders who learn and grow and change for the better in their political careers? We should challenge them, but ultimately, we will not change our political system exclusively by relying on new elected officials. We need to help some of the current crop to move toward us.

Senator Warren inspired many of our members by calling out the corporate agenda. We loved her articulation of transformational change in the power of who runs our economy and who it works for. She understood the need to call out the ways in which racism serves not just as a tool of economic power for a white elite, but as a means of social control of Black and Brown people, especially in our system of mass incarceration.

Ultimately Senator Warren received the second most votes from our members in our endorsement process. So where did she miss? As we engaged with her campaign, we noticed a gap between its people-power rhetoric and its behavior. It largely hired local staff who had worked for other presidential or traditional business-as-usual campaigns. They delayed committing to events with our members until the last minute.

At the Iowa People's Presidential Forum, a gulf opened between the senator's noncommitment on our Homes Guarantee platform and our members who had experienced foreclosure and the hard end of the housing crisis. Her staff seemed to have an academic understanding of policy and power, but they were averse to policy decisions being made by the most impacted people. Senator Warren declined to register for our Las Vegas forum, claiming a schedule conflict. This tipped us off to a common candidate strategy: if you don't want to engage, blame your calendar.

These moves fed a feeling among our members that Senator Warren would frequently be a champion of our issues and worldview but would not ultimately be accountable to us. This contrasted strongly with Senator Sanders' orientation.

While our members overwhelmingly voted to endorse Senator Sanders for president in 2016, a repeat was not guaranteed in 2020. Our members saw a partner in struggle with his anticorporate analysis that had never changed. In the hardest days to be a politician questioning the economic structure of our country, Senator Sanders had not wavered. That consistently inspired our members to see that Senator Sanders would not waver in our aligned worldview. And in 2016 his candidacy had almost single-handedly made Medicare for All—one of our flagship issues—relevant in the political discourse.

Not that there weren't faults. Senator Sanders seemed to understand race and racism only as an outcome of the struggle for economic power. Of course, we partially agree with that analysis. But we also find it insufficient. Over the decades racism has metastasized into a weapon of not just economic control but social control. Senator Sanders' words in the wake of the 2020 Black Lives Matter uprisings made the gap clear. Far from transforming our public safety system, and necessarily decreasing the number of police, he argued that police should be paid more.

But Senator Sanders overwhelmingly won our members' support by how he and his campaign engaged. Senator Sanders' campaign took the "Not me, Us" slogan from rhetoric to actuality. When he developed his housing platform, he leaned on the thinking of our members who had lost their homes in the foreclosure crisis and largely built out an agenda patterned on our Homes Guarantee. He participated in a tour led by Iowa CCI Action of corporate agriculture problems in northern Iowa. After he spoke briefly, he invited our members, rural dwellers and family farmers alike, to propose solutions in front of the national media. His campaign treated our members with respect when times were hard. When it was too risky for him to make our New Hampshire People's Presidential Forum due to his recent heart attack, he rescheduled and met our members in a New Hampshire barn just weeks later. These moves underscored for our members that Senator Sanders, and his campaign staff, understood that the real goal of his candidacy was not just to elect him president but to actually build the movement to govern through his candidacy. That was revelatory for our members, and I think is the heart of why they overwhelmingly backed him with 73.6% support in our final endorsement vote.

So we had an endorsed presidential candidate—we only needed to elect him! This is where I believe the biggest failings of our People's Presidential Campaign took place. While we did help Sanders' candidacy, we did not do so to the scale of our capacity or his need. Why? A combination of factors ranging from poor planning, unfocused capacity-building, and in general a lack of understanding of how to add value to a presidential campaign that was its own people-powered juggernaut.

What did we learn? We as a progressive movement need to take primaries seriously. We have moved to endorsing candidates, which is positive, but it's one small move. We have to build the real capacity to push our candidates over the top in primaries, similar to the capacity we legitimately built in general elections.

Part of this is reserving the time during primaries to go all-in for our endorsed candidates, so we don't work multiple projects at the same time. This is frequently a stress because of legislative sessions that run the first half of the year. From January through June our member organizations are both advancing policy in a legislative session and trying to win party endorsements and March–June primaries for their candidates.

Part of it is building up the funding muscle so we can pay for calls, texts, voter databases connected to mobile phone applications, literature, and organizer time to scale. This would help us make the most of the value we have to add. Presidential campaigns, especially on and after Super Tuesday, have no way to build the depth of relationships in a given jurisdiction that community organizations have. Community organizations could be the campaign in some communities. To do it legally we need to structure contracts to supplement small in-kind expenditures with movement candidates.

Finally, we need a robust collaboration infrastructure among movement organizations during primaries. In January 2019, in conjunction with the Center for Popular Democracy Action, we joined seven other

Bernie-backing groups to form an independent expenditure coalition called People Power for Bernie. But, formed late, we had not built the mechanism of a collaboration infrastructure: a shared strategic plan for our efforts, common usage of a single online voter file, and clear workload delineation. As one of the co-organizers of the group, I'd take accountability for this as something I should have incorporated into my planning from the 2018 launch of our 2020 presidential work, asking questions like these: How will we collaborate with allies? What infrastructure will we need to set up in advance? On what timeline? While we each did some individually effective work to move votes for Bernie, we left the power of effective electoral collaboration on the table, and failed to equal more than the sum of our parts. With earlier organizing and joint strategic planning we can collaborate to more effectively deliver votes for a presidential candidate in future primaries.

The pivot to Biden

Ultimately, Vice President Biden beat Sanders in the primaries. Sanders' strong performance did shift the terms of the debate and advanced real political power for us on the left. But we were still faced with a difficult pivot.

In 2016, given Secretary Clinton's nonresponsiveness and nonalignment with our movement, we decided not to endorse in the presidential election and just focus on down-ballot races. In June 2020 we convened our delegates for a conversation about the presidential election. Our hard-won consensus: Vice President Biden was a flawed candidate, but rounding up votes for him in the key swing states was the only way to defeat the existential threat of Trump and make some gains on our agenda. At stake was not just a question of Trump versus Biden. Large numbers of people felt the conflict between two giant worldview questions: whether to support a politics of division and scarcity, or a politics focused on caring for our neighbors, rooted in abundance. We would not endorse in 2020. However, we would do the work to elect Biden president.

It helped that after the primary, the campaign more consciously engaged us and other movement organizations. They assigned us a key staff point person, organized weekly check-in calls with us, set up meetings between us and point people on key issues, coordinating on joint phonebanks and a town hall forum. We were not able to impact their approach (I'm not sure if that was them or us), but we were definitely in regular communication and trying to collaborate.

In our back pocket we had the deep canvass experiment we had developed to learn how to move voters from Trump to Biden. In traditional canvassing the goal is to train volunteers to obtain an ID (a support ranking on a scale of 1–5, to determine whether the voter supports our candidate, supports the opposition, or is undecided). Then the canvasser delivers a two- or three-sentence "message" about why our candidate, a Democrat, is the next best thing since sliced bread and will finally, finally, be the person to make healthcare or education better. Traditional canvassing is verbal direct mail. The volunteer is treated like cannon fodder, rather than a sentient being with their own perspectives and experiences.

Similarly, the voter is treated like a mailbox, an empty canister to deposit a message in. Success is based on the number of IDs collected. This lets whoever is paying for the program—the foundation, candidate, party committee, or major donor—feel like they are politically sophisticated and getting their money's worth because the work is "metric-based" and "data-driven." This imports the logic of corporate America and Silicon Valley into elections. What traditional canvassing doesn't do is sustain and build a long-term volunteer base. It leaves voters' worldviews as is. It doesn't even work effectively to move voters to vote for Democrats against Republicans. Deep canvassing flips the script.

How does deep canvassing work? We rely on long-form conversations and ask the volunteer to leave the Fox News and MSNBC talking points at home. Instead, we train volunteers to share their own personal stories of how a system harms them or people they love, and ask voters to do the same. In 2019 we ran an experiment in rural areas and small towns in North Carolina, Pennsylvania, and Michigan to see if we could move voters who were with us on issues like universal healthcare and Medicare for All, but who were opposed to including undocumented immigrants in those programs.

Frequently those voters, once they heard the idea of immigrant inclusion in universal social programs, would move away from supporting the programs. In the deep canvass conversations, voters and volunteers shared health crises that crushed their families financially, or their experiences as immigrants and reasons for crossing the border. People cried in these conversations—and they could make a difference. We found after running a randomized control trial that such exchanges persuaded 8% of people who initially opposed immigrant inclusion to support it. But we didn't stop there. We tested and developed a series of questions and phrases that began to move the core worldview that underpins why people are conflicted on an issue like including undocumented immigrants in Medicare for All.

For the 2020 presidential election we explored how to move voters from Trump to Biden. We tested 27 scripts in our iteration phase with canvasses from Wisconsin to Pennsylvania. The learnings were similar to immigration: we had to ask voters where they were at; share and ask for stories of needing care, and then propose a worldview shift. We named Black, Brown, and white people and our common struggles and Trump's use of division to try and break that commonality and our collective power. Ultimately, we ran a giant differences in differences experiment (a controlled before-and-after study),[8] which proved that in a highly polarized country we could move 3.1% of voters from Trump to Biden. As a subset we were able to prove our ability to move 8.5% of independent women. Two independent researchers, Josh Kalla and David Broockman, determined that our deep canvassing methodology was 102 times more effective than the average presidential persuasion methodology. They reached this conclusion based on a meta-analysis of 49 general election persuasion experiments.[9]

But we were also confronted with COVID-19. Our main theory of change was that one-on-one in-person conversations with people in their communities could best break down Trumpist politics. With COVID we could not ethically run door-knocks and in-person organizing events. We were pushed to phones and texting. However, in this model lay an advantage: if we weren't restricted to terrestrial organizing, we could organize volunteer deep canvassers anywhere. We eventually had volunteer bases in all 50 states and overseas. We held online live streams with prominent progressive elected officials like Senator Sanders and Representative Ocasio-Cortez, as well as people from our own movement like Pennsylvania Representative Rick Krajewski and Illinois State Senator Robert Peters. We invited musical guests like Vic Mensa and Speech from Arrested Development. During the live streams we constantly posted and pitched, asking attendees—anywhere from 80,000 to more than a million of them—to join us at the next deep canvass training and call shift.

Doing deep canvassing by phone worked. In a year of increased social isolation, surprising numbers of people picked up the phone, talked with us, and shared intimate details of their lives as we shared ours. This was buttressed by impressive data work. We worked with graduate students at the University of California, Berkeley, to develop a machine-learning model to find people who would pick up the phone and to identify a larger-than-average number of undecided voters. In general, the targeting used machine learning; we used machine models to find undecided voters or Trump supporters who could be moved and machine models to find people who would pick up the phone. This work took some of our biases out of the work of persuasion. For example, while the conflicted voters we talked to were majority white, Black, Brown, Indigenous, Asian and Pacific Islander, and other people of color voters were represented in our universe at a share greater than their general presence on the enriched voter file we used.

For the first time we hired a massive national team of organizersto mobilize volunteers across the country to participate in phone deep canvassing and texting to supplement the operations of our state member organizations in the key swing states.[10] This ended up being a key decision. We added tens of thousands of volunteer shifts and millions of additional interactions with voters. Leaning into volunteer power gave us this capacity. Volunteers were trained not just to talk to voters, but to develop and run events and to train other volunteers. When right-wing activists hacked into our texting system, volunteers organized to repel them. This required a step forward in agency. Volunteers weren't there just to complete a task: they would learn and decide how to execute events and our overall strategy. This also built a base of people engaged in deep canvassing for the long run.

Ultimately our work had impact. The number of voters we deep-canvassed was greater than the margin of victory for Biden in four key states: Arizona, Wisconsin, Michigan, and Pennsylvania. We succeeded in building a long-term national volunteer base that went on to deep-canvass to turnout disaffected voters in Georgia and in the 2021 New York City, Minneapolis, and Buffalo elections. In 2021 we are expanding our deep canvass experiments by testing our ability to turn out infrequent, but worldview-aligned, people in the municipal elections in Massachusetts, New York, Minnesota, and Pennsylvania.

As the Biden team transitioned into government, they continued to connect with us and other progressive organizations. While we have "access" to the administration, the question going forward will be whether we can turn that access into concrete policy changes. That remains to be seen.

In 2022 we will target our deep canvassing to inoculate and inspire voters in Republican-held swing-state Senate and House races from North Carolina to Washington State. While the progressive movement has made great strides in electing champions in safe blue turf, the story is much more complicated in swing districts. Federal elected officials like Joe Manchin (D-WV) and Krysten Sinema (D-AZ) are allowed to define electability with a soft-on-race, pro-corporate centrism. With tons of organizing in Republican-held districts and places like West Virginia and Arizona, we know this is a mismatch; voters are with us on many populist issues. However, meaning-making on race has been ceded to the right. Right-wing candidates attack demands for racial justice as divisive and unfair, equating the Black Lives Matter uprisings with the January 6 attack on the Capitol and rolling back advances on racial equity at the state level with legislation attacking teachers and public sector workers who teach the truth about racial inequity while mainstream Democrats remain silent. We will use deep canvassing to dive into race with voters to inoculate them against right-wing race baiting and move them toward us on our agenda. We will be engaging and backing candidates who will advance our agenda as well as using deep canvassing to move voters towards us on critical issues. This strategy, including preprimary endorsements, challenges us to grow from our 2020 experience and prioritize primaries as well as general election organizing. In addition to this work at the federal level, we will focus on our down-ballot candidate pipeline to get more people from the multiracial working class who practice Movement Politics into elected office to co-govern with them. To join us, sign up at www.peoplesaction.org.

Acknowledgments

Our work building Movement Politics and our 2020 People's Presidential campaign rested on the labor of tens of thousands of people. If you made a phone call, sent a text, or are just an active member of People's Action, you made all of the above happen!

Credit to the entire Leadership LAB in LA for teaching me and others about deep canvassing. Huge thanks to Steve Deline and Ella Barrett who spun off from that group to form the New Conversations Initiative and have supported deep canvassing at People's Action every step of the way. Props to current and former People's Action staff Brooke Adams, Adam Kruggel, Mehrdad Azemun, Bree Carlson, Marlene Paez, Tim Wilkins, Catherine Curran-Groome, Matthew Rodriguez, Winnie Zhang, Susmik Lama, Jessica Burbank, Vishal Reddy, Isabel Bloom, Camile Duria, Derrick Crowe, Ross Floyd, Laurel Wales, Sondra Youdelman, Michaela

Lovegood, Daniel Espinosa, Nigel Tann, and Danny Timpona, who led specific parts of this organizing—but really the whole People's Action staff and leadership over the last decade made this happen. Thanks to our Board President Lizeth Chacon. Board member and PLAN Action Director Laura Martin led our 2020 strategy committee that guided this whole effort. Thanks to Seed the Vote, POD Save America, Movement Voter Project, Rural Democracy Initiative, SEIU and Way to Win for their partnership. People's Action is anchored in and made up of our member organizations, and they all powered our forums and throwdowns for the primaries and general election. In lead roles were GroundGame LA, San Francisco Rising, Progressive Leadership Alliance of Nevada (PLAN) Action, Living United for Change in Arizona (LUCHA), Colorado People's Action, Iowa CCI Action, TakeAction Minnesota, Citizen Action of Wisconsin, The People's Lobby, One People's Campaign, Michigan People's Campaign, Pennsylvania Stands Up, Down Home North Carolina, Rights And Democracy, New Hampshire Youth Movement, and Student Action. Staff at Community Change Action grounded us in their experience running forums in 2008 and 2016.

Notes

1. The Community Reinvestment Act worked to reverse red lining, a systematic refusal on the part of banks to lend money to borrowers in low-income neighborhoods, especially in communities of color. The CRA forced banks to lend money in low- and moderate-income neighborhoods.

2. To "bird-dog" a politician or a policy simply means to follow persistently to ensure accountability or action. Indivisible talks about it also as a tool for getting candidates and electeds on the record. See "Bird-Dogging Guide: Get Them on the Record," https://indivisible.org/resource/bird-dogging-guide-get-them-record.

3. As our group Maine People's Alliance did in Lewiston and GroundGame LA did in California.

4. 54 Yes votes, 3 Abstentions, and 2 No votes.

5. Healthcare provides a great example. From 2006 to 2016 hundreds of millions of dollars were spent on candidate and independent expenditure ads driven by for-profit consultants that included contentless phrases like "quality, affordable health care for all" or "mend it, don't end it" (in reference to the Affordable Care

Act). Those same consultants told candidates in swing congressional districts that Medicare for All was a sure loser with voters. In contrast, our experience organizing in swing districts is that voters know that small tweaks won't help them, and Medicare for All performs well in swing districts. In this way the for-profit political consultant class helps limit possibilities for transformational change in healthcare.

6. Community organizing has for years engaged with powerful elected officials. We receive phone calls from electeds telling us why they voted this way or that. We call them before a vote to put pressure on them to vote the right way. All of this is a tactical intervention by community organizations to try to alter an outcome right before it occurs or by an elected official to mitigate fallout from taking a bad vote. With "movement co-governing" we orient toward a long-term strategic relationship with our elected officials. We plan together when we will advance different issues or bills. We plan together the "inside game" of our aligned elected official moving other elected officials in City Hall to support our position and the "outside game" of rallies and protests to create the public pressure needed to advance our position. We treat the elected official not as a target, but as a collaborator. The elected official doesn't treat us as yet another "interest group" but as a powerful actor with whom they should jointly move a shared agenda.

7. Due to scheduling issues (the date we picked ultimately immediately preceded a Democratic Presidential Debate) we offered candidates in contention for our support small group meetings with our members (New Hampshire Youth Movement and Rights and Democracy) in New Hampshire.

8. Because of the COVID-19 pandemic we were not able to run deep canvassing by door-knocking in this 2020 anti-Trump experiment. We had to canvass by phone, so we were not able to run a randomized control trial (RCT) experiment. Difference in differences is a methodology that assesses the impact of an intervention (in this case, deep canvassing on voters' views of Trump) over time. It holds a treatment and a nontreatment group so even though we know other variables impact a voter's perception of a candidate over time in the real world, both these groups are getting that real world exposure, but are held separate for the study so we can see how our work impacts them over time.

9. Joshua L. Kalla and David E. Broockman, "The Minimal Persuasive Effects of Campaign Contact in General Elections: Evidence from 49 Field Experiments," *American Political Science Review* 112, no. 1 (February 2018), pp. 148–66.

10. Largely hired from Senator Sanders' presidential campaign.

20

Fight the Right, Build the Left: Seed the Vote's Work in 2020

Jill Shenker, Rose Mendelsohn, and
Jason Negrón-Gonzales of Seed the Vote

In the 2020 general election, Seed the Vote (STV)—a project that didn't exist two years before—established partnerships with grassroots groups in four states and mobilized over 9,000 volunteers from across the country to make phone calls and knock on doors to defeat Trump and halt the most dangerous advances of far-right authoritarianism. We built infrastructure and relationships that not only made a difference in states like Arizona and Pennsylvania on November 3, but also allowed us to deploy over 448 volunteers to Georgia in the January 2021 Senate runoffs, boosting the work of grassroots groups in the state and denying the GOP control of the Senate.

Through a year of intense engagement in key races, STV leaders and volunteers acquired rich experience and learned a tremendous deal about electoral work and the way leftists can effectively intervene in that arena. Many people who had only done electoral work at the local level—or not done it at all—came away much better prepared to take the skills they sharpened, and the nimble STV structure, into battles ahead. The project was launched in a state of emergency, and although we achieved our goal of avoiding a second Trump term, we're clear that the dangers we were resisting in 2020 have not at all disappeared, and that the electoral terrain will continue to be key in the fight against the racist authoritarian right.

This article is one attempt at telling the STV story and sharing what we've learned. The first section covers the background and formation of the project. After that, we recount the work we did, how we did it, and the lessons we learned. We finish with some thoughts about the critical work ahead for us and for the left overall.

Background: Pivoting from defense to offense

Many Bay Area organizers who would go on to start Seed the Vote have similar stories about the early evening of November 8, 2016. As we were knocking on doors, flyering for local candidates, and campaigning for ballot initiatives, we were also anxiously checking our phones as the presidential race turned bleaker by the minute. Those of us who were engaged in electoral politics had focused all our election energies on local races, and the juxtaposition between the exciting things we were fighting for locally and the reality of what a Trump presidency would mean for our communities was starting to sink in. On November 9, a few people got together and started discussing what was to be done. We realized that we needed to pay attention to national work in a way that we hadn't prioritized before, because Trump and his politics were an existential threat to the communities and issues important to all of us.

These early conversations were focused on building strategic alignment and figuring out how to build infrastructure that could move masses of people to respond to the attacks that would surely come once Trump took office. What emerged was Bay Resistance—a rapid response network built to counter Trump's hateful policies by activating individuals and families to defend our communities and our movements. By the time the inauguration came around on January 20, 2017, Bay Resistance had already developed a core set of principles, a mass texting system for people to join, and thousands of physical invitations to invite people in. This set the stage to help mobilize thousands of people to San Francisco airport a week later for an action in protest of Trump's Muslim ban.

That began four years of rapid response mobilizations, mass trainings, and strategy sessions about how to orient newly mobilized masses of people in the Bay Area toward racial justice work led by existing grassroots groups.

In early 2019, during a Bay Resistance steering committee meeting, one of the committee members pitched the need to pivot from resisting Trump's policies to helping remove him from office. After three years of exhausting work responding to attack after attack, and focusing on defensive fights at the expense of more visionary campaigns, it was not a hard sell. A few members from the Bay Resistance steering committee joined with other local organizers to start convening a group to further flesh out these ideas. As we delved deeper into these early conversations, some people were not overjoyed about the idea of investing our resources into the presidential race without knowing who the Democratic nominee would be. Regardless, they came to the meetings because we had spent the last three years under Trump—and many more before that—working together and growing our relationships. Through various campaigns, mobilizations, disagreements, and coalitions, we had built enough trust to get us started. We used those early discussions to build alignment and, in the end, almost everyone who was part of those meetings would stick around for the long haul.

We knew that despite our desire to contribute to the national election, there was little meaningful ability to do that in our state because California's Electoral College votes consistently land Democratic. We needed a plan that would enable organizers and activists from the Bay Area to effectively support work in battleground states, and that's how the basic function of Seed the Vote was born. Our movements across the country have so much technical capacity to offer, but we don't always know how to prioritize the deployment of our forces. We have organizers, trainers, fundraisers, writers, communications specialists, electoral campaign specialists, technology specialists, and more. Since getting rid of Trump and flipping the Senate weren't on the ballot in California, we knew that we had to bring these capacities to support work happening in states that were actually up for grabs. While this approach seemed basic, we were making an argument for something surprisingly uncommon and practically challenging. As the project grew, we were able to mobilize people to support swing state efforts not only from the Bay Area, but from places across the country that were not at play in the presidential election.

Over the last few decades, even in important elections that the left wanted to impact, like the reelection of Bush in 2004, or Trump versus Clinton in 2016, it has been uncommon to see the left coordinate around moving capacity from progressive hubs to battleground states. There are plenty of legitimate reasons for this related to limited capacity and resources, the prioritization of local work over national fights, the absence of strong relationships across geographies, the limitations of 501(c)(3) funding, and the challenges of having outsiders involved, to name a few.

However, while the left generally wasn't engaging in this kind of strategy, the right was. Through the Obama era we lost congressional seats, state houses, governorships, and eventually the presidency to Trump. It is beyond the scope of this chapter to review how and why this happened, but as we continued to largely stay in our areas of strength, our national reality was getting worse in painful ways. As we grappled with this reality we began asking ourselves a series of questions: Was it good enough to win local campaigns when we were getting killed by Trump and the Republicans at the national level and seeing the local impacts of that? How could we help defeat Trump even though our state was not at play? How could we do this in ways aligned with our values and in support of building long-term grassroots power?

These questions and others led us to coalesce around the assertion that the left and social movements needed to prioritize defeating Trump in 2020, and that by supporting the strategies of grassroots organizations rooted in communities of color, we could win. These organizations had been fighting alongside people in their communities for decades. They knew how to build a field plan and messaging that would turn out their people. We built this project—with the initial internal name "Fight the Right, Build the Left"—oriented around three main goals:

1. Motivate people in our movements to prioritize the presidential election.
2. Add capacity to the electoral campaigns of people of color-led grassroots organizations in key swing states.
3. Do the work in a way that strengthens our movements.

By the fall of 2019, we landed on the name Seed the Vote and publicly launched with a call to action for people to commit to volunteering with an organization called Living United for Change in Arizona (LUCHA) for two weeks leading up to the general election. We secured commitments from over 150 organizers and activists, many of whom became volunteer leaders in the project over time. We continued to make these asks far in advance, to get left leaders to prioritize and commit to action for this election.

In March 2020, when the COVID-19 pandemic began, we pivoted to phonebanking and broadened our volunteer recruitment and partnerships nationally. In Arizona, we partnered with LUCHA and UNITE HERE Local 11/CASE Action. In Florida, we partnered with the New Florida Majority (now Florida Rising), Dream Defenders, and Florida for All. In Pennsylvania, we partnered with PA Stands Up, Pennsylvania Working Families Party, and Asian Pacific Islander Political Alliance (APIPA). In Georgia, we partnered with Asian American Advocacy Fund PAC, Georgia Latino Alliance for Human Rights Action, Mijente PAC, the Southern Crossroads chapter of Showing Up for Racial Justice, New Georgia Project Action Fund, and UNITE HERE.

By November 2020, Seed the Vote had become an enormous volunteer powerhouse of organizers, activists, and community members coming together to build progressive turnout and win up and down the ballot. We recruited and engaged nearly 9,000 volunteers to defeat Trump and flip the Senate, including over 1,270 volunteers who did in-person canvassing in Arizona, Pennsylvania, and Georgia.

Looking back, there were a few key elements of our work that both led to our success and brought up challenges and questions about the future of this type of work. Those elements were nimbleness and starting early, relational organizing and relationship-building, and an intensive door-knocking strategy. The throughline that allowed for all those elements to be successful was the strength of existing relationships and the intentional nurturing of new ones.

Key elements of our work

Nimbleness and timing

This project would not have happened without a few key leaders in the Bay Area seeing a need and prioritizing bringing people together to start discussing it early. We were all busy running local campaigns, but we were also attuned to national politics and its impact on our local organizing. There were three main assertions that made up our initial assessment. The first was that defeating Trump was a hugely important task because Trump stood in the way of our other aspirations. The second was that his defeat was possible but not inevitable, and so our work could actually make the difference. The third was that nobody in our local left movement ecosystem had a plan yet to harness our collective resources and help defeat him.

Seed the Vote's origins show us the importance of building organizational cultures and infrastructure that can be nimble and that allow us to make choices and prioritize work outside of our organization's core efforts when needed. Prioritizing the presidential election and building STV necessitated tapping experienced organizers to take substantial leadership on specific pieces of the project, and staff members taking time off from their community organizations to take a role. One reason we were able to be nimble, adapt to shifting organizing conditions (namely COVID-19), and do a lot of work with limited funds was that we could hire skilled and experienced organizers for part-time and short-term work who could jump in and contribute at a high level quickly. We were also able to bring in key volunteers with specific skill sets that allowed them to take on roles often reserved for staff. All of this was only able to happen because key organizations made an assessment that this work was urgent and would not happen if they didn't create the room and flexibility in their work plans to permit staff to take leave to work on it. Without this realization and decision, Seed the Vote may not have happened.

Much of our nimbleness was tied to the talent we were able to draw. While we ideally hoped to recruit a lot of people, we also knew that we had more capacity to bring in smaller numbers of experienced people than we did to bring in masses of people. So, for example, when we decided last-minute to run an Arizona in-person door-knocking program (under the leadership of UNITE HERE and LUCHA) we prioritized tapping people who could effectively serve as field leads on very short notice. They were able to develop a rigorous and effective field program for hundreds of volunteers without much prep time or supervision. The same thing happened in Georgia when we decided to leverage our capacity and throw down with the local groups there for the January Senate runoff.

None of this nimbleness would have been possible without our partners' flexibility and willingness to work with us. We weren't part of their initial field plans, but they made room for us to play a role and to adjust that role as we went along. This was no small thing, since they were already working at capacity and running large field programs.

Part of being nimble meant starting early and being open to adjusting as conditions changed on the ground. Seed the Vote launched 13 months before the general election, with exploratory and planning conversations beginning even earlier. Many of the early volunteers became leaders in the project and did important groundwork such as building local and national partnerships, fundraising, communications work to influence narratives, volunteer recruitment, and getting buy-in from movement leaders. However, most of the voter contact work did not start until three months prior to the election, and we saw our volunteer numbers skyrocket at that time. Seed the Vote essentially became part of an "advance team," a small group of people who prepared infrastructure for others in the movement to join after the primaries.

One story that shows the importance of nimbleness is that of our in-person collaboration with the Pennsylvania Working Families Party (WFP) to turn out voters at Philadelphia early voting sites. During the final month leading into the election, we (with contributions from a sister project based in New York City called Water for Grassroots) recruited 592 volunteers to complete 1,063 days of voter engagement in Philadelphia. This work included voting center outreach, where we talked to people who were near open poll locations and helped them make a plan to vote. It also included supporting WFP's Joy to the Polls effort, which brought music to voting centers across the city. Finally, it included participating in racial justice and postelection direct actions.

We decided early on that we wanted to support work in Pennsylvania because it was the tipping point in many Electoral College scenarios. We started phone banking with PA Stands Up in July of 2020, but it was unclear whether there would be any on-the-ground work that made sense for us to join. However, because of the importance of the state, the fact that we had a base of volunteers in the Northeast, and our confidence in being able to do in-person work safely, we made ourselves available and on-call to support groups there in person should the opportunity arise.

One group that we stayed in touch with was the Pennsylvania Working Families Party. Once the call came in September 2020, we had to balance moving very quickly with being patient and graceful. WFP had a lot to do to prepare the program before we could start playing our role, and voting centers were a new thing for everyone. We also didn't have a relationship with them going into this project, so we tried to be conscious of our position as outsiders and build trust as we went. We weren't pushy, but we showed up in ways that gave WFP the confidence to bring us into a coordination role quickly. The balance of deferring and stepping into leadership wasn't always easy, and we didn't always get it right. There were bumps along the way and times where we slowed the work down by being overly cautious, but overall, taking on this role was worth it and greatly increased Seed the Vote's impact in Pennsylvania.

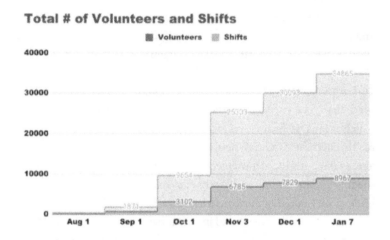

Total # of Volunteers and Shifts

Our plan to be nimble and timely was challenged during the spring and early summer of 2020. The global COVID-19 pandemic turned the world upside down, the Presidential primary had been decided in favor of Joe Biden, and the police killing of George Floyd kicked off unprecedented uprisings and demonstrations against police violence and racial injustice. As leaders of Seed the Vote, we felt the urgency of defeating Trump was further reinforced by his administrations' costly response to the pandemic and the uprisings, but the rapidly shifting conditions during this period made it difficult to figure out how to continue to build our capacity to defeat him. We weren't sure if door-knocking was safe. Our partner organizations and volunteer pools were stretched thin, because people were focused on mutual aid and organizing around police violence, housing relief, stimulus checks, and dealing with personal and collective grief. Our community-based partners in swing states had to throw down for more immediate things impacting their local bases, whereas Seed the Vote had a very specific mission to support those very same organizations in their plans to defeat Trump. Internally, the work felt somewhat stuck during this period. In retrospect, it's clear that this was not necessarily a failing on our part, but a result of the external conditions being what they were. We did what we could then to shift our strategies based on COVID-19 restrictions, to reground in our role, and to get ourselves ready for when attention returned to the presidential election, which we knew it eventually would.

Our organizing approach

Seed the Vote created a structure rooted in relational organizing, which means we focused on recruiting volunteers and organizing people through their existing networks. STV emerged from conversations among Bay Area social movement leaders, and as it grew, we intentionally sought out one-on-one and group conversations with more movement leaders. We knew that movement leaders are powerful influencers in our communities who we needed to inspire others to get them involved. This was one of the main features that set Seed the Vote apart from most other national electoral efforts—it was started by social movement organizers rather than people who do traditional electoral work, and we created this for other social movement leftists to plug into.

Everyone was encouraged to recruit more people, and leaders were supported to do targeted, consistent outreach with clear, specific, and very ambitious asks. We created Seed Pods, small groups of connected people who phonebanked together. This allowed people to recruit friends, family, and movement comrades into the project and provide support and accountability to each other. We created a similar structure called Branches, for established organizing networks that wanted to plug into Seed the Vote together. Through Pods and Branches, volunteers

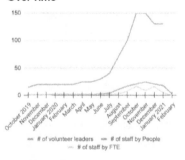

# of STV Staff and Volunteer Leaders Over Time

— # of volunteer leaders   — # of staff by People
— # of staff by FTE

were motivated to participate and benefited from working with a consistent group of people who they were personally connected to.[1] While we provided training and support for these groups, we also relied on the fact that organizers would be able to recruit their own people into the work, pick up on the content quickly, and be able to run with it. This all allowed us to scale up with limited staff capacity.

We relied on volunteer leaders just as much as staff. We recruited and were driven by over 150 volunteer leaders who played essential leadership roles in all aspects of the work. While we were able to hire a substantial number of temporary and part-time organizers during the height of election season, volunteer leaders played a critical and essential role in building and sustaining the work. Most of our leaders were organizers and activists who were mainly interested in engaging in GOTV efforts connected to long-term power building, though that wasn't the case across the board. Our leaders had skills and expertise to offer, and a need for somewhere to plug in that aligned with their values. As with the Seed Pods, we capitalized on the experience of our volunteers generally throughout the project by offering them substantial trust and responsibility for the work.

We also provided leadership opportunities that were accessible and celebrated. There were varying levels of participation, types of leadership opportunities, and time commitments. In reflection, leaders shared that they appreciated the opportunity to share their talents and get involved in a range of ways, and that they felt supported and appreciated in the roles they took on. As one volunteer wrote:

> As a community organizer for over two decades, I appreciated the way STV made it possible for both long-time and brand-new organizers to get involved. It felt great to know that I was making a contribution without having to be responsible for creating and holding the whole project. Knowing that I was just one of many people coming together enabled me to identify a clear role and purpose during election season.[2]

Though we did not set out with this intention, Seed the Vote became a political home for people who were looking for opportunities that aligned with their values rather than a candidate or a party. The strategy of investing in grassroots organizations led by people of color resonated with our volunteers, and by conducting volunteer engagement and outreach nationally—with a tighter focus on recruiting people in social movement organizing communities—Seed the Vote was able to attract many of the volunteers local partners wanted.

It's worth mentioning here that while we were successful in recruiting a lot of movement organizers into this work, there were still many organizations and individuals that did not join us. While we did not experience as much ideological pushback as we expected from groups on the left, most of the dissension came in the form of nonparticipation. We just couldn't convince as many people as we wanted to prioritize this work.

Another place where we learned important lessons around relationships was with our partner organizations. STV partnered with organizations in battleground states that are building long-term political power in working-class communities of color. Their nonstop work between election cycles led to the historic turnout in 2020. This work enables them to defend a Senate majority in 2022, and it keeps pressure on the Biden administration to deliver for our communities. Our intention was to follow their leadership while bringing meaningful capacity to boost our collective efforts to defeat Trump and strengthen movements. Building the partnerships was a dance in which we tried to make offers without being pushy, build trust, and navigate dynamic conditions and situations together.

In some cases, we had long-term relationships with people at our partner organizations, but in most cases, we did not. One of our top reasons for starting the project early was to ensure we had time to build trust and offer real support before things got hectic. It was important that we showed up as intentional community organizers who prioritized relationship and trust-building, not political consultants who prioritized results. We also tried our best to be cognizant of the complex local contexts and play an appropriate support role. We had a small team of dedicated people in Seed the Vote who led the collaborations, which helped us learn and apply lessons over time and from one partnership to another. We found that things ran the smoothest once we set up regular weekly meetings, and when our point person in the partner organization was someone with a significant level of experience and power in their organization, even though these were the people who are most stretched. While we had some concerns about having multiple partner organizations in a single location, it was also helpful because some partnerships ended up having many limitations while others flourished. Some factors that affected this included their staff's capacity to collaborate, how much volunteer help was needed, and whether our volunteer demographics were a good fit with the voters they were targeting.

We learned and experimented with what roles we could play, and it varied over time and with each partnership. In some cases we ran phonebanks or in-person canvasses, while in others we sent volunteers to activities hosted by the local organizations. In some places we had access to and could help manage the backend of the predictive dialer,[3] and in other places we ran the entire out-of-state volunteer program for a partner.

In our independent evaluation interviews, local and national partner organizations shared that they were able to build trust with Seed the Vote because we "threw down." As one of our partners wrote,

> They were able to come into a city that is largely used to working with themselves and not typically as easily convinced to work with outside organizations. [Seed the Vote] really built trust and made it easy to see them as a resource and never tried to have influence in how we moved and how we approached the work … They just came with their resources and said you're doing this really cool thing. We'd like to help. This is what we got.[4]

As Seed the Vote goes forward, we look forward to deepening many of these relationships and strengthening the work we do with our partners.

One question that remains unresolved for us is how our model contributes to helping our partners build power. One popular theory of movement-building is that we change society by organizing oppressed people to take power and leadership in their own local communities. Our model asks people to engage in short-term and tactically important work with allied groups based elsewhere. Those two things aren't necessarily opposed, but there can be tension between the two.

As we move forward, we are still struggling with that question and others related to power building in electoral work. What does it take for us and our partners on the ground to have the scale and technical expertise required to have an impact? How does this work relate to our theory of change, theory of power, and the priorities of the left in this political moment?

While we are still grappling with these questions, we think that building longer and deeper relationships with our partners will help us get closer to answering them. For example, round one of Seed the Vote was mostly focused on recruiting and supporting as many volunteers as possible to plug into our partners' work. But in round two, if we can start talking to partners earlier, with an existing relationship to build off of, we can have more sophisticated conversations about what kinds of capacity we can add to their work that will not only help them win, but support their longer-term power-building goals. As we work to expand the number of leftists and social movement organizations that engage in the 2022 elections, there will necessarily be hard conversations about strategy and priorities that force us to continue clarifying our positions and our role.

Door-knocking

Knocking on doors was the focus of our pre-COVID-19 field plan, but between March and August 2020, we did not think it would be possible for health reasons. The decision to pivot at the last minute to knock on doors in person was not made lightly, and it ended up being hugely valuable.

The ability to build relationships and organize people in our physical communities is a foundational strength for our movements, and much of that is dependent on our ability to gather in person and speak face to face with our people. Many of the activities that are directly connected to the work we do were halted when the pandemic reached the US in 2020. Unions stopped doing house visits, community members could no longer testify at City Hall, and electoral campaigns simply stopped all in-person door-knocking operations.

In September 2020, we decided at the last minute to knock on doors in person in Arizona. That decision was not made lightly. We worked with UNITE HERE and LUCHA to organize a massive 400-person volunteer canvassing operation in Arizona, and learned from UNITE HERE's model to implement adequate safety protocols so that there wasn't a single outbreak of COVID via community spread.

Traveling and taking time off during a pandemic was not easy for anyone, but once people started knocking on doors, they didn't want to stop. After months of limited human connection leading up to one of the biggest elections of our lifetimes, getting to talk to people face-to-face and working collectively with a team toward an immediate and high-stakes goal was electric for our volunteers. We had people who signed up for a week and then stayed for a month, people who negotiated complex family plans to extend their trips, and even someone who drove home from Arizona to California to then turn right back around and stay until the election. One of our team leads in Georgia told us:

> Talking to people on the doors about what issues they cared about was invigorating for many volunteers who were engaged in political work back home, but didn't often get to have those kinds of in-depth conversations with working-class people about what actually mattered to them. People left their time in Arizona and Georgia fired up to keep having conversations like that afterwards, and we've even

seen groups of Seed the Vote volunteers seek out door knocking opportunities together since the election.[5]

It's clear that door-knocking wasn't only important in helping us reach enough voters to unseat Trump, but that this was also a rare opportunity for many activists and organizers who weren't engaged in this tactic in their day-to-day work back home.

We adopted UNITE HERE's intensive door-knocking strategy, which meant we not only helped people make plans to vote when we were at the doors, but also did multiple follow-ups afterwards to make sure they were able to complete their plans. Volunteers extended their trips because they could feel the difference we were making at the doors, one by one by one. The same thing happened in the Georgia Senate runoffs in January. Volunteers planned to come for a few days and ended up staying until the election, in some cases, leaving and coming back for the final week. The average volunteer stayed in Georgia for 10 days, despite this being an election that no volunteer had planned for ahead of time.

By the end of the election cycle, we had recruited and supported 1,270 in-person volunteers across three states. Some 230 of these volunteers were in Arizona, and most of them stayed for a week or more; 592 were in Pennsylvania, where they collectively completed 1,063 days of in-person outreach. There were 448 in Georgia, where they completed a combined 4,159 days of canvassing. The results of the election made the impact of this work crystal clear. In Maricopa County, Arizona—which ended up being a crucial county in deciding the federal election—Biden won by 45,000 votes. The Democratic Party did not knock on doors there, and the Republican Party did. Seed the Vote volunteers knocked on 45,562 doors, yielding over 14,000 direct conversations. Combined with the many doors knocked by our partners at UNITE HERE and LUCHA, it is not a stretch to say that our door-knocking efforts made a big contribution toward the razor-thin victory for Democrats in Arizona and Trump's defeat nationally. This made it clear to us that we almost completely ceded what gave us our edge.

A parallel case study in California made it clear just how important door-knocking was to our movements, especially in 2020. Emily Lee, director of San Francisco Rising Action Fund and a member of the Seed the Vote coordinating committee who knocked on doors for a month in Arizona, describes it this way:

> Two campaigns in San Francisco (Prop G) and in California (Prop 15) lost by less than 2 percentage points in November. These campaigns did not do any in-person voter outreach work and relied on phoning, texting, and paid ads. However, our opponents' massive spending against Prop 15 confused our voter base just enough for people to vote against their own interests. If our campaign had actually mobilized a door-knocking program in our key geographic areas, I believe we would have won by that same narrow margin. It's fair to say that only one organization has successfully run massive campaign operations at a statewide level with the appropriate level of COVID safety protocols, and that is UNITE HERE, which ran the largest canvas field program in Arizona and Nevada. Being embedded with their program has made me realize that our sector can and should be replicating their approach across the country if we seek to win and advance a racial justice agenda in the next four years. We should continue to integrate digital and remote organizing techniques, especially in our communities who lack digital access, but we also cannot relinquish what sets us apart and gives us our edge to victory.[6]

The decision to follow the lead of UNITE HERE and switch back to door-knocking in the 2020 general election was crucial to our success. It is a tactic that continues to deliver for electoral work and for our movements more broadly.

Unite for a generational fight

A redwood tree's roots don't go very deep, but they do reach outward toward other trees, and they intertwine. In this way, entire forests are

held together by interlocking roots, and it allows the trees to better collectively withstand the forces of nature that may tear them down. The
interlocking roots also allow entire forests to move water and nutrients
to places where they are most needed. Taller trees take in water from fog
and pass it onto shorter trees, and better resourced trees are able to move
some of their resources to other trees that need it more throughout the
forest. Perhaps it is no wonder that the idea for Seed the Vote was born
in the Bay Area, where our redwood forests are a defining feature of our
community.

Much of the US left understands that, in this moment, the threat of
the far right is greater than Trump the person. The existence and danger
of the far right in the US is not new, but conditions over recent decades
have brought us to a new and heightened moment of danger, both here
and globally. While our defeat of Trump struck a blow for the forces
of justice and democracy, none of the underlying dynamics that led to
Trump's rise have changed. We believe that we must continue to respond
with people power and organizing. The reality is that the enduring fight
against the far right is going to be a generational fight for us, and we
hope that Seed the Vote can contribute to expanding our ability to win
on one of the fronts of that battle. The next few years will be crucial in
loosening Trumpism's grip on our federal government. Seed the Vote
was a success, and we are planning to reactivate this project for the 2022
election cycle. We will partner with grassroots organizations in three
to six states that are battlegrounds for Senate and House seats, and add
on-the-ground and remote volunteer support tailored to the needs of
each organization and race.

We built Seed the Vote with the idea that interstate support was
necessary for victory in the 2020 election. We went through ups and
downs with the pandemic, but held on to the core thread that progressive and left activists needed to support the fight in the battleground
states. When Trump lost in some of those key battleground states, and
when the Senate races were won in Georgia, the work was anchored by
groups that had been present doing work on the ground over the last

decade or more, but outside supporters made important contributions. This type of active solidarity may be less common in community organizing, but it's fairly common in the union movement. If 15 workers from a union local are unfairly fired and they decide to hold a worksite action, dozens if not hundreds of workers from other unions will join them. The workers unite to show up together where the fight is happening. In 2020, we wanted to approach our work in the same way. We know that voting and the electoral system in the United States is unfair. The Electoral College and Senate give undue weight to areas of the country that are older, more rural, and more white, and the Republican Party is doing everything it can, everywhere it has power, to disenfranchise voters of color.

We believe that our experience and the lessons we learned along the way are important to the battles ahead. The far right isn't backing down, and neither should we. The electoral arena is a key front in the fight against the far right, and we have to show up and continue engaging in it. We must continue to experiment with new models of organizing and new infrastructure that makes the most of the strengths we have in our movements across the country and builds power for the long haul. We must build infrastructure that is nimble and reactive, and we must constantly reassess our conditions and change our course of action as needed. We must continue to prioritize building long-term relationships rooted in trust and respecting each others' areas of expertise. We must lean on our networks and make bold asks of our comrades. We must stick to the door-to-door and in-person tactics that are at the root of our people power. If we do this, and if we can redirect our strengths and resources to the fights that need them the most and ultimately impact all of us, we will put ourselves in the best position to defeat the far right and move closer to the thriving multiracial democracy that is possible in this country.

Notes

1. Seed the Vote, 2021, *It Took All of Us. Organizing Works. A Report on Seed the Vote's 2020 Elections Experiment to Help Defeat Trump and Build Our Movements*, www.seedthevote.org.

2. Seed the Vote, *It Took All of Us*, p. 14.

3. A calling system that calls through many people quickly on behalf of the caller, so the caller doesn't have to dial manually or wade through lots of voicemails.

4. Seed the Vote, *It Took All of Us*, p. 23.

5. Seed the Vote, *It Took All of Us*.

6. Seed the Vote, *It Took All of Us*, p. 26.

21

Win Justice and Beyond: Winning Elections While Building Power for the Long Term

Deepak Pateriya

Introduction: apologist or idealist?

Parts of this chapter will sound to some readers like they're coming from an apologist for the timid inadequacy of what has passed for a Democratic Party in the United States these last few decades. Other parts will sound to other readers like happy talk from an idealist pining for some left-wing mass movement fantasy of an earlier era.

For example, I believe primary challenges to moderate and obstructionist Democrats with candidates from the left is important—if and when it's based on an unromanticized analysis of local power. At some times, in some places, our base and our movements lack the necessary power, so those challenges can backfire. In those times and places, we have to work with those Democrats, apply pressure smartly with the power we do have, and aggressively grow our organized bases to change the facts on the ground over time.

I also believe, under the current realities of political power and ideological alignment in the US, that lining up behind whoever wins a Democratic presidential nomination (or US Senate nomination for that matter) and throwing left movements' full electoral energy behind ensuring they win is the right and necessary thing to do. While we help elect those often mediocre candidates, we have to simultaneously work every day to build an organized and disciplined mass base and voter turnout apparatus large enough and powerful enough to command attention, instill fear, and dramatically shift the center of gravity of US electoral politics. We have to do all this without jeopardizing the short-term objective of keeping white supremacist authoritarians away from the nuclear codes and veto pens.

These are two of many parts in a tricky balancing act—not for the faint of heart, the closed of mind, the fearful of tension, or the too rosy of vision. We can't just be marginal electoral actors from the left. Neither can we just be unquestioning subjects of the Democratic Party as it exists. This broader balancing act is a strategic necessity during a period in US politics that in my view requires leftists, progressives, and liberals to struggle together to act as a united front in the electoral arena.

I see none of this as apology or idealism.

In the first part of this chapter, I'll describe details and share lessons and implications from the grassroots electoral power building work I've been involved with over the past several election cycles, including the Win Justice collaboration in 2018 and 2020. In the latter part of the chapter, I share some personal thoughts on imperatives for all of us on what it's going to take to build the power we need to win for real.

Building toward the 2020 election and the Win Justice collaboration

In both the 2018 and 2020 elections, I had the privilege of co-leading the Win Justice collaborative electoral project—one of the largest grassroots direct voter contact efforts in the country. Win Justice was a joint effort of Community Change Action, the Service Employees International Union (SEIU), the political arms of Planned Parenthood and Color of Change,[1] and all of our respective state affiliate and partner organizations.

One of my roles at CC/CCA was overseeing and growing the electoral program from 2012 until I left the organization in the summer of 2021. For me and Community Change/Action (CC/CCA), the Win Justice effort was informed directly by our experiences in the preceding several election cycles. Below I begin with some brief notes on that history before sharing the story of Win Justice and its purpose, strategies, program, and impacts. All of this work by Win Justice and CCA has, in my view, been contributing toward building electoral power to achieve our vision of justice, at the scale necessary to actually achieve it, while sustaining that balancing act of a united front.

Community Change/Action (2004-14): Building community-grounded voter engagement capacity and sophistication

Community Change (CC) is a national 501(c)(3) nonprofit organization working with grassroots community groups to build power for economic and racial justice and immigrant rights. Community Change Action (CCA) is its 501(c)(4) political and advocacy sister organization.[2] CC/CCA does this work with grassroots groups across the country through organizing, leadership development, policy advocacy, and voter engagement. The voter engagement efforts began in 2004. From then through 2014, we focused especially on building core capacity and skills for voter registration and turnout, increasing our sophistication with voter data analysis and management, and creating new 501(c)(4) arms for many 501(c)(3) groups that didn't have them. All of this was driven by the philosophy that we must strive for our voter engagement and turnout work to be integrated with, and in service to, building our base, leadership, organizations, and power for the long term.

On the 501(c)(4) partisan side of the work, we began positioning CCA and grassroots 501(c)(4) groups as players within the mainstream, progressive electoral landscape. This included the national and state-level "501(c)(4) voter tables" (where most of the key organizational players doing partisan voter turnout work—including organized labor and environmental and other single-issue or constituency electoral groups—sit together to coordinate and minimize duplication of activities during each election cycle), and also with key national and state-level political donors.

Community Change Action (2015-16): Scaling national partisan voter programs

Starting in 2015, Community Change Action and local partner grass-roots groups in the immigrant rights and economic and racial justice movements decided we had to take a leap in scale and impact on the electoral power front.

We were clear at this stage that building the kind of power in the electoral arena that we really needed, and being recognized for it, meant doing the types of large-scale partisan voter engagement work that is best done through political action committees (PACs). We founded and launched a federal "independent expenditure" SuperPAC (Community Change Voters) and affiliated state-level political action committees, which were all owned and controlled by Community Change Action. Creating these political arms,[3] and the infrastructure to manage them well,[4] was key for enabling CCA and our local partner groups to raise and spend larger amounts of political dollars and run larger scale partisan voter operations that are recognized by DC political operatives as impacting election outcomes, in federal and state-level races—the White House, US Senate and House, governors, state legislatures, etc.

We built a collaborative plan and strategy with local partner groups in three strategic states (Colorado, Nevada, and Florida) where the potential voting power of immigrant, and pro-immigrant voters of color could help turn statewide elections in key swing states for control of the White House and US Senate, while simultaneously advancing electoral goals at the municipal and state levels.[5]

This 2016 effort yielded some important accomplishments and also lessons for the future. First, even though we lost the White House, our program did help win a number of key races, including electing Democratic US Senator Catherine Cortez-Masto, the first Latina US Senator— and a number of down-ballot races and ballot measures that were significant for our movements locally in Florida and Colorado—including flipping control of both the Nevada state Assembly and state Senate to Democrats, and a successful Colorado minimum wage measure.

We also moved a plan to try to shape what the "political story" of the election would be after November. We wanted to cultivate and promote an analysis among mainstream political circles that immigrant and pro-immigrant voters in key states were essential to the wins and that Democrats in Congress would face an imperative to act on comprehensive immigration reform in 2017, after having failed to do so under Obama. We landed some high-profile news pieces but, in truth, this plan didn't work out, given the outcome of the presidential election.[6]

We had initial success in putting CCA and key local groups on the radar of the political establishment (donors, labor, state tables, political operatives), as actors that could build and deliver impactful voter turnout programs at statewide scale in multiple states; and as actors that could be entrusted with PAC contributions in the hundreds of thousands and millions of dollars. This success was built on an early planning and coalition-building process, starting a year ahead of time, with deliberate work in each state to define shared goals, strategies, plans, and roles.

Together, we were able to raise $15 million (a majority PAC and some 501(c)(4) funding), position our collaboration as one of the largest independent expenditure direct voter contact efforts focused solely on voters of color in each of those three states (Colorado, Nevada, and Florida), and engage a total of 750,000 voters.

We also began to demonstrate that we could use old-fashioned organizing approaches—at scale,[7] and coupled with state-of-the-art technology—to reach, motivate, and turnout many so-called "unlikely" voters in our communities, who have historically been ignored by traditional candidate and party campaigns. In 2014 and 2016, we were often laughed out of rooms of mainstream politicos when we said we planned to spend significant time and money to turn out voters who were in our base demographics but who had never (or almost never) voted in previous elections. It was the accepted wisdom then that spending precious campaign money trying to turnout "unlikely" voters was the equivalent of setting the money on fire because "those people won't turn out," or it will cost more than it's worth to reach them. We believe that our efforts in

2016, along with the work of many others over the past few years, have exposed the backwardness of this logic. [8]

This also included the lesson that local experience and knowledge really matter—especially within diverse and complex communities of color. For example, CCA and our local partners worked with BlueLabs to create a voter file model for identifying,[9] understanding, and engaging specifically with Puerto Rican voters in Florida. Historically, traditional campaigns and party efforts had a habit of considering all Latino voters as if they were a monolith (that is, making the mistaken overgeneralization that all Latinos in Florida are anti-Communist Cuban-Americans and should be engaged accordingly). The research and organizing in this project became one of the foundations for continuing deep work among different communities of Latino voters in Florida, and an important lesson for us.

Why Win Justice?: Rationale and strategic purposes

Building on past strategy lessons and our collective movement's urgency after the defeat of 2016, in the summer of 2017 CCA approached the Service Employees International Union and the political arms of Planned Parenthood and Color of Change with the idea of a collaborative effort for the 2018 elections. After a series of exploratory discussions, we all identified strongly shared views for how progressive electoral politics should be done and agreed to launch a joint project for the 2018 elections. Win Justice was born—and it would eventually play a large national role in both the 2018 and 2020 elections. In 2018, we targeted more than 2 million voters across three critical swing states and raised and spent $21 million in PAC and 501(c)(4) dollars. In 2020, we targeted 5.5 million voters across four swing states with a $31 million program.

We set out to build and run a large-scale partisan program that would help change what had seemed to be the common sense about how Democrats and progressives can win in state and national elections by:

1. Listening to, engaging, and motivating the base—especially voters of color, but also a targeted group of aligned white voters (instead

of what Democrats had been doing by focusing disproportionate energy on a small number of "swing" white voters and taking the base of color for granted).

2. Confidently articulating a genuine progressive vision that speaks to these base voters' values and concerns (as opposed to just trying to convince them that the other side is worse).

3. Investing in so-called "low- and mid-propensity voters" among our communities who have rarely or never voted before (instead of only prioritizing voters who always vote).

4. Expanding the understanding of where actionable wisdom comes from during election time—to help shape message, messengers, and strategies. Community and labor organizers and grassroots volunteers are talking to many thousands of voters every day during elections; we need to systematically capture, in real time, and respect their insights about voters and what moves them. Professional pollsters aren't the only ones with that wisdom and insight.

5. Doing our voter turnout work in a way that consciously builds ongoing power and independent community and labor organization for the long term (instead of the typical "parachute-in" or "pop-up" election operations that swoop into communities, do transactional get-out-the-vote efforts, and then disappear the day after Election Day, or worse, just spend billions on TV commercials).

We believed that it made sense for our four national organizations to be the ones to build an effort like this for several reasons.[10] We each had a deep base and established trust and credibility among key constituencies of voters and in key geographies—through our national organizations and with our affiliates and partner organizations in states. We each had an existing track record and capacity for scaled programs of partisan PAC and 501(c)(4) voter engagement. We shared a high level of alignment on the analysis and goals above, as well as a strong existing foundation of political and operational trust among our organizations from past work together.

What Win Justice did in 2018 and 2020: Focus, strategies, program, and results

The states: We decided to choose a set of national swing states (important for control of the White House, US Senate, and US House) where our organizations and state partners/affiliates had significant capacity and interest, and where our coalition of base voting constituencies were large enough to help sway the statewide outcomes. For 2018, Win Justice chose Florida, Nevada, and Michigan. For 2020, we continued in Florida and Nevada, and added Wisconsin and Minnesota.

The state affiliate and partner organizations for Win Justice 2020 were: Florida (New Florida Majority, Organize Florida, SEIU Florida, Florida Immigrant Coalition Votes, Dream Defenders Action, Faith in Florida Action, Florida Planned Parenthood PAC); Minnesota (SEIU State Council, Planned Parenthood of Minnesota Political Action Fund, Unidos Minnesota, Faith in Minnesota); Nevada (SEIU Nevada Local 1107, Planned Parenthood Votes, PLAN Action); Wisconsin (Voces de la Frontera Action, Planned Parenthood Advocates of Wisconsin Political Fund, SEIU).

For 2018 they were: Florida (New Florida Majority, Organize Florida, SEIU Florida, Florida Immigrant Coalition Votes, Florida Planned Parenthood PAC); Nevada (Planned Parenthood Votes, PLAN Action); and Michigan (MOSES Action, Michigan People's Campaign, Michigan Planned Parenthood Votes, SEIU Healthcare Michigan).

The voters and geographies: We defined universes of voters that made sense for WJ as a collaborative effort across all our organizations, that created the potential for statewide and national impact on the election outcomes, and that also aligned with our organizing and power-building goals. Specifically, our largest focus was on a wide range of voters of color, and we also planned to engage a targeted set of supportive white voters (including women, young people, and union supporters). In line with our strategies and purposes described above, within all these demographics our priority was on the "low- and mid-propensity" voters and newly registered voters, who are often ignored by traditional campaigns.

We also had a keen eye on key geographies within each state for targeting our voter universes and voter engagement program plans. These geographies and districts were prioritized to align with the medium- and long-term state level power building goals and strategies of the Win Justice partner organizations in each state. In concrete terms, we prioritized areas where we could impact state and local election outcomes (in addition to federal races) and where the in-state partner organizations had either existing bases or goals for new base organizing and growth. In total, Win Justice targeted just over 2 million voters across three states in 2018, and 5.5 million voters across four states in 2020.

The voter engagement program: Working together across the WJ national and state-level partner organizations, we designed a multi-pronged grassroots approach to engaging, motivating, and turning out our voters while growing our bases, organizations, and power. Our program design was informed by a few key principles. Direct contact and two-way conversations with voters needed to be priorities, rather than one-way paid advertising. Known and trusted local leaders and organizations would be the best messengers, especially to new and infrequent voters (for example, Faith in Minnesota's roots in the Black community through their Barbershops and Black Congregation Cooperative, or Voces de la Frontera Action's deep trust in Wisconsin's Latino communities from decades of organizing and mobilizing tens of thousands of people in immigrant justice fights. And we would aim to win the election and simultaneously make our organizations and movements stronger by developing our capacity and leadership and recruiting new people to the cause.

These principles applied to both the 2018 and 2020 Win Justice program. Of course, in early 2020 we had to quickly adapt to only using the many remote modes of voter contact for most of the cycle. In a few places local partner groups decided to resume door-knocking in the final weeks before Election Day, with strong COVID-19 protocols. Much has been written elsewhere about these necessary adaptations to remote voter work during the pandemic in 2020, so I'm not going to delve deeply into that dimension of WJ's 2020 efforts. With those caveats, these were WJ's strategic voter engagement program elements, covering 2018 and 2020:

- *Canvass (door-to-door direct voter contact):* We ran large-scale paid, and some volunteer, door canvasses, with canvassers recruited as much as possible from existing memberships and grassroots volunteer bases and nearby communities. Canvassers were trained more like organizers. They learned to ask questions, have conversations, and listen, before effectively moving to encourage and affirm support for our candidates, and how and why to vote. In most places, our canvasses also included follow-up volunteer and member recruitment efforts with "leads" identified during door canvass conversations with voters, and follow-up done quickly by dedicated teams.

- *Relational voter organizing:* Using organizer-friendly mobile apps such as Impactive (formerly OutVote),[11] in both 2018 and 2020, Win Justice ran one of the largest relational voter organizing programs in the country. Of course, all good organizing is relational, and using these tools doesn't mean technology takes the place of organizing. What it does do is provide a mechanism for thousands of volunteers, members, and staff of our organizations to link their own personal contacts (friends and family) with the detailed data on the voter file, communicate systematically and convincingly with those friends and family (over text, social media, email, etc.) and track and measure their impact within the voter universe for our election program. For more on how relational voter organizing works and how we measured its impact, see this *New York Times* op-ed by Win Justice 2018 Director Kristee Paschall,[12] and this article in *Mother Jones*.[13]

- *SMS/text messaging:* Our approach here focused on two-way texting conversations with voters (not spam text messages), and involved primarily volunteers and members and staff of our organizations as the texters.

- *Online organizing and digital engagement:* "Organizing" and "engagement" here are key. We didn't only do one-way paid advertising on social media channels. We were organizing, recruiting people, experimenting with approaches that motivated people to become volunteers engaging their own social networks. In addition to Facebook, we were active and experimenting on Instagram, WhatsApp, YouTube, TikTok, and other platforms where voters in our communities are active. We were constantly developing grassroots toolkits to help volunteers communicate effectively with their own family and friends.[14] One exciting note on digital engagement is that we also believed that it would work best to ask volunteers, voters, and local organizers themselves to create the messages and content to encourage our voters to turn out (rather than relying only on professional staff or consultants in DC to design content—even though some of that is good too!). We did exhaustive research and tests comparing the effectiveness of both kinds of content. The "grassroots organic content" often out-performed the "professional" stuff, as in WJ 2020's compilation of four grassroots videos from different local volunteers and organizers about why they each are voting,[15] or the short video from Liz Alvarez, a healthcare worker who's active with Voces de la Frontera Action in Wisconsin. Liz says in part that she is voting because "my hope is for a government that will protect its people and their well-being, so get out there and vote."[16]

- *Volunteer recruitment, training, and leadership development:* This was built into many aspects of the voter contact work, as noted above as part of canvassing and digital engagement. Another example was the Color of Change series of Black Women's Brunches in communities across key states during the election.

They invited people through online ads and SMS outreach to be part of community-building gatherings, and then provided paths for their energy to do political work as volunteers.[17]

- *Vote by Mail and Early Vote (VBM/EV):* Well before it became a necessity because of the COVID-19 pandemic, many of us ran concentrated programs to organize our communities to vote by mail or at early vote centers, with much larger quantitative goals than were traditionally viewed as important. This has proven useful especially (but not only) with new and infrequent voters, because it creates more time for the voter education and process support they need (especially in the face of voter suppression schemes). In WJ 2018 we tied VBM and EV programs to community-specific cultural events (such as "Souls to the Polls" in Black communities and "Early Vote Fiestas" in Las Vegas Latino neighborhoods complete with taco trucks and mariachis). In the 2018 midterm elections, among our WJ Nevada voter universe, over nine times as many voted early or by mail than had done so in the previous midterm election in 2014. In Florida it was more than three times as many.

- *Phonebanking and mail* were supplemental, not leading, parts of the program.

The state and local power building and agenda: These priorities were also integrated into the original targeting of key races/elections and geographies, and into our messaging. In each WJ state, in-state and national leaders prioritized state and local races and ballot measures to be incorporated into the WJ program in addition to the federal races. This often included progressive candidates who came from the membership or staff of partner organizations—creating an additional motivating element for local voters and activists. For example, in 2020 we helped elect Angie Nixon to the Florida statehouse from Jacksonville; Angie had previously been a senior staffer for SEIU in Florida and served as Win Justice 2018 Florida state organizing director. We also prioritized state ballot measures that were important for in-state movements. These included Florida's 2018 Amendment 4, which restored voting rights for people who were formerly incarcerated, the 2018 Nevada measure for automatic voter registration, and the 2020 Florida measure for a $15 minimum wage.

How Win Justice was built and run

How Win Justice did what we did in 2018 and 2020 also mattered. We took care to do the goal-setting, strategy-making, political space-claiming, fundraising, and operationalizing in ways that served both the short-term goals of winning the elections and the long-term goals of building power and strengthening our organizations and movements.

We started early. We decided to work together and began planning more than a year out from Election Day (for 2018 and 2020). National and state partners worked together to develop the plan (key states and races, voter and geographic targeting) in consultation with other key players such as labor, climate groups, donor tables, and party-aligned independent expenditure committees, in order to (a) assert our shared political space and roles as WJ in the 2018 and 2020 election landscapes, (b) ensure positioning of our effort within key donor spaces to attract the scale of money we would need, and (c) get early recognition and validation for the WJ experiment and our way of doing voter turnout.

For as many aspects as possible of the operation and staffing, we used and expanded our existing organizational capacities, bases, and staff teams rather than outsourcing. Often these kinds of large-scale national election efforts are re-created from scratch every two years. They are disconnected from existing organizations in communities, and they don't add value and strength to our organizations after Election Day (often they deplete capacity and subtract value). Almost all of the staff and grassroots volunteers for this large operation were lent, assigned from, or hired into, our existing organizations—nationally and locally. We hired a small core of dedicated staff for the Win Justice effort, only five people in 2018 and nine in 2020. These teams (led by Kristee Paschall

in 2018 and by Kenia Morales in 2020) were essential to the success of
Win Justice, and a huge part of their work was supporting the existing
staff and volunteers within the WJ partner organizations in carrying out
the program.

We raised the money together, into shared pools that we managed
and prioritized together, based on our agreed plans and strategies. We
tapped into and enhanced the fundraising relationships and positioning
of all of our national and local partner organizations.

A final note on the "how" of working together. It goes without saying
that impactful coalition-building and experimentation across organizations and constituencies takes honesty, trust, courageous conversations,
and a lot of emotional labor under any circumstances. In an existentially
high-stakes environment like election 2020—well, it takes even more of
all those things. The Win Justice collaboration was no exception. We
navigated through the hard work of coalition, not always perfectly, but
the results speak for themselves. We also made the healthy decision in
early 2021 to declare victory and end the WJ collaboration. The organizations will keep working together in different ways, but we remembered
the lesson that not every movement structure we create needs to go on
forever.

The results: Win Justice's victories and program impacts

In 2018, Win Justice helped win two US Senate seats and two governors'
seats (all in Michigan and Nevada), 10 US House seats, and 19 state legislative seats.[18] We also played a huge role in passing Florida's Amendment
4, restoring voting rights. In 2020, Win Justice was central to delivering
Wisconsin, Nevada, and Minnesota for Biden-Harris. We helped win
one US Senate seat (re-electing Tina Smith in Minnesota), four US House
seats, and 34 state legislative seats. In both years, the Win Justice collaboration also set and achieved a number of goals related to ongoing power
building and organization strengthening, including new volunteer and
member recruitment and engagement, staff training and capacity building on a range of electoral skills and operations, and improving the posi-

tioning of the local and national partner organizations as players in the electoral landscape and with key political donors.

Acknowledgments

The voter engagement programs described here were done through the hard work of many members, leaders, and staff within CCA, the Win Justice national partner groups, and the many local grassroots organizations mentioned above who were central to it all. I especially want to acknowledge the leadership of Grecia Lima at Community Change Action, Arisha Hatch at Color of Change PAC, Jennifer Lawson at Planned Parenthood Action Fund (PPAF)—along with Deirdre Schifeling who was at PPAF in 2018, and Maria Peralta at SEIU in making Win Justice the success that it was.

Looking ahead: Imperatives on the path to real electoral power

Including the several election cycles described in this chapter, I've spent decades organizing at the intersection of aspirational power-building for systemic social change and necessary campaigning within the compromised reality of contemporary electoral politics. Informed by the Win Justice experience most recently and the earlier work, including my formative years in the 1990's learning grassroots electoral politics with Anthony Thigpenn at AGENDA/SCOPE in Los Angeles, these are some of my own thoughts on what is required if we want to build the scale and depth of power needed in the electoral arena to be able to durably govern the country and enact our vision for justice.

What must we do? And what will it take for us to do it?

1. First, as I noted at the start of the chapter, it is "united front" time right now for leftists, progressives, and liberals, and will be for a number of years and elections to come. *Much* of our collective energy and current power has to be aligned in the short and medium term toward beating white supremacist authoritarianism and the hegemony of capitalist economics and consciousness

(rather than arguing among ourselves over our *relatively* smaller differences). For the long term we have to organize and grow our power.

2. We must build multiracial organized mass bases and wide grass-roots leadership, through an ecosystem of movement organizations, with a resilient core of shared values and vision. The bases and power of our combined movement ecosystem must eventually constitute a political super-majority of the country (not just the 50% +1 needed to win an individual election but the 70% to 75% needed to boldly govern), which means we must organize and align large majorities of all communities of color plus a strategic portion of white people. We can't win the country with our current base of activists alone, nor can we win it by organizing people of color alone. We can't wait for demographics to shift. They aren't destiny. White supremacy is powerful and the historical fluidity of what and who is "white" continues. Plus, the world is on fire and people are dying—now. On the electoral front, this is the basic political math,[19] and organizing that's needed to consistently win statewide elections and to contest in enough states to take national power.

   - By organized base and grassroots *leadership*, I mean democratic organizations with high participation, ownership of goals and strategy, and felt agency by large proportions of rank-and-file members. I mean groups with strategies centered on organizing the power of large majorities of communities and workplaces taking disciplined action together—not only staff-driven strategies of mobilizing lists of activists who are already with us.[20] Building to a political super-majority means organizing well beyond those lists of activists.

   - We must build these bases and organizations with sufficient political, ideological, and resource independence from Democratic Party (more on money in point 7 below).

- I say an "ecosystem" of movement organizations because no one organization can do it all. No one organization should try to do it all. No one organization should say they are doing it all—not to funders and not to the rest of us.

- Within the ecosystem we must consciously nurture and sustain national vehicles for sustained alignment on strategy and program (electoral and otherwise) across the states, bases, constituencies, sectors, and organizations. As I discussed earlier about Win Justice, any such movement-building work across lines takes consciously dedicated time, energy, and emotional labor.

- Electoral power is critical, but it's only one of the dimensions of power we need to build. Our movements also need to be building worker/economic power; ideological and cultural power to evolve mass consciousness; advocacy power at state and federal levels; etc.

3. We have to **confront systemic oppression, including anti-Black racism,** head on, as central to how we organize and fight. We have to do this **while also building the multiracial political supermajority** mentioned above. All communities of color, women, and other communities facing systemic oppression and exclusion must be supported and respected in organizing and building their own base of power and space for leadership. But if we only build those separate bases and spaces, we will lose. Across those bases and spaces, across those communities, we must also build the shared analysis, common vision, aligned strategies, and deep well of trust required to go into sustained and messy struggle, together.

4. **The US two-party system isn't going anywhere soon.** While we may have longer-term aspirations for a different political system, in the short- and medium-term we need to build power and fight in an assertive and smart way that makes our people, our values, and our agenda the center of gravity of the Democratic Party.

5. As I also noted at the start, we have to **build and contest for electoral power** at a scale that is commensurate with the degree of societal change we seek. **We can't be only marginal players,** nor can we solely rely on left electoral strategies or tactics that only work in a few parts of the country.

   - Don't get me wrong: concerted electoral efforts from the left are necessary and good. We need some organizations articulating a left pole in US elections. It is important to challenge moderate Democrats from the left in primaries, in those districts and during those years where that might actually succeed. Small-scale voter projects asserting space in particular communities with experimental methods are also necessary.

   - But that alone is insufficient. We as a progressive grassroots movement also have to build and run voter programs, independent of the Democratic Party, that engage and turn out voters at the scale necessary to meaningfully affect statewide and national election outcomes, and control of the White House, Congress, governors' offices, and state legislative chambers.

   - And we have to be seen to be doing so (see point 8 below).

6. Our own organizations have to cultivate, within our own memberships and staff, the hard technical skills, tools, technology, logistical/operational capacity, and culturally competent **knowhow to do large-scale voter engagement and turnout from inside our base organizations.** This does include some specialized intermediary groups that exist within, and are accountable to, our movement ecosystem. But we have to stop relying on and enriching the kinds of outside consultants, operatives, and private firms-for-hire that aren't accountable to our movement and base, and don't share our goals.

7. Our organizations have to **consistently and independently secure tens and hundreds of millions of political—PAC and 501(c)(4)—dollars,** every election cycle, in order to make any of

what I'm saying here possible to do. In the long term we must try to generate our own resources at this scale from and with our base. But outside of a handful of the remaining large national unions, our movements are very far from realizing this ideal. In the meantime, we have to raise most of this money from individual political donors and institutional sources. We have to do it while being smartly honest with donors about the grassroots, power-building, and politically progressive way we intend to do our voter engagement. We have to be consciously trying to actually bring *some* of those donors and institutions along with us to our new "common sense" for how to win elections. Doing this money-raising and spending well and at scale means:

- (a) Assertively positioning and promoting our organizations and our approaches in that money world.

- (b) Effectively translating and code-switching about our work, understanding where donors are and what they care about, and finding the intersections with our own goals and programs.

- (c) Building the finance and legal systems and discipline in our organizations to responsibly manage this kind of money at the speed and scale needed (without breaking laws, opening up our organizations to right-wing smears, or turning donors away for good because of some financial or legal misstep).

8. We need to do effective public positioning and strategic story-telling—about our vision, but also about the electoral power we're exercising behind it. Elected officials, political operatives, donors, journalists, and other elite influencers have to know we exist, know our agenda, and know we're moving significant electoral program and money that's helping elect (and beat) candidates and shape election mandates. **We can't just run big programs and help win elections—we have to "get credit" and be feared for our hopefully growing electoral power,** to translate into serious governing influence on public policy and state resources.

Notes

1. Planned Parenthood Action Fund and Color of Change PAC.

2. *501(c)(3)* refers to a section of the US tax code governing nonprofit organizations with charitable and educational purposes. 501(c)(3)'s cannot undertake any partisan political activities, such as supporting or endorsing parties or candidates for elected office. Contributions to 501(c)(3)'s are tax deductible for the donors. 501(c)(4) is the section of the tax code governing a different type of nonprofit that can spend a portion (not all) of its resources on partisan political activities. Contributions to 501(c)(4)'s are not tax-deductible for the donors. 501(c)(3)'s can, and often do, create related 501(c)(4) arms with shared missions and collaborative activities, provided both "sister" entities carefully abide by the respective laws and regulations.

3. Under current campaign finance rules, this type of SuperPAC is one that can take contributions of unlimited size, and all donors and all expenditures by a PAC are legally required to be publicly disclosed (no "dark money" here). While an independent expenditure (or "IE") SuperPAC can actively campaign for (or against) a candidate or a party, it cannot "coordinate" its activities and spending with any candidate or political party (essentially meaning it cannot make a deal with a candidate that says it will "cover" certain voters and turn them out for the candidate so the candidate's campaign can spend its money on other voters). A SuperPAC can spend 100% of its money doing this type of partisan ("vote for …" or "vote against …") work; whereas a 501(c)(4) must use at least half of its spending in any given year for nonpartisan activities. In a number of states our federal SuperPACs are required by state laws to set up affiliated "state political committees" in order to spend money on state-level elections (such as races for governor or state legislative seats).

4. To make this work, we also had to ensure we had high-quality legal, accounting, and campaign finance management in place for CCA (and also to work intensely with local community organizing partner groups to develop their corresponding capacity and systems as well). This election-related legal and finance work is very specialized and takes either dedicated capacity or focused training for organizational legal and finance teams.

5. The state partner organizations in the CCA 2016 program were Florida (New Florida Majority, Florida Immigrant Coalition Votes, Organize Florida, and SEIU), Colorado (CIRC Action Fund, Colorado People's Action, Generation Latino, Protégete, SEIU Colorado, and Colorado Latinas Rise), and Nevada (PLAN Action and Culinary Workers Local 226).

6. See this article about CCA's work: Emily Bazelon, "Are Get-Out-the-Vote Efforts Targeting Latinos Working?" *New York Times Magazine*, November 4, 2016.

7. See Community Change Action 2016 Program Voter Impact Analysis, https://communitychangeaction.org.

8. These "unlikely" voters are also referred to, in the electoral geek lingo, as "low-propensity voters"—as in, they have a low propensity or likelihood to vote. Our view has long been that this is more of a self-fulfilling prophecy. Democratic candidates and party operations have for decades focused almost exclusively

on those voters who already usually vote, in their turnout operations, in their public messaging, and frankly, in their approach to governing. Since 2017, some focus on these voters has increasingly become a somewhat valued practice by liberal/progressive "independent expenditure" groups, and supported by some mainstream donors.

9. BlueLabs (https://bluelabs.com/) is one of the leading Democratic-side voter data and analysis firms.

10. For more background and information on our four organizations, see SEIU, www.seiu.org/; Planned Parenthood Votes, www.plannedparenthoodaction. org/elections/vote, is the PAC of Planned Parenthood Action Fund (a 501(c) (4)); Color of Change PAC, https://votingwhileblack.com/ is the PAC of Color of Change; and as already described earlier, Community Change Voters is the PAC arm of Community Change Action, https://communitychangeaction.org/2020-power/.

11. Impactive, www.impactive.io/; Impactive was formerly known as OutVote.

12. Kristee Paschall, "What if Democrats Tried Real Outreach?" *New York Times*, January 9, 2020.

13. Pema Levy, "The Secret to Beating Trump Lies with You and Your Friends," *Mother Jones* (November/December 2020).

14. For example, see this CCA toolkit "Organizing in a Time of Physical Distancing" from summer/fall 2020, https://docs.google.com/document/d/1OYxg-tOYAuJJ-QD0TDfcjj_Wh9htNHDTTPLDbWEcu-jI/edit.

15. See the WJ 2020 grassroots video compilation "Why I'm Voting," https://drive. google.com/file/d/1cib3Fy_5ZjA85rCT2ox09OVj-SJXWQku/view.

16. See Community Change Voters video "Why I'm a Voter" from Liz Alvarez, https://yourvoice.communitychangevoters.org/video-single/1602175752097.

17. Color of Change Black Women's Brunch series page on Facebook, www.facebook.com/colorofchange/posts/the-black-womens-brunch-series-is-gearing-up-to-hit-cities-across-america-in-201/10155832059021067/.

18. See detailed reports on the results and impact of Win Justice's programs: Win Justice 2018, https://communitychangeaction.org/wp-content/uploads/2021/08/Win-Justice-2018-Post-Election-Report.pdf, and Win Justice 2020, https://communitychangeaction.org/wp-content/uploads/2021/08/Win-Justice-2020-Post-Election-Report.pdf.

19. For a quick example, we can look at the state of Nevada. Its population is about 3.1 million people, and is approximately 50% white, 29% Latino, 9% Black, and 8% AAPI. The voters who actually turned out in 2020 are approximately 75% white, 14% Latino, 2.7% Black, and 3.1% AAPI. We obviously have work to do increasing turnout (and winning citizenship for undocumented immigrants). But even in a perfect world of full immigrant justice, equal turnout rates among races, and 100% support by all people of color for progressive agendas and candidates (none of which is assured), we still need an important portion of white people to be organized and part of our movement, vision, and voting bloc in order to have the super-majority political base needed to consistently win elec-

tions and enact our progressive/left vision. See TargetSmart, https://targetearly.
targetsmart.com/, and US Census Bureau, "Voting and Registration in the Election of November 2020," April 2021.

20. For further reading that strongly informs my views here—beyond the strictly
electoral context—see Jane F. McAlevey, *No Shortcuts: Organizing for Power in
the New Guilded Age* (New York: Oxford University Press, 2017), and Charles
Payne, *I've Got the Light of Freedom: The Organizing Tradition and the Mississippi Freedom Struggle* (Berkeley and Los Angeles: University of California
Press, 2007).

22

Building and Transforming Power: Lessons from the 2020 Elections

Alicia Garza

When I was a young organizer-in-training, mentors told me that ending social ills—war and militarism, racism and white supremacy, state sanctioned violence, environmental destruction, and more—would require building a viable left that could contend for power in the United States. They told me that power did not exist primarily inside protest and other forms of resistance, but rather in the hands of the state. As long as that was the case, we would have to build a left that could contend for and transform state power. In other words, to change power, we needed a left that was *in* power.

Noting that hindsight is 20/20 doesn't begin to capture the regret over the loss of precious time that, especially these days, feels like a limited commodity. The crises that have been sharpening for some time now have accelerated dramatically in the last decade. In my home state of California, dystopian tales from the Octavia Butler novels that I once considered science fiction are turning out to be prophecies: Dry riverbeds where beautiful, rushing waters used to flow. Fire seasons that yield fire tornados, causing destruction at a scale not seen in my lifetime. In fall 2020, wildfires burning across the state joined the regular fogbanks of my coastal region to yield an entire day when light never emerged from the predawn darkness.

For the left, joining electoral organizing to power-building has long been like trying to fuse oil with water. Reform work has often been cast aside for the sake of more revolutionary work, as if the two are not intricately connected. As a result, we have failed to build the power necessary to engage in the revolutionary work that commands so much of our attention. This has come at great peril, because, to be honest, we've not been great at revolutionary work either. Still, too many are searching the past for examples of left transformation, rather than making history ourselves. We should understand how we got here, but it is just as important to study who we are right now, culturally as well as materially. We have to design—and test—new strategies to help us win hearts and minds and contend for many forms of power, including state power.

I have always understood the work of reform to be that of advancing small victories that create more space for survival, and the work of revolution to be that of re-imagining a new economy, society, and democracy that transform all of our lives. These definitions, while perhaps not the most profound, can serve as guideposts to understand how to strengthen our work to achieve the change that we seek.

As we create space for survival, we should not too readily dismiss the impacts of reform work, especially in our current political and social context. Revolution cannot happen without reform—new structures, processes, and relationships of power cannot exist absent direct challenges to the current structure.

This is why the failure of the US left to engage symbiotically with the electoral arena has been so detrimental. Without electoral power, the US left has little hope of influencing allocation of resources, who represents us, what their agenda is, who shapes the story of who we are and who we can be, and whether actions that counter our agenda will lead to any consequences.

Elections are a vehicle for millions of people to express their desires for their families, their communities, and their workplaces. The arena is ripe for left organizing, particularly because of the deepening crises that so many of us experience viscerally each and every day. The United

States is undergoing unprecedented changes, from shifting attitudes on policing and racism and the surfacing of white nationalism and white supremacy, to a global pandemic that is shifting our relationships, to ongoing and worsening climate catastrophes. A viable, responsive, visionary, and grounded left has never been more necessary. We need to make the changes that we seek legible to millions of people who are desperate for relief, and we need to make clear the path to achieve those changes. Elections are one of many tools that we can use to begin to build the world that we want to see.

Over the last decade, left forces in the United States increased their engagement in electoral organizing, and in 2020 these forces participated in ways not seen in my lifetime. This growth in participation and engagement may be seen as largely defensive, a move to ward off the worst impacts of re-electing a neofascist. Black communities, immigrant communities, and women, along with other marginalized groups, were the targets of backlash from white nationalist forces, joined by corporatist forces, who fought back against the victories won through organizing by those same communities. Much like the Moral Majority of the 1980s, a new movement emerged that fought to reclaim power and once again dominate the country's politics, decrying socialism and communism as core threats and using healthcare, asylum, gay marriage, abortion, civil rights, and the election of the first Black president of the United States as core examples of a looming threat to their established way of life.

Finding a leader in Donald J. Trump, this movement rooted itself in a leap forward in conservative values, what can now be understood as Trumpism. In the 1980s and 1990s the corporate wing of the movement was in the lead, pushing for deregulation, unfettered profit, and global dominance, with China as its core competitor. The religious wing became the mobilizing force that could cement power for the corporate wing, and both largely repudiated the blatantly white supremacist faction.

In the 2000s and 2010s the conservative movement allowed white nationalism to emerge from underground, using it to help mobilize resentment, fear, and anxiety against a convergence of movements that threatens the hegemony and power of the corporatist wing. Faced with increasing economic anxiety from a growing segment of the American population, including white communities, white nationalism was weaponized to distract from the corporate wing's disastrous economic policies that have driven more and more people into poverty and desolation. This economic anxiety, coupled with demographic change that will render white people a minority for the first time, provided fertile ground for the 2016 election results.

The election of Donald J. Trump was the culmination of a strategy long utilized by the conservative movement in times of crisis—distract, deter, and dilute the salience of the values and policies that threaten to redistribute power while also changing how power operates.

The left itself was also transformed. For the last two decades, the US left has been forced to reckon with race in a new way, none more salient than the push to address and engage with the impacts of racial capitalism and state-sanctioned violence. The rise of US-based racial justice movements like Black Lives Matter, Not One More, and others compelled the US left to move past a tepid racial justice analysis and address race and class simultaneously. Marginalized communities largely led this push and moved the US left to a reckoning that is transforming the left itself.

With respect to electoral organizing, segments of the US left are pushing beyond a strategy of nonengagement to using electoral organizing as defense, with an eye on long-term power-building. While still certainly uneven, the engagement of leftists of color in the fight to claim the country's politics is a significant development, one that must become more than a trend. It must become a lifestyle. In order to build and seize power and transform how power operates, we must take electoral engagement even further to incorporate electoral strategies that shape our larger fights and help us win. We can learn significant lessons from the engagement of left forces in the 2020 elections. A few are recounted below.

Who will believe in us if we don't believe in ourselves?

For decades, the US left has been ambivalent at best about the potential of electoral organizing as a strategy for building power. In the meantime, the policies and procedures that govern our lives are untenable, creating misery and devastation not just here at home but around the world. Politics as it stands has never delivered what we need, and so politics in its current form cannot stand.

The organized left is not alone in its cynicism about politics—the as-yet-unorganized in our communities are rightfully cynical as well, because for decades we have gotten little from politics in its current form. Cynicism among both groups is dangerous, combining "can't do" with an absence of any alternative vision.

For decades US international policy has invested in bashing socialism and/or other left alternatives as dangerous big-government conspiracies, or as taking resources from hard-working people and giving them to people who don't work hard and are undeserving. Moreover, too few socialist experiments have succeeded, bringing corruption rather than transformation of a society and its economy. As a result, some have been politicized by the failure of socialist experiments, and their anti-government rhetoric has given strength to the battering ram once championed by former British Prime Minister Margaret Thatcher—that poor people have no alternative to an economic system that preys on them and requires them to sell their labor simply to survive.

In US elections, the idea of socialism is unpopular because of smear campaigns against left alternatives and the weakness of our organizing vis-à-vis the hegemony of US international policy.

If our communities understood socialism as access to affordable and quality housing, jobs that pay a decent wage, food on people's tables, or even guaranteed income, everyone would love socialism. But socialism continues to live in the heads of the left, not in our homes, communities, or workplaces. While this remains true, the conservative movement will continue to succeed in making socialism a boogeyman. Talking about socialism in the abstract, without models or policies that can help win over hearts and minds, is insufficient. This is particularly true in the realm of elections. We must win victories that improve the material conditions of those who receive nothing from politics, and contextualize those wins to help people understand that these are steps toward a new way of governance.

Too often, when we engage in electoral politics we prioritize candidates over organizing. A smattering of progressive or even left candidates, without a strong base that demonstrates a mandate for change, does little to interrupt a political machine that enjoys hegemonic dominance due to lack of a clear, viable, and sustained alternative.

Such was the case in the 2020 presidential primaries, when Senators Bernie Sanders and Elizabeth Warren both presented viable alternatives to today's economic status quo. Yet, rather than organize as many people as possible to support either one of them for the Democratic nomination, the US left turned to splitting hairs about which was further left. This exercise was largely futile because the country's political nucleus not only is not left, it may be closer to right than centrist. Securing a win for a left candidate in this political context would have been a significant victory.

Had the US left been less enamored with the *idea of* socialism, and more focused on a strategy to build the left and its power by winning immediate material gains for our communities, we might have secured a different future—and, interestingly, a different party apparatus. Yet left strategy in this realm has largely focused on changing the party apparatus without doing the work needed to organize the unorganized, or focusing on individual candidates rather than making governance structures more accessible and equitable.

When we over-promise or are insufficiently ambitious about the possibilities if we wield power, we breed cynicism about any alternative to the status quo. The US left has experimented with cultural reforms when what we need to combat cynicism about political possibilities is a deep and rigorous engagement in rewriting the rules and procedures that govern our lives. Amilcar Cabral once said, "Always remember that the people are not fighting for ideas, nor for what is in men's minds. The people fight and accept the sacrifices demanded by the struggle in order to gain material advantages, to live better and in peace, to benefit from progress, and for the better future of their children." When the US left engages in fights over policy and governance, and advances candidates who will effectively fight to change the rules that have been rigged against us, the result will be tangible changes in the lives of our communities, making change real in practice, not just in theory. It will shift the lives of those left behind by politics—and engage them in the process of changing their own lives.

We must fight harder for racial justice than our opposition fights for white supremacy

In his re-election campaign, Donald Trump not only weaponized racist tropes, he also called white nationalists to arms, to mobilize to defend white supremacy against all enemies. White supremacists did, indeed, mobilize, marching through the streets of Washington, DC, and cities across the country. These were clear voter suppression tactics, as the Trump campaign knew that it had to both mobilize white resentment and prevent Black voters and voters of color from voting in order to stay in power.

The US left did not drive white supremacists underground. For the most part, communities of color, immigrant communities, and Black communities are familiar with the use of racial terror to subvert and undermine our will. And yet the US left does not invest significantly in mobilizing and activating white voters, whom our opposition targets, as antiracist voters.

Fighting for racial justice doesn't merely mean marching in the streets for justice for those murdered by the police, like George Floyd or Breonna Taylor. Fighting for racial justice, especially in an election cycle, means talking to white communities about the ways in which whiteness is mobilized against *their* material interests as well as against the interests of communities of color and Black communities. The discomfort with talking about race—or refusal to do so entirely, or bastardizing explicit discussion of race as "divisive identity politics," especially in an electoral context—undermines our ability to build and transform power. This is particularly so because transforming power must also mean dislodging white supremacy from the structures and policies that govern society.

Don't let the perfect be the enemy of 'good enough to fight the fascists'

Deepening crises, combined with strong organizing, created the conditions for the presence of two presidential candidates who had a strong message of promoting economic justice through curtailing the power of corporations over our economy and our democracy. Senator Bernie Sanders popularized the idea of democratic socialism in mainstream discourse, and Senator Elizabeth Warren brought a strong regulatory approach to corporate influence over the financial sector and the social safety net. They were contenders in a sea of corporate apologists who favored small adjustments in a fairly entrenched status quo.

One would think that the left's strategy in this period would have been to join with as many forces as possible to push both candidates as far as possible in contending for the Democratic Party nomination for president. But the left quickly devolved into camps organized around which candidate was further left, rather than accepting that either would have represented a huge leap forward. The fight should never have been about who was "most left," but rather about building the power of the progressive left and wresting power from the moderate wing of the party, as well as defeating this phase of fascism.

The Black Voters Matter Fund, spearheaded by LaTosha Brown and Cliff Albright, understood this strategy well. It mobilized Black voters to the polls on what was often dubbed "the Blackest bus in America," and gave Black communities the tools and resources needed to activate, educate, and organize themselves.

Black Voters Matter Fund understood that it didn't need to go all in for a candidate in order to get Black communities engaged and involved. Through efforts that were largely nonpartisan, it focused on the issues that mattered most to communities that have been left out and left behind, facing cynicism and legitimate distrust of politics and politicians from Black communities that were used to broken promises.

Perhaps the most significant part of the work was showing Black communities our own strength. Our communities often feel powerless to change our political system, but the Black Voters Matter Fund reminds us that we do have power—especially when we come together and not only make demands but act together in the service of those demands.

That work paid off. Black voters led a multiracial coalition to victory over fascism in the 2020 presidential election. We did it again in January 2021 when two Democrats were elected in Georgia, resulting in a 50–50 split in the United States Senate, with the first Black and Indian woman vice president available to cast tie-breaking votes.

Black Voters Matter Fund didn't spend its time lamenting that Joe Biden and Kamala Harris weren't good enough. Rather, it turned to building a base of power to which Biden and Harris would have to be accountable.

Use culture as a weapon, or it will be a weapon used against you

To build power we must change both policy *and* culture. Hegemony guides our understanding of right and wrong, belonging and exclusion, who is deserving and who is not. We must prevail in both realms, and elections are an opportunity to do so. "Defund the police" was a counter-hegemonic concept that broke through the conventional wisdom that to challenge law enforcement would undermine a campaign. Too many on the left have wrung their hands over how our opposition will use our most visionary demands against us, but too few of us have invested in thinking creatively about how we can use ambitious demands to our advantage. We are at a historical moment of unprecedented skepticism about the ability of police and policing to keep us safe. Instead of retreating from counter-hegemony we should lean in. Defund the Police, Black Lives Matter, Medicare for All, and so many other visionary concepts have captured the hearts and minds of our people, and will continue to do so—but only if we do not back down.

Stories and storytelling are magnificent tools to help people envision what is possible. Stories connect us, helping us to understand one another better and appreciate where we stand in relationship to each other. We should never underestimate the importance and influence of the conservative storybook. The stories they tell are compelling in ways that encourage people who are hurt by their agenda to believe instead that the agenda operates in their interest. The conservative playbook is full of stories that identify an enemy and a source of suffering that aims to detract and distract from the true sources of the pain.

Our stories must move beyond reliance on facts and figures—particularly in a world of disinformation and misinformation. We must rely instead on what we long for and how to chart a path to get there, together. Our stories must reach farther than they do now—beyond the already converted to those who are longing but haven't yet found a home for their longing. In elections, we tell stories about candidates, but we don't tell stories about communities, and about what makes us a community. We tell stories about what we don't have and what's wrong, but we don't tell stories about what we do have and what we get right when we come together and fight for what's ours.

Conclusion

Increased engagement by the left in electoral organizing and power-building efforts is an important shift that, if sustained, could fundamentally reshape this country's political terrain. Such a strategic approach to electoral organizing is needed if we are to build the kind of political power that will improve the lives of our communities.

Acknowledgments

This book, like the political work described in every chapter, is a collective product. The editors were only one component of the dedicated team that took *Power Concedes Nothing* from an evening's musing to a published reality in less than ten months, and we want to say a special thank you to the following people.

Marcy Rein and Karl Kumodzi went one extra mile after another in working with writers, conducting interviews, and editing copy both for political clarity and accessibility. Sandra Hinson added her editorial skills and political savvy to the project for the final push to completion.

Marcia Henry pitched in on the editorial side when help was most needed. Lucía Oliva Hennelly and Tyger Walsh provided vital support throughout the project.

Book production manager Steve Hiatt did far more than design and execute or supervise every aspect of the book's physical production. His expertise concerning all aspects of publishing, from editorial style through promotion, guided us all through these crucial stages of work.

Guillermo Prado at *8 point 2 design* scrambled to make room on his schedule to design the book's cover and internet presence. Thanks to Annemarie Strassel and Sarah Eidelson at UNITE HERE for obtaining permission to use the compelling photograph on the front cover, and to Andy Hsiao and Rishi Awatramani for providing valuable advice and support. We are grateful to Colin Robinson and everyone at OR

Books for taking on this project and working with us on an accelerated schedule.

Institutional support was indispensable in producing this volume. *Convergence – A Magazine of Radical Insight* (formerly *Organizing Upgrade*) sponsored the project. *Convergence* is a web-based vehicle for the broad left to debate strategy, share lessons, and strengthen alignment between its component parts. Clear-eyed about the danger from the racist and authoritarian right, and the centrality of racial justice struggles to all of US politics, *Convergence* invested considerable resources to produce this volume.

Finally, the editors are deeply grateful to all the individuals who authored or co-authored a piece for this book, or who took time to provide an interview. We know it was not easy for any of them to carve out the time to do so; organizers are incredibly busy people whose schedules are often disrupted and reshaped by forces well beyond their control. Time for reflection and summation is scarce even in times less fraught than today. The fact that close to 40 very busy people still found ways to think deeply about and share their experience and insights is the bottom-line reason this book exists.

— Linda Burnham, Max Elbaum, and María Poblet

About the Contributors

Cliff Albright is a cofounder and executive director of Black Voters Matter Fund, an organization dedicated to expanding voting rights and access and increasing voter registration and turnout. Cliff hosts a weekly radio show in Atlanta and has contributed articles to the *New York Times*, *Washington Post*, the *Guardian*, and other publications.

Jules Berkman-Hill served as the deputy organizing director at PA Stands Up from 2019 to 2021. She is currently managing a state House campaign in Pennsylvania and supporting local organizing as a volunteer.

Linda Burnham served as national research director and senior advisor at the National Domestic Workers Alliance for nearly a decade and co-authored, with Nik Theodore, *Home Economics: The Invisible and Unregulated World of Domestic Work*. She was a leader in the Third World Women's Alliance in the 1970s, and co-founded, with Miriam Ching Louie, the Women of Color Resource Center, serving as the organization's executive director for 18 years.

Vivian Chang is the civic engagement manager of the Asian Pacific American Labor Alliance, AFL-CIO, where she oversees APALA's programs on voting, immigration advocacy, the Census, and redistricting. Her most recent electoral experience includes serving as deputy field director of the Asians for Ossoff and Warnock campaign, mobilizing volunteers to help flip the US Senate and elect Georgia's first Black senator.

Yong Jung Cho was the national constituency organizing director of Bernie Sanders' 2020 presidential campaign. She is currently the national field director of the Green New Deal Network.

Larry Cohen is the board chair of Our Revolution, the successor to Bernie 2016. From 2005 to 2015 he was the president of the Communications Workers of America and has been on the Democratic National Committee since 2005, serving as the vice-chair of the Unity Reform Commission, established in 2016.

Sendolo Diaminah is co-founder and co-director of the Carolina Federation. Previously s/he served as training director for Black Organizing for Leadership & Dignity (BOLD), developing somatically-based leadership curriculum for organizers and executive directors.

Eli Day is a Detroiter, writer, and the communications director at We the People MI.

Neidi Dominguez was the deputy director of states in Bernie Sanders' 2020 presidential campaign. She is the executive director of Unemployed Workers United.

David Duhalde got his start as a campus-based and nationally elected leader within the Young Democratic Socialists of America. Since then, he has served as DSA's national youth organizer and deputy director. He is currently the vice chair of the Democratic Socialists of America Fund, a 501(c)(3) educational nonprofit that works to advance socialist education and public policy.

Max Elbaum has been involved in peace, antiracist, and radical movements since joining Students for a Democratic Society (SDS) in the 1960s. The third edition of his book about the US revolutionary efforts that emerged from the 1960s upsurge, *Revolution in the Air*, was released in 2018 by Verso Books. He is currently on the editorial board of *Convergence* (formerly *Organizing Upgrade*).

César Fierros Mendoza began his political career working as an Obama organizer, then transitioned to congressional work with Rep. Raúl Grijalva and with Rep. Ruben Gallego through the Congressional Hispanic Caucus Institute. He currently serves as the communications manager for Living United for Change Arizona (LUCHA).

Alicia Garza is the principal at Black Futures Lab and co-founder of the Black Lives Matter Global Network. She serves as the strategy and partnerships director for the National Domestic Workers Alliance, and is a co-founder of Supermajority, a new home for women's activism. She is the author of the critically acclaimed book *The Purpose of Power: How We Come Together When We Fall Apart*.

Stephanie Greenlea is executive assistant to the secretary treasurer at UNITE HERE, where she also leads work in the Immigration, Diversity, and Civil Rights Department and the union's Black Leadership Group.

Ryan Greenwood has been an organizer with the United Electrical, Radio & Machine Workers of America, served as executive director of Progressive Minnesota, and co-founded the local People's Action member organization TakeAction Minnesota. He co-founded the Movement Politics program at People's Action, has served as its director for the last seven years, and now serves on the Movement Politics Staff team.

Alex Han was the Midwest political director of Bernie Sanders' 2020 presidential campaign. He is the executive editor of *Convergence* (formerly *Organizing Upgrade*).

Arisha Michelle Hatch is the vice president and chief of campaigns at Color of Change. Before coming to Color of Change, she worked as a lawyer and organizer for Barack Obama's presidential campaign in 2008, and later served as national organizing director of the Courage Campaign, which lays the groundwork for progressive change in California.

Sandra Hinson was a policy analyst, writer and editor at the Grassroots Policy Project from 1994 through 2019. Prior to joining GPP, she worked on access to healthcare with the Communications Workers of America.

Beth Howard, from Eastern Kentucky, is a leader in Showing Up for Racial Justice (SURJ), a national organization that brings hundreds of thousands of white people into fights for racial and economic justice. Beth is deeply committed to liberatory organizing strategies to build a multiracial poor/working-class people's movement in Appalachia and the American South.

Hany Khalil has been the executive director of the Texas Gulf Coast Area Labor Federation, AFL-CIO, since 2016. He taught social studies at Houston public schools for nine years and is a vice president of the Houston Federation of Teachers.

Karl Kumodzi is an organizer, trainer, and the deputy director of organizing at Blackbird, where he works with grassroots organizations across the US and the world to strengthen Black organizing and left social movements. He was a 2014–2015 Gardner Fellow at the Center for Popular Democracy.

Timmy Lu is the founding executive director of AAPIs for Civic Empowerment (AAPI FORCE) and AAPI FORCE-EF, organizations dedicated to building the political power of Asian American and Pacific Islander grassroots communities. He currently serves as an executive committee member of Million Voters Project and is a co-founder of Asian American Power Network, a new national alliance of Asian American grassroots 501(c)(4) organizations.

Jon Liss has organized for racial and social justice in Virginia for more than 40 years. In 1986, Jon co-founded Tenants and Workers United (TWU) and served as the executive director of TWU until 2011. In 2007 he co-founded the Right to the City Alliance. In 2007, he co-founded New Virginia Majority and currently serves as one of the organization's co-executive directors.

Lycia Maddocks, a citizen of the Quechan Indian Nation, is a skilled relationships and communications strategist with years of experience in leading campaigns to advance the political power of Native people and to expand the exercise of sovereignty by tribal nations. She is on the leadership team of the NDN Collective, an Indigenous-led organization dedicated to building Indigenous power.

Jay Malone is the political and communications director for the Texas Gulf Coast Area Labor Federation.

Thenjiwe McHarris has over 15 years of experience in grassroots organizing, movement building, international policy, and advocacy work. She currently leads Blackbird's organizing team and before that she served as senior leadership in the US Human Rights Network and led advocacy efforts at Amnesty International.

Rose Mendelsohn spent several years coordinating Bay Resistance, a rapid response mass-mobilization network in the Bay Area, before becoming Seed the Vote's organizing director in 2019. Since the 2020 election, Rose has been running a digital organizing fellowship with Bay Rising, and supporting mutual aid and fundraising projects locally.

Andrea Cristina Mercado is co-executive director of Florida Rising, formed through a merger of New Florida Majority and Organize Florida to strengthen strategic campaigns that center Black and Brown communities. She is one of the co-founders of the National Domestic Workers Alliance and led the California Domestic Worker Coalition, a statewide effort to include domestic workers in labor laws, which successfully passed Domestic Worker Bill of Rights legislation in 2013.

Laura Misumi sees her work at Rising Voices as an opportunity to build power with Asian American women and families in Michigan. She formerly served as managing director for Detroit Action; staff attorney for Service Employees International Union (SEIU) Healthcare Michigan; and as workers' rights staff attorney at the Community Development Project of the Urban Justice Center in New York City.

Maurice Mitchell is a nationally recognized social movement strategist, a leader in the Movement for Black Lives, and national director of the Working Families Party. Following the murder of Mike Brown he relocated to Ferguson to support organizers on the ground, and then co-founded and managed Blackbird to provide strategic support to Movement for Black Lives activists across the country. Since taking the helm of the Working Families Party in 2018 he has worked to make WFP the political home for a multiracial working-class movement.

Rafael Návar served as the California state director for Bernie Sanders' 2020 presidential campaign starting in 2019 and was subsequently appointed to lead Sanders' campaign in New York. He was the only Latinx state director for the Sanders campaign, and was senior advisor for Mijente and Georgia Latino Alliance for Human Rights' historic outreach to Latinx communities in the 2021 Georgia runoff election. From 2012 to 2019, he served as the national political director for the Communication Workers of America, and he is a co-founder of Mijente.

Jason Negrón-Gonzales is co-coordinator of Seed the Vote, a collaborative project to mobilize organizers, activists, and volunteers against Trump in the 2020 election. He was a founding member of Movement Generation Justice and Ecology Project and is a shop steward with the San Francisco nurses group of SEIU 1021.

Adelina Nicholls is a co-founder and executive director of the Georgia Latino Alliance for Human Rights (GLAHR), a community-based organization that organizes the Latino community in Georgia to defend and promote their civil and human rights. Adelina is a fierce advocate for the protection and extension of the rights of immigrants in America.

Deepak Pateriya served as chief of staff and later managing director of Community Change and Community Change Action (CC/CCA) from 2012 to 2021. He co-founded Win Justice, the 2018–2020 electoral collaboration of CCA, the Service Employees International Union (SEIU), Planned Parenthood Votes, and Color of Change PAC. He previously worked for SEIU and the United Food and Commercial Workers, and from 1995 to 2003 he worked at SCOPE/AGENDA in Los Angeles, as organizer, lead organizer, and director of SCOPE's national training program.

María Poblet was instrumental in building Causa Justa/Just Cause (CJJC), aggregating the power of three different neighborhood-based Latino and African American organizing groups in the San Francisco Bay Area. She served as CJJC's founding executive director, helped build Bay Rising, the Right to the City Alliance, and the US chapter of the World March of Women. She is currently executive director of Grassroots Power Project (GPP).

Ai-jen Poo is the executive director of the National Domestic Workers Alliance, director of Caring Across Generations, co-founder of SuperMajority and a trustee of the Ford Foundation. She is the author of *The Age of Dignity: Preparing for the Elder Boom in a Changing America*. Together with Alicia Garza, she co-hosts the podcast Sunstorm.

Marcy Rein is a member of the editorial board of *Convergence* (formerly *Organizing Upgrade*). She co-authored *Free City! The Fight for San Francisco's City College and Education for All* with Mickey Ellinger and Vicki Legion, and with Clifton Ross, she co-edited *Until the Rulers Obey: Voices from Latin American Social Movements*.

W. Mondale Robinson was the founder of The C. Institute, an NGO concerned with equitable governance and inter-social treatment for persons of African descent in countries where they are a minority population. He also founded Black Male Voters Project, the only national organization with the sole purpose of increasing Black men's participation in electoral politics.

Art Reyes III is the founding executive director of We the People MI. He was born and raised in Flint, Michigan, and hails from three generations of UAW members who fought to give working-class people the dignity we all deserve.

Jill Shenker was the 2020 political director of Seed the Vote. Previously she worked with the San Francisco Day Labor Program and Women's Collective and helped found the California Domestic Worker Rights Coalition. She was a co-founder and later field director, then international organizing director of the National Domestic Workers Alliance.

Mohan Seshadri is the executive director of the Asian Pacific Islander Political Alliance, Pennsylvania's first and only statewide Asian American advocacy and political organization. Before launching API PA, Seshadri served as executive director of the Governor's Commission on Asian Pacific American Affairs.

Jacob Swenson-Lengyel served as the director of communications and narrative at PA Stands Up from 2020 to 2021. Previously he was a program manager at Narrative Initiative, served as deputy director of communications at People's Action, and worked at Interfaith Worker Justice. He is on the editorial board of *Convergence*.

Nsé Ufot is the chief executive officer of the New Georgia Project (NGP) and its affiliate, New Georgia Project Action Fund (NGP AF). Under her leadership, NGP has registered over 500,000 Georgians to vote.

Diana Valles, an immigrant from Mexico, began working at the Stardust Resort and Casino in Las Vegas as a guest room attendant in 1988, where she also joined the Union Committee. She began working for the Culinary Workers Union Local 226 as an organizer in 2005, and today is the director of internal organizing.

Aisha Yaqoob Mahmood is the executive director of the Asian American Advocacy Fund. She is native to the South, founded the Georgia Muslim Voter Project, and worked as the policy director for Asian Americans Advancing Justice – Atlanta.

Mario Yedidia is the national field director and western regional political director for UNITE HERE. He has directed or helped lead large programs in Nevada, California, Georgia, and Washington State, and he currently lobbies for hospitality workers in Sacramento.

CPSIA information can be obtained
at www.ICGtesting.com
Printed in the USA
JSHW032212140422
24961JS00004B/12